SHARMA BOOKS
5545A/62, Ansari Road, Darya Ganj
New Delhi-110002 (India)

ARMY 2020

SHAPE, SIZE, STRUCTURE AND GENERAL DOCTRINE FOR EMERGING CHALLENGES

ARMY 2020

SHAPE, SIZE, STRUCTURE AND GENERAL DOCTRINE FOR EMERGING CHALLENGES

Edited by

Lt Gen **Vijay Oberoi**, PVSM, AVSM, VSM (Retd)

Director, Centre for Land Warfare Studies

Knowledge World

New Delhi

in association with

Centre for Land Warfare Studies

New Delhi

Knowledge World
5A/4A, Ansari Road, Daryaganj, New Delhi - 110002

Published in India by Knowledge World

First reprint in 2005

ISBN: 81-87966-33-5

Typeset by Dharana, New Delhi; studiodharana@vsnl.com
Printed at Glorious Printer, New Delhi

Published by Kalpana Shukla, Knowledge World, 5A/4A, Ansari Road, Daryaganj, New Delhi - 110002; www.knowledgeworldonline.com

CENTRE FOR LAND WARFARE STUDIES (CLAWS)

CLAWS was established in December 2003, as an independent think-tank, devoted to the promotion and furtherance of intellectual pursuit in the art, science and literature of land warfare. The vision of the centre is to be a pioneer in futuristic thinking about all aspects of land warfare, as they relate to operations within the region.

The centre hopes to attract leading strategic thinkers, defence analysts and academicians to deliberate over every facet of land warfare, from the minuscule to the mega, so that it can be disseminated to the professionals of the armed forces, as well as to all citizens of our nation. The effort would be to develop a strategic culture in general and professional nuances in particular, so that the armed forces and the political leadership, on the one hand; and the academia, the intellectuals and the man on the street, on the other, benefit from it.

In March 2004, CLAWS had organised its inaugural seminar in New Delhi. This book contains the proceedings of the seminar, as well as the papers presented during the various sessions.

CONTENTS

CONTRIBUTORS

Lt Gen Vijay Oberoi (Retd) is the Director of Centre for Land Warfare Studies (CLAWS).

Lt Gen K.S. Brar (Retd) is a war veteran and a former General Officer Commanding in Chief (GOC-in-C) Eastern Command.

Ambassador Ranjit Gupta is a former diplomat and an expert on international relations.

Vice Admiral P.S. Das (Retd) is a former Flag Officer Commanding in Chief (FOC-in-C) Eastern Naval Command.

Lt Gen V.K. Singh (Retd) is a defence analyst and a former Director General of Military Operations.

Air Cmde Jasjit Singh (Retd) is a war veteran and Director of Centre for Air Power Studies.

Brig (Dr) Arun Sahgal (Retd) is a senior fellow at the IDSA and a former Director, Net Assessment.

Dr Manoj Joshi is a leading defence analyst, media person and an expert on strategic affairs.

Brig Rahul K. Bhonsle is Commander of a Mountain Brigade.

Prof Badal Mukherji is Director, Delhi School of Economics.

Col (Dr) P.K. Vasudeva (Retd) is an economist and educationist.

Lt Gen V.K. Kapoor (Retd) is a former Commandant, Army War College, Mhow.

Lt Gen N.S. Narhari (Retd) is a former Commandant, Army War College, Mhow.

Dr Bharat Karnad is a leading defence analyst and an expert on the nuclear doctrine.

ACRONYMS

ADC	Aide-de-Camp
AJT	Advanced Jet Trainer
APEC	Asia-Pacific Economic Cooperation
ARF	ASEAN Regional Forum
ARTRAC	Army Training Command
ASEAN	Association of Southeast Asian Nations
ATACM	Artillery Tactical Missile
ATGM	Anti-Tank Guided Missile
ATV	Advanced Technology Vessel
AVSM	Ati Vishist Sewa Medal
AWACS	Airborne Warning and Control System
BARC	Bhabha Atomic Research Centre
BFSR	Battle Field Surveillance Radar
BIMSTEC	Bangladesh-India-Myanmar-Singapore-Thailand Economic Cooperation
BPO	Business Process Outsourcing
BSF	Border Security Force
CAS	Chief of Air Staff
C^3I	Command, Control, Communication and Intelligence
C^4I^2	Command, Control, Communication, Computers, Intelligence and Information
C^4I^2SR	Command, Control, Communication, Computers, Intelligence, Information, Surveillance and Reconnaissance
CAR	Central Asian Republic
CBIRT	Chemical Biological Incident Response Team
CBM	Confidence Building Measures
CDS	Chief of Defence Staff
CEP	Circular Error of Probability
CGE	Central Government Expenditure
CI	Counter-Insurgency
CIS	Commonwealth of Independent States
CISC	Chairman Integrated Staff Committee
CISF	Central Industrial Security Force
CLAWS	Centre for Land Warfare Studies
CNS	Chief of Naval Staff/Comprehensive National Strength
COAS	Chief of Army Staff
CONUS	Continental United States
COSC	Chief of Staff Committee
CPO	Central Police Organisation
CRPF	Central Reserve Police Force
CTBT	Comprehensive Test Ban Treaty

CVC	Central Vigilance Commission
DAA&QMG	Deputy Assistant Adjutant and Quarter Master General
DAE	Department of Atomic Energy
DCB	Ditch cum Bund
DOE	Department of Energy
DRDO	Defence Research and Development Organisation
EBO	Effect Based Operations
EEZ	Exclusive Economic Zone
ELINT	Electronic Intelligence
EMP	Electro-Magnetic Pulse
ERF	Extra-Regional Force
EU	European Union
EW	Electronic Warfare
FEST	Foreign Emergency Search Team
GCC	Gulf Cooperation Council
GDP	Gross Domestic Product
GNP	Gross National Product
GoM	Group of Ministers
GPS	Global Positioning System
GS	General Staff
GSLV	Geo-Synchronous Launch Vehicle
GSO	General Staff Officer
GSQR	General Staff Qualitative Requirement
HAL	Hindustan Aeronautics Limited
HRD	Human Resource Development
IAEA	International Atomic Energy Agency
IAF	Indian Air Force
IB	International Boundary
ICBM	Intercontinental Ballistic Missile
ICK^2	Information-based Command and Control
IDS	Integrated Defence Staff
IDSA	Institute for Defence Studies and Analyses
IEA	International Energy Agency
IFF	Identification Friend or Foe
IO	Indian Ocean
IOR	Indian Ocean Region/Rim
IOR-ARC	Indian Ocean Rim - Association for Regional Cooperation
IRBM	Intermediate Range Ballistic Missile
ISF	Internal Security Force
ISI	Inter-Services Intelligence
ISR	Intelligence, Surveillance, Reconnaissance
ISRO	Indian Space Research Organisation
IT	Information Technology
ITBP	Indo-Tibetan Border Police

IW	Information Warfare
J&K	Jammu and Kashmir
JDAM	Joint Direct Attack Munition
JTOT	Joint Technical Operations Team
KT	Kilo Tonne
LAC	Line of Actual Control
LCA	Light Combat Aircraft
LIC	Low Intensity Conflict
LICO	Low Intensity Conflict Operations
LIW	Low Intensity Warfare
LoC	Line of Control
LRRP	Long Range Recce Patrols
LTTE	Liberation Tigers of Tamil Eelam
MAD	Mutual Assured Destruction
MBT	Main Battle Tank
MD	Missile Defence
MEA	Ministry of External Affairs
MFN	Most Favoured Nation
MGO	Master General Ordnance
MLRS	Multi-Launcher Rocket System
MoD	Ministry of Defence
NATO	North Atlantic Treaty Organisation
NBC	Nuclear, Biological, Chemical
NDC	National Defence Council
NEST	Nuclear Emergency Search Team
NMD	National Missile Defence
NNMA	Non-NATO Military Ally
NPT	Non-Proliferation Treaty
NSC	National Security Council
NWFP	North-West Frontier Province
OOTW	Operations Other Than War
ORBAT	Order of Battle
PGM	Precision Guided Munition
PLA	People's Liberation Army
PMF	Para-Military Force
POK	Pakistan Occupied Kashmir
POTA	Prevention of Terrorism Act
PRC	People's Republic of China
PSU	Public Sector Undertaking
PVSM	Param Vishist Sewa Medal
PWG	People's War Group
QR	Qualitative Requirement
RAPID	Reorganised Army Plains Infantry Division
RBI	Reserve Bank of India

RDD	Radiological Dispersion Device
RMA	Revolution in Military Affairs
RPV	Remotely Piloted Vehicle
RR	Rashtriya Rifles
SAARC	South Asian Association for Regional Cooperation
SAM	Surface to Air Missile
SCP	Strategic Configuration of Power
SEAD	Suppression of Enemy Air Defence
SEAL	Sea, Air, Land
SFC	Strategic Forces Command
SFF	Special Frontier Force
SIGINT	Signal Intelligence
SIMI	Students Islamic Movement of India
SLBM	Submarine Launched Ballistic Missile
SLOC	Sea Lanes of Communication
SM	Sena Medal
SOF	Special Operations Forces
SRBM	Short Range Ballistic Missile
SSBN	Ballistic Nuclear Powered Submarine
SSM	Surface to Surface Missile
TA	Territorial Army
TAR	Tibet Autonomous Region
TGM	Terminally Guided Munition
TMD	Theatre Missile Defence
UAV	Unmanned Aerial Vehicle
ULFA	United Liberation Front of Assam
USI	United Service Institution
USTRADOC	United States Training and Doctrine
UYSM	Uttam Yudh Sewa Medal
VM	Vayusena Medal
VrC	Vir Chakra
VSM	Vishist Sewa Medal
WMD	Weapons of Mass Destruction
WPI	Wholesale Price Index

FOREWORD

Restructuring of the Indian Army does not merely mean changes in organisational structures. It includes restructuring of the field force, efficient management of internal and external conflicts, optimisation of doctrine and concepts, upgrading human resource development (HRD), streamlining logistics and modernising the army training methodology. Restructuring should be compatible with the likely security environment and battlefield milieu; it should be a balance between manpower, weapons and force multipliers; and should conform to the availability and allocation of funds.

The future world is likely to be as volatile as any in the history of mankind. Our potential adversaries will be well armed, and are likely to confront us in many conventional as well as unconventional ways. Any instability in our neighbouring countries and the extended region of our interest, directly or indirectly, will impinge upon India's security. In the coming decades, the role of the army will continue to be "to preserve national interests and safeguard territorial integrity and unity of the country, against any external or internal threats, by deterrence or by waging a war."

The Indian Army, being a dynamic institution, has adapted to the changing environment in the past in a pragmatic manner. Change, in the coming decades, is likely to be much faster, for a number of reasons. Technology is rapidly changing and if the army does not absorb it at the same rate, it is likely to be left behind. Great changes are also taking place in our society. Being the army of a democratic country, all societal changes do have a profound effect on the structures and functioning of the army. Some other obvious reasons are the war on terrorism, the volatile regional environment and internal dynamics with a security bias.

Future wars will be conducted with the aim of achieving a situation of political advantage, and not merely victory. Traditional war-making concepts of capturing territory, destruction of military forces or strategic resources, and attacking fortified defences are becoming less relevant in modern warfare. Low intensity conflicts are likely to be the preferred mode of waging war in future.

All operations on the future battlefield will be joint and combined, and there will be a substantial increase in the employment of the third dimension, for both operations as well as logistics. Warfare in the information age will require highly complex planning and coordination to tackle both friendly and enemy situations, as well as the creation of a favourable public opinion. Operations in the future may not be easily divided into conventional conflicts or low intensity conflicts. The shadow of nuclear weapons would also influence the planning and conduct of operations.

The army needs to increasingly focus on the operational level of war, as the outcome of any future war will largely depend on the success or failure of operational level battles. In order to effectively plan, coordinate, and execute rapid, simultaneous, and decisive operations, to the depth desired, the army needs to restructure and reorient its philosophy of conventional war-fighting. The army needs to develop a force capable of rapid deployment, with in-built speed, lethality, and information dominance that will enable it to conduct decisive operations. The structure of the army should also be such that it can meet challenges across the entire spectrum of threats that are likely to manifest themselves.

Internal threats to India's security are mostly non-military in nature, although some require military force to deal with them. The proxy war in Jammu and Kashmir (J&K), initiated by Pakistan, and insurgencies in other parts of India, especially in the northeastern states, require military force to tackle them.

Organisations as large as the Indian Army inherently resist change, forgetting that changes in the emerging security environment and the future battlefield milieu, as well as societal changes, demand change. Considering the momentous changes taking place in the global, regional and domestic environments and their impact on security formulations, the army needs to restructure, so that it continues to be the potent force that it is and serves the nation with efficiency and élan.

Combat power is not simply the sum of machine performance. It requires individual and organisational competence and synergy as well. Machines can assist, but warfare continues to be an intensely human activity. Meeting challenges amid the more fluid, lethal and dispersed conditions of future combat will require superb training and leadership. In the complex battlefield of the future, it would be essential for the army to develop its human resources to a high pitch, so that they are able to meet the challenges of the future.

The enormous human potential in the army, its judicious harnessing, moulding it to exacting standards, providing it special skills and injecting a high level of motivation, are essential prerequisites for the achievement of excellence. Emphasis on the development of personality, leadership traits and core military values, will have to increase. Motivation will continue to be an effective and economically low cost force multiplier in the coming years and decades. Numerous trends will shape military leadership in the coming years. The traditional 'hands on' leadership will remain essential, but future leaders will have to reorient themselves for joint operations, much larger peace-keeping operations, the stresses and strains of low intensity conflict (LIC) and non-combat roles.

The preceding paragraphs encapsulate the major issues that were discussed during the maiden national level seminar of the CLAWS in March 2004. This volume is not only a compilation of some excellent papers that were presented at the seminar, but also includes the details of the interactive sessions, which were an essential and invigorating part of each session. The book also includes the details of the inaugural and the concluding sessions, which were extremely useful in setting the stage for the seminar and highlighting the issues of importance respectively.

The essential point that emerged from the inaugural session was the importance and indeed the dire need for joint operations. The three Service chiefs were unanimous in espousing the need for the three Services to operate in a joint manner in all aspects of war-fighting.

The seminar was divided into four sessions, in a sequential manner, so that a holistic view could be taken of the subject in its entirety. The first session of the seminar looked at the future and dealt with the security environment and the threat perception that was likely to evolve in the coming years and decades. The papers presented were of high quality and amply reflected the professionalism and experience of the speakers. Incisive comments by the discussants as well as by the audience added to the quality of the discourse. The coverage of the speakers was vast and included the international, regional and national environment, and how the security dynamics would affect us. The factors affecting the region as well as the extended neighbourhood were brought out in fair detail. The unipolar nature of the world, the emergence of China on the world scene, the impact of 9/11, the nuclear dimension, and the impact of domestic forces on the security environment, were discussed in detail. As was intended, the first session set the stage for delving deeper into the subject.

The broad topic for the second session was "national aspirations" and the part the military had to play in achieving them. The intention was to have a pragmatic look at what the nation should aspire to, in the light of the emerging threats and challenges, which were so succinctly brought out during the first session. The focus was on the shaping of military strategy to meet the challenges, the recommended strategy, coping with proxy war, the dire need for sustainable development, a vibrant defence R&D base and self-reliance, and rapid technology integration. Considering the size and potential of India, a strategically autonomous perspective was recommended. Many speakers highlighted the importance of joint warfare. A capability approach, instead of the traditional threat approach, was also highlighted. The stress was on India striving to become a developed country rapidly, for which adequate military capabilities were the *sine qua non*. Developing our human resources and modernising training capabilities were also stressed.

Budgeting was the subject of the third session. Having analysed the threats and challenges, and deliberated on the aspirations of the nation, a look at finances was the next logical step, before the specifics of restructuring were debated. The budgetary aspects that were analysed included the past trends, likely future allocations, and pragmatic projections. It was brought out that defence budgets in the past had been modest, with accretions only after a conflict or war. Resultantly, the modernisation of the armed forces was in fits and starts.

It was highlighted that in recent years the defence budgets were at an all time low, which precluded any meaningful modernisation. This had resulted in the combat potential of the army being adversely affected. Speakers also highlighted the archaic and cumbersome procurement procedures, which resulted in large sums being surrendered at the end of each financial year, further reducing the combat potential of the armed forces. The general consensus, at the end of the session, was that for an army of the size India was fielding, a defence budget between three to three and a half per cent of the gross domestic product (GDP) was essential. The non-lapsable defence fund, which had been instituted recently, received favourable comments. The lack of accountability, especially of the integrated finance in the Ministry of Defence (MoD), also received adverse comments.

The final session focussed on the need for the restructuring of the force and doctrinal changes needed to enable the Indian Army to continue to be a potent force, which would be able to successfully fight the nation's wars in 2020 and beyond. Thought-provoking papers were presented during this session and many suggestions were offered. Keeping in view the changing nature of war, which pointed towards increased low level and sub-national level conflicts, it was argued that the army should restructure its formations and units to meet the emerging challenges. Small, mobile and information technology enabled units were recommended. A number of speakers recommended major increases in the size of our special forces, as it was felt that they would increasingly be required to meet future challenges, particularly in asymmetric situations as well as in low intensity conflicts. Some felt that the nation needed forces only at the two ends of the conflict spectrum, viz. nuclear forces and forces to fight low intensity conflicts. However, the general consensus was for an army of full spectrum capability.

It was recommended that the nation's nuclear forces be vastly enhanced and made more potent. This would increase their deterrence value, and would also enhance the nation's strategic autonomy, increase international political leverage and bargaining power, as well as immunity from politico-military pressures and from economic and technology sanctions. A substantial nuclear capability, including sizeable numbers of thermonuclear devices in our nuclear arsenal, would enable the nation to play a substantial role in shaping the world order. A substantial increase in our missile forces, along with the fielding of qualitatively better and longer-range missiles, was also recommended.

It was appropriate in many ways that the first seminar of the newly set up CLAWS was on the extremely important subject of restructuring the Indian Army to meet the challenges of the third decade of the 21st century. The eminent analysts who participated in the deliberations and the highly aware audience amply justified the selection of the subject. The seminar was extremely well received by the audience, a large number of whom were serving officers from the three Services. The media, as well as the retired community, both civil and military, were also well represented and took an active interest in the proceedings.

We, in the CLAWS, have enjoyed putting this volume together, in the manner in which it is presented. The views contained in this volume are those of the authors in their individual capacity, and do not necessarily reflect the thinking or policy of any organisation or institution. However, I am solely responsible for any infirmities, errors or shortcomings in this volume.

The CLAWS hopes to conduct seminars and other events in the same genre in future and plans to publish the proceedings so that they are available in the public domain. This is in conformity with one of the aims of the centre, which is to spread the word about matters military. We hope this volume will whet your appetite to remain current with important security-related issues.

Delhi Cantt.
November 2004

Lt Gen Vijay Oberoi
Director
Centre for Land Warfare Studies

Inaugural Session

Welcome Address : Lt Gen Vijay Oberoi, PVSM, AVSM, VSM (Retd)
Director, CLAWS

Inaugural Addresses : Gen N.C. Vij, PVSM, UYSM, AVSM, ADC
Chief of Army Staff

Admiral Madhavendra Singh, PVSM, AVSM, ADC
Chief of Naval Staff

Air Chief Marshal S. Krishnaswamy, PVSM, AVSM, VM**, ADC
Chief of Air Staff

WELCOME ADDRESS

Lt Gen Vijay Oberoi, PVSM, AVSM, VSM (Retd)
Director, CLAWS

Gen N.C. Vij, Chief of Army Staff, Admiral Madhvendra Singh, Chief of Naval Staff, Air Chief Marshal S. Krishnaswamy, Chief of Air Staff, former chiefs, commanders-in-chief, delegates, friends from the media, ladies and gentlemen.

It is my privilege this morning to welcome you to the inaugural seminar of this newly formed Centre for Land Warfare Studies, or CLAWS for short. This centre has been recently set up with a variety of objectives, but perhaps the foremost is to look deeply into all aspects of land warfare, with the twin aims of learning and disseminating nuances, especially those of a futuristic nature, to all concerned. Let me add that the persons concerned are not just the personnel of the army, the navy and the air force, but all decision and opinion-makers and indeed all citizens of our country who may have an inclination to know more about matters military. Although the phrase Land Warfare stands out prominently in the name of the centre, as we all know, no operations at any level are possible today unless they are joint in nature. The centre will, therefore, endeavour to always focus on joint operations while organising its events.

Ladies and gentlemen, the subject of this inaugural seminar of the centre is as displayed i.e. "Army 2020: Shape, Size, Structure and General Doctrine for Emerging Challenges." We have a large number of eminent panelists who will deliberate on every major facet of relevance to the subject over the next two days, in a total of four sessions. The four sessions are being chaired by Gen V.N. Sharma, former COAS, Lt Gen V.K. Nayyar former governor of Nagaland and Manipur, Shri Mohan Guruswamy of the Centre for Policy Alternatives Society and Gen Shankar Roy Chowdhury, also former COAS and currently a member of the Rajya Sabha. We also have a number of eminent speakers on each panel. I am sanguine that their individual and collective wisdom will ultimately result in a broad but coherent picture of what the Indian Army of 2020 should look and feel like.

Ladies and gentlemen, land warfare has evolved over years, decades, centuries and, indeed, millennia, because it is dynamic in nature. It is not just about weapons but about everything, from individual soldiers to organisational structures, to joint and combined operations, to logistics, to the bewildering variety of weaponry, technology and doctrine, and a host of variables and imponderables; all this and more, the centre will focus on, and hopefully meet the objectives it has set for itself.

May I also draw your attention to the logo of the centre, which encapsulates in three small words what we intend to achieve: "Victory Through Vision."

Ladies and gentlemen, as you were informed, the chief guest for today's inaugural function was His Excellency, Dr A.P.J. Abdul Kalam, our Rastrapati and the supreme commander of the three Services. However, he was constrained to opt out as the schedule of the general elections has been announced and he feels he should not participate in any event till the elections are over, lest his presence be misconstrued in any way. His presence would have been a great honour indeed. I am sure we all understand his desire to scrupulously adhere to all aspects of the strong democratic process of our nation. The Hon'ble Defence Minister, Shri George Fernandes, who had also agreed to grace the occasion, has also conveyed his inability to attend, on account of the general elections.

Ladies and gentlemen, I am indebted to the chiefs of staff of the army, the navy and the air force for accepting our request at short notice to take on the mantle of chief guests for this morning's inaugural function. It is a privilege and I am honoured to have them amongst us. Your presence, sirs, and support will undoubtedly give a major fillip to our fledgling organisation. Let me also welcome every one present; the former chiefs, commanders-in-chief, the distinguished delegates, the participants, members of the media and serving and retired officers of the army, the navy, and the air force, for accepting our invitation and being with us today.

Thank you, ladies and gentlemen. •

INAUGURAL ADDRESSES

Gen N.C. Vij, PVSM, UYSM, AVSM, ADC
Chief of Army Staff

Thank you very much Gen Oberoi, my two esteemed colleagues, Admiral Madhvendra Singh, CNS and Air Chief Marshal Krishnaswamy, CAS, all the former chiefs from the army and the air force, former Defence Secretary Mr Yogendra Narain, many senior officers from all the three Services, and distinguished panelists, ladies and gentlemen.

It is indeed a pleasure for me to be here today to participate in the inaugural session of the CLAWS. The need for such a forum was long felt, in order to have some independent and unbiased opinions on certain matters which are critical to the land forces, or to warfare as such. As Gen Oberoi has mentioned, the phrase "land warfare" really doesn't mean much, as today is the time of jointmanship, as it has been for quite some time. Since World War II, especially, there has been a requirement for all the three Services to operate together. As a matter of fact, operations on land and in air have become totally synonymous. In a war situation, the navy also plays a very important role.

We have wanted to set up a forum of this type for quite some time, so that we can take advantage of independent opinions and, fortunately, we now have one. I am sure you are aware that the world over, most armed forces have the benefit of 'think-tanks' like CLAWS, and their opinions carry considerable weight. In the USA, they have the RAND Corporation and the National Defence University. They also have the Association of the US Armed Forces. Similarly, in the UK, you have the UK Defence Forum and the Royal USI, and even in India, we have, very fortunately, the Centre for Air Power Studies. The navy also has a similar forum. When some scholars, retired senior officers and eminent thinkers suggested the setting up of such an organisation, we welcomed the idea and assured our support, including the provision of logistical support from time to time. This discussion has brought us together today. In our discussions, I have suggested that the centre should come out with unbiased, well considered views, but these should not be devoid of the practical realities of the times through which one would be passing. It should also be a thought process which will be all encompassing, keeping in mind the requirements of all the three Services, with special emphasis, of course, on land warfare.

Let me clarify that the views they come up with would be the views of the think-tank and should not be taken as the official views of the Indian armed forces or the Indian Army, because the exercise would be purely academic, so that maximum benefit accrues to the people who are still in uniform.

The subject of the seminar is of a very topical nature. All armed forces need to have a plan and a vision for the next 20 to 25 years to focus on. The Indian Army also has such a vision up to 2025 and it is on account of that vision that this particular subject has been selected for the seminar. We need to evolve a broad doctrine for the army at the end of it. We are in the process of evolving one, and we already have a rough draft. Your deliberations will perhaps help us to finalise it; we shall look at them very seriously and analytically to see how we can use them.

After this, you will perhaps go through the process of setting up a long-term plan of your own, as to what you would like to do over the next few years, and later over the next 20 to 25 years. I would recommend that you have an annual agenda for the centre which can be decided by your advisory board and, of course, if you consider it fit, you can consult us. We could also give our suggestions from time to time, so that your work is of contemporary use to us.

Lastly, let me leave a thought with you. While we do need to study warfare and past events very carefully, there is also a need to reflect on pitfalls. Please remember that we do not fight the next war with the last war's tactics and systems. We should plan for future wars with the help of our experiences of past wars, and determine what we need to change to achieve victory.

I would like to thank you, ladies and gentlemen, for coming here in such large numbers. I am sure your presence will add great value to the learning process for us in the armed forces. I would like to thank our former chiefs as well as my two esteemed colleagues for joining us this morning. It indeed gives a lot of credibility to the forum.

Thank you. •

Admiral Madhvendra Singh, PVSM, AVSM, ADC
Chief of Naval Staff

Gen Vij, Air Chief Marshal Krishnaswamy, Gen Oberoi, Gen Shankar Roy Chowdhury, distinguished guests, ladies and gentlemen.

The other day you must have read an article "Dear Indian Army: Thank you." It was written by Admiral Nadkarni, and today another admiral stands here to voice more or less the same sentiments, in this sea of olive green. Of course, I do not have to read that article or attend this seminar to realise the value of an army, and indeed to realise the value to our nation of the Indian Army, because frankly, the man standing before you is one who is already converted.

I was born in the Indian Army. I have learnt many things from the Indian Army, much of what you will be discussing. One learnt as a young boy, along with people of the Indian Army. In those days, hunting was allowed, *shikar* was allowed, and I recollect that many of the things I learnt just chasing game as a young boy, apply equally to what the army does: whether you call it outflanking, whether you call it surprise, or whether you call it stealth, camouflage, manoeuvre, economy of force et al. What I would like to say is, whether it is *shikar* or outwitting our enemies, we remain the same even today. The tools have changed, the technology has changed. Today one hears a lot about information warfare. It was as important in days gone by as it is today. It's just that you have tools like satellites, unmanned aerial vehicles (UAVs), surveillance radars, etc, to get that information.

The subject chosen, of course, is very timely, very apt, but crystal gazing at the best of times is a bit hazardous and should normally be done only by fortune tellers, but armies, navies and air forces have to be planned. They have to be planned for the future, based on trends and these trends, we know very well, we have studied them and I have no doubt that the people who are here in the seminar know these trends, and based on these trends, obviously, certain recommendations will be made. In seminars like this, ladies and gentlemen, we must always challenge some assumptions and I would not go only for the assumptions which are totally army dominated; there are many other assumptions which need to be challenged, such as what many people are saying, that wars between great powers are no longer likely. The fact is many people have said this before, many people said prior to World Wars I and II that wars are unlikely, but throughout history, give men, or even women for that matter, something to quarrel about, and they will, and, in fact, the map of world today, if you really look at it, has been drawn by their quarrels. Another assumption is: wars will be short and they will be swift. So thought Kaiser Wilhelm prior to World War I. In fact, he told his troops that they would be back before the leaves fell. It took five seasons of falling leaves before the war ended. The same was the case with the Iraq and Iran War, and even the latest war, where the Americans fought the Iraqis with hardly any opposition, but it lasted six to eight weeks, and in certain ways, it still continues. For a short war, the army, navy and air force will act in a different manner and for a long war, they will again be different. While we hope for a short war, we must always be prepared for a longer one. There are a few who say that there are many scenarios in our country where it is a single Service that matters and another Service really does not. Perhaps this is true in peace time, where an army is fighting another army, but when countries go war, it is not the navy fighting a navy or an air force fighting an air force, it is a country fighting a country, and when that happens, no matter where you apply force, it matters. While you are, of course, planning the army of the future, as two of my distinguished colleagues have already said, please think jointly. As we say in the Defence Services Staff College, please "think purple."

It is not the jointness of the armed forces that matters, it is the jointness of every arm of the country, every arm that can give some muscle to the war. For jointness is what matters between the armed forces in this day and age of networking. Standard operating procedures should be the same and, finally, we should train, work and exercise with each other far more than we have been doing in the past.

Stand-off precision attacks, as I have said in another forum, are going to become another principle of war shortly. Certainly, we do not see the enemy at sea, yet we fire off miles and miles away; the air force does the same. Ultimately, that will happen to the army also. People are already thinking about why large armies come into contact. Why must you actually come into contact? Of course, I agree that the infantry is the "Queen of the Battle" and the infantry has to finally go in. Yet, the fact is that we have to think of precision stand-off attacks. Must you go into contact, if you can finish off the enemy in some other way? While you are thinking of modernisation of your army in the year 2020, please do not forget to modernise the man, and in this respect, to modernise the man, you have to change his attitudes, his mindset, and his leadership styles. The old ways may not necessarily suffice in the future. Ultimately, as the old saying goes "It is the man behind the gun that matters," and, therefore, I say, you must modernise the man while you modernise your equipment in the army.

Finally, of course, you cannot have an admiral not saying something about the navy. You all talk of manoeuvre: I would like to remind you that the largest manoeuvre space in the world is the sea. Seventy per cent of the earth is covered by the sea, and it represents the largest manoeuvre space in the world.

This has been proven in recent history, whether it is the Falklands, the Gulf War or even Afghanistan, where troops were landed from ships in the heart of Afghanistan. Throughout history, navies have transported and supported armies wherever they needed to go, and I can assure you that this navy intends to do the same. I would like to wish the seminar all success, Gen Oberoi, and may your deliberations ensure for all of us in the armed forces "Victory Through Vision."

Jai Hind. •

Air Chief Marshal S. Krishnaswamy, PVSM, AVSM,VM**, ADC
Chief of Air Staff

Gen Oberoi, my esteemed colleagues, respected former chiefs, ladies and gentlemen.

For me it is indeed a great pleasure and honour to be here this morning. As far as the air force is concerned, we are very much part of these deliberations and the thinking process. It is of great importance to us, because, as was so well said by Gen Vij, in future conflicts, whatever type they may be, we all have to fight together. It will not be the army's war, it will not be the navy's war and it will not be the air force's war. It will be our war. When the country is at war, every citizen has an important responsibility. We have a great responsibility entrusted on our shoulders; hence, we must put to the best use all we have to achieve our objectives, because this is what we owe to our nation. In a democracy, we take up arms to resolve issues as a last resort, after all other means like diplomacy and so on have been exhausted. Therefore, it is a combined responsibility that we have to achieve our objectives, because that is what we owe to the nation. What is interesting and important today is that the times are changing, and they are changing rapidly. Perhaps, my watch is ticking faster than before! I feel in my job that by the time we take a decision, events have overtaken us from all sides. Let me give you an illustration. We are used to working in a certain way; as a nation and as a democracy, we have our own way of thinking; as human beings we react and we perform the way we have been brought up, tempered with age and years of service behind us. We have a certain pattern that is difficult to change. It influences our thinking. All these thought processes and what we have on our minds get formatted in our brains over the years. Our actions depend upon what is stored in our minds. But today the challenges that face us are actually challenging our thinking abilities. We need to determine whether what we have stored in our minds continues to be valid today.

The global situation is changing. We have a very learned audience here today and I am sure they are looking at things globally. We can no longer be only India-centric. Take, for example, Kargil – the conflict was highly localised, it may even be called a skirmish, but it took on a global proportion. Every country in the world was suddenly interested in what was happening in Kargil. Kargil was unheard of before, but across the world they knew that something had happened in Kargil. So, whatever happens today has certain global dimensions. The other factor is the media: information travels so fast, nothing is secretive, nothing can remain unanalysed everything gets known very quickly today. Also, there is a demand for action from people occupying responsible positions. What are you going to do about it? An average citizen is much better informed today. In a democracy , the tax payer wants to participate, and question decisions. In the armed forces, as we are the soldiers, the airmen and the sailors, whatever we do has to be professional, has to be top class. We are accountable to our people in a democracy. That is a great challenge. We cannot give reasons and excuses on any matter. Everything has to be open and it has to be debated. There is a greater demand on accountability now. Information and knowledge are important: the information will be there, but the knowledge of what exactly is going on and where is likely to be limited. So, it gets very reactive. The world today, and how it will be shaping up in the next two decades, is of great importance to us. It is not just our own nation on the move. When we talk about war-fighting and about the employment of the military, it is very important to have a good perception of the world at large, of the superpower and other powers, and how these equations are developing. Hence, everything we do has worldwide implications and has to have worldwide acceptance. Today, war-fighting has changed in many ways, especially in the forms of fighting. There is great concern about the people across the world today, including in our country. Human rights have assumed much greater importance. The activists against human rights violations have very firm demands. Public opinion strongly demands that innocents should not be touched in any type of war-fighting. This is both a constraint and a great responsibility, which is now forced on us. We can no longer just send planes with 1,000 pound bombs. The 1,000 aircraft bombing raids of the past are now history. We can't just fire an artillery barrage of the type that we saw in the last war and last operation. We have to be very precise about what exactly the objective is. Future military conflicts will be very demanding, very specific to what the objectives are. And all of it is, of course, going to be photographed and passed on in almost real time, to the public, wherever they are. Therefore, war-fighting is going to have very major changes. It has to have acceptance worldwide.

The other constraining factor, of course, is resources. No military in the world, whether American or any other, is happy with the resources or the budget it gets. India is no exception. We are very much aware that we are a developing country. There is the so-called feel-good factor, but at the same time, we are familiar, as citizens, of where the poverty line is, where the money should be spent. There is a large demand for our resources to be spent for the people. Our great country is committed to the upliftment of our people and we must now certainly ensure that our citizens get what they have not been able to achieve, or get, in the last 50 years of our independence. Therefore, our major focus is on our people, and when it comes to finances, we shall always be on a tight budget, but we shall still be expected to perform according to the responsibility entrusted to us. The responsibility is very compelling and very demanding, but our performance has to be very professional. At the same time, what strikes us, the people in uniform in a democracy, is that the military is somewhere in the barracks or in our local flying areas, as we call it, or in our own ocean–training. What happens there is not of great consequence or importance to the average public, unless we come in for exposure and demonstration, exercises and parades, and so on. Normally, in peace time, the public is not really involved in how you train, how you recruit the people joining the military ; it is of the least consequence to the public, but it is of importance to us. Therefore, public attention gets diminished in peace-time. However, we do not want war. It disturbs our tranquillity and yet it has an impact, mostly a negative impact, because it is not known as to what exactly the Services are doing. So in peace time, the impression of the military is that we are government servants, public servants (*government ki naukari*) and, therefore, we are focussed on the bidding of the government. We carry on, and what propels us is the next promotion, where do we go from here, what is the size of our force, what are our emoluments, and so on. The drift sets in. We are, after all, each one of us, citizens of this country and, therefore, the drift may set in, but then we have to draw ourselves back, and focus again on the importance of being a soldier, an airman and a sailor, and that we have a job to do, that we are not merely government servants, not merely public servants, we are the military. We wear a uniform and there is honour and focus in what we do. So, we have to periodically reassess ourselves and, therefore, who we shall have in uniform is a very important matter. The military is highly respected in our country and we will have to make sure that the quality is maintained, 24 hours a day, every day, and that has to be ingrained in our system.

As far as the system is concerned, modernisation must, of course, go on, but to the extent it is affordable. It is our responsibility to modernise, but the thinking behind it is very important. We can fight with swords, we can fight with anything as long as we have the motivation and the people, provided the people who man the weapons are well motivated. We have seen many examples of this in Afghanistan or elsewhere in the world, or what the Liberation Tigers of Tamil Eelam (LTTE) is doing in Sri Lanka. These are highly motivated fighters. We are not questioning here what the cause of the fighting is, but these people who have taken up arms, have done so with great bravery and so-called focus. It is very important that the motivation of our military is also focussed.

In the end, let me talk about resources. I would like to say that budgets are very difficult to get, but we are focused on expenditure, we are accountable as to how we spend our money. Therefore, in this game we have realised that we can save on expenditure and be very cost conscious, and yet be very productive, militarily speaking.

The new challenge today is how we manage our expenditure. We need to bring in some discipline, some specialisation in our expenditure, so that we are that much more accountable and answerable. We have to motivate our people, the best of the people, to join the Services and to remain motivated and carry on doing what they are expected to do. In peace time, we should train, but when called upon, we shall strike and strike so hard and strike so precisely that we do not harm or disturb peaceful citizens. We will secure our objectives in the time required and to the extent required, and then withdraw to the barracks. I believe that is the challenge that faces us today and that is where and how we shall gain respect for our defence services, from our own nation, our own citizens and of course, our friends the world over. I shall put this as an objective to be achieved for myself and, of course, for the gathering here. I am sure we all generally agree on this, and it shall be a pleasure for us to participate and work together in unison, with a tri-Services posture, towards these objectives. My best wishes to the new organisation, the centre as you call it. I am sure it will go from strength to strength, and it shall throw up ideas on subjects that we can ponder upon.

Finally, I would like to say that while we keep attending seminars, where so many papers are read, and we applaud them, what is important, and I look forward to it, is the action plan to carry out these ideas. I hope that we can implement even five per cent of what we say, what we see and hear. While implementation is very important, it cannot be done by individuals or by a single Service; it is a national commitment. The government, the public, all of us together, must implement what we believe is a good idea.

Thank you very much. My best wishes for the seminar. •

APPROACH PAPER

ARMY 2020: SHAPE, SIZE, STRUCTURE AND GENERAL DOCTRINE FOR EMERGING CHALLENGES

Lt Gen Vijay Oberoi, PVSM, AVSM, VSM (Retd)
Director, CLAWS

General

The Indian Army is the fourth largest in the world, in terms of numbers, as well as in terms of some items of capital equipment. Since Independence in 1947, the army has been engaged in active operations on a sustained basis, with only short periods of peace. These challenges have helped the army to earn a formidable reputation of a force that delivers, usually against heavy odds.

Over the last decade and a half, while the professional levels of its officers and men have been sustained and even enhanced in many respects, the fighting potential of the force has unfortunately decreased. There are many reasons for this. Some of these are:

- A lack of vision and knowledge of security-related issues amongst the political leadership, as also the bureaucracy.
- Stunting the logical progression and growth of the army on misconceived notions, by withholding or decreasing budgetary allocations.
- A potentially damaging resistance to change amongst the army brass.
- Short command tenures amongst senior ranks, which inhibit futuristic thinking.
- Hesitation amongst most senior officers to take risks.
- A status quo mentality among a large number of decision-makers.

The result is that while accretions have taken place in the number of persons in uniform; in the number of additional units and formations; and the quality and quantity of armaments, the overall structure of the army and the methods of doing business continue to be much the same as they were five decades ago.

There have been broadly two major structural changes in the size and organisational structures of the army. The first was the post-1962 expansion, and the second was in the mid-Eighties. However, the impact of these changes was soon lost, as there was no matching change in doctrine. Resultantly, the army has generally remained static, both structurally and in doctrinal terms, except for incremental changes, to meet challenges as they arose. What the army has lacked is a futuristic vision and a firm resolve for change, as also the courage to adopt the innovative and shun the predictable.

In the over five decades since Independence, vast changes have occurred in the security environment, within the country, in the region of immediate concern, and at the global level. The last decade and a half has been of special importance, on account of the ongoing Revolution in Military Affairs (RMA). The time is perhaps ripe to plan for radical and fundamental changes, so that the fourth largest army in the world does not just remain large in terms of numbers, but also carries the necessary punch, so that it is capable of meeting the challenges which the first two decades of this century are likely to throw up.

Global and Regional Environment

The global military environment will continue to be influenced by the unilateralism of the sole superpower, the USA; the growing potential of regional powers, particularly China; the war on terrorism; the vast potential of the information revolution; the spread of fundamentalism; and the social upheaval in many developing countries due to the rising expectations of their people. The scenario is further complicated by a rise in trans-border terrorism, sponsored ethnic strife, and low intensity conflicts.

The 21st century had opened with the global environment focussed more on economic issues and multilateral and bilateral cooperation amongst nations. However, after the events of September 11, 2001 (9/11), security issues have re-emerged and taken centre-stage. In addition to terrorism, the world continues to be plagued by conventional military threats, as well as non-military threats. This state of affairs is likely to continue in the next two decades.

In broad terms, the following security-related trends are likely to manifest themselves in the coming decades:

- While the risk of a nuclear war stands greatly reduced, the possibilities of nuclear proliferation are on the increase.
- On the conventional plane, while limited conventional conflicts are still likely to occur, they are gradually giving way to trans-border terrorism, engineered ethnic strife and sponsored insurgency.
- The international players, individually or collectively, are likely to intervene, not only to limit the duration or extent of a conventional war, if fought, but also to ensure that it remains below the nuclear thresholds of warring states.

Changing Nature of War

Rapid advancements in technology, in the fields of information, nuclear energy, biotechnology, aviation and underwater operations, are changing the concept of warfare. In the field of information technology (IT), digitisation, networked communications, electronic warfare (EW), as well as information warfare (IW) have highlighted the importance of systems integration and the concept of "system of systems."

RMA, which is manifested by high technology weapons, sensors, communications and IT, will increasingly impact on all types of military operations. Evolving technologies are resulting in a transition from "information in warfare", through "information dominance" to "information control." Warfare in the information age, irrespective of whether it is nuclear, conventional or low intensity in nature, will require highly complex planning and coordination, near real-time and total situational awareness, decision support systems and massive data-base and information-exchange capabilities to tackle both friendly and enemy situations. Technology has made information more readily available, and it has now become a weapon of choice. The Indian Army needs to focus on IT and IW, in a big way in the coming years and decades.

In conventional operations, the front, depth and rear areas would be engaged simultaneously with real time surveillance, integrated command, control, communication, computers, intelligence and information (C^4 I^2), target acquisition and highly lethal precision weapon systems. The battlefield will become more digitised, more transparent and would experience a major increase in deployment of electronic devices, signalling the growing primacy of the electromagnetic spectrum. Rapid escalation will also reduce space for conventional warfare. The ability of ground forces will depend upon the speed with which they can move, concentrate and regroup rapidly over any type of terrain.

The proliferation of all types of missiles; the versatility of modern aviation platforms; the precision guided and terminally guided munitions (PGMs and TGMs); and multi-dimensional manoeuvre vehicles are some of the breakthrough technologies which have changed the nature of warfare. Technology is now evolving exponentially, which means the rate of change is accelerating.

Missile defence (MD), whether at the national or theatre levels, is another technological advancement which will have a major effect on warfare in future. MD is a strategic shift from a doctrine of deterrence to that of interdictory interception.

Concepts and methodologies of waging war are also changing. Asymmetric warfare, non-nuclear deterrence, regime change and preemption are the new buzzwords added to the lexicon of politico-military terminology. It is now difficult to divide operations into conventional and low intensity conflicts. The modern battlefield demands that wars be fought in all six dimensions – space, cyber, air, land, sea and sub-surface.

Today, joint and combined operations are the norm. IT, in all its manifestations, affects decision-making. At the same time, IW, including the creation of a favourable public opinion, is a necessary adjunct to the higher direction of war. Military planners will need to give considerable thought to the likelihood of terrorist threats also, while formulating plans for military operations. Resultantly, greater numbers of troops and equipment would be required to cope with such threats.

Overall, the army will require flexible, highly tolerable organisations – from individuals to subunits and units to formations – to meet the diverse needs of future operations. The fast pace of operations, day and night battles and high attrition rates will result in greater physical and psychological strain on all combatants. This will have to be factored in by leaders at all levels.

Threat Perception

India's sphere of influence needs to encompass not just the South Asian subcontinent, but also the northern Indian Ocean area, from the eastern seaboard of

Africa in the west, to the Malacca Strait in the east, and must include Iran, the Central Asian Republics (CARs) and China. India's credibility, as a regional power will be contingent upon institutional stability, economic development and military strength, including nuclear deterrence.

The long stretches of disputed borders with China and Pakistan and sizeable areas under their illegal occupation, are unlikely to be resolved in an early timeframe. They will continue to generate tensions and instability at periodic intervals. Our vast island territories also need to be guarded.

In the last over two decades, the army has been heavily committed in dealing with internal threats like insurgencies, terrorism and proxy war. This has undoubtedly been at the expense of its war-readiness, as well as the desired quality of life. As low intensity conflicts will increasingly manifest themselves in the future, the army has to restructure itself, so that while it combats insurgencies and manages high-grade political violence, it continues to retain its combat edge. Having two sets of forces, the traditional army for deterrence and waging war and an internal security force (ISF) for combating LIC is perhaps one answer. Major reforms and restructuring would be required for this.

India's military strategy needs to be effective across the entire spectrum of possible conflicts, from a high intensity conventional war under the backdrop of a nuclear threat, to low intensity conflicts which may include high intensity insurgency, militancy and terrorism.

National Aspirations and Desired Capabilities

India aspires to be recognised as an economic and military power of some reckoning, with a permanent membership of the UN Security Council. To achieve these objectives, India needs to ensure a peaceful internal environment, security from external threats and capability to project power in the region. Such an aspiration requires India to modernise its armed forces and equip them with contemporary techno-equipment to meet the expanded roles they would need to perform, while ensuring sustained economic growth and development.

India needs to develop the capacity to influence the affairs of the region by maintaining a limited force projection capability to influence events in the area of its interest. If India wishes to be a leading nation in the 21st century, she would have to configure her military forces accordingly. The army will have a major component in any force projection capability.

The force structure of the army should be such that it is able to achieve the objectives the nation expects from it. We need to be regional players of eminence, as well as have a say in global strategic formulations. The army's capabilities, therefore, must include the following:

Nuclear: We need to refine our nuclear doctrine, which should continue to be primarily for deterrence, but for use in case we are forced to use the nuclear option. Our retaliatory capability must be potent, comprehensive and timely. This entails, besides a range of warheads, the requisite delivery and support systems. We need to build up our current missile capability substantially so that the army is equipped with a full range of missiles, capable of reaching all possible targets.

Conventional: Credible conventional deterrence will continue to be important. The conventional capability of the army must be comprehensive against our likely adversaries, The army must maintain an effective superiority in conventional forces vis-a-vis Pakistan. The army must also have the capability for punitive response to provocations short of war. The challenge China is expected to pose in the mid and long-terms requires that our deterrence capability be upgraded, by adding a potent offensive capability to our current posture.

Low Intensity Conflict: The army needs to support the counter-insurgency strategy of the nation, without diluting its conventional capability. It must have adequate capability to fight high-grade.insurgency in any part of India, as well as proxy wars of the type currently being waged by Pakistan in Jammu and Kashmir. This may imply a separate force, which must be equipped, manned and trained specifically for this role.

Peace-Keeping: The army will have to play an enhanced role in peace-keeping operations, mostly under the aegis of the United Nations, but perhaps under other circumstances too.

Budgetary Aspects

The growth of the Indian Army in the past has been haphazard and as a reaction to contemporary crises. Declining budgetary support and archaic financial management procedures further aggravate the situation. Currently, financial allocations for defence are in the region of 2.5 per cent of the GDP. The share of the army varies, but is generally around 52 per cent of the budget allocations. Is this sufficient for a million-strong army? The answer is obviously in the negative. Most modern militaries are sustained with a budget that varies between 3 and 4 per cent of the country's GDP. It has been analysed that a defence budget of over 4 per cent is likely to have an adverse effect on the overall growth of a nation. On the other hand, sustained modernisation of the military is not possible with a defence budget of less than 3 per cent. In the context of India, a financial allocation of about 3.5 per cent will meet the requirements of both national development and military modernisation. Our capacity to spend enhanced allocations also needs to be upgraded by modernising our procurement procedures.

Economic policy-makers in India have, unfortunately, viewed the defence expenditure through the narrow prism of fiscal policy, rather than through the looking glass of technological upgradation, foreign and defence policy imperatives, and self-reliant industrialisation. It is necessary to acquire a broader vision on the relationship between defence spending and national development.

Defence expenditure constitutes one of the major items of Central government expenditure (CGE), and given the fluid nature of the current world order and the challenging domestic and regional security environment, will continue to retain this position. A viable and pragmatic defence posture can only be attained and sustained by well-planned deployment of financial resources, in accordance with clearly defined long-term objectives. It needs to be appreciated that procurement and upgradation of equipment for modernisation has to be a continuous process. It cannot be sustained on the basis of ad hoc allocations and political proclivities.

Force Restructuring and Doctrinal Challenges

Organisations as large as the Indian Army inherently resist change, forgetting that the army is a reflection of the society it serves, the changing security environment, and the future battlefield milieu. Considering the momentous changes taking place in the global, regional and domestic environments and their impact on security formulations, the army needs to restructure so that it continues to remain the potent force that it is and serves the nation with efficiency and élan.

Restructuring does not merely mean changes in organisational structures. It includes optimisation of doctrine and concepts, restructuring of the field force, efficient management of internal conflicts, upgrading HRD, streamlining logistics and modernising the army training methodology. The imperatives of restructuring are:

- Compatibility with the likely security environment and battlefield milieu.
- Balance between manpower, weapons and force multipliers.
- Conforming to the availability and allocation of funds.

Future wars will be conducted with the aim of achieving a situation of political advantage, and not merely victory. Traditional war-making concepts of capturing territory, destruction of military forces or strategic resources, and attacking fortified defences are becoming less relevant in modern warfare. Instead, the aim of future military operations will be to bring about strategic dislocation.

Deterring war would be the primary aim of the army. This is only possible if it maintains a potent force in being. Once deterrence fails to checkmate the adversary, then there should be no hesitation in selecting the military option, which also includes preemption.

The army's overall strategy must be proactive, with doctrinal shift from attrition to manoeuvre warfare. Other important concepts which need to be debated are the need for simultaneity of operations; relevance of tactical and logistics pauses; and above all, the need to focus on one front at a time, so that overwhelming force is brought to bear on the front which is activated.

The army needs to conceptualise the integrated battle at the operational level and the major focus must be to target the minds of the enemy's military and political leadership.

Future conflicts must be won quickly and decisively, with few friendly casualties, in a time-frame that makes simple attrition methods of war-fighting obsolete. In future operations, army formations would need to gain destructive positional advantage over the adversary. This is possible only if the army develops the ability to manoeuvre rapidly.

The army needs to restructure and reorient its philosophy of conventional war fighting. The army should concentrate on three-dimensional warfare, which entails doctrinal changes like shifting focus from the battlefield to battle space.

Restructuring, to coopt the vertical velocity of attack, will vastly increase the tempo of land operations. Army Aviation needs to play a vastly enhanced role in land operations in the coming decades. This is only possible if it grows dramatically, both qualitatively and quantitatively.

The army needs to redesign its combat forces, with an emphasis on deployability, manoeuvrability, battle space awareness, lethality and survivability. At the same time, the army must transit from manpower orientation to high technology.

Linear tactics, which have long been the forte of the Indian Army, need to be discarded. The focus on adhering to detailed orders, with nearly every aspect of the operation centrally controlled and 'synchronised', needs to give way to a bold and offensive approach. Innovative methods need to be planned for restoring mobility in the mountains, where long periods in a defensive mode have fostered a defensive mentality.

The army's logistics structure is archaic, unwieldy and not cost-effective. It largely follows the system that had existed prior to Independence, when India acted as a logistics base for the British Indian Army fighting World War II in many overseas theatres. Over the years, some changes have been made, but no major restructuring has been carried out.

In the complex battlefield of the future, it would be essential for the army to develop its human resources to a high pitch, so that they are able to meet the challenges of the future.

Technology is advancing at an astonishing pace. The fruits of the information age – precision and information – coupled with future breakthroughs in mobility, could lead to significant new capabilities at every echelon. There is a need in the army for a doctrinal shift towards mobility and agility, on the one hand, and greater reliance on technology, on the other.

Conclusion

National security requires preservation and protection from all types of external and internal threats and pressures. The Indian Army has met the security challenges posed to the nation since Independence with courage and professionalism. By its actions, the army has ensured that the values that are dear to the nation are preserved and indeed enhanced.

Future wars will be technology driven. The next few decades of the 21st century will bring new challenges. The army, being a dynamic organisation, has to anticipate these challenges so that corrective measures to counter them are thought out and implemented in advance. The essence of the military profession is preparedness. As the nation's ultimate weapon, the army must never compromise with excellence. It must remain geared to impose the nation's will at all times and at all costs. Therefore, it is essential that it is always structured and equipped to meet the challenges of the future.

Combat power is not simply the sum of machine performance. It requires individual and organisational competence and synergy. Machines can assist, but warfare will remain an intensely human activity. Meeting these challenges amid the more fluid, lethal and dispersed conditions of future combat will require superb training and leadership.

The mission of the army will continue to be to fight and win the nation's wars and conflicts. Implied in this is keeping all the components of the army trained and well maintained, so that they are ready and capable of achieving decisive victory on any battlefield.

The Indian Army must continue to open windows to the future and maintain its cutting edge. Only then can it sustain its proficiency and professional excellence.●

Session I

Future Security Environment: Changing Nature of War, Threat Assessment, Battlefield Milieu and Impact of Technology

Panel Chairman : Gen V. N. Sharma, PVSM, AVSM (Retd)

Panel Discussants : Prof Satish Kumar
Lt Gen Satish Nambiar, PVSM, AVSM, VrC (Retd)

Paper Presenters : Lt Gen K. S. Brar, PVSM, AVSM, VrC (Retd)
Ambassador Ranjit Gupta
Vice Admiral P. S. Das, PVSM, UYSM, VSM (Retd)
Lt Gen V. K. Singh, PVSM (Retd)*

**The paper of Lt Gen V.K. Singh could not be presented during the seminar, but has been included here.*

PRELIMINARIES

Lt Gen Vijay Oberoi

Ladies and gentlemen, we now start the seminar proper. The subject of the first session is "Future Security Environment", which will encompass the changing nature of war, threat assessment, battlefield milieu and impact of technology. The panel consists of six eminent persons. Gen V.N. Sharma, former COAS, is the chairman. We have two discussants, Lt Gen Satish Nambiar (Retd) and Prof Satish Kumar, and there are three paper presenters: Lt Gen K. S. Brar (Retd), Ambassador Ranjit Gupta, and Vice Admiral Premvir Das (Retd).

Gen V.N. Sharma

Well ladies and gentlemen, the first session is very important; we have to start thinking as to what the future will bring. In the past, all of us have been accused of fighting the last war. This is perhaps because both technology and thinking are moving so fast that it is not easy to keep pace. What we think of today, may not come to pass tomorrow, and what we think is not necessary, may well be essential. I am sure our speakers and later on all of you, will bear in mind that the human mind and human brain are the fastest of the lot. Imagination must be utilised, and people who do not agree with your views must not be discouraged. If you encourage dissent, at least you are alive to the fact that something may happen that is different to what you thought. From our experience in the past two-three wars that we have fought, I refer particularly to 1965, 1971 and 1999, what we thought was going to happen, did not happen. What our intelligence told us was going to happen, did not happen. It was not only because of the new equipment that people were using, which we knew about, but rather the different manner of employing that equipment and the new tactics, new techniques of the tactical battle that sometimes we were confronted with. Therefore, let us give a clear thought to the future and see what our speakers have to say. Do not be afraid to speak up after that with your views; all of us must accept dissenting views, particularly if you can give us some good reasons for them, so that we can take note of them. We will now start with the presentations.

ARMY 2020: FUTURE SECURITY ENVIRONMENT AND THREAT PERCEPTION

Lt Gen K.S. Brar,PVSM,AVSM,VrC (Retd)

Introduction

Some scholars have termed the 21st century as the century of ascendancy of Asian power and have gone to the extent to suggest that it could even be a challenge to US unipolarism and superpower status. This view is based on the assumption of a relative decline in US and Russian power, and increase in Asian power, particularly that of China, Japan and India. According to one perception, this provides an incentive for a realignment of interests between the US and Russia in order to contain the new Asian centres of world power. This, however appears a bit far-fetched in the author's opinion. The US has the politico-military wherewithal to balance on its own the growing power of Japan and India. But it will need strategic partners to regionally balance China. This is where India's and also Russia's importance lies as strategic partners of the US in such an eventuality. But as everything else, nothing is predictable at this point of time.

India's regional security has been affected by a collusive nuclear weapons- cum-missile development between China and Pakistan, the spread of Islamic fundamentalism, the growing nexus between narcotics trafficking and terrorism, ethnic diversity, the proliferation in lethal weapon systems, besides many other factors. The aim of this paper is to analyse the emergence of security trends and challenges in India's immediate and extended neighbourhood and threats to its national security in the mid and long-terms (2020), so that it provides a framework for the formulation of a national security strategy. Since long-term threats cannot ever be predicted with certainty, as perceptions and relationships may change from time to time, these need to be constantly reviewed and updated periodically. In the 21st century, which has just begun, we find a world order that continues to be in a state of transition after the disappearance of bipolarity, and new challenges and threats to national security are surfacing. While conventional war is becoming increasingly unviable as an instrument of foreign policy, it has been overtaken by a mixture of sub-conventional conflicts, armed violence and terrorism. To be able to evolve sound strategies for meeting the emerging threats to a country's national security, it is also necessary to take into account the developing structure of global and regional economies, communications and technologies.

Although Asia is fast emerging as a formidable economic power, turbulence and instability in the region are prone to conflict due to nuclearisation, arms proliferation, political transition, unresolved territorial disputes, and spread of violence. In South Asia, there can be little doubt of the fact that India is a unipolar power, particularly if the external influences of the US, Russia and China are delinked from the region. The strategic realities of the region are that:

- India is the predominant power in the region in terms of geographical size, human resources, economic strength, industrial infrastructure and technology, in comparison with any of its neighbours.
- Challenges to the above potential can be expected only from the US, Russia and China.
- Pakistan, a long standing ally of the US (more so in the past) and China, despite its possession of nuclear weapons, is in no position to challenge India.

South Asia: Regional Trends

Wary of China, India will increasingly look towards the US, but its need of oil and desire to balance Arab ties to Pakistan will lead to a strengthening of ties with the Persian Gulf states also. The South Asian region in 2020 could be perceived as follows:

- India will remain the unrivalled power, with a large and strong modern military, including naval and nuclear capabilities; and a dynamic and growing economy as the world's fourth largest economic power. Indian democracy will remain strong and it will have robust technological modernisation comparable to global standards.
- Pakistan will be more isolated, fractious, and dependent on international financial and economic assistance. It will not have recovered from decades of political and economic mismanagement, divisive politics, lawlessness, and ethnic friction. Democratic reforms will not produce much change in the face of opposition from an entrenched political elite, and radical Islamic parties. In a climate of continuing domestic turmoil, the government may be able to wield its governance confined to the heartland (Punjab); and in the worst case scenario, some crystal gazers even feel that Pakistan may be a 'failed' state by that time, although it would be in India's interest to have a stable, mature and democratic neighbour instead.

Pakistan

The first salient trend is that all the South Asian states are increasingly taking their bearings from strategic developments along a wider canvas, rather than the local arena alone, and their responses will, thus, contribute to the elimination of the subcontinent's traditional isolation. The Indo-Pak security competition, which has been the most familiar feature of local politics, will continue, but it will be less a bilateral affair than a unilateral one. Pakistan, by virtue of its weakness, fragility and continuous fear of India, will attempt to compete with the latter to preserve its security and autonomy. Having lost its traditional Cold War supporter, the US, as a future ally, Pakistan will increasingly attempt to rely on Chinese protection, weaponry and technology. India, on the other hand, would replace the previous 'Pakistani obsession' to look beyond the constraining environs of South Asia to pursue larger great-power capabilities that have eluded it so far. This new approach, centred upon economic strength and maturity, will build closer relationships with its neighbours in South Asia and, of course, the US, giving India the capacity to stand shoulder-to-shoulder with the great powers in Asia and beyond. This fact notwithstanding, the Indo-Pak scenario would still be dangerous and a cause of concern for a number of reasons, some of which are given below.

First: territorial disputes have resulted in three and a half wars (if Kargil were to be considered a half war) and a continuing proxy war waged by Pakistan in Kashmir for over a decade. Even if the present day ceasefire and peace overtures were to fructify into a final settlement of the Kashmir issue, Pakistan is unlikely to give up its motives for continuing an undeclared war against India, by once again encouraging and supporting militancy and secessionist movements in other border states such as Punjab, and the Northeast (in collusion with Bangladesh) as it feels threatened by its strong and powerful neighbour, India.

Second: the nuclear programmes in both countries are still in a state of precarious evolution, with somewhat uncertain levels of deterrence and 'command and control' systems which are yet to be put in their place. Besides this, there will remain a danger of Pakistan's nuclear weapons falling into the hands of terrorist groups, which could end up in a catastrophe. Thus, the possibility of an occurrence of 'crisis instability' in Pakistan cannot be overlooked.

Third: the internal weaknesses of the Pakistani state, largely influenced and controlled by radical Islamic fundamentalist groups and the dominance of the military over elected institutions in all matters of governance and decision-making at the national level, are matters of worry and deep concern.

Fourth: severe economic disparity vis-à-vis India and the inability to overcome domestic discord, could prompt Pakistan to embark on diversionary brinkmanship with India, leading to military confrontation.

In the years ahead, what needs to be watched is whether Pakistan would give up its obsession of Kashmir, having come to realise that the present insurgency and war of proxy has run out of steam and reached the limits of its success, or, would it choose to escalate it by enhancing either the quantity or quality of support to the insurgencies, either in Kashmir or any other geographical part of India. This would determine India's security responses during the '*near term*' period, in terms of a more aggressive strategy of military retaliation. At the same time, the region could witness instabilities as a result of nuclear proliferation by either or both countries. The determinable factor would be the kind of nuclear weapons, delivery systems and doctrines that may be developed by both countries. The issue of stability assumes a fair degree of urgency in the context of both countries acquiring relatively short-range ballistic missiles, perceived to be armed with nuclear warheads, even if the survivability quotient is low. History and past events have shown that even though there may be some form of civilian government today and in the future, which could, in a sense of optimism, realise the '*no win*' result of low level conflicts with India, and it acts with maturity, its writ would not run if radical Islamist parties were a threat in being to the government in power; with the result that India may have to face up to undesirable policies and cross-border activities. We need to accept, at the same time, the fact that Pakistan cannot be coined as a "failed state" as long as it has some external help (from China?) to bail it out. India would welcome a stable, peaceful and responsible neighbour instead.

During the transitional mid-term period (2010-2015), we could witness power transactions, as a consequence of uneven growth of capabilities between the two nations. For instance, a dramatic growth in Chinese economic and military power, and, at the same time, a strong India as an economic power. If India's economic strength is perceived by China as capable of altering the prevailing balance of power between India and Pakistan, it could have a role to play in protecting a weak Pakistan, by forging a strategic relationship with it and, in the same stroke, offsetting India's aspirations of becoming a strong and dominant regional power in South Asia; a development such as this could provide Pakistan incentives for continued conflict with India under China's security umbrella. Similarly, a growing strategic relationship between the US and India, as has already begun, could lead to a forging of greater ties between China and Pakistan, thus, deterring India from taking any punitive action against Pakistan in the face of provocation from the latter.

- In the long-term (2020), keeping the above connotations and emerging trends in mind, we could perhaps draw a reasonable conclusion that the possibility of a deliberate major war between India and Pakistan is increasingly unlikely, because the political objectives that could be secured through the instrument of war are fast disappearing. As the economic and political transformations in both countries surface, it is more likely that these two South Asian neighbours would be forced into mutual accommodation, even if some outstanding issues between them remain unsolved. This is also because Pakistan, the weaker of the two, will increasingly find it a Herculean task to resort to force for territorial gain, while India, the stronger state, would rather remain preoccupied in asserting its claims of acquiring global recognition rather than resorting to military action in the subcontinent. Needless to say, such a posture would be welcomed by both the US and China as they would not be faced with the dilemma of intervention in support of one state or the other.

In summary, therefore, it would be reasonable to assume that the threat perceptions involving India and Pakistan would manifest themselves in the period leading onto 2020 (the long-term) as follows:

- Indo-Pak border unrest may continue in varying degrees to be the dominant form of conflict, because neither would achieve gains from an all-out decisive war, keeping in mind the military balance and the influences and pressures from extra-regional powers such as the US and China. However, either one, or both, may support insurgencies in the other's territory, and yet restrict the levels, keeping in mind the nuclear factor, so that low intensity clashes do not escalate into a full scale military conflict.

or

- The possibility of low level insurgencies and local conflicts inadvertently escalating into a larger conflict, accompanied by nuclear brandishing, in the wake of serious instability in Pakistan or a takeover by a Islamic fundamentalist regime in that country.

or

- A war of desperation launched by Pakistan, in case India's economic and military strength implies the isolation of the former and an increasing neglect by the international community, in particular the US, of its outstanding territorial claims; even at the cost of dismemberment of the nation state.

China

China is located on India's northern border and its growing nuclear and military power, its phenomenal economic growth and its enhanced industrial capacity, make it a vital strategic concern of India. India and China are two large land powers, with less asymmetry in their power relations in comparison with that of India and Pakistan. Historically, China continues to be an aggressive and expansionist state, and its military and economic rise will remain a threat to India unless the border issues between the two countries are settled. Its aspirations to become a major power centre in the international system apart, China desires to remain the sole power in Asia and views India's defence and economic growth as a direct threat to its dominance in the region. Currently, China demonstrates a desire to maintain "peace and tranquillity" in its neighbourhood for it to be able to pursue its economic reconstruction and modernisation, unhampered during its quest for superpower status. In the long-term, however, China views India as an arch rival in attainment of its global and regional aspirations; hence, its defence paradigms are aimed at marginalising India into a sub-regional power, by increasing Chinese leverage in South Asia. Chinese moves to contain the Indian strength are based on its policy of "encirclement" of India. China's transfer of nuclear and missile technology to Pakistan and its assistance in developing the Gwadar and Pasni ports on Pakistan's Makran coast, its gradual penetration of Myanmar where it has established a radar base in the Coco Island, which is in close proximity of the Andaman and Nicobar Islands, its deployment of nuclear forces in Tibet and other bordering provinces, besides the inroads it has made in Nepal, Bangladesh and Sri Lanka, are already perceived as a long range strategy of outflanking India.

China today is the fastest growing economy in the world with a growth rate of over 12 per cent per annum, and it is anticipated that it may overtake the US by the year 2020. India's growth rate has been steady at 5.5 per cent of GDP and it has, in fact, achieved a growth of 8.4 per cent in the second quarter of 2003 (July-September), with prospects of a 9 per cent growth in 2004. In every likelihood, by the end of the next 10-15 years, India would be the fourth largest economic power in the world and China would have to contend with the former being a dominant power in its own right in South Asia. In the next ten years or so, up to 2015, a Sino-

Indian conflict seems unlikely, as both countries would be looking towards completing their economic, political and military transformations. The balance of power along the Himalayan borders dividing the two countries, unlike 1962, is stable and the Chinese would have to make major strides in improvement of logistics capabilities to be able to sustain a conventional war against India in the near and mid-term periods. The possibilities of direct Sino- Indian confrontation may, however, grow during the long-term (between 2015-2020). These could include either border clashes on India's northern borders, or even naval skirmishes in the Indian Ocean as India builds up its naval strength. Much depends, however, on the future relationship between the two countries, the economic and political changes that take place, as well as the *inter alia* relationships with extra-regional powers such as the US and Russia; and perhaps, even Japan, which would by then be a major economic power.

Taiwan, an economic giant and a bone of contention between China and the US, will influence futuristic relationships between these two countries, since a democratic Taiwan has no desire to unite with China. Although Taiwan has opened up its trade with China and has heavy investments in that country, it has, meanwhile, acquired adequate military strength to counter any threat from mainland China. Should China decide on settling scores with Taiwan and forcing its reunification through military means, it would invite US intervention. Even if there was to be no open conflict between China and the US on this issue, any mutual mistrust and misperceptions between the two major powers is bound to affect the South Asian security configurations. Similarly, the recent improvement in US-India ties and the likelihood of an increasing gulf between the US and Pakistan (once US interests in Afghanistan and Iraq are fulfilled) would be seen by China as a direct threat to Chinese predominance in this region. In such a case, there could be closer linkages between China and Pakistan, which may provide scope to Pakistan for any misadventure against India. These extra-regional factors will need to be carefully analysed and war-gamed, to fit into India's futuristic threat perceptions.

Even if there was to be Sino-Indian conflict in the long-term, as a result of clashing interests, it is more likely to be fought in the air or in the Indian Ocean and there is less likelihood of a major land battle due to topographical constraints and other factors, though it cannot be ruled out, and force structuring would have to take this into account while evaluating the threat levels.

Military planners need to take into account the fact that even if the Chinese were to maintain a force level of 9-10 divisions in Tibet, they would be able to augment that force level by induction of additional forces from bases in Yunnan, Sichuan, Qinghai and Xingxiang. The Chinese ability to augment present force levels in Tibet and fight a campaign for several weeks is being continuously improved with development of road networks leading to the border, the completion of the oil pipeline from Lanchow to Lhasa, a number of all weather airfields in Tibet, which would be operational all the year round, and the Golmo-Lhasa railway. The People's Liberation Army (PLA) is fast upgrading its ballistic missile inventory. It already possesses the DF-41 and DF-42 missiles, with ranges of 8,000 and 10,000 km respectively. Also, development of the JL-2 SLBM (submarine launched ballistic missile) is well underway. China's growing influence in the Indian Ocean region (IOR), with its nuclear submarines, is well known; in its policy of "strategic encirclement" of India, it is looking towards acquiring naval bases in Myanmar, Bangladesh, Sri Lanka and Pakistan, with air/overland routes to such bases. By the year 2020, China would be close to having a powerful "Blue Water Navy" dominating the Indian Ocean, an additional threat dimension, the implications of which merit attention.

India's Smaller Neighbours

Bhutan. Bhutan is a landlocked Himalayan kingdom having common boundaries with China and India. It is fully dependent on India for its survival and has resisted Chinese attempts all along of making inroads into the country in the political, diplomatic and economic fields, lest it comes under Chinese influence and domination, as has happened to Nepal to a considerable degree. China is keen to develop its roads leading on to the Bhutanese border, as this could provide China an additional route of ingress into India in a future Sino-India war. There have been no irritants between Bhutan and India and both countries continue to maintain very friendly relations. The rise of the Nepalese population (40 per cent as of now) could gradually shift the demographic pattern in the country, and eventually the indigenous population of Drukpas(Bhotias and Lepchas) may be reduced to a minority, which could have some implications, in the context of Nepalese migrations in India's Terai region and their presence in large numbers in the Darjeeling Hills district, in close proximity of Bhutan; these elements could be influenced by the Maoists in Nepal in creating internal problems for India. Apart from the foregoing, we can rule out any security threat from Bhutan, apart from a thin possibility of China violating its sovereignty in order to create an additional route of ingress into India.

Nepal. Nepal has a perennial problem of the tussle between the monarchy and its political leadership. The recent violent activities of the Maoists inside Nepal have posed a very serious problem, and although Nepalese security forces presently control the capital, Kathmandu, and some of the major towns, in other areas, the Maoists run their diktat, and law and order has virtually broken down. The Maoist movement is changing rapidly from an insurgency into a people's uprising and these new security challenges in Nepal pose a spillover threat to India. The open borders, with a population of eight million Nepalese in India, increase the prospects of weaponisation in the states of UP and Bihar, besides a long-term threat of subverting the Gurkhas in the Indian Army. The stakes in the internal disorder and political instability in this Himalayan kingdom are as high for India as for Nepal, since it could gradually manifest into an internal security threat to India. Relations between India and Nepal have had their ups and downs over the years, but it would be safe to assume that India faces no military threat from Nepal. In the long-term, however, with China active in the development of infrastructure in Nepal and spreading its influence within that country, we cannot rule out the possibility of the latter being used as a conduit in case China wages a war against India. To offset this, there is a pressing need to project an honest desire of regional cooperation and solidarity; and to demolish any feelings of suspicion or mistrust that Nepal may have towards India.

Bangladesh. There is no serious problem with Bangladesh, except for the sanctuaries and covert support provided by that country to Indian insurgent groups in the Chittagong Hill Tracts. After many years of military rule, Bangladesh has settled down reasonably well to a mature civil administration. The main problem confronting the country is its shattered economy, as a result of which it could fall an easy prey to aid offered by external powers, even at the cost of its sovereignty. These could be Pakistan in the short-term, though very limited as the former is itself in poor economic shape; but more probably, by China in the long-term, as it could exploit the situation in its "encirclement" policy towards India. A major worry for India is the close proximity of the Bangladesh border to the vulnerable Siliguri Corridor, through which all lines of communication run to Assam and all the northeastern states of India. This corridor is sandwiched between Bangladesh and Nepal and in any future war with either China or Pakistan, it will have to be safeguarded against an attack launched by Bangladesh to sever the Northeast, in collusion with either or both Pakistan and China, particularly the latter in the long-term period (2020).

Myanmar. After over twenty-five years of little or no contact with Myanmar, India has now established a relationship with it, motivated primarily by security concerns. Myanmar borders four of India's northeastern states, namely, Nagaland, Manipur, Mizoram and Arunachal Pradesh, and the border between the two countries serves as a convenient gateway for insurgents working towards the destabilisation of India. Although presently there is a lasting peace with the Naga rebel groups, and the backbone of the United Liberation Front of Assam (ULFA) in Assam has been virtually broken, there is a diminishing likelihood of a nexus growing between India's rebel groups and the Chin and Karen rebel groups operating in Myanmar, as has been the case in the past. To that extent, the fears of Myanmar being used as a platform to destabilise the northeastern states has subsided. But a worrying factor from India's security point of view is that of increasing Chinese involvement in Myanmar, as it gives them the potential to deploy their sea power in India's maritime areas of interest, and to eventually directly threaten India's eastern flank. Developments regarding the establishment of a Chinese electronic listening post in the Coco Islands, just off the northern tip of the North Andaman Island, assistance to the Myanmar junta to improve and develop naval ports and facilities on the Arakan coast, and military assistance to the Myanmar government, are well known.

Sri Lanka. Sri Lanka has a long history of the Sinhalese-Tamil divide and there seem to be very slim hopes of a peaceful resolution to the ethnic conflict, which has been raging in the island country for many years. The impact of the ethnic conflict has its ramifications in Tamil Nadu and has every possibility of entry of external influences, basically, China,on the pretext of assisting Sri Lanka in dealing with the insurgent problem; thereby also gaining ground in its strategy of encirclement of India. Sri Lanka, however, as in the case of Bhutan and Nepal, poses no threat to India.

India's Extended Neighbourhood

Afghanistan. While the Taliban has been dispersed by the American coalition forces, and there is presently a representative government in Kabul, future developments need to be carefully watched. Prior to the US intervention in Afghanistan, we are aware that the worsening situation in Kashmir coincided with the rise of the Taliban. The existence of a client regime in Afghanistan had allowed Pakistan to create strategic depth in Taliban controlled Afghanistan, out of reach of the Indian armed forces. Furthermore, Pakistan was able to divert troops toward the Indian border, taking advantage of a friendly regime on its western flank. Pakistani militants were reinforced by foreign elements that had taken part in the war against the Soviets and were available to Pakistan for the insurgencies and terrorism that it directed against the Indian state and its people. Additionally, the narcotics trade originating in Afghanistan was used to fund the covert operations of the Inter-Services Intelligence (ISI) against India. In the long-term, the stability of Afghanistan would depend on the Northern Alliance and the majority Pashtuns being able to provide good governance, so that the warlords are marginalised. Afghanistan would need the support of Pakistan because of the influence the latter wields on the Pashtuns; in return, Pakistan would not like to see Afghanistan and India developing close relations for reasons mentioned earlier. We can safely conclude that India faces no threat from Afghanistan as there is no clash of interests between the two countries.

Central Asian Republics

The end of the Soviet Union created a new political entity on the vast expanse of Eurasia. Five new republics, Kazakhstan, Kyrgyzstan, Tajikistan, Turkmenistan and Uzbekistan emerged, each with its own national identity problems. The geographical significance of this region is that it lies at the crossroads of Russia, the Middle East, South Asia, and the Far East. Given the internal weakness of its component states, coupled with the military power of the states surrounding it, there is a clear danger of turmoil in Central Asia adversely affecting Asian security as a whole. Ethnic and religious tensions, energy politics, and great power rivalries all intersect in the area connecting Central Asia to Asia. The emergence of a predominantly Muslim and multi-ethnic CARs has, thus, added a new strategic dimension to the geopolitics of the whole of Asia and more so, to the countries located in its close neighbourhood. India's security concerns related to this region are as under:

- Central Asia lies between two nuclear powers, Russia and China, and at the interface of Russia and the Islamic world. It shares borders with Afghanistan and Pakistan, both of which have been a major source for the spread of religious extremism. The spread of religious fundamentalism and influence exerted by Islamic extremist groups in the region could invigorate similar elements active in Kashmir. Both Pakistan and China would try and build up an anti-India rhetoric to India's detriment, in order to serve their own interests. This, despite the fact that the spread of Islamic fundamentalism is a cause of worry to China itself, already having an Islamic underbelly in Xingxiang.

- Central Asia has become a major source and transit point for drug trafficking. This region is a major route for transportation of narcotics from Afghanistan to Europe. These states being internally unstable and economically weak, have found the drug trade to be very lucrative; in the southern part of Kyrgyzstan alone, four million people are involved in the dealing, growing or processing of raw materials, as a result of which it exports more narcotics than Myanmar and Thailand. As drug trafficking is a major source of financing terrorism, it is of serious concern to India which has been, and is likely to continue to be, on the receiving end of terrorist related activities.
- The Central Asian region also remains highly vulnerable to the smuggling of fissile material for weapons of mass destruction (WMD). As it is, this region lies between two major nuclear powers, Russia and China, and in close proximity of two smaller nuclear weapon states, India and Pakistan. Uzbekistan has the world's third largest uranium deposits, whereas Tajikistan has uranium enrichment capability and Kyrgyzstan has a lot of nuclear waste left over as a legacy of the erstwhile Soviet Union. Kazakhstan was a nuclear test range during that era, and has qualified technicians well versed in nuclear technology. The region, thus, could be a hot-bed for proliferation of WMD and a source of clandestine supply of nuclear devices to the likes of Bin Laden and similar terrorist outfits.
- A number of major powers such as the US, Russia and China are trying to spread their sphere of influence into Central Asia and are busy cementing partnerships and building a new cooperative framework with some of the republics. The US and China are both eyeing the phenomenal large reserves of oil and natural gas located in the region, with the former anxiously exploring every means of developing an infrastructure for exploitation of this natural wealth through a pipeline below the Caspian Sea, whereas China is exploring a potential project that would allow for diverting the resource through a pipeline in the easterly direction. Although most technical experts believe that these ambitious projects are not feasible in the immediate or short term, they may well be viable in a 10-15 year period. Other countries, such as Turkey, Iran, Saudi Arabia, Afghanistan, and Pakistan are also furthering their influence in the region, whereas Japan and South Korea are establishing economic ties with them. It is possible, therefore, in the mid and long-term, that there may be a clash of interests between the external powers vying for their slice of the cake in the new opportunities that present themselves in the region. This could lead to Central Asia becoming a flashpoint for rivalry and conflict. India, as an emerging regional power in South Asia, is naturally interested in any changes

occurring in its extended neighbourhood, which may have implications for its security.

Technology Advancement and Battlefield Milieu, 2020

The battlefield, in 2020, would witness high technology in almost every department of war. The impact of technology on the conduct of warfare would appear in a number of dominant trends; namely, extension in the reach and range of weapons, volume and accuracy of fire, systems integration, and increasing transparency on the battlefield. Unlike past wars, when the accuracy of weapon systems was compensated by heavy volume of fire, the future development of guided weapons will add a new dimension altogether. Induction of various kinds of missiles, laser-aimed weapons, target designators, and smart munitions will add to the achievement of precision fire. Two to three rounds of PGMs would be able to achieve the same destruction power that 300 conventional artillery rounds were able to achieve earlier. Thus, with an increase in the induction of PGMs, there will be a major reduction of logistics required to support an army during combat. In addition, high technology will be an influencing factor on organisations, tactics, equipment, and planning differentials between the combat arms and the logistic units. Advances in communication technology, computers, information systems, and surveillance and target acquisition systems will provide field commanders much better means of command and control over large formations during battle. However, no matter how advanced information technology may become, it would not totally eliminate the human angle and uncertainties in the fog of war. By compressing greater firepower, a smaller force will be able to achieve decisive results, as a consequence of greater lethality, accuracy, mobility, and extended ranges of weapon systems. Manoeuvre capabilities will also increase manifold, with the ability to converge speedily at a decisive point. In the 2020 battlefield scenario it would also be possible to process intelligence using advanced communication and computer systems, thus, expanding the commander's vision and detection ranges, besides improving the quality of information and instant dissemination to subordinate commanders, via real-time digital transfer. Micro processing technology will enable an army to conduct and dominate sophisticated information operations; in other words, to observe, to orient, to decide, and to act.

Getting down to the specifics of a likely battlefield milieu in a war with either Pakistan or China, the following merit consideration:

- With advances in satellite imagery as well as aerial and ground based sensors, there will be an increase in the "warning period" available before the outbreak of hostilities.
- Effective night vision devices will add a new dimension to night fighting capability; particularly so in the plains and semi-desert areas of Punjab and Rajasthan, in the context of an India-Pak War; and slightly degraded in mountainous terrain in the case of a Sino-India War.
- Whereas mechanised forces will have a major role in a war with Pakistan,

they will have limited utility in a war against China. Instead, air mobile forces will play a predominant role in the latter case.

- Wars will be short, swift, and limited against a nuclear backdrop. However, the tempo will be enhanced on both sides, using high-tech night vision and surveillance devices, and a broad spectrum of sensors.
- The integration of command, control, communications and intelligence (C^3I) systems would lead to faster decision-making and responses.
- Besides forces earmarked for conventional battle, we should expect to see 'rapid action' forces, lightly armed and equipped and backed up by a sound infrastructure of tactical airlift aircraft, intelligence agencies, and counter-terrorist organisations which would infiltrate, close in, and destroy those who engage in unconventional warfare, such as Pakistan.
- A land battle launched by China, though unlikely in any great measure due to terrain and logistic restraints, would see the employment of airborne forces targeted to seize deep objectives, duly supported by PGMs and seaborne weapon systems.
- Whereas an India-Pak War is more likely to be fought inside Pakistani territory, the reverse would be likely in the case of a Sino-India War, which would be fought on Indian soil and over the skies above.
- The stronger power would attempt to lengthen the duration of the war to its advantage; this would imply a longer duration war with China than one with Pakistan.

The US as a Predominant Determining Factor in Power Equations and Conflict Resolutions in Asia

Any prediction of regional threats, power equations and the shape of future conflicts in the India-Pakistan-China context would have to take into account America's increasing domination in Asia and the impact it would make in the mid and long-term periods.

Only time will tell whether the "war against terror" launched by the US will eventually lead to another war, or a clash of civilisations, or a nuclear war of *jehad* in South Asia. China would be apprehensive of the fact that it could be, unwillingly, drawn into a conflict with the US, not in context with an Indo-Pak military exchange, with the US using India as a surrogate, but for other reasons. The top leadership of the Taliban and Al Qaeda, having fled into Pakistan's North-West Frontier Province (NWFP) and Pakistan Occupied Kashmir (POK), there is every possibility that the war could gradually zero in on Pakistan as the new battlefield. If this were to happen, it would put China in a dilemma, as any open support for its long time ally, Pakistan, would jeopardise China's relations with the US and India. On the other hand, with non-intervention on Pakistan's behalf, China would fear that India may be prompted to settle its score with the latter once and for all and thereby tilt the regional balance of power decisively in its favour.

Growing Chinese strategic pressure in the Malacca Strait has already led to maritime collaboration between the US and India, and their navies are jointly patrolling the strait. More significantly, the US-India strategic relationship has scaled new peaks, with a series of measures taken by the US, normally reserved for its close friends and allies. For instance, joint exercises in Alaska that would boost India's high altitude warfare capabilities in the Himalayan glaciated areas where it faces Pakistan and China; joint airborne exercises in Agra; joint naval exercises in the Arabian Sea; training of India's special forces; intelligence sharing; sale of military hardware such as radars and surveillance high-tech equipment, besides giving Israel the clearance for the sale and delivery of the Phalcon AWACS (airborne warning and control system), something earlier denied to China for fear of enhancing its air surveillance and early warning capability in the Taiwan Strait. All these are a clear and implicit signal to China and Pakistan of India's growing closeness to the United States and its strengthening of military prowess. China has become increasingly concerned with the gradual shift in the regional balance of power in South Asia, driven by a US-India strategic relationship, wherein Washington refers to India being a "counterweight to China" in US perceptions and national interests; and, at the same time, Pakistan's gradual descent into a "failed state."

Another disturbing factor, not only for India but also the US and China, is that should a post-Musharraf Pakistan disintegrate or be taken over by Islamic extremists, there would be a heightened level of instability that will rock the region and increase tensions between all the major players. Even more serious and dreadful is a scenario in which Pakistani nuclear weapons fall into the hands of the extremists, forcing India to militarily intervene in Pakistan.

Conclusion

In summary, we can expect Pakistan, for some years, to remain dysfunctional and torn between the demands of military rule, democratisation, and theocratic pressures from the Islamic fundamentalist and *jehadi* groups, which are increasingly growing stronger. Pakistan, having supported insurgency and militancy in the Northeast and Punjab,has been waging a proxy war in Kashmir for over a decade. It perceives India as a serious threat to its security and exploits every opportunity to weaken or fragment the Indian state. Having possession of nuclear weapons, Pakistan's behaviour cannot be predicted, particularly as it has acted irrationally in the past. Also, what needs to be taken note of is the fact that Pakistan is not prepared to abrogate the first use of nuclear weapons and, in fact, threatens to use them in the event of India crossing into its territory. Pakistan could, therefore, be termed as a "first strike and last resort" nuclear threat. In the ultimate, what we need to understand is that it is unlikely that the misperceptions in Pakistan's mindset towards India would permanently disappear, and even if there is not another war between the two countries, it will be an "uneasy peace". Notwithstanding the foregoing, India has military superiority over Pakistan and is capable of winning a war on its own.

China perceives India as its only rival in Asia and would like it to be weak. We could safely assume that after another two decades of economic progress and military modernistáion, China would be in a position to assert itself in the pursuit of its national interests and goals. By the year 2020, China will be an increasingly influencing factor, not only regionally, but even globally, and in the event of a clash of interests on political, territorial or economic issues, India could become a victim to its use of military force to achieve its ends. China already possesses a substantial nuclear capability, relative to India. While India will, in the next 10-15 years, try and narrow down the gap, it would perhaps end up developing a relatively small, mobile, deterrent force, either land or sea based, or both, oriented towards counter-value targets. However, because India and China are both large land powers, with less asymmetry in their power relations compared to Pakistan, it seems very unlikely that nuclear weapons would be used in a Sino-India conflict even in the long-term. The likelihood of a future conflict being fought in the air (including space) or naval skirmishes in the Indian Ocean appear more probable than a land battle of any magnitude.

In the final analysis, however, China's response to a future India-Pakistan War is likely to be shaped by its desire to protect Chinese national interests, no matter at what cost. Geostrategic concerns may compel her to side with Pakistan, while publicly calling for restraint by both sides. In the triangular equation, China will ensure, by whatever means, that the balance of power in the region remains pro-China and is not allowed to tilt in India's favour.

With regard to the smaller South Asian neighbours, we cannot ignore the asymmetry that exists between India and them, in terms of demography, technological capabilities, and military strength. It is for India to remove any fears among its neighbours, which could be a logical consequence of this asymmetry, lest some of them look for balancing equations from other countries outside the region. There is no direct military threat from any of them; at most, some of them may be used as conduits by China in furtherance of its goals of weakening India, in whatever small measure it is possible. Any such activities would be within manageable limits as far as India is concerned.

Central Asia, as discussed earlier, has strong possibilities of becoming a flashpoint in superpower rivalry and this could have serious security implications for India in the long-term period. India will need to project its influence in the region through defence and economic cooperation and building a friendly relationship with the CARs at all costs.

As discussed earlier in this paper, the United States will be a major player in determining the power balance in Asia, and in the future resolution of conflicts in this part of the world. •

INDIA'S FUTURE SECURITY ENVIRONMENT

Ambassador Ranjit Gupta

Introduction

Whilst there is a host of factors that determine a country's external security environment, the three most important factors are:

- the policies and attitudes of its neighbours;
- the policies and attitudes of the major global powers;
- the policies and attitudes that the concerned country adopts towards its neighbours and the major global powers.

The last 60 years have witnessed three landmark watershed events which have decisively reshaped the global geopolitical landscape.

Watersheds in the Global Geopolitical Landscape

The Cold War

The first was the Cold War. In the wake of the Allied victory in World War II, the past Germany-centred intra-European rivalries were replaced by a new ideology-based rivalry between the US-led Western democracies and the Soviet Union-led Communist bloc. Vanquished Japan joined the Western camp. The process of decolonisation started and a huge number of independent states emerged, with the rival blocs seeking to line them up in their respective camps. This rivalry lasted for 40 years and was called the Cold War.

During the Cold War period, India was surrounded by a network of alliances which greatly aggravated India's geopolitical difficulties. One neighbour, Pakistan, was the hub of India's security threats. Another neighbour, China, with which we have an even longer border, had been almost as hostile. To make matters worse, these two established an exceedingly close, lip-and-teeth, strategic, military and political alliance. The world's most powerful nation, the US, also established an alliance relationship with Pakistan, and for the latter half of the Cold War, the US also had a strategic partnership with China. In addition, the US also established a web of alliances in West Asia and Southeast Asia, and Pakistan was a member of both. The dynamics of Cold War politics and India's insular economic policies ensured that India had marginalised itself from the international mainstream. India never conceived a long-term strategic vision of its future, beyond being the leader and spokesman of the emerging Third World; this gave India very considerable international prestige and influence, but it started waning from 1955 or so and after 1962 went into free fall. Thus, India progressively lost clout, even within the Third World, while ensuring a poor relationship with the powerful Western World. At the end, India's only friends were countries of the Soviet bloc, Bhutan, Cyprus, Maldives and Mauritius. Finally, India's most stalwart friend, the Soviet Union, disappeared and India itself was on the verge of financial collapse. Thus, during this period all three important determinants of our external security environment were adverse. A more nightmarish external security environment is difficult to imagine.

Disintegration of the Soviet Union and End of the Cold War

The second landmark watershed development was the disintegration of the Soviet Union and the collapse of the Communist empire, and these marked the end of the Cold War. Consequently, two very important things happened:

India's Isolation Compelled it to Reorient its Policies

With the initiation of economic liberalisation and reforms, India began its transition from the earlier collective national consensus on building a socialist society to a consensus on building a modern, free market one. This heralded the era of seeking to integrate the Indian economy with the global economy. It also resulted in a new emphasis on economic issues in the making of foreign policy. Another welcome transition was the shift from "Third Worldism" to the promotion of its own national interest; from abstract idealism to greater pragmatism. Anti-imperialism, which had been at the heart of India's struggle for decolonisation had degenerated into knee-jerk anti-Westernism; very significant dilution if not abandonment of this traditional anti-Western mode of thinking, as a natural reaction to events, was the third important transition.

The results have been impressive. The long emaciated relationship with the US, now the lone superpower, has been transformed, and is the best ever in the last half a century. Relationships with the European Union (EU) and major European countries have acquired a new substantive economic dimension and strategic features, with their publicly expressed support for India's Permanent Membership of the UN Security Council. These transformed relationships with the Western world have not come in the way of India maintaining its traditionally robust and strong relationship with the new Russia, after disturbing hiccups in the first few years. India has successfully established dynamically growing relationships with both West Asia and Southeast Asia, and has become a substantive player in both these regions. In West Asia, this is manifested through the establishment of diplomatic relations with Israel and the development of a strong and growing strategic partnership with it; the development of symbiotic links, particularly in the energy field, with Gulf countries and becoming a Dialogue Partner of the Gulf Cooperation Council (GCC), one of only three countries; and, an impressive Indian presence of more than 3.5 million people in the Gulf countries, more than the total expatriate population in the Gulf region from all other countries of the world combined; a vitally transformed relationship with Iran, and vibrantly developing relationships with the CARs. Similarly, in Southeast Asia, India has become a full Dialogue Partner of the Association of Southeast Asian Nations (ASEAN) and a member of the ASEAN Regional Forum (ARF); the economic relationships with ASEAN as a collectivity and with individual member countries have been developing and growing strongly in recent years; the signing of free trade framework agreements and establishment of mechanisms such as Bangladesh-India-Myanmar-Singapore-Thailand Economic Cooperation (BIMSTEC) augur well for the future; defence cooperation, particularly in the naval sphere, and strategic relationships with several countries of the region are developing rather satisfactorily.

India has been posting impressive economic growth rates in the recent past; its global trade has been rising impressively; there has been a dramatic turnaround in India's global economic standing and one manifestation is our healthy foreign exchange reserves, now more than US $ 107 billion, as contrasted with less than US $ one billion in 1990. Another manifestation is global acknowledgement of India's prowess in the 'knowledge' sector, particularly in the IT software field. Outsourcing IT enabled services to India by the advanced countries has become the latest fad.

Conducting our nuclear tests after a lengthy period of succumbing to international pressure and overcoming the expected adverse international fallout within just a few years has been a major watershed achievement. India has the third largest army in the world, the second most powerful navy in Asia, a very capable air force and impressive indigenously developed missile capability. India is amongst the top five countries of the world in space technology.

In just over a decade, India's position has been totally transformed and India has emerged on the global scene as a significant political, military and economic power with a new sense of self-confidence. The other side of the coin is that the world at large today acknowledges India as a significant player on the global stage. India is better placed today than it has ever been to handle the multiple security challenges that it faces. It has now acquired, more than ever in the past, the leverage and the opportunity to shape its security environment by judiciously exploiting the favourably emerging global strategic scenario.

A Dramatically Changed New World Started Emerging

The US emerged as the sole global superpower. The US' alliances with Pakistan and China became redundant. Strategic issues that stood between India and the US started dissipating. A rising China emerged as a very significant player in East Asia in particular. New equations and relationships started developing. But perhaps the most important new development was the phenomenon of international terrorism. Flush with success by defeating a superpower in Afghanistan, Islamic *jehadi* warriors turned their attention to new targets, mainly the US, the remaining superpower, now perceived as the main oppressor of Islamic countries and peoples, and India. While sporadic attacks against Western interests started taking place with greater frequency, it was India that faced the concentrated brunt of terrorist attacks, consciously steered and directed by Pakistan. Unfortunately, India's complaints and warnings did not elicit the kind of attention that they warranted.

This new emerging world is not divided between two superpower controlled rival ideological blocks but between areas of relative stability, growing prosperity and increasing interdependence and areas of relative instability, internal socio-political fragility and economic stagnation; between democracies and dictatorships of various hues; between globalising societies and those resisting change and integration. This latter group consists primarily of countries ruled by authoritarian regimes, countries with extremely weak institutional infrastructures and economies, countries on the verge of becoming failed states. **It is a remarkable** fact that individuals and groups indulging in international terrorism have, without exception, originated in and been nurtured, given sanctuary, facilities for living, training, travelling and funding and arms by countries which fall in this latter category. Also, all known WMD proliferation has taken place between countries with authoritarian regimes. Thus, the primary security challenges that the world faced as the 20th century ended emanated from this group of countries.

In the past, it was mainly inter-state rivalry, whether on an individual basis or as part of alliances, that determined the security environment of different countries. While such traditional security threats continue to exist, non-state actors have become a far more important security threat, not only to individual countries but to the world at large. They leapfrog boundaries and create mayhem, spread death and destruction, subversion and internal destabilisation and, thus, effectively undermine national security. And, national security threats are the greatest where state hostility is combined with state promoted activity of ostensibly non-state actors. This was specially the case in respect of India. Thus, while during the decade of the 1990s, India's external security environment in the overall global context improved dramatically, India's security environment on its northwestern borders deteriorated equally dramatically.

The Events of September 11, 2001 (9/11)

The dawn of the 21st century saw the emergence of a unipolar world with the US commanding economic, military, political and technological preeminence and predominance unprecedented in human history. President George W. Bush, who assumed office in January 2001, made it abundantly clear that the US intended to maintain this position of unchallenged preeminence into the future. Yet, for the first time in its history, the US mainland was subjected to attack on September 9, 2001, by foreign elements and the targets were the symbols of its military and economic might. **The events of 9/11 constitute the third major landmark watershed development**. Cross-border terrorism emanating from Pakistan and Afghanistan had been India's main security threat for the past decade. The events of 9/11 finally resulted in US realisation that this is an exceedingly serious threat to itself and to the world at large. Following 9/11, Indian and US security concerns converged for the first time ever.

A wounded and deeply angered Goliath has unambiguously signalled that it intends not only to subdue David but to crush him. The US has informed the world that while it desires international cooperation in this endeavour, it will act alone if necessary. 9/11 concentrated international attention on these two countries and on the larger hinterland to their west and north – the Gulf and Central Asian regions. The US is leading the fight in respect of these international security concerns. The codename of this operation is the **War on Terror**.

Thus, it is clear that India's external security environment since its independence has been determined primarily by the policies of the US, China and Pakistan, acting individually and collectively, and India's own policies. In the new post 9/11 world and in the context of the War on Terror, past equations and relationships are changing. These changing interrelationships will determine India's future security environment.

The United States

The two major developments in the War on Terror so far have been:

- Regime change in Afghanistan; and
- Regime change in Iraq.

There have been five immediate and significant geopolitical consequences of these US actions:

- The US has established a long-term physical military presence in an arc from Pakistan and Afghanistan through the Gulf and into Central Asia. The announced purpose is the elimination of terrorism at its sources and the democratisation of the region. Some movement in this direction is already evident.
- Although evidence has been lacking, US involvement in Iraq was postulated on the basis of the Iraqi regime's alleged links with Al Qaeda and its alleged WMD programmes. However, US action in Iraq has succeeded in focussing ameliorative attention on WMD proliferation – the recent renunciation of its WMD programmes by Libya; disclosures by Iran of sources of its nuclear material procurement and its agreement to cooperate with the International Atomic Energy Agency (IAEA) regarding its nuclear programmes; North Korea being persuaded to engage in multilateral negotiations relating to its nuclear programme; and, the public exposure of WMD proliferation from Pakistan and its commitment to ensure that this does not take place in the future.
- Under the umbrella of the war on terrorism, Japan, though geographically very far from Iraq and Afghanistan, has taken actions and adopted policies which are in dramatic contrast to its post-World War II political and military policies. Its deploying ships in the Indian Ocean, sending troops to Iraq albeit in a non-combat role, initiating moves to review Article 9, the kernel of its 'pacifist' Constitution, joining the US in theatre missile defence (TMD) research and development, etc, represent the political and military coming out of Japan onto the global scene.
- China has found it prudent to adjust its policies – in strong contrast to the

policies of some of the US' traditional allies and many Third World countries, China's approach to the Iraqi issue has been much more circumspect. It has generally decided to cooperate with the US wherever possible, adopt a passively accommodative posture otherwise and not antagonise the US in any way. China's proactive involvement in seeking a resolution of the nuclear issue in North Korea is one example. China's reactions to Japan's new assertiveness are uncharacteristically muted. China's reactions to unprecedentedly provocative policies being pursued by Taiwan are notably non-belligerent, in marked contrast to the past. There is a noticeable change in China's attitude towards Pakistan and its policies. China is exhibiting a newly found reasonableness in its attitude towards India.

- Pakistan has come under very severe pressure of a kind it has not faced since its independence. It is not unreasonable to assume that through its continuing and growing military presence in Pakistan and stronger than ever diplomatic and economic leverage vis-à-vis Pakistan, the US will seek to establish strategic influence over Pakistan's nuclear assets as well as the Pakistani military. Pakistan is unlikely to be able to enjoy the luxury of being able to pursue the policies that it has been smugly doing since 1989 in particular.

Clearly, therefore, the consequences of US policies since 9/11 have been directly beneficial to India and manifestly serve its immediate as well as longer-term geopolitical and national security interests. It is my view that the evolution of events since the assumption of office by President Bush and particularly after the events of 9/11 provide India with a remarkable opportunity to consciously forge an Indo-US strategic alliance. Many in India will question this assessment in the light of Musharraf being mollycoddled and praised, and Pakistan being given very generous economic and even military assistance

However, a closer examination suggests that this picture may begin to look a lot different once we consider the following factors dispassionately.

First, the overarching theoretical rationale for this is rather simple and straightforward. Given overwhelming US power and its determination to wield it, the chances of success of any policy that we pursue vis-à-vis any country or issue will, in the future, more than ever before in the past, depend to an increasing extent on the attitude and policies that the United States adopts towards those countries and issues and towards our policies. There can be no question but that the US will seek to pressurise India, alliance or no alliance, relating to issues on its own national interest agenda. There will inevitably be differences, even acute differences, on many issues, as there always have been even between the closest of allies. However, it will be easier to address these pressures and differences if we are in a partnership relationship rather than in an unhappy and questioning mode regarding US motivations, intentions and policies. This is the reality and it is not only expedient but prudent to accept it.

Second, the overall US strategy vis-à-vis Pakistan is in the longer-term security interests of India. This will be evident from the following:

- US has long castigated North Korea as a rogue state, but has been exceedingly wary of taking military action against it for fear that that would inevitably invite devastating North Korean missile attacks on Japan and South Korea and inevitably draw in US involvement, with unpredictable but potentially devastating consequences. Thus, the use of force against it was perceived as being self-defeating and counter-productive.

• Broadly similar considerations have determined the present US attitude towards Pakistan. Pakistan is a nuclear weapon state and is militarily far more powerful than either Iraq ever was or North Korea is. Though a seriously debilitated Iraq proved no challenge in the actual war, the US is facing enormous problems and taking heavy casualties in the post-war scenario; indeed, the situation is broadly similar, though on a smaller scale, in an even weaker country such as Afghanistan. If regime change had been attempted in Pakistan or had the US engaged in intrusive military intervention, the fallout would have been hundreds of times worse than in Iraq, in a country full of armed *jehadis*, capable and powerful armed forces which would have been thoroughly alienated and, a relatively huge radicalised population. Several retired Pakistani generals have publicly stated in the past that should there be attempts to neutralise Pakistan's nuclear assets, it would immediately lash out against India (and Israel). Given the nature of the Pakistani state and Pakistan's past policy record, such statements cannot be ignored. In addition, any attempted regime change would have resulted in widespread chaos, which would have inevitably spilled over into India in a highly destabilising fashion. A chaotic, disintegrating Pakistan would be an enormous threat to India's security.

• The US is in the process of establishing an intrusive long-term physical presence in Pakistan with the latter's acquiescence, which was never permitted even when the US and Pakistan had a formal military alliance. In the short-term, this will have a chastening and moderating effect and in the longer-term a cleansing effect. All this takes time, as the situation in Afghanistan has clearly shown and the situation in Iraq is starkly exhibiting. There has been an effective ceasefire across the Line of Control (LoC) for the last two months; infiltration of terrorists into Kashmir has diminished noticeably; Pakistan is responding to Indian peace overtures in a more meaningful manner than it has ever done in the past; Pakistan has given a commitment that WMD proliferation will not take place, etc. Whether we admit it or not, to a very considerable extent, all this is due to strong behind the scenes pressure that the US has been consistently exerting on Musharraf.

• The past US relationship with Pakistan and its military was in the context of the Cold War. If one were to objectively review the entire spectrum of global events throughout the duration of the Cold War, it will be observed that India and the US were on opposite sides of the fence on virtually every issue. Hence, the US-Pakistan relationship inevitably got invested with an anti-India flavour, which was most noticeably evident in 1971-72. The Cold War has ended, the Soviet Union, India's stalwart and all-weather friend, has disintegrated and hence, the present US-Pakistan relationship has a conspicuously different dynamic. Indeed it has a pro-India bias. Additionally, the US has dismantled the strategic depth that Pakistan had created in Afghanistan through the Taliban regime and the new dispensation in Afghanistan created by the US is once again an India friendly one.

Thus, the strategy of betting on Musharraf to help change Pakistan rather than taking him head on has considerable merit.

Third, there are several other persuasive reasons for an India-US strategic alliance:

- India's first priority must be rapid economic growth and technological advancement. This will be best served by the closest possible relationship with the US.
- The US had already anticipated this possibility when for the first time the US National Security Strategy Report (the current one was issued in September 2002) mentioned India at some length and the evolving future of Indo-US relations was elaborated in very positive terms. Since then there has been very impressive forward movement in Indo-US economic relations and defence cooperation. Just last month, identical statements were issued by Prime Minister Vajpayee and President Bush significantly entitled "Next Steps in Strategic Partnership."
- As we move further into the 21st century, the spread of democracy is going to be one of the most important foundations for peace, stability and prosperity, particularly in Asia. In this endeavour the US, the world's oldest democracy, and India, the world's largest democracy and the first in Asia, are natural partners and allies and can together play a vitally important role in furthering this process.
- Israel has been the most trusted friend and steadfast ally of the US in West Asia. The Indo-Israeli relationship is developing very satisfactorily, without in any way adversely impinging on its traditional relationships in West Asia in general and the Gulf region in particular. It is a relationship of great strategic importance to India. Similarly, Japan is the most important and steadfast ally of the US in East Asia. In the past three-four years in particular, there has been a very noticeable and significant forward movement in Indo-Japanese interaction. In the longer-term, a strong relationship with Japan will be in the mutual interests of both countries. Coincidentally, India, Japan and Israel are the oldest democracies in Asia and this is another binding factor. However, strong relationships with these two countries can only exist, let alone be sustained, on the basis of an unalterable precondition – India maintaining a very strong relationship with the US. Happily, it is in US interest to have strong ties among India, Japan and Israel and the US has been consciously encouraging this.
- For decades, India has had an extremely close relationship with Vietnam and continues to enjoy enormous goodwill in that country. The US is in the process of establishing a close and potentially strategic relationship with Vietnam.
- India has the world's second largest Islamic population and yet there has been no involvement or association of Indians with Al Qaeda and linked ter-

rorist organisations. India has virtually no indigenous Islamic terrorist movement like in many Islamic countries. The Indian example demonstrates brilliantly that Islam and democracy are compatible. India has excellent relations with the countries of the Islamic heartland in West Asia, as well as with the Islamic countries of Southeast Asia. Thus, India is a valuable bridge to the Islamic world and has a potentially very important role to play.

- Nearly half of the entire seaborne commerce of the world moves across the waters of the Indian Ocean. Seventy five per cent of this commerce is between and to/from countries external to the region; 20 per cent of this freight traffic is oil and gas. These proportions are going to increase over time. This underlines the global economic and security importance of the Indian Ocean. India abuts into the Indian Ocean. The security role that India's strategic location devolves on India cannot be overemphasised. Security of sea traffic is of vital concern to the dynamically growing economies of the Asia-Pacific. Being in the Indian Ocean, it is of paramount importance to India. As the world's largest trading nation by far, this security is of particular interest and importance to the US. This makes strong Indo-US cooperation in ensuring security in the Indian Ocean an imperative necessity.
- The increasingly significant role that the Indian community is playing in the US is itself becoming a strategic bridge between the US and India.

In the light of what I have said, it is my assessment that an India-US strategic alliance would be the best option for a secure and prosperous future for India. It would provide a values-based foundation for a stable and secure Asia. Having a strategic alliance with the US does not rule out having friendly, cooperative and close relationships with other significant powers such as Russia or China; indeed, the US itself is engaged in doing precisely that. We need to be proactive in furthering the concept. Looking forward, once India and the US have had their elections this year, India should prepare for a US presidential visit next year to announce a historic Joint Declaration of a shared vision for Asia's future. The choice is ours to make – we can be on the right side of historical trends or choose to swim against the tide.

China

World history is a chronicle of rising powers changing the existing status quos. China is the world's major rising power. China's civilisational ethos, historical legacy and contemporary political discourse suggest that it is only a matter of time when China will seek to reassert its position of predominance in Asia. China has more neighbours that it shares boundaries with, land and/or maritime, than any other country in the world. All its neighbours are Asian countries. Not one single neighbour poses a military threat to China. In modern times, China has not had the good fortune of having as peaceful and non-threatening an environment as it has around it today. Yet, China is consciously and deliberately developing military capabilities to ultimately match those of the only superpower in the world. What does this suggest?

China does not share common socio-political values with India, nor a common vision of Asia and the world of tomorrow. China thinks and plans long-term and strategically – it realised early on that India is the only potentially realistic hurdle in its quest for reestablishing dominance in Asia. But before I proceed further, let me state emphatically and clearly that I fervently believe that a good, harmonious, cooperative and friendly relationship between India and China is an almost essential *sine qua non* for peace and stability in the world in general and Asia in particular. It is desirable and indeed necessary to constructively engage China. But this has to be on the basis of parity, equality and mutual respect. Therefore, in charting our future relationship with China we have to bear in mind the following factors.

The Record of India-China Relations

The record of India-China relations would clearly indicate to any objective observer that despite India's passionate advocacy of a meaningfully friendly and cooperative India-China relationship ever since the establishment of the People's Republic of China (PRC), Chinese policies and attitudes have been one of unremittingly undermining India's security, both internal and external, its relationships with other countries and its legitimate aspirations to play its rightful role on the international stage. India unilaterally gave up its historically inherited rights in Tibet and formally accepted China's forcible takeover of Tibet; when China was diplomatically isolated, India was the leading campaigner on China's behalf on the international stage and even sacrificed the possibility of its own Permanent Membership of the Security Council in favour of China; China has physically occupied large tracts of Indian territory and continues to claim even more and finally invaded India in 1962; China's actions in 1962 were consciously designed to humiliate India in the eyes of the world and particularly Asia; both before and after this aggression, China actively aided insurgency movements in the Northeast. Since then, China has very successfully strategically girdled India through the development of an exceedingly close strategic, military and political relationship with Pakistan knowing full well that Pakistan's cardinal foreign policy principle is unmitigated hostility towards India; and, furthermore, in tandem with its surrogate ally, North Korea, China has deliberately helped Pakistan to become a nuclear and missile power in violation of all international non-proliferation norms; China has consciously cultivated Myanmar and has become by far the most influential power in that country and has created for itself significant military and strategic assets in Myanmar with a view to a future role in the Bay of Bengal and the Indian Ocean; it has developed a strong economic, political and military relationship with Bangladesh, the creation of which it had strongly opposed – indeed, the fact is that it enjoys more influence in Bangladesh than India does. It has consistently nurtured and stoked anti-Indian sentiment in Nepal. It has assembled impressive military and strategic assets in Tibet, which have profound implications for India's security concerns. Notwithstanding all this, India once again took the initiative to try and reestablish a friendly relationship with China with Shri Vajpayee's visit to China as external affairs minister in 1979. While he was still in China, China attacked Vietnam, at that time perhaps India's closest friend in Asia. In this part of the world symbols are very important and through this action China indicated in crystal clear fashion just how little it cared for Indian sensitivities. In fact, ever since the inception of the PRC, international relations related discourse in China has exhibited a patronising attitude towards India when it has not been downright contemptuous. Clearly, China has not been a benign neighbour.

China's Opening to the World

Since Deng Xiaoping took over as China's undisputed leader in 1979/80 and launched the programme of "Four Modernisations," successive Party Congresses have emphasised that domestic concerns must have priority over foreign policy and national security came to be synonymous with the preservation of peace and stability internationally and particularly in China's immediate neighbourhood so that nothing could derail the process of modernisation and the development of "comprehensive national strength." Pragmatism and moderation became the highest virtues and mending fences with neighbours a priority. Even while the relationship with the USSR was still strained, China resolved its border problems with it. It has also done so with another traditional antagonist, Vietnam. It exhibited flexibility even on the sensitive issue of Taiwan by accepting the concept of peaceful reunification as the basic principle though refusing to renounce the possible use of force. Even more significantly, it agreed to Taiwan's membership of the Asia-Pacific Economic Cooperation (APEC), the first multilateral organisation to which Taiwan has been admitted since its diplomatic isolation began at the end of the 1970s. After the disintegration of the Soviet Union, China moved rapidly to establish cordial relationships with the newly emerged CARs and has formed the Shanghai Cooperation Organisation with them and also settled its borders with them. It had earlier settled its borders with Afghanistan, Myanmar and Laos. Its border settlement with Pakistan involved the latter surrendering Indian territory in occupied Kashmir to China. China has resolved its border problems with 11 out of its 13 neighbours.

With the end of the Cold War, its strategic partnership with the US ended. This compelled China to dramatically change its attitude towards ASEAN. As a first step, using the leverage of its huge market and extremely impressive economic growth rates, it developed increasingly productive and mutually beneficial economic relationships with ASEAN countries. This induced increasing goodwill and confidence between both sides, enabling China to establish the most extensive network of institutional interaction that any country has with ASEAN. It followed the same economic strategy vis-à-vis Japan, South Korea and Taiwan, and has become their leading trade partner. These countries together have become the world's most dynamic economic region with China as the fulcrum. With Russia demoralised and its relations with the US see-sawing, China moved dexterously and forged a strategic partnership with Russia, and has become its largest weapons customer. Meanwhile, China continued to assiduously cultivate and deepen its relationships with Pakistan, Bangladesh, Myanmar and Nepal. China reacted to India's nuclear tests in the most strongly critical terms while expressing understanding of Pakistan's retaliatory nuclear tests.

With China's relations with the US on a steady downward trajectory, except in the economic field, China has been exhibiting great tactical agility and dexterity to salvage what it could by cooperating with the US wherever possible, being passively accommodative otherwise and taking care always not to antagonise the US. This attitude of cooperation and accommodation has been particularly evident in the aftermath of the events of 9/11. The result has been that recently Secretary of State Colin Powell stated that US-China relations today are better than they have ever been since the Nixon visit of 1972. More hyperbole than accurate description of the factual situation, this statement nevertheless underlines the enormous efforts that China has made, and is making, to have a truly meaningful relationship with the US.

Thus, it has established excellent relationships with every single neighbour. China's most extensive territorial and border problems have been with India and yet they remain the only unresolved land borders of China, along with Bhutan. Clearly, India has been the only exception to China's conscious, deliberate and calculated mending of fences with the rest of the world. Part of the reason, as Chinese strategic analysts readily admit, is that for China, South Asia has always been the lowest priority area amongst its neighbours. Yet China had no hesitations in being hyperactive in cultivating anti-India relationships in this region.

China Smiling at India

It is a fact that there have been a series of high level visits exchanged between India and China since the early 1990s. These were made possible by yet another Indian initiative – Prime Minister Rajiv Gandhi's visit to China in 1988 during which he indicated that India may be willing to consider a political solution to the border issue. These visits laid the groundwork for China beginning to show a relatively positive attitude towards India, beginning with Pakistan's adventure in Kargil, and becoming more noticeable after President Bush assumed office, and the events of 9/11. I would suggest that for the present, this is primarily a tactical shift of approach due to the following four factors.

First, the dramatically changed geopolitical ground realities. China respects power and firmness – India is very much on course regarding the first attribute and needs to embrace the second. China has noted India's emergence as a major power in political, strategic, military, technological and economic terms on the global scene and the world's welcoming of this new Indian status. I have earlier spelt this out in some detail. Most importantly, India's relationship with the US has been dramatically transformed.

Second, the very considerable reinvigoration and strengthening of the US' military alliances and relationships in the Asia-Pacific – the military alliance with Japan has deepened and acquired a dramatically new outward looking orientation; the US-Taiwan military relationship is now stronger than it was when the two had a formal military alliance; the strengthening of its military and security relationships throughout Southeast Asia. There is incrementally increasing defence cooperation with India which has also publicly expressed support for the US idea of missile defence. And the establishment of long-term US military presence in China's western neighbourhood – in Afghanistan, Central Asia and Pakistan. All this is very deeply disturbing for China.

Third, China's longest standing and closest strategic ally, Pakistan, is now under severe pressure as never before in its history due to its publicly exposed central role in international terrorism and WMD proliferation. Pakistan's value as a strategic ally is beginning to look more and more questionable and could cause China avoidable trouble. Thus, China has virtually lost its main strategic pressure point vis-à-vis India.

Fourth, there is palpable discomfort and unease throughout the world with growing manifestations of aggressive US unilateralism. China is aware of the deeply ingrained sense of anti-Westernism in the psyche of the Indian political elite and intellectual circles. It wishes to tap this before it dissipates completely. By appearing to be relatively amenable, it is seductively suggesting that the Asian countries should band together to stand against US led Western hegemonism – something which evokes deep resonance in India.

The Border Problem

All indications suggest that India is very keen on an early settlement of the disputed territorial issues with China. It would also appear that the settlement is going to be broadly on the basis of the existing ground realities, with minor modifications. That would mean that China would retain Aksai Chin. Aksai Chin is of very great strategic importance to China and is the real prize that it is after. This provides India leverage for firmness and if there has to be a compromise, then it must be part of an overall political package, which must include the following elements:

- China must return some territory which is part of Aksai Chin and under their control as well as some adjoining Chinese territory to enable India to construct an all weather road linking Himachal Pradesh with Leh in Ladakh; this is strategically important for India.
- There can be no question of the transfer of populated areas of the Northeast to China, for example, Tawang.
- China will also have to concretely exhibit a respect for, and sensitivity towards, India's legitimate security and strategic concerns, including our need for appropriate nuclear and missile assets.
- There is increasing global acceptance of the desirability of India being a Permanent Member of the Security Council – China must accept this too.
- China must respect our political and security sensitivities in the subcontinent and desist from abetting, promoting and encouraging anti-India policies and sentiments in our neighbouring countries.

In terms of all objective criteria, India and China are peer powers and China must accept this reality. An acid test of China's sincerity about the future of its relationship with India would be an equitable settlement of the territorial dispute, the most serious issue in Sino-Indian relations, somewhat along the lines that I have indicated. Simon Garver, who is not biased in favour of or against either India or China, in his well-researched book on Sino-India relations says: "The contrast between New Delhi's handling of its rapprochement with Beijing and Beijing's handling of its rapprochement with Washington... and Moscow... is very instructive... A sense of strength and confidence underlay Beijing's handling of rapprochement with Washington and Moscow (even though China was quite weak)... the overriding Chinese sentiment (was)... China could afford to wait... sooner or later (they) would accede to China's core demands... New Delhi's handling of rapprochement with Beijing, in contrast, seems to (be) underlaid by a sense of weakness and helplessness. The dominant Indian sentiment seems to (be) that India did not really have much leverage vis-à-vis China and thus there was not much reason to expect China to feel compelled to accede to Indian demands." China, of course, has always been aware of these realities and, hence, it can afford to appear reasonable towards India. In the event that the territorial dispute with China cannot be resolved on this basis, this will be a clear indication that China continues to harbour ulterior motives vis-à-vis India; on the other hand, if the dispute is resolved without these elements, it would represent yet another surrender by India, encouraging China to feel ever more confident that India is the one country it has mastered in handling. If one gives in to a bully he will keep on extracting more – this has been the story of India-China interaction in the past 50 years.

Unless we exhibit firmness, I fear we will have frittered away the favourable geostrategic position that we are in today and in the bargain face, aggravated security challenges from China in the not too distant future as China's comprehensive national strength and influence inexorably grow.

Pakistan

Ever since its independence, Pakistan has had a single point foreign policy agenda – implacable hostility towards India. This has been manifested in initiation of four wars of aggression in 1947, 1965, 1971 and 1999 and a proxy war through state sponsored cross-border terrorism, first in the Punjab and then in Kashmir since the mid-1980s. In carried out a barbaric genocide as a conscious policy and killed three million of its own citizens in East Pakistan in 1970-71. It installed an evil, barbarous and medieval regime in Afghanistan and together Pakistan and Afghanistan became the epicentre for radical, fundamentalist international terrorism, posing the most serious threat to global security in decades and to India in particular. Pakistan's polity is dominated by the military, partnered by *mullahs* and feudal elements. It has been the most egregious WMD proliferator in partnership with its dictatorial friends, China and North Korea. It has pathetically low human development indicators and its economy is in shambles. It has been on the verge of being a failed state for decades. The nature of the Pakistani state and its policy record would objectively lead to its being classified as one of the world's worst rogue states but ironically it has survived all these years only because it has been treated as a frontline ally by the United States while being lethally armed by China, which has made it into a nuclear weapon power. Its strategic and military doctrine specifically provides for first use of nuclear weapons.

Pakistan's demographic profile suggests that by 2010, it will have a population of 200 million of whom 80 million will be unemployed or underemployed and 35 million people will be in the age group of 16-24, potentially the most volatile segment of poor societies. It simply does not have the natural resources, the human skills, the economic infrastructure, and civil society networks that can meaningfully support a population of that size. This socio-demographic profile will worsen in the next decade. It should be readily evident that this is a recipe for disaster in the making, with potentially frightening consequences for its neighbours, India in particular. The US is undoubtedly aware of these realities and now has the possibility of addressing the potentially serious problems that lie ahead

Pakistan remains the primary threat to India's security. However, for the first time since Independence there is a realistic possibility of this threat being neutralised. Prime Minister Vajpayee has been engaged in a concerted attempt at making peace with Pakistan. US policy has been an enormous factor in boosting these efforts. I personally am optimistic that the situation is likely to take a positive turn in the near future. However, in politics nothing is certain and we must remain on watchful guard.

Bangladesh

Some countries are islands, others are landlocked; Bangladesh is 'India-locked'. There is no other major country in the world which has this unique geographical characteristic. This fact has, and will continue to, inevitably dictate Bangladesh's policy orientations. If Bangladesh had visionary leaders, the policy choice was simple and straightforward – the development of an extremely close and symbiotic economic relationship with India. This in no way diminishes let alone extinguishes an independent political identity. The EU and ASEAN countries provide excellent role models.

Bangladesh is the world's most densely populated country. Its large population relative to its size, its terrain, its paucity of natural resources, and the lack of meaningful economic infrastructure has ensured that it is one of the world's poorest countries. Poverty is one of the most useful tools for political demagogues. Bangladesh is the world's most corrupt country and unfortunately its political leaders are selfish, self-centred and self-serving. Manipulating the population on the basis of 'anti-Indianism', arising out of Bangladesh's unique geographical characteristic is the easiest way to secure and retain political power. China and Pakistan have been actively involved in nurturing this approach. The legacy left behind by its almost three decades of existence as part of Pakistan is more easily politically exploitable than sentiments of gratitude for India's help in obtaining its independence. All this means that it will take time for a viable mutually beneficial relationship to emerge between India and Bangladesh.

But there is some reason for hope, because Bangladesh is fundamentally different from Pakistan and in due time these differences, rather than past affinities, will come to the fore. A change of mindset in Bangladesh is very much more on the cards than a change of mindset in Pakistan. To encourage this, India has to behave like an elder brother, not as the big brother. India can afford to be more generous than it has been. India should also consciously use a multilateral approach in developing mutually beneficial economic linkages and BIMSTEC provides a very useful mechanism; a multilateral approach, by definition, elicits less suspicions.

By itself, Bangladesh does not pose a security threat to India. However, there are two worrisome aspects. Bangladesh territory is increasingly being used as a base for insurgents and terrorists who strike in India. India has been providing infomation, but so far Bangladesh has remained in denial mode. This attitude will have to change. If Bangladesh responds, well and good, but India cannot wait indefinitely; should appeals to reason and persuasion fail, then India needs to consciously seek the help of the international community to avoid the necessity of possible preemptive action. The second and more serious aspect is illegal migration from Bangladesh. Informed guesstimates suggest that well over 20 million Bangladeshis are now in India and their numbers continue to rise. This is changing the demographic composition of the Indian states bordering Bangladesh with potentially serious socio-economic consequences. This ingress of huge numbers of people is an increasingly serious security threat. One cannot ignore the fact that in today's world the most serious security threat is posed by non-state actors. Once again, Indian representations evoke denials that any such thing is happening. The lengthy border does not lend itself easily to modalities such as fencing, and Bangladesh, in any case, opposes such an approach. Greater firmness is unavoidably necessary. Deployment of vastly increased paramilitary forces may become unavoidable. International opinion needs to be sensitised to this growing problem. In an increasingly globalised world, a cooperative international effort is desirable, since all such activity has a potentially cascading destabilising effect. A self-confident India should not be wary of internationalised approaches to seeking solutions of the problems in its neighbourhood.

Nepal

Nepal by itself also does not pose a security threat to India. However, India has open borders with Nepal, permitting free and unrestricted movement to Nepalese citizens. Others inclined to cross the lengthy porous border do not feel restricted by the few designated entry points. The policing and surveillance infrastructure on the Indian side is pathetically primitive and underdeveloped. All this constitutes an enormous security risk. This needs priority attention, particularly in the context of the serious security threat posed by non-state actors. One has to bear in mind that there has been an alarming increase in the numbers of mosques and *madrasahs* all along the border region and these have been set up and are run with foreign funding.

These issues relating to Bangladesh and Nepal are not new. In addition, both Bangladesh and Nepal are endemically poor, with prospects for economic growth in the short term being rather slim. Both also exhibit endemic socio-political instability and Nepal has been wracked by the growing Maoist insurgency. Chinese influence is strong in both countries. ISI cells have been in existence in both countries for long, and have been coordinating anti-Indian activity within both of them and from their soil against India. We have a tendency to allow matters to drift and fester and begin to attend to them only when they reach crisis dimensions. It is important that these issues are seriously addressed on a priority basis so that they do not become totally unmanageable and add to the already existing security pressures.

India's Internal Security Environment

India's evolving external security environment will be determined in the context of the scenario I have sketched. However, *diplomacy will have to be complemented by conscious and continuous development and maintenance of military capabilities* commensurate with the capabilities of potential adversaries, not only to deter ulterior intentions, but to withstand strategic blackmail. In an era of growing globalisation, increasing interconnectedness and interdependence, India's security perimeter must be considered as extending from the Persian Gulf to the Strait of Malacca and including Central Asia and the Indian Ocean. India has extensive land boundaries covering very varied and difficult terrain, and which are particularly vulnerable to contemporary non-traditional forms of security threats. These facets would need to be factored in to ensure appropriate and adequate military preparedness. Happily, in recent years there has been more conscious attention to our national defence needs; nevertheless, public interest and awareness need to be consciously cultivated to ensure that fulfilment of defence requirements will remain a national priority. In this context, may I say that seminars such as this one are a very useful contribution to national purposes.

Maintenance of internal stability is of even greater and paramount importance. This is dependent upon the nature and quality of governance, socio-cultural societal harmony, broad based economic growth and balanced regional development. The vast Hindi speaking heartland of India, with its huge impoverished population, continues to exhibit progressively deteriorating governance, characterised by political populism, rising corruption, rampant fiscal irresponsibility, economic stagnation, a virtual breakdown of law and order, an increasing nexus between criminality and politics, and virtually non-existent civic consciousness. There are many other parts of the country steeped in backwardness. The depressing situation in these huge parts of the country stuck in almost medieval backwardness needs to be consciously and proactively addressed as a matter of the highest national priority. And, I have not even mentioned insurgencies of assorted kinds in various parts of the country, which are essentially due to people having lost hope in their future.

The recently released *National Security Review 2003* should set alarm bells ringing. The editor, Prof. Satish Kumar, has said and I quote: "India has fared poorly on human development indices. The internal security scenario is grim on account of poverty and unemployment." The study has factored in India's population, while rating its national security index; had population been left out, India's rank would have crashed to 26 out of 50 countries covered. Additionally, a country which ranks 124 out of 173 in human development indices cannot hope to be considered a front rank global power. If meaningful action is not taken on a priority basis to remedy this abysmal situation, the respect, admiration and influence abroad that India is now so happily beginning to enjoy, will prove transient and ephemeral and our security environment will continue to remain endangered not so much due to external factors but due to severe internal shortcomings. *An internally strong and stable India is a necessary precondition to an externally influential and secure India.* •

CONTOURS OF INDIA'S EMERGING SECURITY ENVIRONMENT

Vice Admiral P.S.Das, PVSM, UYSM, VSM (Retd)

Preamble

The emerging security environment is full of uncertainties. Within a short span of three years, a well entrenched Taliban regime in Afghanistan has been thrown out, an equally dominant Saddam Hussein has been destroyed in Iraq, nations which had adamantly thumbed their noses at the sole superpower, Libya and Iran, have become more 'amenable', and Pakistan's unabashed proliferation of terrorism and nuclear technology has been exposed and admitted. All of these may be unconnected and yet, there may be some underlying threads of connectivity. In this state of uncertainty, it is wiser to predicate assumptions on factors which have greater permanence and are less likely to change quickly. Geography cannot change; the country's national interests also have some permanence. Finally, since intentions could alter quickly, capabilities merit greater attention. It is in this overall context that India's emerging security environment should be viewed.

The Global Environment

The world has become increasingly unipolar in the last decade. The presumption that America's unilateral and aggressive' postures flow from the neo-conservative nature of the Bush Administration or that they are the direct fallout of attacks on the Twin Towers, does not stand scrutiny. Key US strategic goals and objectives, as spelt out in the Clinton National Security Strategy of October 1998, are almost exactly the same as those spelt out in the Bush Security Strategy of September 2002. They stress a world political order amenable to America's values and interests, an economic dispensation in which its interests would be enhanced access to critical raw materials, exclusive control over cutting edge technologies, non-proliferation of WMD and, generally, a world in which America's preeminence would remain undisturbed and unchallenged. Both terrorism and WMD predate the Bush period; similarly, preemption is not its invention. The attacks on 9/11 have been a watershed, not so much because they have altered the course of American strategy but because they have allowed the country to link its larger strategic goals with the war against terrorism.

On another plane, the emerging security environment has shifted focus away from Europe to the Asia-Pacific. The countries of concern, the failed states or rogue states not amenable to the USA or hostile to its interests, are located in this region, as also the non-state actors. A very large reservoir of the major critical raw materials, oil and gas, is to be found here. The one country which can, potentially, be a challenger to US strategic interest, China, is in Asia. It is not surprising that in this environment, America has military presence stretching right across Asia and very comprehensive capabilities at sea which can be brought to bear quickly and decisively.

The Indian Ocean

The IOR is an important element in the security environment in the Asia-Pacific and in Asia, in particular. Many countries relevant to America's concerns are littorals of this ocean. The critical energy resources flow out of its sea lanes to a number of countries whose economies are dependent on them. This gives great strategic significance to the region. It also has vulnerabilities as these sea lanes pass through very narrow channels both eastwards and to the west, and can easily be interdicted or disrupted. Most regional countries are still to become politically stable and many regimes are authoritarian and could destabilise easily. Lying in the centre of the Indian Ocean, India has important concerns and interests.

India is as dependent on energy imports from the Gulf as is America. Their quantum will double by 2020. More than 97 per cent of India's trade moves through the Indian Ocean. We are affected by narco-terrorism, both on land and at sea. India has very important economic interests, both in the Gulf countries and in the ASEAN group. The region has also seen considerable militarisation in the last ten years. Situated as it is, India has no option but to interact with and, in consequence, be affected by, developments in the region.

Other Factors

Terrorism has emerged as a non-traditional threat even more potent than conventional military concerns. Until now, it remained focussed on land and in the air. It has begun to exploit the medium of the sea and warships of the superpower have been attacked. It is not impossible that attacks of greater lethality may be undertaken. Apart from capabilities and structures internal to the country, terrorism requires engagement with others around us.

The nuclear environment is another factor which impinges on India's security interests. On the one hand, it has strengthened our political capabilities in global interface but, on the other, it has brought severe constraints in the use of conventional military power. The space that was available earlier for pursuance of politics by 'other means' has diminished greatly.

Technology has become essential to military capability. Much more than numbers, it is access to cutting edge technologies which will differentiate the 'haves' from the 'have nots'. Whether in weapons and sensors, intelligence and reconnaissance or in command and control, inadequate technology can act to our very serious detriment.

Need for Engagement

The emerging environment necessitates engagement, politically, economically and militarily, with countries external to this region as well as those littoral to it. Inevitably, military engagement will need to have greatly increased maritime interfaces. These responsibilities will increase with growing economic interests.

The major external power is the USA. India has some differences with America, especially in the respective approaches to the nuclear Non-Proliferation Treaty (NPT) and economic issues, but it also has converging interests on others e.g. the fight against terrorism, proliferation of WMD, safety of sea lanes in the Indian Ocean, etc. This synergy has strategic overtones and has resulted in increasing defence interaction between the two countries with stress on cooperation at sea. This relationship is likely to continue and will add to relationships with other players like the UK, Australia and France.

Russia is a natural ally with whom India must maintain strong interfaces. The same is true of Japan. Because of Cold War suspicions, the Indo-Japanese relationship has remained dormant. In the changed environment, development of interfaces between the two countries merits urgent attention.

China is now importing increasing quantities of oil from the Gulf. Along with its other Indian Ocean interests, this makes it an important external interest. In recent years, India's relations with China have improved and this is likely to continue, given economic and political compulsions. However, there is need to keep a careful watch on China's port development programmes in Myanmar and in Pakistan, as these could provide China with the Indian Ocean capability that it does not presently have.

As far as the regional and neighbourhood countries are concerned, India has defence cooperation agreements with many, and close cooperation with them is necessary to counter non-traditional threats to our security and to be seen as reassuring, generally. Pakistan, alone, remains a question mark and despite recent overtures, it is unlikely that the essentially confrontationist posture can disappear, given fundamental realities. However, as long as clear superiority is maintained, its ability to pose any military challenges is doubtful. Its support to proxy war in Kashmir and elsewhere is, however, likely to continue, its magnitude dependent on global pressure and India's own strengths.

In brief, in the next 10-15 years:

- American preeminence in a unipolar world order is likely to continue and efforts at multilateralism will be cosmetic.
- The global security environment will be Asia-Pacific centric with the major focus on Asia. India's own concerns and interests must recognise this development.
- As India's economic interests grow, the focus of our security concerns will move seawards and require increased capabilities.
- The nuclear environment has greatly diminished the political space for military options.
- Non-traditional threats will play an important role in the security calculus.
- Engagement with like-minded countries at every level has become necessary.

Impact on Military Strategies

In this background, the following compulsions on India's military strategies can be expected:

- Full scale military conflict between India and Pakistan or between India and China is no longer a viable option.
- Even short and sharp conflicts will attract quick international intervention and space for them will have to be created politically with clear and well defined aims.
- Consequently, conventional deterrence is more optimal through air and sea power.
- Transnational terrorism will become more potent through use of sophisticated technologies requiring military response, apart from other means.
- Military power will continue to remain an important adjunct of state power and its impact will shift seawards.

Military Strategies for 2020

Dimensions of India's military strategy which will best cope with the security concerns and interests of the future can now be defined. These are:

- Proactive military engagement in peace with regional countries as well as external powers, which have interests in the region. Interfaces at sea will play a lead role in this. There must be sufficient capabilities for the interaction to be meaningful.
- There must be credible deterrence at the conventional level against potential adversaries.
- A certain 'threshold' against military intervention by a major power should be maintained.
- Creation of force structures which can counter high-tech terrorism, including at sea.
- Networked forces capable of operating through integrated command and control, and supported by effective intelligence and information.

Conclusion

In the emerging security environment, India's security concerns are not just military. Economic interfaces and linkages will become increasingly important as also threats from non-traditional sources. Engagement will become critical in safeguarding and enhancing security interests. This applies to military interfaces as much as to those in other fields, and sea power will play an increasingly dominant role in these interfaces. Credible capabilities are essential in meaningful engagement. These cannot be created optimally unless a holistic view is taken and integrated planning and integrated command and control mechanisms are of the essence. This is the great challenge that confronts the military leadership of today. •

FUTURE SECURITY ENVIRONMENT

Lt Gen V. K. Singh, PVSM (Retd)

Introduction

It is appropriate that the first session of this seminar looks at the future security environment, as it is the security environment which would eventually dictate the shape, size, structure and doctrines of India's Army of the future. This paper attempts to analyse the likely security environment over the next decade, likely threats to India in this period, and the battlefield milieu in which these threats will need to be met, thus, setting the stage for a discussion as to the structures and doctrines required to deal with these threats.

The Global Environment

Three major factors that will shape the global environment over the next decade are as follows:

* The use of its power by the USA.
* The struggle within Islam.
* China's efforts to achieve superpower status.

There are, of course, other factors, such as growing economic imbalance between nations, as well as between various strata within a nation; population movements; the growing demand for energy sources and for water. These can also impinge on the security environment. However, the three noted above will have the main impact.

The USA and its Actions

The USA will remain the sole superpower for the foreseeable future. Whether the US uses this power to stabilise the world and bring peace to warring regions, or uses it to force its view on others, with no regard for local or international opinion, can have a vital impact on the security environment over the next few years. If the US continues to act unilaterally, it can, as it has in Afghanistan and Iraq, achieve regime changes, but it is doubtful that it can achieve long-standing change without international support. On the other hand, if its unilateralism leads to resentment within the region, it could lead to greater tensions in the area and to instability. Instability, particularly in West Asia and Southeast Asia would have a direct impact on India's security. If, however, the US was to use its enormous power to back the United Nations and carry the bulk of the world with it, it could be a major factor of stability. Much will depend on the nature of government that takes charge after the presidential elections due later this year.

The Conflict Within Islam

All discussions on the international security scenario focus on the impact of Islamic fundamentalism and militancy on the world environment; few analyse the fact that Islamic fundamentalism and militancy affects Muslim society worldwide much more than it affects non-Muslims. The struggle within Islam is twofold. The first is between those who wish to put a modern face on Islamic thought and those who believe in a strict adherence to their interpretation of the teachings of the Prophet. The second is the struggle between authoritarian regimes, which seem to rule a majority of Islamic states and those who wish to overthrow the existing authority and establish regimes more representative of the people. To the extent those engaged in the struggle see others, i.e. non-Muslims supporting the existing structures within Muslim society, they also become targets of attack. This struggle within Islam is what causes unrest and instability within the Muslim world and this can have a direct bearing on India's security. India lies in the middle of an arc of Muslim nations, which stretches from North Africa through West Asia, South Asia and on to Southeast Asia. Two of India's immediate neighbours, Pakistan and Bangladesh, are Islamic nations. India itself has a large Muslim population that cannot remain unaffected by the general turmoil in the Islamic world. India, therefore, needs to watch the struggle carefully and to isolate itself from it to the extent it can.

China

China's avowed aim is to become a superpower, capable of challenging US hegemony. To reach this status, however, China must establish its dominance over Asia as a first step. There is only one nation in Asia that can pose a challenge to China and that is India. But even before this, how China deals with the Taiwan question and its sea boundary disputes with its Southeast Asian neighbours will be a pointer to its intentions and policy towards the use of its growing economic and military power. An aggressive China can destabilise East and Southeast Asia with inevitable repercussions on India. China, in any case, is India's major neighbour with a disputed border. It is also the largest supplier of arms to India's other neighbours, Myanmar, Bangladesh and Pakistan. China's actions, therefore, will not only affect the international security environment but directly affect India's security concerns.

The Regional Scene

When considering the region of concern to India in respect of its security; the region we need to look at is the arc that stretches from the Gulf of Aden to Southeast Asia. Central Asia and the east coast of Africa are also of interest, but for the purposes of this study we will confine ourselves to the earlier formulation of West Asia through to Southeast Asia.

West Asia

West Asia is vital to India for three reasons. First, as its major source of its energy requirements; second, as a market for Indian skills in that it supports a large Indian expatriate community, whose remittances add greatly to our foreign exchange earnings; and third, the area lies athwart our sea lines of communications to Europe. Unfortunately, West Asia has many factors that can lead to instability in the region. The unsettled Palestinian question creates strains in the region and leads to terrorism. The US interest in the oil wealth of the region often leads it to ride roughshod over local sentiments The large US military presence in the Gulf states and Saudi Arabia, while protecting the existing regimes, leads to resentment in certain sections of society and in turn to turmoil and instability. It is well to remember that Osma bin Laden's initial aim was to drive US presence out of Saudi Arabia.

The struggle within Islam, described earlier, is present in the area in a major manner with underlying tensions created by people wishing to change the currently authoritarian regimes in the area. There are also regional rivalries, particularly between the Arab states and non-Arab Iran. While these are at a low key today, they could flare up and add to the instability of the area. While instability in West Asia may pose no major threat to India, it would have a major economic impact. Instability in the region may also draw India militarily into the region as part of an international or regional stabilisation force.

Southeast Asia

Southeast Asia is important to India as a market and an investment destination as well as a source of investment. It is also an alternate source for oil supplies from Myanmar, Indonesia and possible oil finds off the shores of Vietnam. Important sea routes to East Asia and to the Pacific coast of the Americas pass through this region. Southeast Asia, mainly because of the successful ASEAN grouping, has generally been stable. Recently, however, there have been some disturbing signs of a rise of Islamic fundamentalism and links to militant groups in West Asia. The situation in Indonesia is of particular interest to India as Indonesia is actually a neighbour and the troubled Acheh province in Sumatra is one of the nearest areas of that country to the Great Nicobar Island. While the Indian Navy is already engaged in working towards protection of shipping through the Strait of Malacca, the Indian Army may need to relook at the strength of its garrison in the Andaman & Nicobar Islands and the necessity for a presence in Great Nicobar. Myanmar also is of special significance to India, as it has a long land border with India. China has an increasing economic and military presence in Myanmar and this could in certain circumstances be inimical to India, particularly in a future Sino-Indian armed conflict. None of the developments in Southeast Asia presently pose a direct military threat but the area will need to be engaged, to ensure that no hostile presence establishes itself in the region.

The Neighbourhood

The neighbourhood is, of course, the most vital consideration for India while examining the security scenario and likely threats. The neighbourhood consists of all the states of South Asia as well as our largest neighbour, China. Given the major role that China and Pakistan have played in our security concerns in the past, and are likely to continue to play in the immediate future, these two will be considered separately.

South Asia less Pakistan

All the countries of South Asia, possibly with the exception of the Maldives, have internal problems and to the extent that all these countries abut on India, these problems can, and often do, spill over into India. The truce in Sri Lanka between the government and the LTTE seems to be getting fragile; any resumption of hostilities will have implications for south India, particularly Tamil Nadu, in the influx of refugees and possibly even armed cadres of the LTTE. This would create an added internal security problem for India. The growing population and lack of employment opportunities in Bangladesh have led to a large influx of people from that country into India causing both population imbalance and resentment in the areas to which this influx has taken place. This creates a security problem for India; presently, there does not seem to be a way out of this unless Bangladesh cooperates. Bangladesh is also a refuge for many of the militant groups operating in the Northeast. Bhutan has just faced a major security situation with the militants from the northeastern states seeking refuge there; this can occur again. There is also incipient tension in Bhutan between the native Bhutanese and Nepalese settlers that can spill into India. Nepal itself has a major problem with Maoist rebels in the country; these rebels have a rabidly anti-Indian stance. While these pose no real threat to India just at present, if the movement stretches into the Terai area and develops linkages with the militant leftist movements in Bihar and West Bengal, our security problems would aggravate.

While Afghanistan does not directly abut on India, it has often been seen as a part of South Asia. It has historically been the bridge between West and Central Asia and the Indian subcontinent. Afghanistan is not yet stable and if instability spreads, it could affect India's growing links with Iran and Central Asia, as well as add to tension within Pakistan, with a possible spill over into India. Stability in Afghanistan is of importance to India's security.

Pakistan

Ever since it was founded, Pakistan has suffered a sense of insecurity vis-à-vis India. Three Indo-Pak Wars since 1947 and a number of skirmishes like Kargil and Siachen have proved to Pakistan that in purely military terms, it can never succeed in imposing its will on India. It has also realised that for all its quest for parity, India's size, resources and economic strength preclude Pakistan from matching India. This realisation led to Pakistan developing a two-fold strategy against India. The first was to stoke and aid any separatist movement in India, so as to break up India, as smaller components could be dealt with in detail. This is what led it to support the Sikh extremists and to offer aid and training through bases in erstwhile East Pakistan and now Bangladesh to various insurgent groups operating in India's Northeast. All this culminated in the ongoing proxy war in J&K where its policy graduated from arming and training local insurgents to raising, training and infiltrating forces raised from its own population. The hope was that such operations would so tire the Indians that they would be prepared for a solution to the Kashmir problem on Pakistan's terms. It is a tribute to India's underlying unity and its resilience that none of these Pakistani efforts have succeeded.

Pakistan's second step was to develop nuclear weapons to offset India's conventional military superiority and thus deter India from taking any military action to punish Pakistan for aiding various separatist movements in India. The result of the Kargil conflict, where India was able to take limited military action in spite of Pakistan's nuclear threat has, it is felt, led Pakistan to realise that nuclear weapons are not a panacea to all its problems with India. It is this realisation, as well as the realisation that militant groups once raised cannot always be controlled and that they can threaten who sired them, that seems to have led Pakistan to react favourably to improve relations between the two countries. However, there have been many false dawns in the history of Indo-Pak relations and it is difficult to be sanguine that the current initiatives will succeed. Much will depend to the continuation of the current regimes in both countries. Elections are due in India and one is not sure how secure President Musharraf is in Pakistan. Progress will also depend on how much pressure the US continues to exert on both countries. Progress, if any, will be slow and halting and it is incumbent on India to keep up its guard and be ready in case there is a breakdown and a recurrence of military pressure in J&K.

China

China has been briefly discussed earlier in the paper and it has been pointed out that much will depend on how China progresses towards its goal of being a superpower and if and when it reaches that position, does it ape the arrogance of the US or does it see its role as a moderate? China also realises that to be a superpower, it must, in addition to economic power also possess military power. It faces no military threat worth the name but has gone about systematically modernising its armed forces, both nuclear and conventional. It has taken to heart the lessons of the first Gulf War and taken steps, not just to obtain modern weapons and equipment but more importantly to modernise its doctrines and training. Current indications seem to point to China being an arrogant, impetuous power. To reach this position, however, China must first dominate Asia and as opined earlier, the only country in Asia that can seriously challenge it is India. China seems to have acknowledged this long ago. Its invasion in 1962 was to show up India to be a giant with feet of clay and diminish its stature in Asia and the world. To keep India confined to South Asia, it subsequently aided Pakistan to ensure that India would face danger from two fronts, and made efforts to forge military links with India's neighbours such as Nepal, Myanmar, Bangladesh and Sri Lanka. The border dispute between India and China continues, with progress in finding a solution being very slow. At times, it appears that China is in no hurry to solve the disputes as its existence gives it an excuse to heat up the border whenever it feels like it.

With a certain rivalry between China and India being inevitable, the question is how they will deal with it and what the result will be. The best result would be if both decided to cooperate to put forward a unified Asian view-point to the rest of the world, like France and Germany in Europe, historically enemies for a long time but now in a cooperative endeavour. The next best is one of coexistence; both carving out spheres of influence and not interfering in each other's sphere. The last is one of confrontation. Confrontation need not necessarily be military, but if it does take place, then it will definitely involve land forces. The Chinese aim would be to do a repeat of 1962, a short swift campaign to inflict a humiliating defeat on India so as to dash its pretensions of being a great power. China is unlikely to attempt this, however, unless it is reasonably sure of success. As long as India retains a credible dissuasive force along its frontiers and builds up a credible nuclear deterrent so as to preclude any nuclear blackmail by China, chances of a confrontation appear remote.

Internal Security

No study of the security scenario facing India can be complete without looking at the internal security situation in India. Some part or the other of India has been in a state of armed unrest and uprising practically since Independence. The Indian Army has been involved in dealing with such uprisings: beginning with Telengana in 1948, to Nagaland, Mizoram, Punjab, Assam, and Kashmir, the story is long and unending. This is not counting the many times when large elements of the army have been called out to deal with civil strife such as caste and communal conflicts. There does not appear to be any respite from this. While Mizoram and Punjab may now be back in the mainstream, simmering problems continue in the Northeast, and Kashmir still remains on the boil. All these ignore the situation in the tribal belt stretching from Andhra Pradesh, Chattisgarh and on to Jharkhand, where various leftist groups have made sure that the writ of the government scarcely runs. One wonders when the army will be called in there.

The disturbing aspect is not that there are these internal security problems, but that successive governments, at both the Centre and state levels, have tended to treat these purely as law and order problems, to be dealt with by deploying an armed force, whether army or police. There seems to be no realisation that violent movements begin by a combination of economic, social, and cultural fault lines and that unless these root causes are dealt with, there can be no solutions to such movements. There is also now a tendency to take shelter behind the excuse of foreign origin of these problems. This belies the fact that in each and every case, even in J&K, militancy started as an indigenous movement and was then abetted and aided by countries hostile to India, whether China or Pakistan or Bangladesh. Only when we are able to work out a coordinated strategy, involving good administration, economic and social upliftment, combined with military force when required, are we likely to be able to have a stable internal security environment. Many believe that the greatest challenge to India's security, territorial integrity and its economic and social progress comes from within and not from external sources. It is difficult not to agree with this assessment.

Likely Conflict Scenarios

Having viewed the security environment, international, regional, in the neighbourhood, and internal, one can now examine the likely armed threats that India may face and the type of conflict that such threats could give rise to. It is obvious that in the foreseeable future India faces no direct sizeable military threat other than from its two traditional adversaries, Pakistan and China. Given the military equation among China, India and Pakistan, a future conflict between any two of them would run the full gamut, from an all out nuclear war, to a limited nuclear war, to an all out conventional war, to a limited conventional war, to a low intensity conflict, using proxies. The Indian Army also faces the challenge of dealing with numerous internal threats. A brief examination of the likely conflict scenarios and the type of operations that may need to be carried out is needed to set the stage for later examination of the capabilities, force structures and doctrines required to meet future challenges.

Nuclear Conflicts

Tomes have been written about the use of nuclear weapons and about nuclear fighting, all in the theoretical field, because there has never been an actual nuclear war, total or limited. The reason for this is that even before President Reagan stated that "a nuclear war cannot be won and, therefore, must never be fought," the basic truth of this had been realised by both the USA and USSR. In spite of the many studies both carried out, in spite of the theories of a limited nuclear war and graduated response, both sides knew that once an exchange of nuclear weapons started, even low yield tactical weapons, it could and probably would quickly graduate to a full blown nuclear war, leading to ''Mutual Assured Destruction" (MAD). As neither of the sides was mad enough to desire MAD, they made sure that situations that could lead to a nuclear exchange were never allowed to arise.

China, India and Pakistan, it sometimes appears, have failed to fully grasp the import of acquiring nuclear weapons and the restraints and responsibilities that such acquisition imposes on those who have them. China talks of using tactical nuclear weapons on the battlefield, discounting the fact that if the adversary possesses nuclear weapons, the next step could be an exchange of weapons directed at value targets, leaving no winners but only losers. Pakistan threatens an outbreak of nuclear war every time there is tension with India, without seeming to acknowledge that a nuclear response could devastate it. Kargil should have shown Pakistan that nuclear weapons do not deter a local conflict. Eventually, all three countries will realise that nuclear weapons should only be used when the very existence of the state is threatened, and that even then, that while such use may cause enormous hurt to the adversary, the inevitable nuclear retaliation may still lead to the destruction of the initiator. Once this is understood then the true value of nuclear weapons would be understood, which is to deter an unbridled conventional conflict; keeping such conflict below what is generally referred to as the "nuclear threshold."

To ensure that a nuclear war does not confront India, one of the essentials, in addition to conventional restraint, is the acquisition of a credible nuclear deterrent. The credibility of the deterrent will depend not so much on the number of warheads held, but on the adequacy and flexibility of the delivery systems and the survivability of the command and control elements. In some manner, these must be demonstrated to the adversary, so that it knows that however strong a first strike it may launch, India is capable of launching a crippling retaliatory strike.

Given these scenarios, a nuclear war involving either China or Pakistan and India does not appear to have great probability. The military balance between China and India is such that it is unlikely that China will ever face a situation vis-à-vis India that it feels the need to use its nuclear option. As regards an Indo-Pak conflict, there should be no situation in which India would feel so threatened as to feel the need to use its nuclear weapons, except in retaliation to a Pakistani nuclear strike. A Pakistani nuclear attack would only occur if Pakistan felt that its very existence were threatened. As this is unlikely to be India's aim, the circumstances for use of nuclear weapons by either should not arise. It would appear that a nuclear conflict involving India, China and Pakistan is a very remote possibility.

Conventional War

The last two decades of the 20th century saw a significant change in which conventional wars would be fought. These changes have been brought about by the application of new technologies to war-fighting, leading to what is commonly termed as RMA. Put in very brief terms, RMA has come about by a combination of extensive use of improved reconnaissance, surveillance and target acquisition systems and the introduction of a variety of precision guided munitions, both linked by automated command and control systems. This now allows detection and recognition quickly, as well at greater ranges, with fire to be delivered on such targets rapidly and accurately. In such a battle, the electromagnetic spectrum becomes of vital importance and victory would go to the side that best uses the spectrum, while denying its use to the enemy. The other major factor that has come about is the realisation that all conflict on land will need to be fought as a land-air battle, and the side that can best coordinate and combine its land and air forces is the one that will win the battle. The other result that arises from RMA and the extensive use of air power is that large concentrations of troops, whereever they may be, and static defences are now more vulnerable than before. The bias will be for smaller, highly mobile groups able to remain dispersed, concentrate quickly for an operation and then disperse again. In this sense, the RMA battlefield is akin to what was imagined for a nuclear battlefield.

RMA, however, poses certain limitations. The first of these is the high cost of acquiring and fielding such systems. Most armies can afford only a limited number of such systems and their availability or non-availability may well determine the duration of a war. The increased lethality of these weapon systems also means that casualties, both in men and material, would be heavy, making a long drawn out conflict difficult to sustain. China, India and Pakistan are likely, given the costs and difficulties in acquisition of the latest systems, to field a limited number of systems, generally a generation older than those fielded by the US or its Western allies.

While considering the nature of conventional war that India may be involved in, either with Pakistan or China, the following will need to be kept in mind:

- All three being nuclear weapon powers, there will be immense international pressure on them to bring about a quick cessation of hostilities, lest it lead to an outbreak of a nuclear war.
- In their own self-interest, so as to prevent a nuclear war, India, Pakistan and China would themselves be compelled to exercise restraint on the aims, objectives and duration of a war. The compulsion would be to keep it below the perceived nuclear threshold of the enemy.
- The international community also now does not countenance the change of accepted borders by force. This, to an extent, acts as a disincentive for going to war to settle territorial disputes.
- The high cost of modern weapon systems and the high rate of attrition would also tend to limit the duration of a conventional war fought under conditions of RMA.

The above considerations lead to the conclusion that any conventional war that India may be engaged in, in the near future, is likely to be a limited war; limited both in the objectives set and the duration of such a war. In the Indo-Pak context, the war, unless it is confined to J&K, would be conditioned by the fact that both sides have vital areas close to the borders and, therefore, the nuclear threshold could be lower. In the case of China, given the nature of the terrain and the likely higher nuclear threshold between the two countries, such a limited war may last longer, albeit at a lower intensity. In such limited wars, the objectives would be limited, and the priority may be to not lose territory, as opposed to gaining territory. Not to appear defeated may well be a victory at the end of a war. However, while these wars may be limited for the duration they last, they will be intense. In fact, given the short duration of the war, the temptation will be to fling everything into the battle at the earliest so as to obtain the maximum gains in the shortest possible time and, thus, be in a favourable situation when the war ends. The short duration of the war also implies that the war will have to be fought with the resources in being at the start of hostilities, of both men and material; there will be no time to raise and train new manpower or to perk up production of equipment and munitions. A fairly large standing army will, therefore, need to be maintained.

Low Intensity Conflict

Given the low probability of being able to achieve one's aims by open hostilities whether nuclear or conventional, there is an increasing tendency, of both state and non-state actors, to take recourse to unconventional warfare. Insurgency or terrorism or a combination of both is often now the preferred option. This certainly is the option that Pakistan has chosen to apply against India, first in Punjab and then in J&K. In fact, in J&K, where many of the militants are Pakistani citizens or come from areas in Pakistani control, they can really be described as Pakistani irregular forces, very much part of the military establishment but not in uniform. President Musharraf has pledged to control such activity; it, however, continues and even if stopped, can be restarted at short notice. We need also to keep in mind that China has in the past aided insurgency in the Northeast and could do so again if it feels like it. The Indian Army has enormous experience in coping with such operations but seems not yet to have refined the doctrines and organisations needed for such conflicts. And it is likely that the army will keep facing such situations, if not from external sources, then from internal sources. Therefore, the threat and the necessity to operate in such a scenario will remain the army's primary task in the period under review and must be factored into any discussion on doctrines and organisations.

Organisational and Doctrinal Implications

While force structures and doctrinal changes are a subject of further study and discussion, it would be useful to sum up some of the implications which arise from the security scenario and threat perceptions considered in this paper. These are briefly enumerated below:

- The major armed threats to India remain those from Pakistan and China and from internal armed movements.
- A nuclear war is unlikely; but to ensure this it is necessary that India build up a demonstrated nuclear deterrent.
- Conventional wars, either with Pakistan or China, will be limited, in both objectives and time. In this context, one needs to relook at the forces, especially offensive forces. Do we need a number of lighter offensive formations instead of large strike corps?
- Modern conventional warfare places a premium on dispersion, mobility and ability to regroup and disperse quickly. What are the types of forces required for such a war?
- While wars may be short, they will be intense and casualty rates, for both men and material, will be heavy. The organisation will need to cater for this.
- Men will be under intense mental and physical strain and our training systems must be able to prepare troops for this.
- Modern wars will require integrated management of the electromagnetic spectrum and air space. Joint doctrines will need to be evolved.
- While RMA places a premium on mobility and mechanisation, much of our land frontiers lie in jungle or mountainous terrain and our future organisations must cater for these.
- Even in the plains, many of our important cities, for example Pathankot, Gurdaspur, Amritsar, etc lie very close to the border. We will, therefore, need

certain static forces to defend these, as there is no space to fight a mobile defensive battle ahead of these.

- LIC will remain a major task for the army. This conflict is also manpower intensive. Can we have common organisations, for both conventional and LIC, and if not, what are the costs involved in having two separate types of forces?
- All land warfare, including LIC, is land-air warfare and our doctrines and training must work to integrate both these forces so as to be able to operate jointly.

Conclusion

This paper has attempted a quick, short survey of the security scenario and the threats India is likely to face over the next decade. It has also touched briefly on the type of wars that the army is likely to be involved in and the implications of these for future organisations. On the security situation, it finds that the external security situation is generally stable though tensions with Pakistan and China will continue. Conflict, if any, with either of them, is likely to be of a limited nature. LIC, both foreign sponsored and indigenous, will remain a major task for the army for the foreseeable future. •

VIEWS OF DISCUSSANTS

Lt Gen Satish Nambiar

Ladies and gentlemen, its a great pleasure and privilege to be here at this flag-off event of the Centre for Land Warfare Studies. In the five minutes that I have at my disposal, I think it would be presumptuous on my part to say very much, after the three superb presentations that you had this morning. What I will try and do is to make a few remarks to reinforce what has been said – where it needs reinforcement; and to make a couple of additional remarks.

The first point I would like to make is to reinforce much of what has been said this morning, in terms of the need to look at all these subjects. You cannot look at the shape, size and structure of the army in the 2020 time-frame, and look at the doctrines to meet the emerging challenges, without having a perception of what has to be done in terms of jointness. There is no other way, and that part has been more than highlighted this morning. I am sure that in the sessions that will follow, one would be looking for the army's role within the overall structure, because I think that while looking that far ahead, one cannot be restricted only to the armed forces. One has to look at this whole process within the rethink and revision of our strategy. National strategy obviously requires clear political direction and, therefore, an understanding of the politico-military dimension of the prosecution of war itself. I am not too sure we have got all that right in our system yet, but hopefully, that will happen one of these days. The remarks I wish to make deal with the type of threats we are looking at, and here I have tried to classify these into four or five types. First is conventional war. While I agree with all those who say it is no longer a serious option that countries can resort to, we cannot discount it totally, particularly in our context. I say this in relation to the fact that our potential adversaries in the time-frame we are talking about remain Pakistan and, to a lesser extent, China. I say lesser extent, purely in terms of our own capability; let me amplify this. China and India, as we all know, are likely to be economic rivals one day. If we do not pose credible deterrence to China, China will just brush us aside. So we must have that credible conventional deterrence. Here, I will just make one or two points quickly, about the type of doctrine we are looking at, and this, I suppose, really relates to the fact the we have to look at operations at three levels: at the frontline; in tactical depth to deal with the reserves; and hitting at the nerve centres. I think someone has called it centre of gravity, which is the enemy's command, and control apparatus, from where the national will emerges. These are the levels where you have to have the capacity to operate, which means your force structures have to be geared to fulfill that role. The second threat that I think will remain is that of terrorism, and here I will only say that this problem of terrorism will be something that we have to handle on our own. I do not think anyone is going to come to our help. Having said that, I would suggest to those who in some ways discount the problem of weapons of mass destruction falling into the hands of terrorists, that I don't think it will be a problem that we alone will have to face. It will, in fact, concern the USA more, and, therefore, they will get into the act. To that extent, we can hope to play a role, or work against this threat, within the international arena itself.

Low intensity conflict is likely to continue for some time, in terms of little insurgencies here and there, which we have to deal with. I would only suggest that when we look ahead, we should not talk of the army getting involved in it; at worst, it should be the Rashtriya Rifles (RR), Assam Rifles and other paramilitary forces, but the army should stay clear. There are three other dimensions which we must look at, in terms of threats, even though these are not direct threats, not the glamorous types of threats which we talk about. I am talking about the internal security dimensions, in terms of the upheavals that could take place in our society with the hitherto depressed classes, the deprived classes, seeking a place in the sun. If that is well managed by our establishment, it will not have any violent repercussions. But as far as the armed forces are concerned, this sort of revival will affect the material that we get into the armed forces. Therefore, the spillover effect is something we should be prepared to handle and, in fact, preempt, in many ways. Related to these last two points, I would like to mention the threat in terms of poverty and disease. These threats are not talked about, but they are serious. A disease like HIV/AIDS is now considered a threat in the international scenario; and it is a great threat to us because it could not only affect the armed forces and, therefore, their performance, but also the eligible human resources pool for the armed forces could be affected by it. Thank you.

Prof Satish Kumar

In the midst of these very distinguished military minds, I do not know whether views of an academic would make much sense, but I will venture to make a few points. The first point I want to make is to put the emerging strategic alliance with the US in some perspective. Two distinguished speakers, Gen Brar and Ambassador Gupta, have given some importance to this emerging strategic alliance. Mr Gupta has built a very strong case for India to have a strategic alliance with the US. I would like to add a word of caution here, lest the niggardly response from the US cause frustration or anger in the minds of Indians later on. My first point is that an Indo-US strategic alliance cannot be based on the fact that one is the strongest democracy and the other the largest, because this introduces the element of sentimentalism in the equation, which ought to be based on balance of capabilities and interests. My submission is that the gap between the capabilities of the US and India is so wide that it is natural for the superior power to treat the weaker power as a junior partner, to be used when the need arises, in fulfillment of strategic needs, like the Malacca Strait last year. The US controls 39 per cent of the world's military expenditure, 33 per cent of the world's GDP, 27 per cent of the world's manufacturing, 15 per cent of the world's trade. Whereas India contributes 1.7 per cent, 1.5 per cent, 1.1 per cent and 0.7 per cent respectively. How much can India catch up, and how soon? It has been suggested by Gen Brar in his paper that in 2020, India might emerge as the fourth largest economic power. I have great reservations about this. I do not doubt the possibility that somewhere along the line, India will be fourth in the hierarchy, but what does it mean if India continues to represent something like 4 or 5 per cent of the total world economy? I think India will not make a difference to the world situation unless it contributes at least 10 per cent to the world economy. Right now, if any country can make a difference, it is Russia in the military field which is currently 7 per cent, and it will be Japan in GDP, which is currently 14 per cent, Japan again in the manufacturing field, which is currently 17 per cent, and Germany in the trade field, which is currently 9 per cent, and perhaps China, if it can maintain its rate of growth of 7 to 9 per cent over this whole period. Therefore, to anticipate and to pin our hopes on the fact that India would emerge as an economic power in the year 2020, which will make a difference to India's international presence, is somewhat uncertain.

According to the estimates of late 2003, the US has 2,55,000 military men deployed abroad for combat and peace-keeping operations, and had sent another 1,36,000 troops from the National Guards and the reserves. But more were needed, and that is why the US sent appeals to various friends across the world to supply troops.

The well known author Paul Kennedy, writing in an article in an Australian newspaper, has said, "Washington frantically denies it has imperial ambitions and I believe those denials to be correct but if the United States increasingly looks like an empire, walks like an empire and quacks like an empire, perhaps it is becoming one just the same." The point that I am making is that there are still vital differences in the capabilities of India and the US, and while forging alliances, one has to see as to what are the expectations from the other side, and what are the benefits India is likely to get, because there are vital strategic differences in the perceptions of the two countries on critical areas. On Central Asia, India thinks that we have common strategic concerns, but the Americans don't think so. On the Persian Gulf, India thinks that we have common concerns and common approaches, but the Americans don't necessarily think so. On non-proliferation, India thinks that we have common approaches and we can handle the problem jointly. There are in fact differences in perceptions on how to approach the question of non-proliferation, as also on the question of terrorism. Therefore, while endorsing the need for building a strategic partnership with the United States, I advocate the necessity of building of countervailing partnerships with other counties, and not bending over and pinning too much hope on the United States alone.

The second point that I want to make, and I will not dwell too much on it, is that I would like to compliment Ambassador Ranjit Gupta on his very thorough treatment of China. If you read the paper carefully, you find that he makes a very stimulating and valid point about the future security environment when he says, "While Beijing has handled its rapprochement with Washington from a position of strength, India has handled its rapprochement with Beijing from a position of weakness." It is a very interesting point, just think about how valid it is. I think it is entirely valid. China's strategic necessity of countervailing and checkmating India through Pakistan, and through India's other neighbours, will always remain.

I fully endorse Ambassador Gupta's five preconditions, fulfillment of which proves that China is not a threat to India any longer. I do not have the time to go through these. China's regional security concerns vis-à-vis the United States, Taiwan, Japan, Korean Peninsula, South China Sea, etc are more important for it than making a substantial improvement in relations with India. I would, therefore, venture to say that asymmetry between India and China in economic and military terms is likely to increase in the next fifteen years, making it necessary for India to upgrade its overall capability, particularly nuclear capability.

Unfortunately, Russia has not been given due importance in this presentation so far, except by Admiral Das, who mentioned it somewhat obliquely. Russia presented its latest Defence Paper in October 2003, the salient features of which are that diluting the role of the UN Security Council and using force on the basis of national decisions would be a serious threat to Russian political and military interests. Russia is concerned over the anti-Russian thrust of the North Atlantic Treaty Organisation (NATO), and its plans to redeploy military bases from Western Europe to Eastern Europe. This will put NATO aircraft within three minutes striking distance of St Petersburg. Next, the Commonwealth of Independent States (CIS) is an extremely important security zone for Russia. Russia retains the right to preventive use of military force, including in the CIS countries, and, last, not necessarily last in the total list, but the last that I could capture in view of the time constraint, Russia could deliver preemptive strikes not only if threatened militarily but also if faced with attempts billed to limit Russia's access to the regions that are essential for its survival, or those important from the economic and international points of view. Nuclear weapons will remain the basis of Russian security. It was after this Defence Paper was published by the Defence Ministry of Russia in October 2003 that Russia opened an air base in Kyrgyzstan in October 2003. Russia, for the first time, is projecting itself as having a global role. That is why Colin Powel published an article in *Izvestia* in January 2004, criticising Russia for human rights violations and curbing the media during the parliamentary elections, trying to indicate that America is now angry with Russia. Hence, President Vladimir Putin has taken the position that he arrested Mikhail Khodorkovsky for trying to give a controlling share in Russian oil to the United States. That is why now certain things are happening. Increasing reassertion of Russia as a power of some global consequence has to be taken note of by India; India cannot afford to dismiss Russia as a very important strategic partner.

Lastly, Mr Chairman, it has not been sufficiently noted that Japan has in the last two years tended to reassert its military role, not only by deciding to send troops to Iraq, through a resolution passed in the Parliament, giving the Self-

Defence Force a vital role. Also, in the year 2002, the Cabinet secretary of Russia went on record to say that Japan could possibly revise its Constitution to change the provision that Japan will neither possess, nor allow, nor manufacture, nuclear weapons on its soil. Which means the possibility that Japan can go nuclear, and you can visualise the consequences if the North Korean nuclear question is not sorted out in the foreseeable future. Therefore, if Japan changes its decision in this respect, you can understand the impact it will have on the non-proliferation regime, and India has to take note of it.

Having said that, Mr Chairman, I will wind up by saying that I agree with every word of the what the previous speakers have said about Pakistan. I maintain what I said last year in my public lecture delivered under the auspices of the Centre for Policy Research. I believe that Pakistan will remain a long-term security threat to India, irrespective of the recent peace initiatives, and there are various reasons for this, including the army's continuing role, religious extremism, the failure of democracy, and the nuclear weapons policy of Pakistan. However, I welcome the possibilities of a rapprochement. As the previous speakers have said, such a rapprochement is not going to make a fundamental difference 20 years from now, as far as our threat perception vis-à-vis Pakistan is concerned. I appreciate the fact that some speakers have devoted some attention to the internal security issues, but I do not have the time to dwell on that. Thank you. •

INTERACTIVE SESSION

Gen V.N. Sharma

Thank you Professor. Ladies and gentlemen, we have little over half an hour for discussions. I will only request that when you raise a question, please do not take too much time. Ask a question and if you want to make a comment, please make a short comment. So, the house is now open.

Lt Gen A.M. Vohra

Thank you, Mr. Chairman, I have been very impressed by the standard of papers presented, but there are one or two issues that I would like to raise. First, I think there is a tendency to overstate the threats. Now, Gen Brar mentioned China's expansionism. Communist China came into being in 1950 and has been mainly concerned about one major issue i.e. One China. Their problem is Taiwan; in addition to that, they are sensitive about their outer provinces like Xingxiang, Mongolia and Tibet, but they have not shown any sign of expansionism. The economy is their core issue and they are doing well in that. Economic interface between India and China is growing and India is no threat to China on economic issues. In the foreseeable future that we are thinking of, China does not pose any military threat to India.

Second, in relation to Pakistan, I agree that it is in great shambles, but I suggest to you that the army is going to continue to be in power to ensure some sort of order; they are visualising a type of democracy in which the army has a major say. That leads me to the second point, which is that in the foreseeable future, wars as such are an improbability because, except in the case of a superpower dealing with somebody, in all other cases, the military balance is such that all wars will be inconclusive. Therefore, no country is keen to go to war. In considering the shape of things to come, we should concentrate on punitive strike capabilities. Thank you.

Lt Gen A.M. Sethna

Thank you, Mr. Chairman, I am offbeat. I am talking of something which is very down to earth : the foot soldier issue, internal security and the army's involvement in it in the foreseeable future. From the point of view of the changes which are taking place within the country, and, if I may use that bad word, 'extremism' within the country, whether we like it or not, the army is involved. I will make a reference to one particular aspect: whether we like it or not, the army is still the last resort for the government. Is the army working on this now, and will it be working on it in the future, to see how it will respond to these situations, which are emerging? I give the examples of Malegaon in Maharashtra; Ahmedabad, Baroda and Godhra in Gujarat; and Chattisinghpura in Kashmir. All three of these, I have been deeply involved in, as a member of the National Minorities Commission. Thank you.

Dr Manoj Joshi

Thank you, Mr. Chairman. I would like to take off from Gen Vohra's remark with regard to China. There seems to be a knee-jerk reflex vis-à-vis China. Mr Gupta pointed out that China has had good relations with all of its neighbours, except India and Bhutan. The obvious question is why? Surely, fifty years after this whole dispute flared up, we should be asking ourselves, whether we could have been in error somewhere? A certain amount of modesty, a certain amount of introspection, I think, is needed with regard to the origins of that border dispute. I also question his point regarding the strategic importance of Aksai Chin. It was extremely important in the beginning because the Chinese did not have the road from Chengdu going, and that is why they needed to come through Xingxiang. At that time, Aksai Chin had a certain importance. But today, Aksai Chin is no longer that important for China. It is certainly not of vital strategic interest, as was made out in the paper. Thirdly, there have been statements about China wishing to band together with other countries against US-led hegemonism. I want to know where these statements are coming from? Certainly, China has not made any call for any "Third Worldism". In fact, if anyone is guilty of trying to raise the banner of the Third World against the First World, it has been India. So, I do not think it is really fair, from an analytical point of view, to put forward such Chinese assertions, unless and until we have much more substantive proof. Of course, we know that the Chinese policy vis-à-vis India has been unrelentingly hostile. They have supplied nuclear weapons and missile technology to Pakistan, but that has a certain context. To extrapolate that the Chinese are out there to do certain things which even they have not claimed, is putting allegations on them. I think today India and China have a historic opportunity to resolve their border dispute. The earlier this is resolved, the better it will be. Then we can get on with the business of competition, which will surely be in the economic field.

Air Vice Marshal Kapil Kak

Thank you, Mr. Chairman, I have just three brief comments. First, is the point about the general narrative saying that there will be no conventional war. May I suggest that if we go exactly a hundred years back to Europe, to 1904, the dominant paradigm was that there will be anarchism and threat of terrorism. In a period of two and half years to be precise, there were seven major assassinations, and the world of Europe then believed that there would be no conventional war. As we know, we had two World Wars, with 81 million casualties. Mr Chairman, the point I wish to make is that the conflict spectrum in which the armed forces, including the Indian Army, will be involved, has widened.

Therefore, conventional war is not passé; we have to be prepared for it. I suggest very strongly that in the context of the nuclear overhang, we revisit the concept of limited war in the South Asian context.

The second point I wish to make, and for which I could perhaps get boxed in the head, is that we are looking at the international power configuration in the 21st century, where alliances are hopelessly outdated. So, I see great potential in the Indo-US relationship. The United States is a great power, a better power, and we must be on its right side, but I think a set of relationships with other major powers, India being a major power, may serve us better than putting all our eggs in the so-called Indo-US strategic partnership. This is particularly relevant when we look at India as a major power itself, having engagements across the political, technological and economic thresholds.

The third point I wish to make is about China. I think we are getting it all somewhat mixed up. There has been a projection that China is a military threat. I do not share that perspective, but we need to look at China in strategic terms as a long-term challenge. China is the longest surviving civilisation in the world today, with a great resilience and historical conflict paradigm. It is also a non-status quo power. I believe India is also a non-status quo power. It has to move forward as a great power and, therefore, conflict is inevitable. My submission, Mr Chairman, is that in no way must India not take an insurance policy vis-à-vis China. It must strengthen its economic, military, technological and, most importantly, its space capabilities, because these are the areas China is moving forward in. There should not be any possibility whatsoever of asymmetry in technological capability between China and India. Thank you.

Lt Gen K.S. Brar

Mr. Chairman, regarding China being a threat, we are talking of 2020, by which time India, of course, will try to narrow down the gap. Our nuclear strength will be slightly comparable to China. We can never match this, but we must have strong deterrence capabilities without fail. The fact is China is spending a lot of money in Tibet, building roads, strategic airfields and railway lines; it has to have a purpose for doing all this; it needs a reason. No one can stop China from being a superpower in Asia, but I do not think it wants to have any other power in Asia compete with it by any means, and China looks at India, the way India is coming up technologically, economically and militarily, and feels that it may be a rival to its total dominance of Asia. It fears that India will be a strong power in South Asia, with regional cooperation with its neighbours, and, therefore, there will be some sort of competition. I do not think China wants that competition. As long as they have some bone of contention, the international border between China and India will remain unresolved. It gives China the leeway to enter into a conflict with India at an appropriate time. We have to be prepared for it. I agree with you that there cannot be a land battle, I cannot see them rolling down the Himalayas and coming in on the Ledo road through Burma or coming down through Bhutan. I do not see that sort of battle. If there is a conflict, it will only be if there is a clash of interests, if they feel that we are coming in their way, becoming competitors with them. I see border skirmishes, I see an air battle, space battle, maritime battle, which will be on a much lower scale, to keep India on tenterhooks, so that China can slow down our development. If there is no threat, then India does not have to worry about anything, It can just look at the economic part. We do not need to go in for better nuclear technology, missiles, long range PGMs and intercontinental missiles, etc. I agree with you that the threat may come or may not come. If it does, it will be in the form of smaller conflicts, when their interests are hurt, and we have to be prepared for it. I would not rule out the possibility in the long-term, unless the border issue is solved, that China is a military threat to India. I strongly feel that in the long-term we have to be prepared for China being a military threat. In what dimension that threat will be is a different matter. Thank you.

Ambassador Ranjit Gupta

Mr. Chairman, I would like to comment on the point about being accused of having put things in China's mouth, that somehow China is propagating the idea of Asian countries getting together to contest US-led Western hegemonism. In my paper, I have not said that. That is a sentiment which is particularly prevalent in India. The Chinese are being reasonable in tapping this sentiment and it will ultimately link up with their own strategic long-term thinking, which is to dominate the whole of Asia. The old feudatory relationship, in a modern form, will come into existence. That will amount to Asia 'banding' together against Western hegemonism, led by the USA or whoever. Thank you.

Vice Admiral P.S. Das

I want to make two brief observations. India needs military power because as a nation state, it requires military power, and not only because Pakistan is a threat or China is a threat. And it is true that the threat of military conflict has come down greatly. We can attend to it by doing two things.

One, by having a military capability, which has a clear superiority over Pakistan. Two, as far as China is concerned, to have what we call in naval parlance a "threshold against intervention," which means everyone should know that for hostile acts there will be some punishment, and that will act as a deterrent. I will not say any more about India and China.

Prof Satish Kumar said something about Russia, and he is right. If there is any natural ally of India today, it is Russia. It is not just because of a background of 35 years. Our interests are common, therefore, he is so right in saying that a relationship with Russia is very much to India's advantage. Except that relationships with America and Russia are not exclusive or that they cannot progress together. There is a need to progress both. Finally, I fully agree with what Air Marshal Kak has said, that today the need is for engagement, including military engagement. In the first fifty years of our independent life, we have remained far from military engagement, have been utterly isolated. It is not possible to be that in the world of today and tomorrow. So, like political engagement, like economic engagement, it will become increasingly necessary for the militaries to get used to the idea of military engagement.

Brig Gurmeet Kanwal

I am struck by a point that Gen Brar made regarding the next conflict between China and India being fought on Indian territory on land, and over Indian skies in the air. I am sure it is a deep conviction, coming from a former Eastern Army commander, based on professional judgment, but if we do foresee a conventional conflict with China over the next 15 to 20 years, then the military strategy, even though it is dissuasive, does not necessarily have to be purely defensive. It must be offensive defence. After all, we must have something to show for our gains at the end of the conflict. I know that infrastructure is lacking, therefore, something must be done about it over the next two decades or so. I know there are very limited reserves; for example, there is no mountain strike corps. So, if the threat is foreseen, the force structure must be raised and, similarly, there are operational voids in the formations over there. They are deployed over large frontages but if at the end of that conflict, we are going to have nothing to show for it, if we are going to again have the Chinese coming down to Tawang or to Teju, then I do not think it should be acceptable to a modern India, which considers itself an emerging regional power. As far as the air dimension is concerned, I don't think the PLA Air Force has the capability to fight over Indian skies. They have the numbers, they have the volume, but not the quality as of today. Of course, the PLA Air Force is also modernising and that needs to be taken into account. Thank you.

Lt Gen K.S. Brar

When we talk of a land battle, an all out war between China and India, I think it is very difficult to visualise that we will go into Tibet, that we will go into Chumbi Valley, or that we will do this, that or the other. But I don't think that India will be in a position to launch a war against China on Chinese territory. I don't think we will see it in our life-times, however much we may want to. I don't say that we must remain passive and defensive. There is a certain amount of offensive defence in our plans, we may be able to bite off a little bit here or a little bit there, but the fact is that if China decides to go to war with us, I don't give that possibility much credibility. I feel that a land war will be extremely difficult. I cannot see the Chinese coming rolling down Tawang to the Brahmaputra Valley, coming down to the Siliguri corridor. The fact is that if there are irritants, and if there are compelling reasons for China to go to war with us, rather than it being a full scale land battle, they would use their air power, their long range missiles, the PGMs and even nuclear weapons. We don't see the possibility of a nuclear war, but the fact is that the threat will remain if there is a wide gap between our nuclear capability and theirs, and we will always be worried about it. So we have to be prepared for a Chinese war against us, whether we like it or not. It may happen, it may not happen. If it does happen, I foresee that it will happen on our territory and not on theirs.

Col A.P. Sharma

Thank you, Sir. I have two observations. The first one is that when the Chinese analysed their security threat perceptions, they factored in comprehensive national power as one of the main indices to assess these. In that, going by the current analysis, the USA and Japan are placed much higher on the ladder than India. But in the next 15-20 years, while they do see India emerging as a possible rival, according to their calculations, our comprehensive national power will not be a match for theirs. In fact, the gap would increase and, secondly, if you study the PLA's modernisation, you find that the centre point is their strategy of limited war under high-tech conditions, and around that is the focus of the complete PLA modernisation. I will not go into this strategy of limited war because it is well known, but two or three factors merit consideration. Firstly, it is proactive, based on active defence; secondly, it is tri-Service, totally integrated; and thirdly, nuclear weapon use is not discounted. Therefore, as a nation, we must consider the Chinese modernisation and their main strategy, which is based on limited war under high-tech conditions.

Maj Gen L.S. Lehl

I would like to make just one point. While assessing the threats, I think we have to get out of the Hindu philosophy of war i.e. waiting till the enemy reaches our border and crosses it. It has happened to us again and again. We have been discussing the guerrilla warfare sponsored by Pakistan and, earlier, by China. It is time for us to think a little about events beyond the borders of our country, like in Afghanistan when the Russians came, we were quite happy, we were not concerned. Ultimately, it led to the trouble in Kashmir, which is still troubling us. Similarly, we have had problems with China in earlier days, so why don't we plan ourselves and get a good base in the Gilgit area? We can have a good base in Tibet and train our forces. When we plan the shape and structure of the future army, I think it should be kept in mind that our role is not just to secure the border, but to a little beyond, before they start troubling us. Thank you.

Gen V.N. Sharma

That is an interesting point for the future sessions. The last two-three questions and the answers given are very valid. We have had a defensive type of attitude for many years because of the way our country thinks, because of the way our political leadership thinks. You can see what America is doing with regard to taking the offensive into what they think is going to be a threat. That's one extreme, but we should not be at the other extreme. I think there is a balance in between.

Col Sanjay Agarwal

I have a point about an aspect which we need to recognise as a challenges when we talk of a long-term vision, as in the Army 2020 vision. It appears that there is synergy within the Chinese establishment between the policy-makers, on the one hand, and the PLA, on the other. It started off with a recognition of the army component or the military component in the force modernisations, and it has continued thereafter. But when we look for such synergy on the Indian side, between the policy-makers and the military component, either it does not exist as satisfactorily as it should or certainly it is not perceived to so exist. I feel this aspect needs to be recognised as an internal challenge for us, wherein we improve both the situation and the perceived situations, and lead on to better handling of both sides. We have to learn how to handle the policy-maker, to understand his problem, so that he can handle us better. I think this to be recognised as a challenge for us. Thank you.

Brig P.K. Chakraborty

I would like to refer to what Ambassador Ranjit Gupta has said, that China has resolved all issues with her 11 neighbours, except for India and Bhutan. But the Spratly issue remains unresolved with Vietnam. The issue of land borders with Vietnam is partially resolved, and Vietnam still happens to be the biggest enemy of China; 900 years of enmity remain unresolved. The erstwhile army commander of the Eastern Command said that the battle will be only on Indian soil. I think he is only referring to the eastern and northeastern borders. If we look at the borders in Ladakh, the areas of Demchok and other areas are suitable for us to plan, what Brig Gurmeet Kanwal just talked about – the offensive – even with our limited capability today. I think what is really lacking in the Indian psyche is the proactive stance. Passivity has been with us right from the early days. I think *Maa Durga* and Indira Gandhi were two people who took proactive actions; one to get us Sikkim. We need to think in a different way vis-à-vis China. Thank you.

Brig B.K. Ponwar

Sir, I would like to go into another aspect of the threat i.e. internal threats. Our nation is facing plenty of them. We are well aware of them. A system should be in place wherein we can manage these internal threats in such a manner that we can be proactive in situations like the Kamatapuri militants in West Bengal, the People's War Group (PWG) in Chattisgarh, in Orissa, and some other states, the Students Islamic Movement of India (SIMI) groups in UP. The political leaders are unable to manage these threats and ultimately the army has to come to their rescue. It has happened over the years in the Northeast, it happened in J&K. We are deeply and extensively involved in both these states, as is well known. How do we work out an orchestration of this internal threat, wherein the politicians have to play their part, the bureaucrats have to play their part, the socio-economic aspect has to play its part, and ultimately, of course, the military has to play its part? At times, it is left only to the military to resolve such conflicts rather than the other issues which are so very important. It was only when the politicians came in that J&K has started to change. It was only when the politicians came in that Mizoram and now Nagaland are moving towards total peace. In fact, Mizoram has already moved towards total peace. It is one of the most peaceful states of our nation. Thank you.

Maj Vivek Chaddha

My point is related to an aspect of what we are thinking of, the Army: 2020 vis-à-vis some of the neighbouring countries, which were listed as minor problems for us. The countries which are posing problems for us are Bangladesh, Myanmar, in the past at least, and Pakistan, which are breeding grounds of terrorism and insurgency, and we seem to be doing nothing about it. Don't you think sir, that we should have a policy of either low intensity conflict or the conventional variety against such erring countries?

Rear Admiral R.B. Vohra

Admiral Das had made a mention regarding the energy requirements of all the countries which are in the Asia-Pacific, as also in the IOR. He said that 4,000 tankers are moving through the Indian Ocean and this is likely to go up to 8,000. Japan is importing almost its entire energy requirements from the Gulf ; China is presently dependent for about 40 per cent, and this is likely to go up to 70 per cent. All the countries are likely to have their requirements met though this route, which is the Indian Ocean, where you have a number of choke points. Don't you think there is likely to be a real problem, since their requirements are growing every year? Therefore, a country like China, which is growing very fast and whose requirements are going to be greater, is going to safeguard its interests in this area. They will make sure that their own forces are geared up for such an eventuality. Can you, therefore, really rule out a conflict? Thank you.

Gen V.N. Sharma

Thank you, ladies and gentlemen. You have raised some very interesting points. I have to end the questions now because we have reached the end of our time. I need to give a few minutes to any one of the panel who may want to say anything. But I am grateful for some very interesting views that came out from the back of the hall and I am happy to see that there is a very good offensive spirit out there. Well done.

Vice Admiral P.S. Das

I want to clarify the picture which was mentioned by Admiral Vohra, about the Indian Ocean scene and this relates to China and the other questions. As part of the modernisation programme of China, the military modernisation, two aspects are critical : modernisation in space and modernisation of sea-going forces both extend China's reach. Let me come to the Indian Ocean now. If this is to be the reach, if China has got such vast interests in IOR, as it is going to have, can it come here? Frankly, presently, no. Even if its navy can be increased greatly, can it operate from here? The answer is doubtful. So what is needed? The requirement is to have shore facilities in this part of the world. Therefore, the two things which are of concern about China are the development of ports in Myanmar and the development of the port of Gwadar in Pakistan. By itself, this would not mean anything, but linked with China's present and intended movements, it will give China an Indian Ocean capability, which it does not presently have. Are we happy with the situation? If the answer is yes, nothing can be done. But if we have some concern over the situation, then we have to structure our capabilities accordingly. Frankly, nobody will be happy with the situation. Will the ASEAN be happy with the Indian Ocean capability of China? Will America be happy with the Indian Ocean capability of China? I frankly do not think so. Nevertheless, there is a need for us to be prepared for this contingency and to shape our plans accordingly. As economic interests grow, inevitably the sea will have to play a larger role in India's security concerns.

Lt Gen Satish Nambiar

Thank you, Mr. Chairman. Just two quick points, Sir. Ladies and gentlemen, within much of what has been said so far, I think what stands out is that in terms of our strategic analysis and analytical capability, it is time we factored in the aspect of military strength as an element of power in international relations. This is something which has not been done and that is why people have written about the lack of strategic thinking in India. At least it is beginning to show. I think much of the discussion today has fortunately brought that out. Particularly for a country like India, given its geostrategic location and size, we cannot hang onto the coattails of some other power. We have to have our own inherent capability, if we are to mean something in international relations, and here, the second aspect comes in, which I think has been talked of – our developing relationship with the USA. It is not developing because the USA suddenly began to like our faces, but because they see that something is to be gained from this relationship. So we have to also work in that context. What do we have to get out of it? Why should we be subservient to them? The point about China doing it from a position of strength and us not doing so, is relevant. We should also look at our national interests point of view. Here, while developing the relationship with the USA, I would like to endorse what Prof Satish Kumar said: we must develop our relationship with Russia and possibly with China, but there again, it should not be one of ganging up against the USA, or when you are working with the USA, of ganging up against China. It should be purely from our national interests point of view. Thank you.

Ambassador Ranjit Gupta

With reference to the point made about Vietnam, 95 per cent of the problem with Vietnam has been sorted out and only 5 per cent remains. I don't think the comment you made was fair, and I was talking about land boundaries, so the Spratlys do not come into it. Thank you.

Gen V.N. Sharma

Ladies and gentlemen, I have just a few points to make before we wind up this session. First, the question of internal security. Points have been raised about this. I would like to divide internal security into two parts. One is the internal security problem created by political and religious movements, and the other is the internal security problem created by terrorism, which is sponsored from outside. Now, what we see in Kashmir and we saw in Punjab, and what we are seeing in northeastern India, is external, state-sponsored terrorism. Arms, weapons, equipment, communications, training and control is by foreign powers, be it Pakistan or China or whoever. The internal movements are the ones which are like the conflagration in Godhra and other places that were mentioned. Let us take these one by one. As far as terrorism which comes from outside is concerned, there is no question that the army has to be involved. The police is incapable of handling it, because those are trained outfits, as flexible as military units, even like military commando units. We need everything, the air force, army and even the navy to counter this, and, if necessary, to carry this across the border. We have to be offensive in our anti-terrorist war. As far as the other type of terrorism is concerned, I agree that the army should not be involved. This type of conflict is basically a result of bad politics, if I may say so. It is one party, or one religious group, agitating for space in the political power system, against the other which creates these conflicts. It is a natural corollary to India's history of the past 100 years, we saw it in Punjab, we have seen it in Maharashtra, we have seen it in Gujarat. The man to man relations are very good between all religions and communities. It is only when politics comes into it, when it becomes a question of getting votes, etc, that you find this type of conflagration taking place. The police cannot control it; often the police itself is controlled by those in power, and often the police is not trained. Hence, there is a need for the political system, the bureaucratic system and the police to gear up and meet the responsibility without waiting to call the army in. Calling in the army to help the police was a British concept, because the Britain used to control this country through the army, but we have passed that stage and we need to mature in this, and, therefore, we need political maturity in the way we go to the hustings for our votes – all of you here who will vote shortly, better make sure that you vote correctly.

A point was raised about oil. It is a very important point. Oil politics runs the world, it runs the armament industry, it runs the drugs world, it runs everything. We need to pay a lot of attention to what is happening in the Persian Gulf, Caspian Sea, and other such areas. You never know what is going to happen in the future. We are talking about 2020. You may require forces to go to the Gulf. You may need expeditionary forces. What sort of organisation do we want for that? It is for the coming sessions to discuss. What sort of organisation, what sort of command and control, and to whom will these people report? A point about our democracy – it is very important. I think the Americans are right when they say that democratic nations do not easily go to war. It is theocratic or dictatorial states who do so very easily. So, we have to have relations with democracies and that is an accepted fact. Russia has rapidly become a democracy. China is a Communist state, but it is acting very much like a capitalist state, in the way its economy is growing. Let us see how the relations develop here, but we have to make sure that in our democracy, the sword is not held by the political leader. That means the political leader has a Cabinet and his people to answer to, and the sword is held by the military, which is under the political order. That is a better balance of the execution of power.

Now, in regard to the 2020 shape of the army, a few points have come out. The US' lessons in Iraq ought to be learnt. You may have as sophisticated a military as you like, but when you come down to the infantry soldier and the tank man and the gunner, you have to occupy territory, you need manpower, you need sophisticated weapon systems, and you need enough manpower to protect long borders, defend nodes, etc, from which mobile forces can emanate to control the countryside. India has got vast land borders. So one cannot say that in the modernisation of the Indian Army in the year 2020, we will go in only for small mobile forces. You have to defend the borders. If you leave the borders open, any joker, including terrorists, will come across and make life miserable for us, and make us weaker in our execution of military plans. There has been a lot of discussion regarding limited conventional war. While nuclear deterrence is important, you also need conventional deterrence of a high order. Conventional deterrence means not only defence but also offensive action. As very rightly brought out by some youngsters, unless you take offensive action, nothing will be gained. We have to dominate the no-man's land, the area which is between you and the enemy. It has to be dominated not only in mind and thought but also physically. So, offensive thinking is very necessary, because if you are under attack, the best form of defence, as Napoleon said, is to attack. About wars coming or not coming, there were two views that clearly came out I would only suggest that human beings don't change. Right from the day Adam and Eve were born, till today, lust, thirst for power, greed, desire and domination of others have been part of the human character, and so it is with nations. Today, you may have a leader who is very peaceful in his attitude, but tomorrow you may have a leader who is very offensive in his attitude. Hence, no country can take chances. Therefore, in the military business, we always say our military power must be based on the military power of those who are surrounding us and those who can affect us from a distance. We have to meet that power, we have to have the capability of doing so. Whether it is used or not used, we can wait and see. But if you don't have it, you can be taken for a ride. Even in the ordinary schools, if you don't stand up to the bully, you could be given a good bashing.

We need to train our bureaucrats and political leaders for the military business, and the way of using the military machine. Unfortunately, this does not exist. They don't like to go back to school. We have been suggesting in our time, to prime ministers and to Cabinet secretaries and everybody else, that just like in the military we keep sending our officers to schools to do courses of instructions right up to the rank of general and equivalent, why cannot the politicians do that? You can't say that you got your vote, therefore, you know it all. You have to be trained. So there is a need for some sort of training for political leaders before they start handling the military machine, and also for the bureaucracy, who feel many times – with due apology to those present – that once you have passed out of the Mussoorie Academy you know it all. No sir, you don't. I think it was Rajiv Gandhi who had suggested that bureaucrats needed to go to the administrative college for a year, where they can interface with colleagues, military persons and business people.

Having talked of an offensive attitude, a proactive stance can only be possible if you have the military capability for that proactive stance, and, therefore, it is important to factor that in when you consider in the future sessions as to what should be the shape and size of the Army 2020. Finally, on India's influence zone; it is not just the immediate neighbours that you have to influence. We are interested in oil in the Gulf. We are interested in the choke points of the Arabian Sea. We are also interested in those nations that can reach out to us by their economic and military power, the United States or Russia or China, or any one. We have to cater for all these in our future thinking. Thank you very much, ladies and gentlemen, for a very interesting discussion and some very pertinent questions that were raised. •

Session II

National Aspirations and Military Capabilities

Panel Chairman	:	Lt Gen V.K. Nayyar, PVSM, SM (Retd)
Panel Discussant	:	Dr Brahma Chellaney
Paper Presenters	:	Air Cmde Jasjit Singh, AVSM, VrC, VM (Retd)
		Brig (Dr) Arun Sahgal (Retd)
		Dr Manoj Joshi
		Brig Rahul K. Bhonsle, SM

PRELIMINARIES

Lt Gen Vijay Oberoi

Ladies and gentlemen, the subject of the second session is "National Aspirations and Desired Capabilities." The panel consists of Lt Gen V.K. Nayyar (Retd), the chairman, Dr Brahma Chellaney, the discussant and Air Cmde Jasjit Singh (Retd), Brig (Dr) Arun Sahgal (Retd), Dr Manoj Joshi and Brig Rahul K. Bhonsle, the paper presenters. I would now request Lt Gen V.K. Nayyar to start the proceedings.

Lt Gen V.K. Nayyar

After discussion of the threats, I think the aspirations are correct issues to be discussed. I now request Air Cmde Jasjit Singh to start his presentation.

ARMY 2020: SYNCHRONISING MILITARY POWER WITH NATIONAL ASPIRATIONS

Air Commodore Jasjit Singh, AVSM, VrC, VM (Retd)

A man's reach should exceed his grasp, or what's a heaven for.
– Robert Browning

As the great poet implied, inevitably there will – and should – be a gap between the aspirations, expectations, and vision for the future, and the realties that impinge on actual policy. It is the vision for the future that shapes progress by channelling energies to achieve what may appear difficult in the contemporary scene. At the same time, it is essential that while long-term idealism should shape our thinking, short-term pragmatism should guide actual policy. This is as applicable in the national context as at the more specific military level. Building military capabilities in general, and that of the army in particular, fifteen years hence requires a judicious mix of what is desirable and what is feasible.

Political Interests and Military Objectives

It is useful to state the obvious at the very outset, that the military power of a state essentially serves – and should be created, structured, and employed for rational achievable and affordable – national political goals and objectives. This is the reason that led Clausewitz to declare, "War is a mere continuation of policy by other means."[1] Since war, as we have understood it, is normally waged with the military power of a state, Clausewitzian logic would lead us to the obvious conclusion that the employment of military power would (and should) be a rational enterprise to serve political goals. This has to be further understood in the context of the times in which Clausewitz lived where the ruler was sovereign, and believed in "the absolute priority of foreign affairs over domestic consideration," the latter virtually having no influence in the decision to employ military power.[2] And, hence the decision to go to war was a rational choice made by the sovereign ruler exclusively on the basis of external considerations and was meant to maximise the power and interests of the state as defined by the ruler and largely impervious to any domestic consideration, beyond what the sovereign chose to include in his deliberations.

But the process of democratisation that the world has experienced since his days no longer supports this basic tenet of Clausewitz, even if authoritarian states may still follow the precept to some degree. For a country like ours, where the process of democratisation and the well-established principle of civil political control over military power and its employment have taken deep roots, the purpose of war would have to be deeply influenced by the domestic dimensions, along with any external consideration. Some would even argue that for a developing country like ours, consideration of domestic factors, especially those affecting the scope and extent of human development, would weigh heavily in such decisions. Where another country wages war against a democracy like ours, the decision to go to war would be heavily motivated by the political rationale and need to protect our sovereignty and territorial integrity, and the core values held dear, rather than an ephemeral contest for power.

But while the rulers of 18/19th century waging wars could take domestic support for granted, the modern political leader cannot. The democratisation of war and the rise of domestic imperatives of national policy, hence, must be taken into account in any consideration of employment of military power in a country like ours. To this would have to be added the element of the existence of nuclear weapons impinging on our policy and security environment. This factor places a certain level and scope of restraint and limitations on the way we can wage a war, as much as it does with respect to the adversary. Some experts have argued that the mere possession of nuclear weapons with adversaries forestalls any probability (if not the possibility) of a war between them.[3] It is true that given the horrendous scale of death and devastation that even a few nuclear weapons can cause, a war which results in the use of nuclear weapons leading to MAD would obviously not serve any rational political purpose. This is why American President Ronald Reagan and Soviet President M. Gorbachev had jointly stated in 1986 at Reykjavik that a "nuclear war cannot be won" and, hence, must not be fought. But what we need to pay special attention to is the use of military power and the phenomenon of war in an environment where nuclear weapons are a reality and part of the adversary's military-strategic capabilities.

At the same time, for a variety of reasons, the role and impact of the perceptions, interests and policies of the international community now impinge strongly on even the build-up of military power in developing countries, leave alone their use by them in war. This is applicable now to intra-state conflicts also, besides the traditional impact on the responses of the dominant powers, because of any potential change in the balance of power. Where the countries concerned possess nuclear weapons, the interest and role of the international community become even more acute, as we have observed in recent years, whether during the Kargil War in 1999 or when our military was mobilised for a possible war during 2002.

National Aspirations

It is against the above backdrop that we need to identify India's national aspirations. Any assessment of aspiration obviously is a complex task, where subjective judgement would tend to play a strong role. There would be a need to bring in as much objectivity into the paradigm as is possible when assessing the expectations of people. It is becoming popular to decry the Gandhi-Nehru vision articulating

India's vision for the future. In specific, a belief seems to have grown that India does not have a "strategic culture" and, hence, is critical of Jawaharlal Nehru.[4] Strategic culture and national aspirations of a country evolve from an amalgam of culture, history, geography, economy, science and technological capabilities and so on. But national aspirations almost inevitably go beyond current realities. It may, therefore, be useful to cite Jawaharlal Nehru at some length on his vision of India of the future:

> Forgetting present problems then for a while and looking ahead, India emerges as a strong united state, a federation of free units, intimately connected with her neighbours and playing an important part in world affairs. She is one of the very few countries which have the resources and capacity to stand on their own feet. Today probably the only such countries are the United States and the Soviet Union – China and India are potentially capable of joining that group – no other country, taken singly, apart from these four actually is potentially in such a position. It is possible, of course, that larger federations or groups of nations may emerge in Europe or elsewhere and form huge multinational states.... Whatever happens, *it will be well for the world if India can make her influence felt. For that influence will always be in favour of peace and cooperation and against aggression.*[5] (Emphasis added).

On the other hand, those that wish to detach themselves from that vision have not been able to articulate a new or different view. In recent years, the Planning Commission attempted to articulate a vision for the country to be realised by 2020.[6] Separately, our current President, Dr. A.P.J. Abdul Kalam and his close associate Dr. Y.S. Rajan have examined India's strengths and weaknesses to offer a vision of how India can be among the world's first five economic powers in the year 2020.[7] Neither of the two touches upon India's military power, although the Planning Commission vision statement does carry a brief reference to peace and security in broad terms. Perhaps Gen K.Sundarji is one of the few in the country that come nearest to articulating a long-term perspective for the future in relation to India's military capabilities and strategies, although his last publication is heavily biased in favour of the nuclear weapons-related aspects of it.[8]

Whose Expectations?

Aspirations in relation to military capabilities are easier to grasp than the broader socio-political expectations. But security is as much a matter of perception as of reality. Every sovereign nation state seeks security at the highest level possible, in turn, generating a level of insecurity in the state from which it seeks to defend itself. The impetus toward such absolutism in national defence is finally circumscribed by resources available in terms of economy, manpower and technology. For every country, there is a natural competition for these resources in other areas of national endeavour. The end result is that, unless building and maintaining military capabilities get released from the larger competition, as may happen in authoritarian and/or security states, a degree of balance and harmony would have to be achieved in arriving at what would be considered affordable and yet sufficiently credible.

This by itself raises the question of whose aspirations and expectations are we trying to assess? In a democracy, this can only be the aspirations of the people at large, although their perceptions would naturally be affected by the thinking and articulation of the elites. When we survey our own scenario, there can be no doubt that the primary strategic challenge and priority for India is to ensure sustained high growth of its human development. This is what the country needs, and this is what the representatives of the people who rule the country would have to pay serious attention to. Our national aspirations derive strength from our democratic credentials, where the people's aspirations reflect the foundations of national aspirations rather than merely those of the elites, as so often happens in non-democratic states. If there was any doubt, the recent elections in four major states of the country where the people rejected fairly efficient governments for their failure to provide for higher levels of human development, testify to the sentiments of the people, the rhetoric of some notwithstanding. Good governance is not just about better *bijli*, *pani* and *sadak*, or eradicating corruption. It is much more about pursuing sound policies that provide for what the people really expect.

The Planning Commission vision is based on an aspiration that would raise India's economic capacity and profile to the level of "upper-middle income" countries like Argentina, Chile, Hungary, Malaysia, South Africa, etc. This vision assumes quadrupling of our per capita income by 2020, which would require an average annual GDP growth rate of 9 per cent over the next two decades. This is not beyond the reach of the country; but it is also a monumental task to be achieved. It is sobering to think that even when we succeed in quadrupling per capita income by 2020 (the benchmark for assessing the needs of the army in our present examination), 13 per cent of our population (an estimated 173 million people, compared to 263 million in 2000) would still be below the poverty line.

An annual economic growth rate of 9 per cent for two decades, by itself, is no guarantee of a better India if is not accompanied by social mobility, distributive justice and elimination of disparities and inequities. The GDP growth has to be seen, among other things, in terms of generation of gainful employment for the hundreds of millions of the workforce, where 10 million persons would be added to that force every year. While the present government has been claiming an annual employment growth of close to 8.4 million additional jobs per year, expert opinion based on empirical evidence concludes that the actual additional employment generation is likely to be around 3.9 million per year.[9] This has to be seen in the context of the impact of unemployment and disparities on economic growth itself.

The world is already in the midst of a revolution of rising expectations, accelerated by the information revolution. Historically, violent revolutions take place during periods of rising prosperity rather than pervasive poverty or widespread affluence. We are at a critical stage in this regard, where we must pay close and serious attention to the issue of rising expectations and aspirations of people and make sure that we do not make the mistake of catering only for the aspirations of the elite. Regional, horizontal and vertical disparities need to be kept to the very minimum, that would assure adequate drive and scope for rapid progress, without impacting negatively on social cohesion and satisfaction levels among the population. This means that human development must receive the highest priority as a *national security objective*. The fundamental precondition for quick and sustained human development is an assured environment of peace. This in turn defines the priorities for building defence capabilities and the Indian Army in the coming decades.

At the same time, it is necessary to recognise that mere aspirations would be inadequate for defining strategic goals and priorities. Meeting aspirations implicitly requires change from the present condition to the desired state. But this in turn requires that one must have the power to make that change; and, at the same time, be cognisant of the reality that change would take a certain amount of time. These considerations would have to be factored into our present discussions on what military capabilities would be needed and wanted by 2020.

National Strategic Doctrine

India's military capabilities would need to be situated in the framework of an appropriate politico-military doctrine that is based on national aspirations. It is obvious that the primary strategic objective during the next two decades, of necessity, must continuously seek durable peace and security, so that socio-economic growth and development can be pursued without adverse impulses. The prevention of war and removal of threat of war become important constituents in such a strategic framework. This would necessitate positive measures that not only reduce the risk of war and conflict, but also in reality include even attempts to understand and reduce the threat perceptions of potential adversaries.

In essence, there is a fundamental need to move from the classical paradigm of competitive security towards a cooperative model of inter-state security.[10] Necessary precautions would, obviously, have to remain in place to cater for a potential adversary pursuing its own objectives and strategies. Thus, *deterrence* would have to be a central factor in the doctrine, while *détente* (at the ideal level) and *peaceful coexistence* (as the optimum framework) are pursued vigorously in a sustained way. The strategic doctrine should be able to synthesise these two apparently divergent, and even conflicting, demands on national strategy formulation.

Given the nature of realities and strategic priority of ensuring peace for human development, the primary strategic doctrine for India in the coming two decades would be the *prevention of war*, whether that war is conventional or sub-conventional, regular or irregular, full-scale or limited. This requires adequate credible deterrent capabilities; and if deterrence fails, to prosecute the war, so as to conclude it and disengage with maximum advantage to our national interests at minimum costs, and in the shortest possible time.

In fact, India had practically, if not formally, adopted the doctrine of war prevention from the very beginning. The holding back of military force during the 1947-48 conflict, the Panchsheel Agreement of 1954, the Tashkent Declaration of 1966, the Simla Agreement of 1972, etc., are all evidence of attempts to apply the war prevention doctrine. But its most visible manifestation came in early 1990 when a resolute policy was put into practice to ensure that the escalating irregular proxy war in J&K, besides the sustained one in Punjab, would not erupt into a regular war, as indeed did happen in 1947, 1965, and (with some changes) in 1971.[11] The coercive deployment of force in 2002 under Operation Parakram was another example.[12] War prevention strategies require a series of steps and guidelines for force planning, the central component of which has to be credible deterrence backed by a capability that can achieve the designated political and military goals, if deterrence fails.

Now, the presence of nuclear weapons impacting on our defence environment and security has made prevention of war, especially one that seeks "decisive military victory," through significant if not substantive destruction of the enemy's military forces or that seeks to occupy valuable or large tracts of his territory, an even greater imperative than ever before. Yet we must have the requisite military power to influence the enemy's policies where they act negatively on our interests. This paradigm requires substantive revision of the way we think about future wars and desirable military capabilities.

Defence Through Deterrence

The strategic priority and core security interest of India will continue to remain the prevention of war into the future through 2020. As it is, the probability of a regular full-scale war in the foreseeable future is low. But if it does take place, its impact is likely to be far greater than that of earlier wars. It also needs to be noted that the next war, if and when it takes place, is most likely to be a limited war (essentially what the Chinese military have been referring to as "local border war" since the mid-1980s), because of the nuclear factor operating in relation to both our major neighbours. Deterrence, therefore, would be the central pillar of defence strategy and would play a major role in preventing war, as well as in fighting a limited war. The credibility of deterrence actually depends upon the credibility of a viable strategy, which would lead to success in case of deterrence failure. Thus, defence strategy must address the issue of war aims in political terms and draw from it the military aims and objectives.

Deterrence may be achieved by **denial** or through **punishment** (or a combination of both). We cannot arrive at rational conclusions regarding the deterrent capabilities needed unless we are willing to objectively look at the relative attributes and characteristics of different components of military power, to provide deterrence through either denial or/and punishment. All components of military power are capable of providing deterrence through denial, especially if close coordination among the three Services is achieved. However, it is in the punishment dimension that the individual components of military power start to have different capabilities and role.

In our context, we also need to consider the scenario where land forces strike inside the territory of the adversary after deterrence has failed and war has been initiated. There would be a high risk of a threat of escalation to and across the nuclear threshold if a deeper strike takes place, although the actual depth for that threshold would be a function of the importance of the area where the intrusion was taking place. The threshold in barren desert area would naturally be higher than, say, populated areas of Punjab. The issue that we will have to come to terms with is the actual scenario of where and when a nuclear threat should be treated as credible. **The challenge for defence strategy is how to apply military power, achieve the desired level of military success and consequent political advantage, but keep the war below a rationally credible scenario of nuclear weapons use**.

Land forces have in the past, and will continue in the future, to remain the core of deterrence by denial. But they have very little capability to provide deterrence through punishment except through defeat and destruction of the adversary's land forces, **before** any other punishment can be visited on the enemy. But in a war, such a situation may not be possible without a high risk of escalation across the nuclear threshold which would not be politically wise or acceptable. A "decisive victory" which would produce the conditions for imposing punishment is no longer a realistic scenario in the presence of nuclear weapons. This also, therefore, raises the question of escalation control which is so critical in a war between countries possessing nuclear weapons. Once engaged in combat, land forces cannot be disengaged unless one side or the other concedes defeat, or a ceasefire is agreed upon. Consequently, escalation control is poor where land forces are employed. A basic political reality must be recognised that between a big country and a small country, a military stalemate would inevitably leave a perception of defeat of the larger country.

Naval forces would provide a balanced set of capabilities for deterrence, by denial as well as by punishment. Similarly, naval forces possess a significant capability in terms of escalation control. This attribute, in fact, had been invaluable in "gun-boat diplomacy." The ability to engage and disengage at will had provided naval power the ability to select the place and time of benefit to it for waging war, and this was a major factor in ensuring that the most successful colonial powers were, in fact, maritime states. But in spite of increasing capabilities of land-attack from the sea, which are partially neutralised by extension of sea denial capabilities by the adversary, naval forces are restricted to the maritime environment. This limits the scope of utility of naval power for deterrence through punishment.

Air power, especially combat air power, intrinsically possesses attributes which provide it with powerful deterrence capabilities through denial as well as punishment. Aircraft can fly across national boundaries and geographical barriers to hit targets deep inside hostile territory. Highly calibrated escalation as well as disengagement control is possible with the use of air power, especially if it can exercise dominance over the adversary's air power. This would be a great asset in a war with limited political-military objectives under a nuclear backdrop.

It is, therefore, essential that when looking at the nature of desirable capabilities for the army in 2020, the most essential is the nature, degree and **role of air and space power** which would operate in conjunction with the land forces. In fact, it would be highly irresponsible and short-sighted to think of Army 2020 in isolation and without a concurrent focus on air power and the Indian Air Force (IAF), the primary wielder of air power in the country. For example, there are signs that lack of modernisation is already reducing the available combat force levels in the air force. One only concludes that it is the Indian Army that would be adversely affected by this erosion of capability. On the other hand, every single indicator actually points toward a much enhanced role of air power in modern warfare; and that role in the context of China's military modernisation, if anything, is going to increase in the coming years and decades in our case. A single Service focus would undercut optimisation of available resources and their synergised impact on the adversary in war.

Resources for Future Defence

Deterrence will remain more critical in the conventional dimension in any war prevention strategy, although deterrence in the nuclear arena will inevitably possess a more apocalyptic dimension. Deterrence will require a capability that is qualitatively and quantitatively superior to that of our likely adversaries. The essential goal would be the capability to dominate effectiveness and the escalation process.

But in the context of affordability it is necessary to note that India maintained a level of spending at an average of 3.0 per cent of the GDP for over 25 years. During these decades, India's economic growth and human development indices kept on improving steadily, even if not so dramatically. This level of spending in the past also provided a capability which helped achieve military victories in 1965 as well as the more dramatic one in 1971. But above all, this capability provided the necessary levels of deterrence against foreign adventure, and the visible effect has been that unlike the earlier era, no war has been launched on us since 1965. This is the practical demonstration of the success of deterrence over three decades till the early 1990s, with a 3.0 per cent investment of the GDP in defence.

But our defence expenditure has been continuously dropping since the late 1980s when it reached a high of 3.38 per cent of the GDP in 1987-88. Our economy had started to pick up after 1993; but, in spite of resources being allocated, we find that substantive sums have remained unexpended for the past six years. The bulk of the unspent amounts relates to capital expenditure where the figure of shortfalls has hovered around at as much as 20-30 per cent of the allocated funds being unspent year after year. The real burden of the low spending has been on modernisation, building up the backlog instead of reducing that accumulated in the early and mid-1990s when the resource crunch affected the country much more.

The recession and retrenchment in the global defence industry is now raising the costs of weapons and equipment.[13] If India has to maintain the force structure and weapons and equipment of the type it has done for the past 10-30 years, the cost is likely to be closer to 4 per cent of the GDP, rather than the earlier 3.0 per cent. This reality was already in evidence in the early 1980s when defence spending started to rise and touched 3.38 per cent, before the cut in spending started to take place. While this level would be affordable in economic terms, politically it may be difficult to achieve, although the Parliament's Standing Committee of Defence had already recommended increasing the defence budget to 4 per cent of the GDP.[14] On the other hand, the 11th Finance Commission (which is a statutory body to distribute resources between Central and state governments) had stipulated that defence expenditure should reach a figure of 3.0 per cent of the GDP by 2004-05 [15] Against this, we will be close to 2.13 per cent of the GDP for the coming year, the lowest figure since the 1962 debacle!

Financial resources obviously would be a major factor in determining the capabilities that we can actually possess (as compared to what we may wish for). The other overriding factor would be the nature of military technology and modernisation that we can acquire. We need to bear in mind that the capabilities for 2020 have already been shaped by the decisions of yesterday and today. And we have experienced substantive funds being surrendered from a level of budgeting that itself was inadequate for defence modernisation for more than a decade and a half, thus, building a major backlog of modernisation that future planning would have to take into account, besides new arisings. There is a clear time lag between the final decision to acquire certain military capabilities, in manpower terms as well as in weapons and equipment. The level of funding available during the next 5-10 years, therefore, would be the determining factor of the capabilities that our army would actually possess in 2020. In turn, this raises the importance of long-term planning, especially the perspective plans and the more definitive Five-Year Defence Plan.

Based on the record of the past decade and a half of the fiscal resources for defence, therefore, it is unlikely that defence spending would go anything above a figure of around 2.3-2.4 per cent of the GDP for the next 15 years. More important, we have experienced a reduction of nearly 2 per cent in the annual allocation of total (Central and state) government expenditure during the past 15 years. Defence spending would have to increase dramatically if even routine modernisation has to be kept up. The core conclusion that can be drawn is that capabilities for 2020 would have to be tailored to the broad level of resources available, regardless of the aspirations or perceived necessities. This may well be around an average of 2.4 per cent of the GDP, equivalent to around 13.5-14.0 per cent of the CGE and in the order of about 8 per cent of the Total (Central and state) Government Expenditure during the next 15 years. The yardstick of defence spending as the proportion of Total Government Expenditure would be a realistic planning parameter. If the government has to cut back expenditure for whatever reason, defence should bear a proportionate share of that cut, rather than what has been happening for a decade.

No serious student of modern day national defence (leave alone any expeditionary force capabilities beyond UN peace-keeping operations), especially in the context of our strategic-security environment of the future, can rationally argue that this level (of 2.4 per cent of the GDP or less) would be adequate, leave alone desirable. In fact, something like 3.0 per cent of the GDP corresponding to about 9-9.5 per cent of the Total Government Expenditure is the minimum required for credible defence in future, since it must also pay for nuclear forces and space capabilities for defence.[16] Incidentally, this level of expenditure would have allocated around Rs. 83,000 crore to the defence Services for the current (2003-04) financial year as against Rs. 89,000 crore that they had projected as required, and Rs. 60,300 crore that was actually provided. But the problems of efficient planning would remain with us, as long as fiscal allocations are not committed on a long-term basis. The trouble is that while the Group of Ministers (GoM) had ruled three years ago that the Five-Year Defence Plan must be finalised along with financial commitments before the commencement of the plan period, the current Five-Year (2002-07) Plan has yet to be approved nearly half way down the plan period!

Army 2020

We need to recognise that our military capability would have to ensure credible deterrence for war prevention in the future, and the Army 2020 would have to fight a war in a nuclearised environment, if deterrence fails. Such a war would have to be conducted under the following overriding factors:

- Political constraints imposed by the need to keep the war adequately below the nuclear threshold. Hence, the military objectives like "decisive victory" to, in the words of a former army chief, "...smash him. You destroy his weapons and capture his territory," would require a full-scale war, and which would most likely spin out of control. No democratically elected leader is likely to allow such a strategy. Military objectives in the future would have to be limited, and, hence, strategy tailored to achieve success within its parameters.
- Resource availability, as noted above, would provide the planning parameters for building future capabilities. This poses serious challenges of choices between a high-technology force and a large size force. The issue of restructuring the army would have to be addressed far more seriously than we have done in the past. A new manpower-high-technology firepower-mobility paradigm would have to be evolved, if we are not to settle for a sub-optimal force for future challenges.
- Whether sub-conventional war (or low intensity conflict, as it is euphemistically called) would/should have moderated or disappeared by that time or not, what is clear is that Army 2020 must focus its energies, doctrine, equipment and training for a high-technology war against professional military forces. Training and fighting sub-conventional wars would lead to a force ready for such a war rather than a high-technology war. Maintaining two armies for the two tasks would simply not be affordable from any perspective.
- Army 2020 would be severely handicapped, if it is not in synergy with a high-technology IAF of the requisite size and quality, along with the requisite space power. There is also need to remember that force-multipliers (or effect-

enhancers) are no substitute for force, except where the enemy does not have similar capabilities, as was the case in the Kosovo, Afghanistan and Iraq Wars.

- Military power in the future would have to be deeply meshed with political-diplomatic policies and goals. The role of our defence forces may require more and more of use of military power for political purposes, without necessarily going into war. Operation Parakram demonstrated the weaknesses in political as well as military strategy.

Land war strategy in a nuclear environment itself necessitates that we closely examine the possible options for the employment of the army in the future. On the face of it, the option of multiple thrusts across the border to comparatively shallower distances would provide greater pay-offs as compared to single (or a couple of) deeper strikes.[17] Such thrusts are less likely to excite an early resort to nuclear escalation than single deep strike corps-based thrusts, while still imposing serious disadvantage on the adversary. The rationale behind the Soviet creation of Operational Manoeuvre Groups and/or German heavy composite brigades would require revisiting from this perspective. And if the adversary goes for a similar force posture, then we would need to ensure something equivalent to the principles embedded in the US AirLand Battle 2000 doctrine and the concept which incorporates combat air power much more synchronised with the land forces than ever before. This may require changes in force structures, doctrine and tactics. A great deal of this can be worked out through rigorous theoretical examination and studies to be backed up by war-gaming. But, above all, it requires much greater flexibility of the mind and intellectual basis of employment of military power in the future.

If there is a single lesson of warfare for the past hundred years it is that land forces cannot achieve their military strategic/operational and tactical tasks effectively without deep synchronisation, bordering on synergy between land and air operations. In effect, air power is the crucial lynchpin without which no military objective can be achieved; and, hence, the key to joint operations. The past two decades have clearly proved that air power now plays a crucial role. A modern army without air power on its side is like the infantry during the pre-medieval times without cavalry, and both without cavalry during the medieval times. In fact, air power itself is extending into space power and we would certainly plan for its effective utilisation in our defence capabilities on priority.[18]

The reason for this is fairly simple, and we need to debate and understand this without getting into turf loyalties and battles, and/or assumption of the relative importance of one component of military power versus the others. Warfare basically revolves around the issues of firepower and mobility. The side that can generate a favourable asymmetry of firepower at the desired point in time and space (through concurrent exploitation of mobility) is much more likely to be the winner compared to those who may seek superiority piecemeal. Such asymmetry has historically been achieved either by exploitation of superior strategy, tactics, and/or technology. Artillery did this in dramatic ways after the 16th century, and horse artillery altered the paradigm due to change in mobility, even where firepower came from artillery with equivalent firepower. Later, the battle tank achieved similar effect; and air power raised the firepower-mobility paradigm to new dimensions.

Conclusion

In fact, it is time we reexamined our principles of war from the foregoing perspective. For example, "concentration of force" in today's wars in reality amounts to "concentration of firepower" rather than force itself. This concentration is further enabled by greater mobility and information power which provides, among other things, high levels of situational awareness. But that awareness may not be a sufficient condition, and one must also know what to do when one is in that situation, and to shape one's own situation to take advantage of that awareness. Advances in modern military technology have been a major cause for this change during the past two decades. This in reality is the RMA. The very logic of force levels and structures has been undergoing change due to this central factor, and we would be committing a gross error by not taking this into account.

One of the key lessons of the Iraq War in 2003 was that the traditional force ratios for the ground offensive were completely turned upside down for a rapid offensive. Basic asymmetry of capabilities between the US and Iraq cannot sufficiently explain this phenomenon.[19] In reality, it was the ability of the US military to generate far greater superiority, amounting to dominance of firepower at a given time and place that held the key. On the other hand, the *fidayeen* attacks sought to generate a favourable asymmetry of firepower at a much more localised level, without a coherent strategy to be able to make an impact at levels above the tactical (which the US soon overcame by rapidly bringing in superior firepower, including by the use of thermobaric weapons). The Army 2020 would need to explore this further to ensure that we have the capabilities of fighting and winning on our terms. •

NOTES

1. Carl von Clausewitz, *On War* (Ware UK: Wordsworth Classics, 1997), p. 22.
2. Gerhard Ritter, *The Sword and the Spectre*, Vol. 1, "The Prussian Tradition 1790-1890" (Coral Gables, F.L.: University of Miami Press, 1969), p. 52.
3. Kenneth Waltz in Scott D. Sagan and Kenneth N. Waltz, *The Spread of Nuclear Weapons: A Debate Renewed* (New York: WW Norton & Company, 2003).
4. For example, see Jaswant Singh, *Defending India* (New Delhi: Macmillan India Ltd., 1999), especially the first chapter.
5. Jawaharlal Nehru, *Discovery of India*, cited in Singh, Ibid., p.46.
6. Report of Planning Commission's Committee on *India Vision 2020*, Academic Foundation, New Delhi, 2003.
7. See A.P.J. Abdul Kalam with Y.S. Rajan, *India 2020: A Vision for the New Millennium* (New Delhi: Viking, 1998).
8. K. Sundarji, *Vision 2100: A Strategy for the Twenty-First Century*, (New Delhi: Konark Publishers,2003).

9. C. Rammanohar Reddy, "In Search of One Crore Jobs a Year," *The Hindu* , February 24, 2004, p.10
10. For a conceptual analysis and principles of cooperative security, see Jasjit Singh, "Cooperative Security: Paradigm Change for International Peace and Security in the 21st Century," paper presented at CSCAP Workshop on *Comprehensive Security*, Kuala Lumpur, August 28-29, 1995.
11. See "It's All Bluff and Bluster", interview with Chief of Army Staff Gen V.N. Sharma, in 1990, *The Economic Times*, May 18, 1993, p.7.
12. It also needs to be recalled that a similar mobilisation was undertaken in 1951 after Pakistan threatened war. For an excellent treatise analysing various dimensions of the use of military force for political purposes without fighting a war, see Barry Blechman, *Force Without War: US Armed Forces as a Political Instrument* (Brookings Institution, Washington DC, 1978) and Stephen Kaplan, *Mailed Fist, Velvet Glove: Soviet Armed Forces as a Political Instrument* (Brookings Institution, Washington DC, 1979).
13. See Aaron Karp, "The Future of International Defence Industry: Implications for India," *Strategic Analysis*, Vol.XIX, No.4, July 1996, pp.557-576.
14. "Defence Policy, Planning and Management", Standing Committee of Defence (1995-96) Tenth Lok Sabha, *Sixth Report*, March 1996, p.37. For a realistic approach to the conflicting demands on national resources, see Lt Gen V.R. Raghavan, *India's Need for Strategic Balance: Security in the Post-Cold War World* (New Delhi: Delhi Policy Group).
15. Report of the Eleventh Finance Commission (2000-2005), Government of India, New Delhi, June 2000, p. 41.
16. For a detailed study assessing future requirements, see Jasjit Singh, *India's Defence Spending*, 2nd edition (New Delhi: Knowledge World, 2001).
17. This had been argued since as early as 1993 when it was clear that Pakistan had acquired nuclear weapons. See Jasjit Singh, "Credible Affordable Defence," *Strategic Analysis*, 1994. The former Chief of Army Staff, Gen S. Padmanabhan, who was the chief and chairman Chiefs of Staff Committee during the period when India almost went to war with Pakistan in 2002 admitted that "doctrinal baggage crippled India's early options in 2002" and indicated that rethinking was now in place for the restructuring of land forces. See "Padmnabhan Mulls Over Lessons of Operation Parakram," *The Hindu*, February 6, 2004, p. 12.
18. See Jasjit Singh, "Space Power and Military Operations," paper presented at the DSSC Seminar on *Exploitation of Space for Effective Conduct of Military Operations*, DSSC Wellington, February 24-25, 2004.
19. Jasjit Singh, "Some Pointers for Our Defence Policy" in Jasjit Singh, ed., *Military-Strategic Dimensions of Iraq War* (New Delhi: Knowledge World, 2004), pp.211-229.

NATIONAL MILITARY ASPIRATIONS AND MILITARY CAPABILITIES: AN APPROACH

Brig (Dr) Arun Sahgal (Retd)

Introduction

Development of national military capability and consequent security needs is directly related to a nation's perception of its overall national security perspective in terms of the threats and challenges it faces. Consequently, the formulation of national strategy encompasses the need to clearly identify national goals and objectives and set out aims for their attainment. The process, of necessity, involves taking stock of the means available to a nation, or what is commonly referred to as development of *comprehensive national strength (CNS)*. A national or grand strategy, suitably employed in the environment in which a nation finds itself [*strategic configuration of power (SCP)*], helps to secure for itself the place that it is seeking in the comity of nations.

The security concerns of a nation can be best addressed by an appropriate blending of the political, diplomatic, economic, military, social, technical and psychological elements, which can be viewed as means or resources to achieve its overall security objectives. The military element is but one of the elements, as dependent on the others as the others on the military element. Nonetheless, credible national military capability is an important component for ensuring security and stability, and provides the desired degree of flexibility to leverage its CNS to its advantage. This is particularly so in the context of India, which apart from facing a multitude of external and internal threats is also beginning to emerge as a major economic player in the world. The formulation of military strategy, within the overall ambit of the national strategy, therefore, forms an important element and dictates the wherewithal and force structures that need to be developed to employ armed forces to secure policy objectives by force, or more preferably, the threat of force (*deterrence*).

It will not be out of place to mention that we have over the years failed to evolve a coherent and viable national security strategy to meet national aspirations. Our overall national security perspective is based on enunciation of our strategic concerns and interests in somewhat narrow terms, without the structured policy framework for their achievement. Axiomatically, while the nation has the military capability and possesses a favourable military balance with its principle challenger (Pakistan), the efficacy of our overall military strategy to deal decisively with the complexities of security challenges such as the ongoing proxy war in

Jammu and Kashmir, recent military stand-off with Pakistan, and even the earlier Kargil crisis, has been found wanting. In the evolution and execution of national security options, there is a tendency to be ad-hoc with knee-jerk responses, often without thinking through the full consequences, together with the possible escalation dynamics and its management flowing out of the same. There is a need to appreciate that the functional efficacy of deterrence is a game of brinkmanship, a competition in risk-taking, where threats to cross thresholds are made in pursuit of national interests or strategic objectives. The process entails preventive moves, perception management and use of international instrumentalities, to gain competitive advantage in an action/reaction cycle. Conflict management, thus, is like an escalation ladder, with intrinsic linkages amongst *deterrence, escalation* and *psychology of perception.*

The aim of this paper is to examine the efficacy of our overall national strategies and consequent military capabilities, to evaluate a scope for alternative strategies in the context of the prevailing military balance, the realities of an intrusive international security environment, and the role it plays in shaping/or constraining our responses. As a first step, there is a need to recognise the fact that in the dynamic and interdependent world, regional instability has a spillover effect, both regionally and extra-regionally. Hence, the ability of a nation state to unilaterally manage any conflict scenario is the function of its CNS and the shaping of its SCP. CNS is the means of assessing the composite of a country's hard national power, soft power, and the grand-national strategy i.e. how national leaders create and adopt an overall national competition strategy, to deal with adversaries/international competition. SCP, on the other hand, relates to the existing security environment and its shaping by a nation to its advantage. Often, a relatively weak national power, by deft shaping of its SCP, can leverage advantage over a stronger power. Here, it would be of interest for us to note the manner in which Pakistan has been able to shape its SCP to its advantage, in terms of being the frontline state of the US in its war against terrorism, as also positioning itself as an important element of the Chinese policy of containing growing American regional influence. Together with remaining an important part of the Arab world, being the only Muslim nation with nuclear capability. Second, and importantly in the context of our regional scenario, the US presence and primacy of its national interests, together with interventionist norms of its political behaviour, will critically impact on defining and shaping regional imperatives. This is particularly so in the light of the fact that with its presence in Pakistan, Afghanistan, Central Asia and Persian Gulf, it has practically become a regional player. Third, and significantly, it is important to note the security interdependence within regional clusters, particularly so in South Asia. A region marked by relative intensity of security relations, in terms of historical enmity or amity, and the potential distribution of power, and their ripple effect on other regional and extra-regional players. In the above context, we are indeed generously endowed both with the legacies of history and extreme religious biases.

Thus, in order to evolve military strategies within the constraints of the prevailing regional realities, we need to clearly understand the impacting dynamics of the security environment, together with their implications on our overall national and military strategies. Together with the above, is the need to leverage SCP to national advantage. In this regard, we have to be cognisant of India's security concerns, as spelt out for the first time by the prime minister at the Combined Commanders Conference late last year. In order to shake India out of its traditional South Asian insularity, the prime minister highlighted India's strategic vision, by unequivocally stating that in addition to traditional threats to its strategic periphery, India's arc of strategic interests encompassed the Asian landmass and Indian Ocean, extending from the Strait of Hormuz in the west to the Strait of Malacca in the east and from Central Asia in the north to the Indian Ocean in the south. The strategic vision so succinctly spelt out must play an important part in shaping our political and military behaviour and responses. Therefore, it is important to note that whereas in the context of the Indo-Pak scenario, our policy options will be dictated by the contours of our overall political philosophy, and how the political leadership intends to employ national power to deal with a crisis situation, in terms of the *desired politico-military objectives* and the *end state*, we will now additionally have to evolve security policies to deal with India's interests and challenges in the area of its extended security concerns, as highlighted by the prime minister. This, in turn, will dictate the overall military strategy. Inherent in the above is the fact that regional realities, together with the *efficacy* and *credibility* of our deterrence, both conventional and nuclear, and the escalation control that we are able to exercise, will determine the efficacy of our policies to achieve national political and military aims. There is a need to evolve policy level options and practical functional military strategy, consistent with the overall national interests and grand national strategy.

Unfortunately, while we have over the years taken pains to develop credible force structures and strategies, these have been single Service efforts, with little or no synergy. This is reflected in the fact that even after four wars and innumerable crises we have failed to evolve a joint doctrine and concepts. Second, and importantly, our approach to military capability development appears to be flawed. Our traditional methods of measuring force effectiveness have remained grounded to force-on-force models that calculate effectiveness on the basis of attritional models, based on exchange ratios dominated by major weapon platforms. These traditional models do not take into account or recognise attempted developments related to information age technological advances or the new technologies that are being introduced. These traditional measures of effectiveness even fall short when they come to addressing stability and security operations on the lower end of the conflict spectrum, like LIC or proxy war, a perspective that is likely to increasingly dominate the conflict spectrum in the future. While the above in itself is bad enough, what is worse is the fact that within the Services there is a belief that joint doctrinal or conceptual thinking is not required. These perceptions are significantly based on an extremely insular and Pak-centric approach. There is no doubt that in the short or even in medium terms, successful countering of the proxy war or Pakistan-related challenges will remain our biggest security threat. However, in the medium and long-terms, India will need to look at security challenges from broader regional and economic perspectives, in line with the strategic vision of the prime minister, if it is to play a significant regional and extra-regional role, to safeguard its interests in its extended arc, or what can be referred to as the *near abroad*.

As a first step, therefore, in the evolution of credible military strategy, it is important to evaluate the political goals of India vis-à-vis its principal competitors, in the backdrop of an intrusive security environment and relative military balance. In the context of the former, it is important to analyse likely future threats and challenges growing out of trends such as strategic realignments in Asia, Chinese transition and its challenges, and opportunities, growing consolidation of radical Islamic fundamentalism, competitive energy scenario, and the need to secure our interests in the near abroad, etc. On the other hand, evaluation of relative military balance should not be a force-on-force analysis, but a detailed analysis of our adversaries' strategic perceptions, doctrine, concepts, military capabilities and, more importantly, political and national will to take risks in the use of force. Therefore, in the above context, and in the backdrop of our recent experiences, we need to reflect upon the following:

- The nature of future threats and challenges and the likely nature of future wars.
- Is our current military strategic thinking and doctrine oriented to address these? The aim is not to merely maintain the integrity of national boundaries, but the full gamut of future military challenges.
- In the prevailing international and regional security environment, and in the backdrop of the nuclear factor, what is the range of military options available, particularly in the Indo-Pak scenario? Is full-scale conventional conflict possible? If future conflicts are likely to remain limited/local, their likely context and dimensions, together with the all important dynamics of escalation management.
- How do we synergise conventional capabilities with nuclear deterrence?
- The need to develop national will and political consensus for use of military force, in pursuance of core national objectives.
- Last, and most importantly, what are the ranges of alternative military strategies available, which address wider national security concerns, allowing India to play a more dominant role in Asia?

Realities of the Existing and Perspective Geostrategic Environment

We need to take cognisance of the incontrovertible fact that post-September 11, global strategic focus has shifted to the region. Coordinates of US presence today straddle the region from the Persian Gulf to South Asia, including Central Asia. This has created a ripple effect on the existing security architecture, leading to sharp realignments and the emergence of terrorism (transnational) as the principal security challenge of the 21st century.

The regional security environment too has undergone a sea change; with Pakistan once again emerging as a frontline state in the US' fight against terrorism, together with the rising tide of Islamic fundamentalism against the Christian West, for their duplicity in equating faith with terrorism, leading to the slow spread of inimical terrorist and fundamental influences in the region, proliferation of WMD, rising incidence of asymmetric warfare and consequences of the future competitive energy environment, in the backdrop of increasing consumption of, and dependency on, Persian Gulf oil. Above all, other factors such as the Chinese grand strategy to be a dominant player in the region and possible Sino-Russian collusion, and other regional realignments that were alluded to earlier, all have a profound effect on regional security and necessitate a range of political and military responses, beyond the construct of our present policies. In this paper, I will discuss the perspectives of the regional security environment, together with their ramifications, not in any great detail as these are generally known and well appreciated.

Likely Security Challenges

As highlighted above, India is likely to face two distinct sets of challenges to national security: near term threats and mid/long-term challenges. These can be broadly identified as under:

Near Term Threats/Challenges

- **Pakistan**. The relationship with Pakistan is too tenuous to provide any definitive perspective of the current peace overtures. It would be safe to presume that it is likely to persist with proxy war as a cornerstone of its India containment strategy. Additionally, in spite of its current tensions with the US over nuclear proliferation, it is likely to remain relevant to the US in its war against terrorism, for stability in Afghanistan and, above all, to ensure definitive control over its strategic assets. Similarly, it will continue to remain relevant in the Chinese security calculus. It, thus, strongly believes that the current regional strategic environment remains critically in its favour in spite of prevailing tensions. Consequently, the centrality of Kashmir, preventing the break-out of a full-scale conventional conflict by balanced conventional capability, supported by a minimum credible nuclear deterrent and erudite management of international perceptions, will remain important percepts of Pakistan's overall national strategy.
- **China**. In the near term, the Chinese threat at best can be summed up in terms of possible border tensions. A clash of interest can also occur in the Indian Ocean rim (IOR) as China increases its forays or questions growing Indian power and legitimacy.
- **Internal Cohesion**. Internal dissonance within the country is on the increase, as a cumulative effect of Pakistan's attempted destabilisation, using terrorism as a weapon, poor governance, criminalisation and communalisation of politics, falling social standards, increasing social empowerment and

failure of the state to provide economic benefits of the same. Consequences of the above are polarisation of society on communal lines, rising incidence of communal and caste violence and strong social backlash against government policies which are unable to adequately address the aspirations of the people.

Medium and Long-Term Threats/Challenges

- **China.** A clash of interests is possible in the medium to long-term, on account of competing interests arising out of regional aspirations, unresolved boundary disputes, or on account of competing economic interests. Infrastructural developments in the Tibet Autonomous Region (TAR), coupled with modernisation of the Chinese armed forces, may provide the desired impetus for any proactive action. Two factors that will dictate the degree of these threats will be:
  - Chinese propensity of a long-term Indian challenge and the credibility of India's conventional and strategic deterrence, underscore this threat.
  - Need to appreciate that any conflict scenario with China carries inherent dangers of escalation and brinkmanship to the nuclear threshold. The credibilty of India's international and regional standing, and ability to link this with wider regional security concerns would be major factors in escalation management. Consequently, managing the future Chinese challenge requires holistic assessment of desired military capabilities, together with leveraging SCP in India's favour.
- **Energy Security.** As mentioned earlier, the relative tapering off of production and increasing demand has led to the energy scenario being in a state of flux. Turbulence in the Middle East, as a consequence of events in Iraq and continuing Israeli-Palestinian tensions, are further contributing to this insecurity. Increasing dependencies are likely to enhance insecurities, and a period of competitiveness in securing energy requirements is likely to ensue in the next few decades. Chinese dependency, which is only 8-10 per cent today, will go up to 85-90 per cent by 2020 and beyond as per International Energy Agency (IEA) estimates. Indian dependency too will increase to 70-75 per cent. Similarly, the oil stakes of other major Asian player e.g. Japan, South Korea, etc are likely to increase. In the above backdrop of turbulence, which is also touching Central Asia in terms of jockeying for hydrocarbon resources and pipeline wars, a scenario of major Asian powers, particularly China, taking positions and using all means to secure their energy needs cannot be ruled out. This could result in a clash between the respective US, Russian and Chinese interests. India too must have the capability to secure and protect its vital energy requirements. This must be done in the backdrop that Central Asian oil is unlikely to reach Indian shores, in the face of Pakistani intransigence. Consequently, India's energy dependency will remain essentially Persian Gulf centric. This has the following security implications:
  - The need to protect and secure both the sources and transportation means. This calls for development of credible maritime, force projection

and strategic lift capability, together with the strategic air component to support such an effort. The security of the proposed North-South Corridor linking India with Central Asia/Russia through Iran will assume importance as an alternative means for sourcing energy needs. So will the Look East policy and relations with Myanmar and ASEAN.

- Coupled with the above is the need to evolve multilateral/bilateral security cooperation with like-minded nations to secure our out-of-area interests. In this, we need to evolve military-to-military cooperative relations with the South Asian Association for Regional Cooperation (SAARC) nations, Japan, Southeast Asia, and other Indian Ocean littoral states. In concert with above, there is a need to consider developing linkages with littoral countries for forward support bases to assist in force projection, should such a need arise.

- **Other Challenges.** Some other challenges that we could face are:
  - The need to secure our economic and trade interests in India's near abroad (extended arc).
  - Dealing with the consequential effects of major realignments in Asia, e.g. consequences of militarisation and/or nuclearisation of Japan; possible nuclearisation of Iran; unification of Korea; Afghanistan lapsing into chaos; turmoil in Central Asia and weakening of the US position, forcing a pullout; Pakistan as a failed state are just a few of the scenarios.
  - Consequent impact of rising incidence of Islamic fundamentalism, and its extension as a crescent linking the turbulent Middle East with Southeast Asia, with Pakistan acting as the pivot.
  - Implosion in a major Asian neighbour or in our extended arc e.g. Indonesia, Saudi Arabia, etc.

Shaping of Military Strategy

Over the last three decades, we have adopted a strategy of conventional deterrence, based on strong offensive capability vis-à-vis Pakistan, with dissuasive deterrence vis-à-vis China, supported by limited out-of-area projection capability for the security of our far-flung island territories. Our approach has essentially been preservation of national and territorial integrity, that has essentially been insular in nature. In the context of the emerging strategic realties in terms of securing India's strategic interests in the near abroad, together with the experience of the recent military stand-off with Pakistan, we have to critically examine the overall efficacy of our military strategies and the desired military capabilities thereof. The issues that bear detailed analysis are:

- Success or failure of coercive diplomacy, signified by the recent military stand-off. Were the intrusive international security dynamics and the relevant military balances capable of substantiating the policy of brinkmanship and deterrence, backed by effective escalation control?
- Was there a clearly identified escalation and de-escalation strategy? Here the

issue is, were we in the position to harmonise political and military objectives, to evolve synergised policy options?

- Given the intrusive regional security environment, the competing interests of regional players, and India's own extended security interests, there is a need to critically examine the nature of future wars and its escalating dynamics. Is limited war a credible option? Will it remain limited (J&K centric)? Is it in our interest? What are the politico-military consequences of horizontal or vertical escalation? What should be our desired politico-military objectives and the end state?
- Another aspect that will have a major bearing on the evolution of policy options is the '*shadow of nuclear deterrence*'. Our perception of Pakistan's nuclear doctrine and deterrence philosophy (strategic deterrence or cultivated irrationality/or brinkmanship) would be major factors in evolving our overall national strategy.
- Next, has our policy of full spectrum capability development, to create the desired '*combat edge*' for strategic/operational advantage, paid the desired dividends? Is there an alternative model to contain, and gain competitive advantage over Pakistan, by a combination of achieving core competency and decisive advantage in selected areas of the conflict spectrum, as also leveraging technological superiority in selected areas to significantly create a favourable military balance?
- Next, and importantly, over the mid and long-terms, India will be faced with many more challenges, particularly those relating to competitive energy requirements and other extra-regional challenges in our extended arc of interest – the near abroad highlighted earlier. This requires a combination of '*power projection capability*' and '*coalition approach*'. For far too long, our subcontinental insularity and largely continental approach has prevented us from forging cooperative defence relationships with like-minded players, to address common regional problems. Similarly, as India's GDP grows to 7-8 per cent and there is increasing volume of trade, the security of sea lanes of communication (SLOC) will become critical.

China has, after detailed analysis of all recent conflicts, adopted a model of war-fighting in a high-tech environment, with the aim of developing technology and concepts to destroy and degrade a technologically superior enemy. Its entire modernisation and right-sizing focus is based on systematic modernisation of the PLA Navy, Air Force, Artillery and RMA technologies in the field of IT, EW, space based systems and IW, in a prioritised fashion. Together with the above, it is laying stress on *institutionalised enhancement of the calibre of its military leadership*, to exploit these technologies. It must, however, be mentioned, it is not planning to change the entire armed forces in one go but to incrementally modernise by initially focussing on the critical 40-50 per cent in the immediate future. We too need to prepare our forces to fight a modern high-technology war relevant to our environment. Two issues that stood out, in a high powered analytical panel on the detailed analysis of the Iraq War, which the author had the privilege to attend, were the importance of network-centric warfare (both defensive and offensive) and the effect based operations. If we want to improve the tempo of future operations, or to significantly reduce sensor to shooter timings, we have no option but to ensure total network connectivity at both operational and tactical levels. In addition, it is important to note that in today's battlefield, the ability to bring force to bear with great precision, from a wide variety of platforms, to attack and reduce the combat power of the adversary with speed, that will cause the desired decisive destabilising effect, causing him to give up even though the majority of his military forces may remain intact, will be the credible battle winning factor. In Western parlance, this approach is referred to as "Effect Based Operations." The main effort is to undermine the opponent's ability to exercise effective command. In a relatively symmetric environment that prevails between us and our principle adversary, it is this technological edge, brought about by precision munitions, battlefield transparency, backed by network centric warfare and IW capability, together with tri-Service operational integration, that will provide the *comprehensive competitive advantage vis-à-vis Pakistan.* A focussed systems approach, commensurate with overall military strategy is required.

Suggested Approach

A pragmatic analysis of threats and challenges flowing from the above dictates that we have to take into account a few fundamentals of the security environment, which will impinge on our future military strategies:

- Presence of Extra-Regional Forces (ERF) in the region and their security interest, particularly those related to terrorism and religious fundamentalism.
- As mentioned earlier, Pakistan has been able to leverage the regional security environment in its favour. It will leverage this, together with US regional compulsions, to persist with its policy of promoting and supporting cross-border terrorism.
- Owing to the centrality of Kashmir in the regional security calculus, all future conflicts are likely to be J&K centric, at least in their initiation.
- Given the presence of ERF and the prevailing conventional military balance, it would not be wrong to assume that the conflict with Pakistan will essentially remain confined to the low end of the conflict spectrum, with propensities of graduated escalation. Escalation to theatre specific or all out conventional conflict, while remaining low, will be dictated by our deterrence capabilities, backed by political will and the abilities at escalation management and diplomatic shaping of the external environment, often referred to as external manoeuvring.
- Pakistan is likely to adopt a three-tier strategy, major components of which will be:
  - *Active LIC,* i.e. promotion and support to proxy war, as also continued subversion of the Indian state, to constrain Indian hegemonic perceptions.
  - Policy of *tactical offence and strategic defence,* i.e. active LIC, while ensuring domination of the LoC, with the ability to undertake shallow/limited offensives. At the strategic level, its aim will be to absorb the shock of the

Indian offensives before launching repost, counter-stroke/strike, employing its strategic reserves.

- Last, but the most important element of the Pakistan strategic triad is *nuclear deterrence, with built-in threshold ambiguity and irrationality.*

• Against China, only a low to possibly medium level threat is envisaged. In so far as Chinese collusive support to Pakistan is concerned, it will be more in the form of diplomatic and material support, rather than any active military collusion. However, Pakistan can and will attempt to exploit the building consensus between Russia and China, to isolate India in the region, particularly as it seeks strategic accommodation with the US. Economic development and military modernisation models and consequent shaping of its geostrategic periphery are likely to shape the Chinese challenge in the medium and long-term.

• In addition to immediate land centric threats, as the Indian economy grows, there will be a corresponding increase in external trade, and energy requirements. The security of our maritime trade and ever increasing energy demand in a competitive energy market will become important factors. Continuous flow of energy and trade would become central to Indian development. The above, together with, the need to secure Indian interests in the near abroad, should entail a critical shift from an essentially *continental approach* of our military strategy to a *combination of continental-cum-maritime approach* i.e. while strengthening conventional deterrence, we must comprehensively develop maritime and force projection capabilities commensurate with our long-term interests, while simultaneously building regional cooperative security relationships.

• The issue of initiating/building regional cooperative initiatives, to address common security interests, must become an important sub-set of our future military strategy. This has the advantage of building regional relations, evolving a multilateral approach to security by building the security stakes of other players, both regional and extra-regional, in addressing the common challenges e.g. energy security, SLOC, etc.

Recommended Approach to Military Strategy

In the context of the foregoing; a three tier comprehensive approach to military strategy is recommended i.e. while strengthening conventional deterrence, we must concurrently develop maritime and projection capability, taking cognisance of long lead times; simultaneously with the above, the focus of our military-to-military cooperation must shift to building relationships in the region, to address common security challenges. A possible outline approach is given in the subsequent paragraphs.

Continental Strategy: Dealing with Threats from Pakistan and China

A relook at our existing strategy to deal with threats from both Pakistan and China is necessary. A shift from the existing strategy of maintaining a credible full spectrum offensive capability vis-à-vis Pakistan and a dissuasive defensive posture with China is desired. Our aim should be to build capabilities to gain decisive competitive advantage in the core areas of the conflict spectrum, while retaining strong dissuasive conventional capability, backed by credible strategic deterrence. In the context of the above, the following strategy is suggested:

- In the face of essentially J&K centric conflicts of the future, the first step should be to enhance our counter-proxy war capability, both organisationally and doctrinally, aimed at increasing the the cost of proxy war for Pakistan.
- To address the issue conceptually, while taking steps to improve organisational and technological capabilities, a strategy of '*creeping escalation*' is recommended, with the ability to escalate both horizontally and vertically in response to Pakistani attempts at escalation. This must be a proactive stance,. with capabilities to undertake such a response with near impunity, employing integrated Special Operation Forces, precision strikes, air power, long-range artillery, backed by credible information operations in an effect based manner, to dominate the operational and strategic space. This requires an inclusive and integrated approach to capability development.
- To ensure that escalation management remains firmly with us, we must continue to build strong dissuasive and strike capability as viable conventional deterrence. However, our approach must be to structure these forces, so that they can be employed efficiently and in a quick response time-frame, to maintain the tempo of operations (network centric and effect based). In the above context, there is a need to review the army's combat organisations and associated operational concepts. These must become more responsive to the likely escalation dynamics, ensuring total control of the battle space at all stages.
- Similarly, we need to have a relook at our air doctrinal concepts/thinking. Our current concepts and doctrinal thinking are based on fighting an all out conventional war. These will need to be fine tuned to the strategy of '*creeping escalation*'. Nonetheless the strategic context of air power will remain relevant, both in terms of China and out-of-area capability.
- Similarly, application of naval power and capability development must underscore the requirements of such a strategy, as outlined above.
- In so far as China is concerned, as mentioned earlier, the challenge will remain muted in the short and mid-terms. However, taking cognisance of infrastructural developments in China, the following approach is desirable:
  - Develop/enhance inteligence, surveillance, reconnaisance (ISR) capabilities over Tibet Autonomous Region (TAR).
  - Force structures to be developed, keeping in view low to medium level threat from China.
  - High level threat should be managed in a similar manner as Pakistan's strategy vis-à-vis India i.e. 'strategically defensive' and 'tactically offensive,' backed by credible nuclear deterrence.
  - Concurrent with above, there is a need to enhance naval surveillance capa-

bility, to cover the Strait of Malacca and the South China Sea. Together with the above, the capabilities of locating and neutralising Chinese nuclear submarines on patrol in the Indian Ocean to be enhanced.

- Last, but importantly, build a credible nuclear deterrence, together with its doctrinal postulates that address Indian security concerns holistically. There is a need to have a relook at the draft nuclear doctrine, taking cognisance of 'Alternative Futures' and their role in promoting the above strategy.

Shift From Continental to Maritime Approach

It would be apparent from the above that in the next few decades, there would be very few provocations to launch major cross-land border operations. If at all, these will be restricted and limited in nature. On the other hand, a look at future challenges would indicate the need for India to extend its sphere of influence with the ultimate objective of shaping the regional environment. It is important that such a capability development process is accompanied by a sophisticated information campaign, so as to not cause unnecessary ripples in regional sensibilities. While the maritime dimension offers the best medium for executing such a strategy, the absence of commensurate maritime capability in the near to medium term requires India to develop cooperative linkages in the IOR to fill the possible time gap.

In order to meet these challenges, particularly the security of our energy needs, and safeguard our interests in Central and Southeast Asia, India must incrementally develop power projection capabilities to include the following:

- Ability to respond quickly to low-end spectrum regional threats (disaster management, piracy/terrorist related incidents).
- Intervention capability to secure energy interests, either on its own, or as a part of a coalition based mechanism.
- Develop capabilities for selective intervention in areas of our strategic concerns e.g. Afghanistan or Central Asia.
- Incrementally enhance periodicity of naval presence in areas of interest in the region.
- Ability to counter increasing Chinese influence in the region, both individually and collectively. It is, thus, imperative to build relations with other important regional powers; this issue must form the basis of India's Look East policy.

In the light of the above, there are a compelling reasons to start making a shift from the purely continental to continental-cum-maritime strategy. The following areas of capability development need to be addressed:

- Creation of task forces with larger endurance.
- Enhancing strategic lift capability, to include personnel, equipment and stores.
- Development of submarine based deterrence capability.
- Development of land attack capability from sea.
- Strategic air power to counter Chinese and Pakistani capabilities, and address out of area concerns.

- Capability to rapidly insert limited number of Special Forces
- Network-centric capability to integrate air, land and sea forces.
- Effect based and precision strike capability.

Regional Engagement Policy: Building Relationships Through Military-to-Military Cooperation

We have generally been insular in our approach on the critical issue of naval cooperation, and recent initiatives at military-to-military cooperation have substantially been US driven. As mentioned earlier, for India to be counted as a regional player, and break away from the existing Pakistan centrality, it is important that we develop regional cooperative security linkages, by a comprehensive regional engagement plan. In building up the above relationships, it is important for India to enter into military cooperation with regional neighbours. Similarly, to build confidence in our extended neighbourhood, it is important to engage countries in our immediate neighbourhood (near abroad) like Iran, Oman, Indonesia, Malaysia, Thailand, etc on regular bilateral or multilateral bases. Our engagement must be focussed and should address India's core security concerns. These must move beyond routine naval exercises to inclusive engagements incorporating the army and air force too.

Next, we must not overlook the possibility of India having to operate as part of a larger coalition effort in an out-of-area contingency in the future. Strategic and perceptional shift and larger operational nuances require analysis, understanding and training for possible coalition operations. Attempting and/or forging such understandings can be used to build confidence among neighbors and could in the long term emerge as a useful tool to build mutual trust, cooperation and security relationships. Contextually, coalition operations should be used as a synergised effort to attain common regional goals. Here, it is essential to point out that big power interests in the region will not always drive such a coalition. These could be structured by India itself, in concert with SAARC, ASEAN and IOR-ARC (Indian Ocean Rim-Association for Regional Cooperation). While analysing the issue of coalitions/partnership operations, it would not be out of place to mention that we have willingly agreed to become a partner in the global war against terrorism. We need to consciously review our stand on this issue and evolve a long-term policy, commensurate with our interests, keeping in focus future security challenges.

Conclusion

This paper is an attempt at holistically evaluating future security challenges to India. The two defining themes of this paper are: one, we need to develop credible effect based and network- centric capabilities to deal with conventional territorial threats. These capabilities must be developed in concert with the likely nature of future wars. In developing these, our concentration needs to shift from an essentially hard power-oriented approach to a focussed soft -power approach in terms of RMA technologies in the field of IT, EW, space based systems and IW in a prioritised fashion. Second, we must be rational in our belief that a purely continental strategy, aimed at securing the country from cross-border threats, has not provided tangible benefits in a larger strategic perspective. In fact, this has made India insular, with Pakistan centricity as a defining norm. Consequently, our regional standing and the ability to play a constructive role, particularly in areas of interest, have greatly suffered. It needs to be appreciated that diplomacy and economics alone cannot always fill the security gap. Military engagement and cooperative security relationships, aimed at securing common interests, are an important construct of any imaginative national security policy. It is in this backdrop that a comprehensive approach at policy formulation has been defined, which attempts to *shift our strategic emphasis from a land-centric to a more comprehensive continental-cum-maritime strategy*. An important percept of the above approach, in concert with the aforementioned strategy, is *creating multilateral and bilateral cooperative relationships* with regional and extra-regional players.

It is strongly opined that such cooperative relationships, apart from addressing common security concerns, also help in building intra and inter-regional influences. As mentioned above, there is no reason why military-to-military cooperation in the region must remain restricted to mere exchange on training courses and periodic visits of senior officers. This can and must be enhanced to addressing joint challenges and threats; towards this, there is a case for joint exercises, patrolling, institutionalised disaster management, and search and rescue assistance. •

NATIONAL ASPIRATIONS AND DESIRED CAPABILITIES[1]

Dr Manoj Joshi

The Problem

The American victory in Iraq, if you ignore the politico-military mess they have made thereafter, has finally revealed the new RMA paradigm. As an Israeli analyst, Isaac Ben-Israel, put it: "The era when victory was obtained by only manoeuvre and capturing the 'high ground' is over. Decisive victory is also yours if you can destroy the enemy's main forces with precision stand-off fire."[2]

In abstract terms, RMA's key component is "situation awareness," viz. the commander's awareness of where the adversary is, and how his own forces are deployed. This has been conferred to an unprecedented degree by air and space-based reconnaissance and surveillance platforms. But in military terms, these abilities are effective only if they are combined with the ability to conduct precision strikes through a range of munitions and missiles.

In the classic concept, victory was attained by manoeuvre, while in the RMA paradigm as revealed in Iraq, victory was gained by high destruction rate of point targets, from stand-off ranges. There have been many claims about the nature of the campaign in Iraq. The most prominent claim is that the Iraqis did not fight, and when they did, they did so through *fidayeen* tactics that were unable to cope with the American firepower. Actually, the Iraqis did fight as per their plan, though they may have been imbalanced by the unplanned American decision to abandon "shock and awe" and race towards Baghdad. The plan appeared to be to give battle before Baghdad and there were efforts to manoeuvre forces.

A US War College analysis indicated that the Republican Guard redeployed four divisions directly across the main axis of the US advance and completed this movement between 24-48 hours before contact, despite the aerial bombardment. At the same time, paramilitary reinforcement was provided to forces in Najaf and Nasariyah.[3] The problem for the Iraqis was that once deployed, they were systematically destroyed by precision, long-range strikes. Even when units did manage to escape this onslaught, and give battle, they were undone by their own incompetence.

According to one source, the Iraqis were left with some 50 of the 10,000 or so artillery pieces they had fielded at the onset of the war.[4] Citing military theory, Ben-Israel has pointed out that a division stops functioning as an organic unit if 10-20 per cent of its weapons and manpower are destroyed. "In practice, the

Americans began moving their forces into Baghdad only after verification.... That over 50 per cent of the Republican Guard division tanks, armoured vehicles, and artillery had been eliminated." This was the primary reason why the Americans faced little resistance entering Baghdad – the Iraqi forces had been destroyed.[5]

On the other hand, in 2002, India mobilised its entire armed forces against Pakistan in the wake of the December 13 attack on Parliament. There have been claims that the Indian side came close to war twice, in January and June, but other information suggests that these actions would not have received political sanction. The first case, the Indian plan for multi-pronged thrusts into POK, lacked the wherewithal for success. In the heavily defended mountain terrain, India simply lacked the ratios required for any kind of success.

The second case, where three strike corps were supposed to have thrust into Pakistan from Rajasthan, was based on the questionable belief that Pakistan would not resort to nuclear weapons in the event of a massive Indian push into its territory. The only viable window of opportunity was in the two weeks after December 13, thereafter it was merely posturing.[6]

As much has been confirmed by Gen S. Padmanabhan, who said by way of *mea culpa* that he simply lacked the shape and size of forces that could have undertaken an action from cold start. In an interview to Praveen Swami of the *The Hindu*, he has implied that the defensive doctrine and the army organisation into holding and strike corps prevented a quicker response.[7] But this is something that the army has been aware ever since it began experimenting with the Reorganised Army Plains Infantry Divisions (RAPIDs); neither for that matter was the army's dissuasive deterrence doctrine meant to be defensive.

Actually, the problem may have been quite straightforward – the army lacked the combat capacity to launch offensive action. At a briefing of the Parliament's Consultative Committee attached to the Defence Ministry, the three Services said "in separate presentations in April [2002]" that India's superiority over Pakistan was barely 1: 1.2, down from 1: 1.7 that obtained at the time of the Bangladesh War.[8] Another report of the same briefing noted that that the ratio that stood at 1: 1.56 in 1990 and had now come down to 1: 1.22.[9] Given the lack of integration among the three Services, there is little that the army or the air force could have done by itself. What the armed forces needed was a joint plan, a doctrine and some degree of wherewithal. While they had the last named, viz. weapon systems and equipment, their more serious failings were in the area of doctrine and planning.

This is the way the adversary saw things. In September 2002, during a visit to the US, Pakistani Army Chief Gen Pervez Musharraf gave a lengthy briefing to the *Christian Science Monitor*. He noted that the Pakistani side had monitored the Indian build-up but had not felt particularly threatened, and that at no point in time had the Indians actually reached assembly positions for an offensive. This was because, as he put it:

> The force levels we maintain, in the army, navy and air force is of a level, which deters aggression... there is a certain ratio required for an offensive force to succeed. The ratios that we maintain are far above that...[10]

The Pakistani dictator went on to add that an Indian build-up was threatening to alter these ratios and there were two ways in which he expected the US to help. First, by proactively denying India US high-technology. Second, by allowing Pakistan to get the F-16s that it had paid for earlier.

On March 18, 2004, the US indicated that it was willing to heed the Pakistani demand when Secretary of State Colin Powell announced that the Bush Administration would seek the Non-NATO Military Ally (NNMA) status for Pakistan. Under this, Pakistan would be entitled to acquire surplus US equipment on a priority basis, as well as have privileged access to US high-tech equipment. So the challenge before us is to create forces that are able to provide genuine deterrent capability in the face of the new RMA paradigm.

Independence and After

In the wake of Independence, India's self-perceptions were shaped in great measure by Pandit Jawaharlal Nehru. In his view, India was a great nation and sought that status from the world. It did not believe in "power politics" and did not seek to become one of the great powers of the world. To this end, he kept the country firmly on the track of non-alignment, refusing to get embroiled in the Cold War politics of the 1950s and 1960s.

In this sense, Nehru's vision put itself squarely against the emerging bipolar international order that emerged after World War II. It came up instead with a model for a multipolar world which sought to influence events by collective moral pressure, rather than economic or military terms. It was one thing to stake out the moral high ground, and quite another to ignore that in the real world military muscle did matter.

The only early Indian leader who understood *realpolitik*, Sardar Vallabhai Patel, died in 1950. He was able to consolidate the Indian state, but was unable to bring his influence to bear on Nehru's somewhat quixotic foreign policy, which was manifested in its dealings with China in the 1949-56 period and its posture vis-à-vis the US in the 1950-53 period, when it adopted a policy of neutrality in the Korean War.

The price it paid for this became apparent when a US alliance enabled Pakistan to emerge as a significant military actor. On the other hand, by ignoring the realities of power politics, India neglected to build up its own deterrent capability and was defeated by China in the 1962 border war, an event that played as great a role in undermining even the status of a great nation that India had sought, as did the failure of the mixed-economy model.

Technology Demonstration as Deterrence

In the 1965-90 period, India sought to build up a military capability based on an arms transfer relationship with the erstwhile Soviet Union. Yet there remained an inherent ambivalence in India's quest.

The contours of India's aspirations are visible in its slow-motion movement to acquire nuclear weapons. It conducted a nuclear test in 1974, yet did little follow-up thereafter. Even as the international arms race continued apace, India sought "technology demonstration" as a means of deterring adversaries.

In the early 1980s, when Indira Gandhi returned to power, India carried out a comprehensive security review. As a result of this, a policy directive was issued asking the forces to maintain a posture of "disuassive deterrence" with regard to Pakistan and "disuassive defence" in relation to China. In short, this meant that the Indian Army could contemplate deep strikes into Pakistan, while with regard to China, it would involve a border defence strategy, ruling out any deep strikes.

Other contours became visible with an acceleration in the nuclear programme and the initiation of the Integrated Guided Missile Development Programme and the go-ahead for the nuclear propelled submarine programme, all in the 1981-83 period. Yet again, the pace of the programmes was such that they seemed to signal that India would remain on the "technology demonstration" mode. This was the period, as we well know, when Pakistan was working feverishly to acquire nuclear weapons.[11]

Under Rajiv Gandhi, India began a more assertive phase in its foreign policy. The bedrock of this comprised diplomatic overtures to the United States, even while maintaining good ties with the now fading Soviet Union. India faced down Nepal and compelled a restoration of democracy there and then began an active intervention in Sri Lanka in 1987, which it was unable to sustain. What also became apparent was that the "deep strike" army strategy against Pakistan had become untenable. On the other hand, India's deployments vis-à-vis China in Op Chequerboard did play a role in getting China to negotiate more seriously on the border. But this was offset by the Chinese proliferation of missiles to Islamabad beginning 1990.

But on both the missile and nuclear fronts, the government maintained its slow-motion pace, despite mounting evidence that Pakistan had crossed the nuclear threshold and was now in the process of acquiring a delivery capability. This was evidenced by the fact that three basic *Agni* tests were spread over five years. In fact, in a reversion to Nehruvian thinking, Rajiv Gandhi's strategy to deal with the crisis was to suggest phased universal disarmament through his Action Plan of 1988.

Coping with Proxy War

By this time, India was involved in a greater threat, one that had emerged from within. The most serious was the Sikh militancy, from around the mid-1980s, aided and abetted by Pakistan, that peaked in the early 1990s. Beginning 1990, Kashmir blew up and in the same year, India faced a fiscal crisis that saw its gold reserves being physically removed to London, to satisfy creditors. The Kashmir militancy, that began as an independence struggle, was soon taken over by Pakistan and became a full-fledged proxy war. But despite evidence of Pakistani aid to the insurgents, India avoided direct retaliation, deterred by Pakistani conventional and nuclear capability.

Freed from their Afghan commitment, Pakistani military leaders now claimed they had the capacity for a deep strike against India. This was the message of Exercise Zarb-e-Momin. In 1990, the United States finally confirmed that Pakistan had nuclear weapons, by refusing to provide a presidential waiver on the Pressler Amendment. The US also confirmed in 1992, that China had been transferring the M-11 missiles, capable of nuclear delivery, to Pakistan, by imposing an embargo on the Chinese and Pakistani entities involved.

Yet external pressures, in the form of the decision of the NPT powers to extend the treaty unconditionally and indefinitely meant that the Indian advocacy of disarmament had become untenable. To close the loop as it were, came the push for a Comprehensive Test Ban Treaty (CTBT), whose provisions required India and forty other threshold countries to sign before it came into force.

The Government of India twice readied to test nuclear weapons, in December 1995 and early 1996, but were forced to call it off. But by this time, another element had come into the equation, the Bharatiya Janata Party, which was committed to taking India across the nuclear threshold. It ordered the test in July 1996, but its government collapsed before they could be conducted.

The Silver Lining

Gloomy indeed as the 1990s were, there was a silver lining in the skies. This was in the form of the economic reforms that the Government of India was forced to undertake in the wake of India's near-bankruptcy. Holding back all unnecessary expenditure, the Indian system began the process of restructuring and reform, a decade behind China. These efforts were immediately blessed by a surge in economic growth.

By 1997, developments in the field of IT had suddenly begun to focus attention on Indian brain-power. In ever larger numbers, Indians began to play a role in the IT revolution, in both India and the US. This in turn bred a kind of national self-confidence that went way beyond the self-laudatory claims of the Nehru-Gandhi era. The United Front Governments of 1996-97 did little to change things. Indeed, their characteristic was to compromise thoughtlessly. On the one hand, Inder Gujral propounded a doctrine whose key element were to offer unilateral concessions to neighbours, regardless of consequences. On the other, the government's weak-kneed concessions on the Fifth Pay Commission led to a near collapse of the fiscal system, particularly of the states.

The Vajpayee Revolution

A much-needed and significant corrective was applied by a new National Democratic Alliance government, headed by the Bharatiya Janata Party. Confronted by the Pakistani test of a new long-range missile, the *Ghauri/Nodong*, capable of reaching the southern extremities of the country, in April 1998, Vajpayee ordered the *Shakti* nuclear tests that were conducted on May 11-13. In retaliation, Pakistan tested its weapons later that month.

The 1998-04 period saw a rapid growth of the country's GDP. Its exports have grown sharply and massive investment in infrastructure, particularly roads, has taken place. It has also seen the growth of the Indian IT industry and the emergence of India as a major business process outsourcing (BPO) destination. India has become more selective in taking development assistance and its foreign economic policy is based on win-win formulations stressing partnership, rather than a donor-donee relationship.

These developments have dramatically affected the country's foreign economic policies. Where once Indian business hid behind high tariff walls, it is now aggressively competing in the world market. A case in point is China. Just two years ago, scare stories on how China would swamp India's industry were seen in the Indian media. Now, the whole tune has changed. Indian businessmen are seeking to exploit the Chinese market, as well as its formidable manufacturing base.

The openness to new ideas was also visible in the articulation of the government's motives and policies by its leading lights – Prime Minister Vajpayee himself, his Principal Private Secretary Brajesh Mishra and the then Deputy Chairman of the Planning Commission, Jaswant Singh. But there have been some nuanced differences between them. Singh was the most passionate advocate of "strategic autonomy" for India, but subsequently, shifted track, and began to see a role for India as a close US ally.

But it has since become clear that the Vajpayee government's strategic vision is multipolar. This has been underscored by his diplomatic activity towards China, Russia, Iran and the European Union. India's nuanced stand on the Iraq War and the prime minister's various references to the need to learn the lessons of the Iraq invasion also indicate this. Significantly, he referred to this event during his speech in Srinagar on April 18, 2003, the one that launched the current Indo-Pakistan détente.

Yet the government has assiduously wooed the US. When President George W. Bush called for the construction of a National Missile Defence (NMD) capability, India welcomed it with alacrity. In the wake of 9/11, India offered its military bases to the US for use, in case Pakistan was recalcitrant. In any event, Pakistan succumbed to the US ultimatum and turned its Afghan policy on its head and offered the needed bases, but in a significant gesture, accepted India's offer to provide escorts for its war-bound shipping traffic from the Strait of Malacca to the high seas.

The massive intelligence failure that led to the Kargil War, served as a backdrop for a comprehensive review of defence policy. What was most significant was that this was a political review, the first ever, led by a GoM, the senior-most in the Union Cabinet. The GoM report has not hesitated to take tough decisions such as the passage of Prevention of Terrorism Act (POTA) or asking the forces to move against Pakistan in the wake of the December 13, 2001 attack on Parliament. The government has also generously funded the armed forces and cleared a number of major deals, such as the acquisition of T-90S tanks, the advanced jet trainer (AJT) and the aircraft carrier *Gorshkov*, with a complement of MiG-29K aircraft. Money has also been provided for the modernisation of the infantry units.

However, two years after the report was approved by the Cabinet Committee on

Security, there is a clear feeling that whatever changes have taken place have been the minimum required by the GoM report. At all levels and each stage, there has been resistance from the various departmental interests. Integration of the armed forces with the MoD has yet to take place, intelligence reform seems stuck in departmental rivalries and the appointment of the Chief of Defence Staff (CDS) remains in a limbo. Neither are there signs that individual Services will, in the spirit of the GoM report, begin deep reforms within their respective spheres.

From Great Nation to Great Power: Triumphal March or Chimera?

Assessing India's national aspirations is not an easy task. In a sense, our aspirations are incorporated in the preamble of our Constitution. But such documents tend to contain high-flying rhetoric rather than practical requirements of a large nation state in a fast-changing world.

Certainly, India would like a permanent seat in the UN Security Council and be seen as one of the great nations of the world. But do we want to become a dominant regional power as an ally of the United States, or do we, like China, seek an autonomous strategic capability? Does India challenge the current balance of power in Asia, or does it seek to maintain it?

There are other complicated issues involved when we try to triangulate the exact meaning of 'national aspirations'. For example, looked at from a certain Tamil viewpoint, India ought to seek a policy of alliance with the LTTE. Indian Muslims would perhaps like India to be stronger in their support for the aspirations of the Palestinians and be tougher on Israel, and have closer relations with other Muslim states. Millions of Buddhists in India deeply revere the Dalai Lama and are interested in the welfare of Tibetans. There is nothing extra-territorial about this, since it is akin to the feelings of one-ness that Hindu Indians have with their diaspora in Fiji or Guyana, or that of the Indian diaspora in the US towards India. Defining national aspirations of a democratic and multi-ethnic and multi-religious country can be a complex affair.

But let us try and determine what these could be. India will willy-nilly be thrust into the role of a great power. First, by the sheer size of its economy, its growing military might and its massive cultural footprint. Second, India would like to be a permanent member of the UN Security Council. Third, it would also like legitimisation of its nuclear status and be recognised as a respectable member of the comity of nuclear weapons and missile wielding powers. Fourth, it certainly aspires to be in the inner club of the economic giants – the Group of Eight or G-8 countries. But none of these groups confers automatic membership; to join up requires certain capabilities, a certain stamina and sustainability.

Desired Capabilities: General

- Everything would depend on sustainable economic growth at a high level and the complete elimination of poverty. Enhanced economic performance and capability are already giving India an edge in its relationship with its SAARC neighbours, including Pakistan. But much, much more needs to be done for India to become a global player of the level of Japan, the EU, the US or China.

India's achievements in IT are only a glimmer of the abilities it could unleash in the areas of manufacturing and agriculture. India's economic profile is heavily skewed, with large states like UP, Bihar, Assam, Orissa and MP having stagnant economies. One of the downsides of Indian economic growth in the past decade has been a virtually nil growth of rural jobs. India may be self-sufficient in food-grain production, but it does not have a healthy agricultural profile.[12] Indian agricultural productivity is low, with yields well below world levels. Second, the level of subsidy: in 2001-02 it was some $12 billion, which is several times more than the $1 billion public and $2.4 billion private investment that went into the sector.

- A secular character and unified society. It must overcome caste divisions that have plagued it through its history. Caste may be part of Hindu culture, but it must not be the basis of discrimination, as indeed it has been. This is easier said than done; political mobilisation across the country is often on caste basis. Fortunately, the reality is that no single caste or sub-caste constitutes the majority in the country, and over time, caste leaders will realise that only through coalitions will they be able to win elections.

Any attempt to treat India's religious minorities, especially the Muslims, as second class citizens, will have serious consequences for national unity, considering that there are currently six states in the Union where the Hindus are in a minority – Mizoram, Nagaland, Meghalaya, Arunachal Pradesh, Punjab and Jammu and Kashmir.Equally important, such a move will be a severe handicap in India's dealings with important Muslim countries in its neighbourhood – Bangladesh, Pakistan, Malaysia, Indonesia, the Arabian Peninsula and Iran.

- Likewise, India has to overcome the divisiveness that it faces because of caste and ethnic pulls. Some years ago, Stephen P. Rosen, published his study of Indian military power.[13] His focus was on trying to find a correlation between Indian society and military power. He found that through its history, military organisation, reflecting the divisions in Indian society, had ensured that India almost never had exportable military power.

He looked at, for example, the Mughals and the Ottomans. Both were Turkic in origin and had founded empires far from their homeland. But where one had been able to export substantial military power, the Mughals had been constantly pressed to keep their empire together against internal dissensions and divisions.

One of the causes was, of course, military organisation. The Turkish military might was based on the *janissaries*, young Christian slaves who were brought up as warriors and paid out of a central treasury by the sultan himself. The Mughal armies were based on the *mansabdari* system, where various nobles got land grants, in return for an obligation to provide the requisite number of soldiers when required. Not surprisingly, it is from these autonomous *mansabdars* that various rebels, including imperial princes, raised their armies to challenge the emperor. The lesson then, as even now, is the primacy in any calculation of the need for the social and cultural unity of the country.

The country should not bother about what brand of Islam someone follows or which party the person belongs to. The key commitment has to be to the Indian nationhood. But this nationhood cannot be defined by the Rashtriya Swayam Sevak Sangh or the Congress; there can only be one benchmark – the Indian Constitution and the political system it has set up.

- Reform its political system to provide good governance. As of now, the political system has become dysfunctional, because it is unable to provide effective governance in large parts of the country. There has been considerable criminalisation of politics, which has its own impact on the country's capabilities. India is only a half-democracy. Fifty years of democracy should have taught us that the right to vote is not the only attribute of democracy, a just society where everyone is equal before the law, or one that provides equality of opportunity regardless to caste, creed or sex is equally important.

Military Aspects of Capabilities

It is desirable that a country of India's size has a strategically autonomous perspective on security and evolves a military capability to service it. Towards this end, it must have a deterrent capability that will take into account all possible threats from every possible source, which includes today's real and potential adversaries as well as friends and natural allies.

For the past fifty years or so, India has been content to build up 'short-legged' capability that would provide an offensive deterrent capability vis-à-vis Pakistan and a defensive one with regard to China. As we see, despite our best efforts, we have not been able to meet our goals. As India's economic and cultural footprint increases, India confronts newer threats and has to examine radically different strategies to meet them. Needless to say, many of these challenges, such as terrorism, are not just to India but to the civilised world at large, but, if India seeks a certain standing in the comity of nations, it must pull its own weight. Further, the first lesson in international politics is that there are no permanent friends or enemies, only permanent interests. In other words, you have to pull your own chestnuts out of the fire.

- The first item in the agenda is integration of the three Services. This is something that has been accepted in principle now by the Government of India, but its implementation seems to be also in slow-motion. This is not to argue that this must be done with haste, rather that the basic decision that this is the way to go must be accepted. Thereafter markers can be laid for the road to the future, the level of integration, depending on resources and requirements.

There can be no doubt that RMA can only operate in an integrated paradigm. Indian military leaders who mouth RMA slogans have set themselves resolutely against integration for no other purpose than that they will lose their empires.

The current situation is abysmal. Each of the three Services makes its own war plans which do, and often do not, have relevance to the other Services. Each of them speaks of "excellent coordination," but the facts are otherwise. The air force, for example has simply not attuned itself to the era of precision long-range strike. Only a small proportion of its weapons are guided and towards physical and electronic suppression of enemy defences. Its strategy, unchanged since the 1965 Indo-Pak War where it fared so poorly, is to seek to attain air superiority over Pakistan by attacking its airfields and bases. But while it swears by the counter-air strategy, it has no coherent suppression of enemy air defence (SEAD) plan and neither is it equipped for the effort. The cult of dog-fighting, mano-et-mano, a holdover from World War I, has served the air force poor. The role of air power is simply too important in fighting a modern war to allow the IAF to make it own plans and doctrines in isolation.

- The country's armed forces must look at a perspective beyond China and Pakistan.Larger national aspirations call for longer-legged military capability - ships with greater endurance, genuine deep precision strike capability with the air force, marine and air assault capability for the army. We may, for the sake of convenience, locate these capabilities with individual Services, but they make sense only in an integrated environment.
- A vibrant defence R&D base and industry. For the past fifty years, India has been trying to set up a defence industrial base, yet we are not too far down the road. There have been four major requipment cycles – 1950s, 1965-75, 1985-95 and 2000. In none of these have indigenously designed weapon systems played a major role.

In the early 1980s, a big push was given to the process with the expectations that the 2000+ cycle would see Indian forces equipped with Indian-made tanks, light fighters, and surface-to-air missiles (SAMs). But as we know, this has not happened.

In 1997, the government announced with great fanfare that a 10-year plan had been made to increase the ratio of expenditure on procurement from domestic sources from 30 per cent to 70 per cent by 2005. This "Self-Reliance Implementation Council" was headed by the then Scientific Adviser to the Defence Minister, A.P.J. Abdul Kalam, who was also the head of the Defence Research and Development Organisation (DRDO). Needless to say, one year away from the target year, we are nowhere near achieving it.[14]

By the end of the decade, the main battle tank (MBT), light combat aircraft (LCA) and the advanced technology vessel (ATV) projects will be completed. The one major Indian weakness remains – weapons systems. The Integrated Guided Missile Development Programme that was begun in 1983, has failed to deliver the *Trishul* and *Akash* SAMs and the Nag ATGM (anti-tank guided missile) by 2004, ten years after the deadline. The *Prithvi* system is a cumbersome dinosaur and the *Agni I* and *Agni II* have yet to join the arsenal in any strength. Developing missiles and precision munitions is the challenge for the DRDO in the next ten years.

- The first stage in the integration must be a deep restructuring of the individual Service. For example, reference has been made above to the adverse Indo-Pakistan ratio. Now it is unlikely that the political authorities would be willing to fund an exercise to restore the ratio to what it was in 1971. The focus of the army must not be on numbers but on quality.

What effective restructuring can mean and the payoffs it can give are evident from the US Army's experience. In the early 1990s, the US Army inventory consisted of 15,120 tanks, of which 7,828 were M-1s, the others M-48s and M-60s, in addition to 900 Sheridans. The artillery component had 491 multi-launch rocket system (MLRS), of which 397 were artillery tactical missile (ATACM) capable. But by 2002-03, the tanks were down to 7,620 M-1A1 and A2s and the number of MLRS had shot up to 830, all of which were ATACM capable. By ridding itself of its tier II and III and light tanks, the US was able to pay for adding precision strike component in the form of the MLRS.[15]

On the other hand, the Indian Army's holding of some 3,000 tanks comprises tier I, II and III tanks, and that has remain unchanged in the past quarter century, despite the strategic transformation of the subcontinental military scenario. It is as though their leaders have heard about some strange thing called RMA, but have never quite got around to adjusting their forces to cater to it.

On the other hand, just how unrealistic some Service chiefs can be was borne out by the demand last year by Air Force Chief Krishnaswamy that the IAF go up to 60 squadrons. This incredible demand must be seen in the context of the current modernisation challenges before the IAF. It has 39.5 combat squadrons currently. At the moment, there are some 325 MiG-21s that need to be replaced, of which the IAF hopes to keep 120 modernised MiG Bisons for another decade and more. The government lacks the resources to replace the balance 225 aircraft on a 1:1 basis. So there will have to be drastic cutbacks in the IAF inventory. Instead, we have the chief demanding a 60 combat squadron air force.

- RMA requirements for situational awareness and precision strike need the control of the air and space. In the Iraq War, the US forces used some 50 satellites for a variety of tasks ranging from surveillance, global positioning system(GPS) for precise navigation and for guiding joint direct attack munition(JDAM), communications, early warning of ballistic missile launches, and so on.

The Indian Space Research Organisation (ISRO) has been an insistently civilian outfit that shies away from participating in any military activity. Sure, they have been responsible for making both the solid-propellent stages for the *Agni* missile, and the launch of the Technology Experiment Satellite in October 2001. India needs to create a dedicated military space programme. The DRDO has a defence satellite programme, but it is simply too unambitious to service the needs of the armed forces.

Any RMA oriented force will require support from Indian made and operated satellite systems. One of the critical areas is the need to make JDAM type munitions that would be immune to any American decision to black-out GPS signals. India has sought to build redundancy by signing up on the GLONASS and Galileo systems, but this may not be enough. The country must have an active military space programme running through its entire spectrum – launch vehicles, control facilities and satellites.

Conclusion

The kind of abilities that India seeks can only come through a system that makes strategic autonomy its goal. While Indian policies since Independence have sought to give the country an independent voice in world affairs, they have not been successful in building up a military-industrial complex around which the country can have a strategically autonomous position in the world order.

Strategic autonomy does not mean a "go-it-alone" strategy. But it certainly calls for alliances and friendships that are based on a mutuality of interests and an ability for both or all partners bringing in their fair share into the partnership. Only an alliance built on strong foundations of national capabilities can be fruitful, otherwise we run the peril of becoming surrogates and being made to serve the interests of the stronger power.

The most important requirement for this is sustainable economic growth, which can underpin the acquisition of the required military capabilities. In other words, the coat must fit the cloth. Only then will these capabilities be credible. The Soviet Union is a prime example of what happens when there is an imbalance in aspirations and the means to fulfill them. Pakistan could probably be cited as another, though it must be noted that Islamabad is remarkably focussed on the fact that the only possible threat it caters to is the one on its eastern borders.

There have been periodic voices demanding that India spend at least 4 per cent of its GDP for defence. Actually, if you count pensions and other related expenditure in the Department of Space and Atomic Energy, India has probably spent that amount anyway. The point is that for a poor country even that expenditure is too much.

The bigger problem is that despite spending a lot of money in the past, the country has not been able to effectively deter Pakistan. The conventional answer to the problem could well be, let us spend more money. I don't think that is the answer. That would seriously undermine our economic future, the key factor in attaining our national aspirations. In any case, the chances that the political authorities will provide more money for defence are next to nil.

In these circumstances, it is the duty of the three Services to set their house in order and integrate their capabilities and plans. Only this way can they make the qualitative jump that is needed for the Indian armed forces to remain credible defence forces; otherwise, they can be content to be a parade-ground outfit, whose main job is to undertake police jobs such as fighting militancy in Kashmir and the Northeast.

Many things are being said today about India's bright future. We don't have to go very far – just to 1990-92 to see the alternate scenario. India was bankrupt, compelled to physically take its gold reserves to London. In Punjab, the terrorists held sway over most of the state, especially at night. Kashmir had just blown up and the Mandal and Mandir movements were tearing the country's social fabric apart.

So when we talk big things today, it must be with a sense of modesty and an awareness that the desired capabilities would have to be attained through a step-by-step approach. They would also have to rest on deeper foundations of economic achievement and social and cultural unity. •

NOTES

1. This is a revised version of a paper presented at the Inaugural Seminar of the Centre for Land Warfare Studies (CLAWS) held on March 4 and 5, 2004, at the Vigyan Bhavan in New Delhi.
2. Isaac Ben-Israel, "Military Dimensions of the War in Iraq." Mimeo, nd np
3. " Iraq and the Future of Warfare: Implications for Army and Defence Policy," presentation made by the US Army War College Strategic Studies Institute to the US House of Representatives Committee on Armed Services, October 21, 2003, in www.globalsecurity.org/military/ops/oif-lessons-learned.htm
4. Conversation with a former RAND analyst.
5. Ben-Israel, n. 2.
6. Lt Gen (Retd) V.K. Sood and Pravin Sawhney, *Operation Parakram: The War Unfinished* (New Delhi: Sage, 2003), pp. 73-86.
7. Praveen Swami, "Padmanabhan Mulls Over Lessons of Operation Parakram," *The Hindu* February 6, 2004.
8. Aloke Banerji, "Slim Edge Over Pakistan," *The Times of India* (Kolkata), June 14, 2002. The report is based on an interview with a senior MP who is a member of the Standing Committee.
9. Rajat Pandit, "Army Seeks Swift Modernisation to Counter Pak," *The Times of India* (Delhi) April 4, 2003.
10. Transcript of interview of Pervez Musharraf in *Christian Science Monitor* posted on September 10, 2002 in *csmonitor.com*
11. See, for example, Manoj Joshi, "Dousing the Fire? Indian Missile Programme and the United States' Non-Proliferation Policy," *Strategic Analysis* (Delhi: IDSA), Vol. XVII No.5, August 1994 pp. 557-575.
12. See Mohan Guruswamy and Abhishek Kaul, *The Looming Crisis in Indian Agriculture*, Monograph of the Centre for Policy Alternatives, New Delhi, n.d.
13. Stephen Peter Rosen, *Societies and Military Power:India and Its Armies* (New Delhi: OUP, 1996)
14. See defence minister's response to Starred Question No 308 of August 13, 1997, in the Rajya Sabha
15. IISS, *Military Balance* 1993-94 and 2002-03

INDIA'S NATIONAL ASPIRATIONS AND MILITARY CAPABILITIES – 2020: A PROGNOSTIC SURVEY

Brig Rahul K. Bhonsle, SM

The new principles of war are no longer using armed force to compel the enemy to submit to one's will but rather using all means to compel the enemy to accept one's interests.

– Qiao Liang,
– Wang Xiangsui

There are things we know that we know ... there are things we now know we don't know. But there are also..... things we do not know we don't know.

– Donald Rumsfeld
US Secretary of Defence

Introduction

Modern India is a nectar of 6,000 years of civilisational and over 200 years of nation building. India as an idea has existed over the millennia. India as a geographical nation state, however, is a result of a combination of terrain fault-lines, British administrative convenience and the Partition. Economically, India has been a prosperous entity gone to seed, due to lack of survival and growth strategies for its teeming millions over the ages. However, the unitary bond in Indians has been strong over the ages. This has been evident with a resurgent, modern India demanding its rightful status of leadership in the world, within five decades of identification with the modern concept of nationhood. Permeation of the urge to excel in Indians has been far-reaching, as signified by the words of a Nagaland student to our President, Dr Abdul Kalam, when he visited Tuensang recently, "Mr. President, I want to live in an India which is prosperous, happy and safe." Such recurrence of national pride within a short period, despite the fissiparity of diversity is unique in the modern world, underlying the strength of the Indic civilisation and its people. India's national aspirations could, thus, be seen to be streaming from this socio-economic matrix and the yearning of its common people such as the Naga student.

These aspirations, in as much as the globalised security environment is concerned, need to be tempered with *realpolitik.* The world is being termed by some scholars like Samuel Huntington as a "uni-multipolar" one, in which resolution of key international issues requires action by the single superpower, the USA, plus a combination of other major states, and in which the superpower is able to veto action by a combination of other states.[1] Uni-multipolarism will have to be balanced with internationalism, with a large number of influential nations continuing to support the United Nations, either due to a genuine concern for equity in world polity or to undercut US influence. Growth of the non-state player, or what some thinkers like James Rosenau have called the "sovereignty free" actor, is another aspect in the strategic dynamics of tomorrow. This highlights the need of building a balanced relationship with other states of the international community, with primacy of affiliation with the United States, be it in the economic or the security sphere. On the other hand, our geographic contiguities include a mass of humanity in South Asia, which is impoverished, underdeveloped, but fully aware of the forces of modernisation unleashed in other parts of the world and, thus, vulnerable to the minions of deviant elements, such as the fundamentalists of all hues and religions. This is likely to create internal and external challenges to our security, which portends antagonistic cooperation, rather than sustained peace and bonhomie. Management of this strategic configuration of power in the subcontinent through deescalating strategies yet advancing military capabilities is essential to enable us to achieve our aspirations of being part of the global orbit of developed states in the modern world. The range of capabilities in a modern military, thus, will have to vary from Clausewitizian organised military forces to Creveldian Trinitarian warriors.

Aim and Scope

The aim of this paper is to provide a prognostic overview of the security capabilities envisaged in our armed forces of 2020, against the backdrop of our national aspirations. While security is increasingly emerging as a holistic concept, separation of the military from its other facets is well nigh impossible. Similarly, jointness decrees that the capabilities of the three Services need to be developed as a synchronous whole. Within this overall ambit, an overview of preferred army capabilities in 2020 has been attempted. The paper has been divided in two rather predictable parts. Part I deals with National Aspirations, including security goals, challenges and opportunities, while Part II focusses on Capability Essentials. In the latter, an integrated vertical and horizontal capability profile has been theorised.

PART I: NATIONAL ASPIRATIONS

India's National Aspirations

India's national aspirations can be summarised in the words of President Dr Abdul Kalam's address to the nation on the eve of Republic Day, January 25, 2003, "To be a developed nation by 2020." The nodal points of Indian prosperity can be denoted as peace, security and national unity. From these simple platitudes, the contours of a developed nation need to be identified. These are amply clear, in as much as its economic, political and socio-cultural aspects are concerned, implying a globalised yet self-sufficient economy, with equitable employment and growth opportunities at all levels of society, a liberal social order, dignity of life and property, effective governance and rule of law, harmoniously blending government and civil society. India has been such a state, a true *Ram Rajya* at various times, albeit for short periods over the ages, be it during the glorious rule of the Guptas, the Mauryas, Ashoka the Great, or in medieval times, the rule of Akbar, the Moghul monarch. These images need to be replicated in the modern day for being denoted as a developed state. In military security terms, it may appear difficult to define the profile of a developed state. Physical security from both external and internal threats, strong national defence, domestic law enforcement and social harmony may appear to be some of its components. Development feeds security and vice versa, as the Planning Commission report states, "*Rising levels of education, employment and income will help stabilise India's internal security and social environment. A united and prosperous India will be far less vulnerable to external security threats.*"

Economic security and ecological balance, contributing to human security are issues which are interlinked with the internal and external security of a nation today, more so, in the modern globalised environment, with the rights of states rendered inalienable and any alteration of geographic boundaries of nation states by coercive power unacceptable. Security and stability are essential for growth and development, for the flow of money, goods and people will happen only where there is security of life and limb, as perceived by the investor. The linkage of national development with security capabilities is well established. There is, thus, need to examine the threats to the Indian security environment, to enable us to derive the desired military capabilities in consonance with our national aspirations of being a developed state by 2020.

India and Indians have traditionally possessed a very high degree of self-esteem. India's peaceful independence movement has been the inspiration of millions across the globe, from Nelson Mandela in South Africa to Martin Luther King's Civil Rights Movement in the USA. This is also epitomised in our leadership of the post-colonial independence movements across the world in the 1940s and 1950s. We have always been a people with independent thought and ideology, signified by our vigorous sponsoring of the non-aligned philosophy by our political forefather, Jawaharlal Nehru, in the 1950s and 1960s. Non-alignment was also a strategy adopted by Nehru as a modest contribution to world peace, through freedom of judgment and action. However, our national aspirations then were not matched by military capabilities, which denied us control of our regional environment. This led us to succumb to faulty strategies sponsored in the name of national interest, such as the Sino-Indian stand-off in 1962. Our inability to harmonise our national aspirations with the military capabilities also resulted in the Indo-Pak 1965 War. These shocks were the inflections leading to a build-up of military capabilities, which exploited opportunities for creating a new strategic balance in the subcontinent, provided by Pakistan's mishandling of the situation in erstwhile East Pakistan in 1970-71. The growth in conventional capabilities over the 1970s brought its own paradox, an adversary who shifted to other strategies: mainly low intensity conflict, terrorism and nuclear parity. Over the years, this brought about an equilibrium in our security thinking, generated by the duality of centripetal and centrifugal forces tearing asunder our aspirations, economic growth, socio-political balance and military capabilities, resulting in security black holes, which our opponent could exploit very effectively all through the 1980s and 1990s, be it in Punjab, Kashmir, Assam or Kargil. This highlights the need for effective dissuasive capability of a nation in all spheres of national capabilities: socio-political, economic and military, in its multiple dimensions of nuclear, conventional, sub-conventional and asymmetric.

India's external threat environment in 2020 is likely to be defined by a resurgent China which would be a power in its own reckoning, and an aggressive Pakistan, whatever its contours in the next two decades, be it as an Islamic fundamentalist state or a modern democracy. Strategic thinkers in the West envisage a dual scenario in the case of Pakistan of the future. The first, an anti-modern vision, which implies a stagnant economy and poverty, provoking its masses towards greater radicalisation and aggression, political isolation and paranoia, leading to Pakistan being a failed or rogue state or even in an extreme case, a failed rogue state, with nuclear weapons, which would be a security nightmare for India for it spells the doom of a nuclear war in which there will be no winners. Even the fundamentalist Pakistani state, with an effectively controlled nuclear capability, poses a grave danger to our national aspirations, for it will mirror image radicalism of the type seen in Gujarat in February 2002. The other, a more benign expression of Pakistan is that of a modern, dynamic, democratic, tolerant Islamic state, with which our security relationship can be more balanced. The demographic implosion from Bangladesh is another facet of the external threat needing attention. In the internal threat scenario, India cannot claim its rightful place in the comity of developed nations unless it resolves its numerous pockets of dissension, either real or imaginary, through improved governance, bridging the development divide and creating an egalitarian society. This will require sagacity and sacrifice of parochial interests at all levels, from the *panchayat* to the Central government. Economic security entails primarily creating growth opportunities for the thousands below the poverty line, interlinking with the global economy and ensuring uninterrupted energy flow for sustained growth. This signifies the fact that national aspirations need to be matched by military capabilities at each stage, and in the modern world is contained in a number of spheres. As a developed nation too, India will have to retain independence of thought, while at the same time continuing to contribute to world peace, regardless of parochial interests. Military capabilities in varied dimensions to support such aspirations are, thus, called for.

What are the catalysts for our aspirations? An economic vitality, which is linking India with the world in rapid strides, indicated by the $ 100 billion plus forex reserves, unprecedented in our history, is indicative of India's surge towards a developed nation. Our capabilities in knowledge based technologies, BPOs, IT enabled services and manufacturing have given us another powerful leverage, which is increasing in its power potential each passing day. A stable polity, based on a realistic assessment of prospects and capabilities by various players, a greater willingness to sacrifice provincial interests for collective good at the national level, is providing India with greater respectability in the international fora. A professional, apolitical military, willing to work purely in the national interest is another asset which can propel us to attaining the status of a developed state.

On the other hand, the great development divide, which separates the vast multitudes of our people, estimated at figures varying from 25 to 33 per cent, which in sheer numbers is gigantic at approximately 300 million living below the poverty line, can act as the greatest brake for our assumption of the mantle of a developed state. For, not only will it stop us from developing economically but the social and subterranean pressures created by this divide in the information age can be exploited by marginalised forces, ever lurking in the background, through narcissistic and kingship networks, laced in half-baked ideological precepts. This will necessitate the need for redeployment of purely external defence forces to internal security duties, greatly denuding our deterrent edge, as has been happening over the past two decades or so. Thus, internal stability through ecological sustainability, social equity, maintenance of federalism with unity and management of diversity, is essential to ensure that our growth to a developed state is not marred by domestic dissonances.

National Security Aspirations

India's national security aspirations, concomitant with our overall goals, need to be clearly stated to envisage the desired military capabilities. Our prime minister has succinctly identified the geographical contours of our projected national aspirations during the Combined Commanders Conference in November 2003. These were denoted as extending from the Persian Gulf in the west to the Strait of Malacca in the east, across the Indian Ocean, Central Asia and Afghanistan, China, Northeast and Southeast Asia. Such a vision is appropriate for a nation on the threshold of embarking on the venture of a developed country. This sphere of interest and influence can be seen to include a security and an economic co-prosperity orb. The rough circle of the SAARC countries and Myanmar coincides with the security sphere, while the economic orbit will include countries in the immediate neighborhood such as Afghanistan, CARs in the west and Southeast Asian nations in the east. The Indian Ocean will form an important outer periphery of this Indian apsirational sphere of influence. In projection of soft power, our Indian diaspora in the world, particularly in the United States, the Gulf countries and Southeast Asia, decrees protection of interests of this community with vigour. As a developed nation of the world community, our ability to keep world peace and amity in human interest would decree a much larger sphere of interest, if not influence, primary amongst which would be the underdeveloped states of Sub-Saharan Africa, where a combination of socio-political and economic factors continue to create tectonic human tragedies, as seen in Rwanda, Congo and Liberia in the recent past.

India's stake in the SAARC region is primary to its achieving its national aspirations. For, the political, social and economic developments in the SAARC nations affect India's polity as well as security. Management of stability in the SAARC states, less Pakistan, is a function of sage political and public diplomacy and economic aid as a sop for support and effective border management. In the latter sphere, military capabilities need to be enhanced. Pakistan has challenged the Indian nation state through its continuous sniping at the very foundations of India as a secular, liberal democracy. Its impact on India's emergence as a developed state, thus, is far reaching, for it has the capability to disrupt our geographical, social, economic as well as information security. Full spectrum military, as well as paramilitary capabilities alone will ensure security against Pakistan. China too needs to be viewed in this perspective, albeit as a major competitor if not an adversary in our strategic sphere. This would in general terms be linked to full spectrum military capabilities of effective border management, surveillance and intelligence, and requisite deterrence as well as dissuasive capability in all spheres of the conflict spectrum; asymmetric, low, conventional and nuclear. Parity with China in numbers may not be pragmatically attainable, hence, it is essential to attain the same in the quality of our armed forces and its technological superiority, which needs to be honed up as a shield, to provide China with an impression of irreparable loss of face in the international community in case of aggression, to which the Chinese are most sensitive.

In the outer sphere, Afghanistan is the primary state of interest. Stability in Afghanistan is essential to avoid its fall under the influence of the forces of fundamentalism, whose ire would be directed against India. Solidity in Afghanistan also implies a tranquil NWFP in Pakistan, thereby eroding the Pathan culture and Pathan Islamic influence of Pakistan's army on its polity. Afghanistan also acts as a springboard for Central Asia and a transit route for flow of oil from Iran once the land pipeline proposal fructifies. Given the geographical separation of the state and Pakistani sensitivities to Indian influence, capabilities may have to be restricted to soft power projection in the state.

Central Asian states will provide the energy resources for the coming decades and are also important due to the proclivities of some of these towards Islamic fundamentalism, though relatively far removed from the Indian territory. Iran and the Gulf states in the Middle East are traditional Indian friends. The large Indian diaspora and economic potential of employment, as well as oil economy, imparts these states a unique influence on Indian polity. That these states are Islamic populates gives us a leverage with our large Muslim population. Southeast Asian countries also have a large Indian diaspora and are important for our economic security, apart from the need to balance the Chinese influence in the region. These nations will also be security dependent on India, for the oil bearing SLOCs passing through the Indian Ocean are under Indian control. These states also come under the influence of the crescent of Islamic fundamentalism which stretches from the Middle East to Southeast Asia, as designated by the Bali bombings, with its expansive portion resting on the Pakistan-Afghanistan-Central

Asia hub. These states are relevant for soft power projection capabilities.

The Indian Ocean is a significant area of Indian interest and is increasingly going to be so. It is important as a global oil transit zone, with approximately 150-200 tankers likely to pass through per day by 2020.[2] China too has a great stake in this region, apart from other developed states such as the United States, Britain, Australia and Russia. Our ability to police this region is, thus, a necessity.

The US is increasingly a dominant player in the area of India's interest and will remain so in the years ahead. It will have a significant influence on supporting our aspirations through economic, technological and even military support. Inter-operability with the United States armed forces, in ways more than our traditional ally Russia would, thus, be essential. This, in no way, lessens the need to balance our relationship with Russia. The Great Bear continues to be important due to its influence in the CARs, energy security, nuclear, military and space technology and common need to combat the forces of terrorism unleashed through the rise of Islamic fundamentalism in the soft Russian underbelly states such as Chechnya.

The EU states provide us a springboard for economic development, employment and support for BPO businesses in the knowledge economy. Israel, on the other hand, is crucial as a provider of military technology for our country, which will enable us to acquire state of the art capabilities at low cost. Technology sharing with Israel, in both the civil and military spheres, is critical in our national interest for growth and development of the economy, particularly agriculture and the military. A stable military-technology relationship with Israel, without compromising on our Arab friends is, thus, called for. Finally, a significant contribution is expected from a developed state as a global citizen. India is regarded by many developing and underdeveloped states as a fair and unbiased player in international affairs and, thus, our ability to assist them in stabilisation of their land and polity within the parameters of international approval is expected.

To summarise, harmonisation of national aspirations, security constants and military capabilities is essential for a holistic appraisal of our needs of tomorrow. This will ensure protection of our land and sea frontiers, and also enhance our global and regional influence, protect economic interests, the well-being of the Indian diaspora and create opportunities for growth and national development.

Challenges to National Aspirations Related to Security

China, the gradually rousing somnolent dragon, can be construed as the prime threat to our national aspirations of being a developed state by 2020. India will be perceived by China as a challenge in its area of influence in Asia and particularly Southeast Asia. China in its most non-belligerent form would pose a security dilemma to us in all the spectrums, nuclear, conventional, sub-conventional and asymmetric. A Sino-Indian stand-off in the Eastern Seas will greatly strain our economic relationship with the ASEAN states. Military parity with China is a strategic necessity for survival, if not for smooth development, though primacy of soft diplomacy to assuage the Chinese threat needs emphasis. On the western front, Pakistan poses a more overt threat, again in multifarious fields, from nuclear to asymmetric. Pakistan is also turning into a net exporter of nuclear technology, if recent reports on Pakistani nuclear polygamy appearing in the Western Press are to be believed. Libya, Iran and North Korea have been part of its past clients. What is of greater concern is the likelihood of this technology passing into the hands of Islamic fundamentalists who have the expertise and enterprising attitude to cash on Pakistani nuclear promiscuity through diverse routes. A surveillance capability of Pakistani nuclear networks may have to be considered as a prime need for our military intelligence agencies. Bangladesh poses a threat of demographic implosion, bringing down growth levels in the most sensitive northeastern area as well as the urban metros of the country. Sheer presence of numbers in the eastern neighbourhood poses varied challenges, which need diverse strategies for us to combat. Nepal is undergoing a major socio-political strife, which is likely to get worse as the years go by, with growing awareness of the masses creating a wide chasm between the elite and non-elite segments of its society, through information proliferation. This too affects a very sensitive portion of our country, both economically and demographically, the northern hinterland of the Indo-Gangetic plains on the Uttar Pradesh-Bihar-West Bengal borders which are grossly underdeveloped. Dealing with neighbours having poorly governed borders and an underdeveloped neighbourhood due to inaccessibility and limited control will provide safe havens for drug cartels, smuggling networks, transnational criminal organisations and terrorist mafias. A dynamic border management policy to combat such varied types of cross-border threats, ranging from Pakistani semi-conventional to Nepali Maoist forays and Bangladeshi migration in large numbers is essential in our constructive national interest, as well as overall human interest in South Asia.

Defence ties with Bhutan, Myanmar and Sri Lanka need to be further strengthened. Maldives too needs to be brought in this ambit, along with the French islands of Reunion, with a large Indian diaspora and a strategic disposition in the least policed area of our interest, the Indian Ocean. In the internal security arena, new challenges will be posed, such as prevention and control of environmental and ecological disasters, securing oil installations in diverse areas, air defence of nuclear facilities, restoring order in case of a nuclear disaster, defence of information, infrastructure, and so on. A large number of these aptitudes will have to be soft rather than in the hard kill dimension, a detailed survey of which is being carried out in the next part of the paper.

A developed state has to base its power configurations within its strategic ambit on deterrence and dissuasion, rather than employment of force. That alone can provide continuity in development, essential for sustained growth. Nations in the superpower mould like the USA are able to successfully manage this duality endemic in power relations. Indian national power will have to be adequate in 2020 to stave off challenges through disincentives offered by perfect deterrence rather than waging wars. The success of capability building implies attaining such power. This will be the essence of change in our force capabilities of the future dictated by global and regional realities.

PART II: CAPABILITIES SPECTRUM – 2020

General

Operation Parakram demonstrated the requirements of the future force in the emerging contemporary environment of a uni-multipolar world. The unipolar power may well undertake unilateral preemptive offensive action against its adversary but will not accept the same by other nations, However, rational be its impulse for the offensive, even while operating in the interest of its multipolar orbit of war against terror. However, short windows of opportunity will continue to be available as was the case from December 13, 2001, to January 2, 2002.[3] War, however, may not be the best option for achieving our security interests in 2020, keeping in view our vision of being an economically developed state, for modern war is an expensive business, which will set back our development goals by decades. Dissuasive capabilities instead should be credible enough to convey a certainty of unacceptable loss in the case of conventional as well as strategic terrorist adventurism, even within this small window to our opponent.

Any assessment of India's future capabilities has to factor in the country's security relationship with Pakistan as an ongoing process, rather than time interposed activities tailored by peace initiatives. Lessons from the post-Cold War world are ominous. While the threat of open wars may recede, new threats constantly emerge to challenge nations. Hence, there is never a case of speculating on the future of armies during periods of détente, but only prophesying on armies of the future. The present economic constriction felt by Pakistan in the past few years and which perhaps is driving President Musharraf towards a peace agreement with India, is due to the three-pronged operational posture required to be adopted by Pakistan's security establishment today, on its west to control the resurgent Pakhtun *jehadi* and Al Qaeda elements, on the east deployment on an active Line of Control against the Indian Army, and an increasingly internal terrorist threat, as demonstrated by two consecutive attacks on President Musharaff in December 2003 before the SAARC summit in Islamabad. This three-pronged squeeze on its economy will have to be continued to force the Pakistan Army to adopt a more amenable policy against terrorism in Kashmir.

Conflict termination and peace-making capabilities within the ambit of the UN, or even other acceptable coalitions in human interest, need to be an add on in capabilities, which our army as well as the armed forces do not possess at present but which a developed nation like India, acting in the human interest, will have to undertake, to project its influence in the world of tomorrow.

Thus, we find that our capabilities need to be based on multiple dimensions such as conventional superiority in the vast swathe of terrain panoramas obtained across our borders, in various facets such as surveillance and information dominance, firepower, shock action and infantry support, as well as logistics, to enable dissuading a potential enemy. In the nuclear field, a credible second-strike capability will be the only effective deterrent, supported by an effective command and control structure. Surveillance and deterrence of cross-border nuclear support mechanisms are also essential, to ensure that Pakistan's capacity for exporting nuclear technology does not fall into hands of non-state actors like the Al Qaeda. Counter-insurgency, terrorism and asymmetrical war capabilities need to be consummate in our forces, along with peace-making and peace-keeping strategies. A model profile of a force of the future is provided by Gen Charles Krulak, an ex-US marine commander, who has described the landscape of future operations as a "three block war." According to Krulak's description of the urban battle space, the armed forces will be expected to provide humanitarian assistance in one part of the city, conduct peace-keeping operations in another and fight a highly lethal mid-intensity battle in yet a third quarter.[4] The Indian armed forces will increasingly have to prepare themselves for a three-block, multi-role type of warfare in the future. All this has to be weaved in a cloak of technology superiority and common doctrines across the Service in the first place and all the three Services later.

The full spectrum of desired capabilities of our armed forces in the world of 2020 is as given in Fig 1. The capabilities envisaged are vertical competencies essential in the armed forces and particularly the army. While these are well identified and accepted, the horizontal capabilities, which transcend vertical competencies, need greater attention. These are capabilities such as information and intelligence building, human resources development, technology assimilation, and so on, which need to be simultaneously fostered, keeping in view the developments in each field separately. Such a network of capability building will ensure that our forces are not only task proficient but also optimally configured to achieve the desired aims effectively.

Fig 1

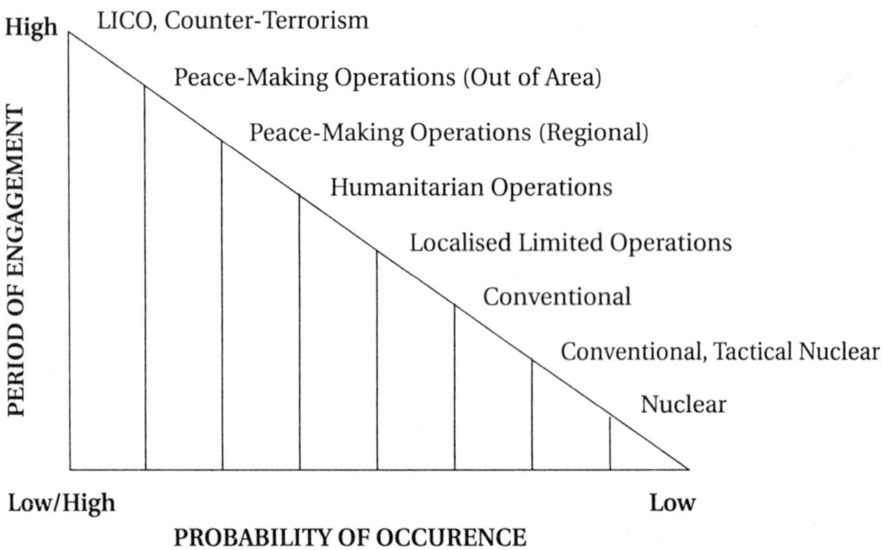

Probability of Occurrence

Conventional Force Capabilities

Conventional force capability is the first and foremost of our security potential building matrix of the future. Notwithstanding diverse manifestations assumed by conflict at present and likely to attain in the future, conventional warfare will continue to be a prime component of national war-making competencies. While war-fighting capability is the prime component of a conventional force, the essence in such an ability for the future may not be winning battles but successfully avoiding the same, through observable dissuasive-deterrence critical mass. Our conventional force capability should, thus, ensure stability for growth sans disruptions like Kargil or threat of disarray post-Kargil, which posed a drain on our economy. Our conventional forces should have the requisite numerical superiority against our belligerent adversary, Pakistan, and force strength to discourage China. If asymmetry is the essence of deterrence, what should be our force balance against Pakistan and China to ensure preclusion of war, thereby shielding our growth and development? This could be viewed through different perspectives. Classically, a country with a purely defensive strategy can envisage sufficient defensive potential with a ratio of 1 : 2 against an offensive adversary. On the other hand, such inferiority may be an invitation for aggression. The ideal ratio will be a function of a symbiotic relationship between capabilities, preferences, credibility and outcomes requiring a separate debate. Suffice to say, the balance has to be achieved without impinging on economic resources for development.

Apart from numerical balance in forces, force structuring should enable enhancing potential and effectiveness. The ability to strike deep through long range, lethal firepower which can be delivered in all dimensions, and shock forces which are capable of rapid deployment both in the plains and the mountains, with greater reliance on helicopters, may be the need of the morrow. While numerical superiority in terms of tanks, guns and personnel can be easily calculated through a swathe of strategic balances, the imponderables are technological superiority, doctrinal and training multipliers. This will be the sum total of deterrence. A perfect model of a future force is available through the concept known as RMA. The RMA based force will be capable of operating in pentagonal dimensions of line, square, time, box and cyber space.[5] Such a force alone will achieve the desired dissuasive capability required in 2020. Costs of such forces will have to be limited through structuring for effects based operations rather than numerical balance.

Exploiting the RMA

American forces effectively demonstrated in Iraq, apart from the subsequent problems of conflict termination, the impact of RMA based forces on the conduct of conventional operations. The singular necessity is to develop RMA capability in our conventional forces, more so in operations in high altitude and mountainous terrain, as in the plains and the deserts. This will not only enable us to overcome the ides of Kargil, but also demonstrate a unique capability much vaunted in the world's armed forces today, as was indicated by the experience of US led forces in Afghanistan. RMA capabilities imply forces fighting through a total transparency of the battlefield, exploiting information superiority through a fused network of satellites, UAVs, air and ground based radars and other 24-hour surveillance systems. Seamless connectivity through computer based communications, generating a command and control which is networked rather than hierarchical, would form the second aspect. Both battlefield transparency and command and control will be integrated with all the three Services, rather than separate stand-alone systems for each Service, except for those in the tactical battle space with limited ranges. Integrated fire support will be the third arm of an RMA based force. Air, artillery, missiles and armoured guns will be fused through digital target integration for precision strikes and high lethality ammunition to cause destructive rather than neutralising effect. The aim would be not only to destroy military targets but also disrupt the strategic command and control by engaging leadership targets through use of special forces, if required. Intimate support platforms need to be provided to the army for a total range of army aviation capability from surveillance, utility, command and control and even deep attacks by UAVs. All this will be supported by effective logistics of modular repairs and replacements in the field. Intelligence, speed, manoeuvre, lethality and precision will be the key parameters on which an RMA force will have to operate. Soldier survivability in an urban environment would be the other key to an RMA based force. Soldier empowerment downstreamed to digitise *ghataks* (infantry) will imply permeation of the RMA to the grassroots level, enhancing the potency of our forces. A link between urban operations in the conventional sphere with the counter-insurgency forces will have to be effectively established to attain a synergy in capacity building of diverse forces.

The capability to deploy these forces abroad in a multicultural environment, under diverse terrain, weather, and socio-political and ethnic environments, is essential for force projection. The Indian Ocean will be an area where base facilities will have to be established and our conventional forces deployed there on a permanent basis. This will have to be divided in two spheres: soft and hard power. Hard power projection, implying new capabilities for inter-operability, capacities for civil and public affairs and media interaction, will have to be considered in the force structures of tomorrow. Soft power projection capabilities will include the ability to provide humanitarian aid and peace-keeping operations.

Force Structuring

Structuring of the future conventional forces also needs consideration in the light of the modes of emerging conflicts, especially in an urban environment. Krulak's Three Block War force appears to be its most articulate but debatable form. "*In one moment in time, our service members will be feeding and clothing displaced refugees – providing humanitarian assistance. In the next moment, they will be holding two warring tribes apart conducting peacekeeping operations. Finally, they will be fighting a highly lethal mid-intensity battle. All on the same day, all within three city blocks. It will be what we call the three block war,"* said Gen Charles C. Krulak. In Block One, thus, forces conduct humanitarian operations in a permissive environment. In Block Two, security operations are conducted in a questionable environment. While in Block Three, high intensity combat carries on simultaneously. These forces are structured to conduct operations in an interchangeable manner. Krulak has cited the example of battles for the city of Grozny to support his theology. He has said that in one city block, marines would be engaged in high-intensity warfare against a well-trained and well-equipped enemy. In another, they might be up against light, irregular forces fighting a gurerrilla-style campaign. In yet another area, marines would be carrying out peace-keeping and humanitarian aid. This concept may be the blueprint for tomorrow but needs detailed deliberation Such diverse demands on the battlefield of the morrow place a high premium on flexibility and leadership challenges, which will be tackled in the horizontal competence building part of the paper.

Nuclear Capabilities

In December 1998, the prime minister spelled out the key elements of India's nuclear policy in Parliament. To recapitulate briefly, salient facets of these include:

- India should maintain a minimum nuclear deterrent and undertake necessary measures to ensure its credibility.
- India has declared a moratorium on undertaking any further underground nuclear test explosions, but R&D activity, including computer simulation and sub-critical tests, will be conducted as necessary.
- Development work on an extended-range *Agni* missile is underway. Additional flight testing will be undertaken in a manner that is non-provocative, transparent and consistent with established international norms and practices.
- In order that our minimum deterrent is credible, we shall adopt and maintain a deployment posture that ensures survivability of assets. Such a posture, obviously, provides for greater safety and security.
- India will not engage in any arms race. We shall not, therefore, pursue an open-ended programme.
- A civilian command and control system, with necessary safeguards, shall cater for all possible contingencies.
- India's commitment to global nuclear disarmament remains undiluted. We will continue to work with other like-minded countries and take initiatives for moving towards a nuclear weapon-free world. We will also seek to negotiate CBMs (confidence-building measures), in both the conventional and nuclear fields, with the aim of reducing lack of trust in the region.[6]

Within this policy framework, the army's role will be to guarantee the second strike capability based on mobile long-range missiles in secure sites with speed, mobility, communications and command and control networks. Once again,how many such missiles within the triad of the nuclear deterrent will contribute to the defence will need to be debated separately. Suffice to say, it is not merely a function of numbers vis-à-vis the primary interest for such a missile – China – for parity in numbers with China's strategic nuclear missiles may not be realistic; however, it should be the sum total of our assured capability for launch, in protection of our vital interest of national survival. The requirement of a tactical nuclear missile capability with the army is still a matter of debate keeping in view the nuances of the declared no first use policy of our government. Again, the need would be to develop an assured capability rather than a matter of statistics, which though reassuring, have to fit into the larger security and policy perspective. The army will also have to provide reliable command and control facilities and ensure the survivability of our command and control structures, as well as leadership. Security of our nuclear power structures and facilities will also be the army's wont, from both air and ground threats. Nuclear disaster management is another facet which has to be brought within the ambit of capabilities of the army in 2020, for, with a growing nuclear power industry, such contingencies though appearing far fetched, need to be factored in a modern state's quiver. A nuclear, biological, chemical (NBC) disaster triggered by a terrorist strike, the "chances of which are that of 100 attempts... 99 would fail, but the single successful one could claim more victims, do more material damage and unleash far greater panic than anything the world has experienced," as said by Walter Laqueur, will also have to be managed by the army, for it alone has the discipline, organisational management and courage required in such extreme situations.[7]

Counter-Insurgency and Terrorism Force Capabilities

Tomorrow's terrorist may not be an insurgent, but will be a highly lethal and potent tool in the hands of the ideologically deviant, with a capability to disrupt the physical, information and economic infrastructure at stand-off distances unimaginable today. The potential of WMD terrorism may not be far-fetched, at least in its biological, radiological and chemical versions by 2020. Under the circumstances, our capabilities to fight terror need to be considerably reviewed. To fight conventional terrorism, greater reliance on special forces will be essential. Special forces, with their nuanced approach to counter-terrorism, are considered most appropriate for the precision required for counter-terrorism operations. The US has gone farthest in special forces proliferation, through deploying three types of special forces in its Special Operations Command, in Iraq and Afghanistan, Special Operations Forces or the Green Berets, Delta Force and Sea, Air, Land (SEAL) Team Six, comprising special hunter-killer teams. For future counter-terrorism, force structuring based on special forces options could be varied, either to convert a larger number of our infantry units to a special forces profile or create hunter killer teams within normal infantry battalions. The US experience in employment of special forces throughout the world needs to be analysed in detail. For it is said that of the 49,000 special operations troops of the US Special Forces Command, 15,000 were deployed in 125 nations across the world in 2003.[8] News reports indicate that plans for accretion of special forces are already underway in our armed forces. Gen Charles Krulak's "three block war force" can also act as a model for structuring forces for counter-terrorism and low intensity conflict operations (LICO). The capability to simultaneously conduct humanitarian assistance, peace-keeping operations and highly lethal mid-intensity combat, within the same battle space, is also relevant in the sphere of counter-terrorism operations capability.[9]

Intelligence and surveillance of terrorist networks and terrorist leaders is an essential facet of capacities for counter-terrorist control. This has to be based on integrated electronic and human intelligence inbuilt at all levels of command, incorporated vertically as well as horizontally within the force, at the operational level. Intelligence in the counter-terrorist operations scenario has to be increasingly aimed at providing real-time information for precision operations. Precision has to be in time and space, to target high value targets such as the militant and political leadership of organisations. The American approach to intelligence building for tracking down Saddam Hussein in Iraq should be instructive of how such a campaign should be planned. Special intelligence teams organised by the US forces in Iraq to track the leadership paid rich dividends. Similarly, special teams should also be organised for tracking suicide squads. Tracking of WMD terror hazards will be another challenge to the intelligence community of the morrow. The overall aim should be to shift the focus of intelligence from a generalised function to a specialised high value one.

The emerging profile of counter-terrorist capabilities, thus, appears to be a defensive component for domination of the area, and offensive component of special forces. Launching precision operations based on real-time intelligence, to eliminate terrorist leaders, capability to carry out surveillance and targeting of sources and network of WMD terror, while at the same time assuaging the general populace to avoid socio-political backlashes, seem to be the force capabilities of the morrow in this sphere. In case of escalation, the ability to carry out surgical trans-border precision strikes, by both air and special forces will have to be a median capability common to the conventional and counter-terrorist forces. This will overcome the essential organisational anomaly highlighted during Operation Parakram, wherein our forces were unable to exploit the short windows of opportunity to strike and, thus, we had to rely on prolonged dissuasive deployment as a part of coercive diplomacy, which was fatiguing to troops.

Security from Asymmetrical Threats

Asymmetrical challenges to national security are the latest form of conflict, which a clever adversary can pose to a nation in the mode of unobtrusive warfare, bleeding a nation through various stratagems like economic, population incursions, trade wars, and so on. The emergence of asymmetrical conflicts is highlighted by the need to humanise war in the contemporary environment, as amplified in Fig 2.

Asymmetrical challenges can be defined as threats, both military and non-military, more covert than overt, which may be slow acting and yet affect the survival of a nation state, a community and society in the long-term, which can either be triggered by an adversary state or non-state or spawned by lack of effective

Fig 2

HIGH INTENSITY CONFLICTS
(Few Possess-Unacceptable Casualties
(SECURITY AGAINST WMD)

⇕

MEDIUM INTENSITY CONFLICTS
(Unacceptable Casualties and Expensive)
(MILITARY SECURITY)

⇕

LOW INTENSITY CONFLICTS
(Unacceptable, Uncivil, Unrestricted)
(POLITICAL SECURITY)

⇕

ASYMMETRIC THREATS
(Soft, Unobtrusive threats to achieve political objective)
(HUMAN SECURITY)

control measures. In the finest traditions of Sun Tzu, two Chinese writers have been the first to publish a treatise on the concept of asymmetrical warfare. Qiao Liang's and Wang Xiangsui's work entitled, "Unrestricted Warfare" was published by the PLA, Literature and Arts Publishing House, Beijing in February 1999 and is freely available on the Internet.[10] Qiao Liang and Wang have identified varied types of asymmetrical threats, some of which are highly exotic, others common knowledge today. Some of the asymmetrical threats denoted by Chinese thinkers are as given below:

- **Use of Non-Lethal Weapons.** These weapons can neutralise the combat capabilities of personnel and equipment without loss of life, giving weapons a humane veneer by controlling lethality.
- **Information Weapons.** Information weapons can come in the form of electro magnetic energy weapons, computer logic bombs, network viruses or media weapons, all focussed on paralysing and undermining the capability and will to fight.

- **Trade Wars.** The forms of trade wars described include use of domestic trade laws on the international stage, erection and dismantling of trade barriers (Super 301) to own advantage, economic sanctions, embargo on export of critical technologies and arbitrary imposition of Most Favoured Nation (MFN) status.
- **Financial Warfare.** This is said to be waged in a manner that saw the collapse of the "Tiger" economies of East Asia in 1997, with flight of international capital at the mercy of day traders and fly-by-night operators working for short-term gains. As per the authors, companies such as Morgan Stanley and Moody's, which provide credit rating reports on nations also participate in financial warfare by denoting targets of attack for the benefit of large finance and investment consortiums.
- **New Terror.** The Chinese ironically defined new terror, or Bin Laden style terrorism, two years before the September 11 attacks. It denotes unlimited wars without rules, with the aid of new technologies and new mediums such as that inflicted by the "Falange armed forces" of Italy that specialise in breaking into computer networks of banks and news organisations, steal stored data, delete programmes and spread disinformation.
- **Ecological or Environmental Warfare.** Ecological or environmental warfare is another technique of conflict in modern times covered by the authors. It envisages manipulation of the ecological system to cause earthquakes, alter precipitation and atmospheric temperatures, gradually developing a capability for causing thunderstorms.

Of particular significance is the grand warfare concept espoused by the Chinese scholars, which combines military and non-military means. It is the employment of a combination of many means that will lead to victory in modern times, say the authors. In the same vein, a nation has to contemplate defence and security in all spheres, military and non-military, such as terrorism, subversive activities, threats to economic growth, drugs and international crime, to ensure all round well-being of the state. The authors have elaborated on the concept of combination by tabulating varied means of warfare and then denoting how each can be meshed with others to achieve a synergistic effect. The means are tabulated under the heads of Military, Trans-Military and Non-Military, reproduced at Table 1 below.

Table 1

Military	Trans-Military	Non-Military
Atomic warfare	Diplomatic warfare	Financial warfare
Conventional warfare	Network warfare	Trade wars
Bio-chemical warfare	Intelligence warfare	Resource warfare
Ecological warfare	Psychological warfare	Economic and regulatory warfare
Space warfare	Smuggling warfare	Sanctions wars
Electronic warfare	Drug warfare	Media wars
Guerrilla warfare	Virtual warfare	Ideological wars.
Terrorist warfare		

How do we combat such threats, most of which lie in the non-military sphere, except for terrorism. Building a secure surveillance and intelligence network and providing a fountainhead of doctrinal support for such threats, with the army's greater strategic insight, appear to mind immediately. This has to be followed by abilities for disaster management, skills to target the opponent's military and civil information spectrum, while securing own information and electronic networks, defensive and offensive psychological operations capabilities, ecological security, effectively networking with civil organisations operating in tandem in this sphere. Prevention of activities of forces that seek to undermine security and stability of the nation in myriad spheres will remain the prime task of military forces, for the nation will continue to depend on them for their integrity, discipline, courage, steadfastness in adversity and sense of sacrifice.

Peace Projection Capabilities

Peace and not power projection would be the order of the day in a modern globalised world. For, even the semantics of power play have undergone a transformation. While terms such as preemptive strikes may be congruous for neo-conservatives in the United States, for sub-regional power players, peace projection will be more appropriate. This will have both hard and soft power projection components. In the hard component, the ability to rapidly deploy conflict control forces in periods of short windows of opportunity to simultaneously deploy troops and equipment, needs to be acquired. Stability and support operations to respond to destabilising events in failed or rogue states without effective governance and order, would be another capability essential for hard power projection. Soft power projection will be another important facet of extension operations in the future. This implies rapid deployment of forces for humanitarian aid in the conflict zones, through a nuanced diplomatic approach requiring great sophistication in higher political and military leadership. Such a strategy would perhaps have eased deployment of our forces in non-conflict zones in Iraq in 2003, despite lack of UN sanctions, purely on humanitarian grounds. Such forces could have an engineer and medical core, supported by infantry units for close protection, communications and logistics support staff. Such forces can also be employed for building infrastructure in, say, Kazakhstan, Tajikistan and Uzbekistan, which have immense potential for such opportunities while fulfilling our larger aspirations of a strong presence in economically vital areas providing energy security. Increased military-to-military interaction through joint seminars, sharing of training facilities and exercises can be conducted, in conventional as well as counter-terrorist operations with countries of the Middle East and Southeast Asia, such as Egypt, Oman, Singapore, Malaysia, Thailand and Laos. Some of the critical peace projection capabilities which can be identified, both under UN aegis and with like minded nations, are as follows:

- Be able to project military power of up to two to three divisions equivalent, to the Middle East and Southeast Asian states.

- Be able to project up to two to three brigade sized forces to other parts of the globe, including Africa.
- Be able to have capabilities for inter-operability with like-minded forces, particularly the USA and EU nations that are presently operating on the cutting edge of modernisation of weapons, equipment and concepts. This will also entail abilities to conduct political and civil affairs, rebuilding civil society institutions and media management.
- Intelligence sharing agreements, both military and particularly terrorist related, with a vast network of nations in virtually all continents, but particularly the USA, Russia, China, EU nations, and Middle East, Central Asian, South Asian and Southeast Asian states, on a regular basis.
- Similarly, defence and military cooperation agreements with the USA, Russia, China, EU nations, and like-minded nations in the Middle East, Central Asian, South Asian and Southeast Asian states.
- Disaster relief forces ready for instant deployment across the globe. This is a major weakness, which needs correction. For, this can build long lasting strategic as well as people to people relations. For instance, immediate aid to Iran during the recent earthquake at Bam would have enabled us to build new relationships with that strategic state in the Middle East, as against moving in assistance along with other nations later.

Thus, peace projection capabilities will have to be multifarious, to include conflict termination, peace-making and nation-building, with the various facets therein such as creation of a security cordon sanitaire, repair infrastructure, building political institutions, restarting economic activity, nurturing civic and political groups and, even in extreme cases, holding elections. The Indian Army had demonstrated such a capability in Sri Lanka in the 1980s; however, management of the political spectrum proved to be a challenge. Such a capability, thus, envisages conflict termination, peace-making and even nation-building.

Lateral Capabilities Building

Intelligence and Information Warfare Capabilities

The army will have to provide the core for intelligence as well as information warfare capabilities in all spheres of security. Human and electronic intelligence capabilities will have to be supplemented by knowledge base building. Regional experts, language specialists, ethical hackers, financial analysts will be shoulder to shoulder with traditional intelligence sleuths. They will have to track such elusive organisations as Brigade 313, an offshoot of the Al Qaeda in Pakistan, to Maoist networks in Nepal and Central India. These will also include nuclear surveillance of the adversary's capabilities and early information of its proliferation, such as how much nuclear material is being produced and productively used within the nuclear establishments of the target nations, say Pakistan and China, how much is likely to be transferred or sold to other nations, how many nukes are available to the Al Qaeda type of organisations, and so on. Maintaining a data base of nuclear scientists and tracking their movements, surveillance of firms at home and particularly abroad which manufacture equipment can have dual use in the making of nuclear weapons, along with surveillance of terrorist groups such as extreme religious fundamentalists and millenarian movements which are most susceptible to use of WMD terror will also be essential. The rigour required can be provided only by the military intelligence community and, thus, this recommendation.

The army will have to remain at the cutting edge of the information warfare capabilities of the armed forces, since a large portion of information warfare capabilities are ground based. The army has a major role to play in the diverse fields of information warfare, be it strategic perception management, strategic systems security, information operations and information security. In the tactical sphere, the information dominance capability will enable our forces to conduct not only decapitating strikes but also precision operations at unprecedented speed, minimising casualties. There is ample scope for improvisation in the field of information operations, as was demonstrated by the Americans who organised a Blue Force tracking system, comprising a dashboard mounted laptop computer, plus roof mounted transponder/receiver capable of receiving signals from satellites, enabling Blue Force tracking for the speeding forces in Iraq in 2003.[11] In the strategic systems sphere, the army will also have to provide the nation foolproof security over the large strategic network of computer systems controlling banking, electricity and power distribution, dams, water supplies, and so on, from potential rivals as well as cyber terrorists. For, the integrity of these vital systems cannot be left to hybrid civil organisations – it has to be assured by militarised security. In the perception management sphere, the expertise has to be to convert images of war into a war of images to own advantage, and effectively generate factoids. Employing the media, both electronic and print as an agent for spreading information within the organisation also needs consideration, for the tentacles of the modern media are far reaching and internal information dissemination cannot match its flexibility and reach. All this requires a total review of our information management organisations as existing today, though the key appears to be delegation and decentralisation of information dissemination, rather than centralised control as existing today. The hierarchy may have to accept loss of temporary credibility to the larger good of rapid passage of relevant information, down to the grassroots level. Development of full spectrum information warfare capabilities will also provide the armed forces ascendancy in conventional warfare, deterrence and dissuasion capability against both Pakistan and China, through a high level of strategic control over the information spectrum, in depth of space as well as time.

Rapid Technology Integration Capability

Technology directions of the future point towards acquisition of state of the art, C^4I^2 capabilities, short take-off and landing platforms, such as helicopters, for high altitude warfare and precision ammunition. Non-lethal weapon capabilities would also be a key operational technology projection for the morrow. This is more than evident through the increase in the budget of the United States Joint Non-Lethal Weapons Directorate from $ 24 million in 2003 to $ 44 million for 2004. Non-lethal weapons are effective not only in counter-terrorism operations, as was demonstrated during the break up of the siege by Chechen rebels on the Moscow theatre but also have great utility in conventional operations, which needs to be fully exploited.

In the recent Combined Commanders Conference, the Prime Minister, Shri A. B. Vajpayee, emphasised the need for smooth two-way flow between technology and strategy. The challenge is to accelerate the process of weapons assimilation between the time these are displayed on Raj Path to their deployment in our operational areas. The budgetary constraints felt so far by the armed forces for procurement and acquisitions will be partially overcome with the constitution of a holding fund, with roll over provision for unspent funds on capital account every year and an envisaged spending of $ 100 billion on the armed forces over the next 15 to 20 years. However, our abilities to effectively utilise these funds has been far from satisfactory. With over Rs 60,000 crore per year, over a period of five years amounting to Rs 300,000 crore, expected to be available to the armed forces, this proficiency needs to be acquired. Technology assimilation, thus, will remain a serious challenge. The multi-tiered weapons and technology integration structure with a crisscross bottom up-top-down approach, with excessive virtualisation, has resulted in excessive delays and time over-runs in availability of state of the art weapons and equipment to the Services. The problem is a complex one, of education and awareness, of approach and attitude, and of fast technological obsolescence in the dynamic modern research and development environment. It is, thus, felt necessary to focus on this essential issue by addressing it as a capability-building norm. Over the next few years, a concerted effort to rapidly acquire, and integrate modern and relevant technologies into our army through processes, structures, organisations, training and human resource interventions, is essential. Our aim should be to reduce the cycle time of processes in technology adaptation and improvement of the supply chain. Our abilities for technology adaptation would have to spread from acquiring knowledge of indigenous as well as globally available military technologies. To this extent, the interface between the DRDO and the army has to be very intimate and fully integrated. A smooth user, developer and research scientist exchange will have to be established. How this can be carried out needs a separate study and analysis. However, the aim was to focus attention on this essential facet of our defence strategic anomaly.

HRD and Training Capabilities

In HRD, the need is to create a learning organisation partaking experiential inputs from diverse fields, and overcome the intellectual ferment and stasis that permeates traditional hierarchical organisations. Implementation of modern management practices such as six sigma, quality circles and adoption of standards in specifications is the need of the hour. A deliberate adoption of information age processes at all levels is also essential. The pressures on leadership and the common soldiery, of operating in an intense RMA based operational environment of the future, can be judged by the spate of non-combat casualties suffered by the US forces in Iraq. From March 2003 to January 21, 2004, 496 US troops were killed, of whom 343 were killed in combat and 153 in non-hostile incidents; 21 US troops committed suicide, making it a staggering 14 per cent of self-inflicted deaths. This is an unusually large number for an army which prides itself on professionalism and signifies the pressures of modern warfare. A review of our human resources development practices is, thus, called for. Bureaucratic hierarchy, procedures and attitudes will have to be replaced by networked functioning capabilities, data based decision-making, decentralisation and exploitation of information networks to impart speed and precision in operations and administrative functioning of the army. Presently, there is a noticeable attitudinal as well as awareness divide at two levels in the army: the senior vis-à-vis the middle management and officer, and other ranks. At the former level, there is a disconnect in appreciation of the larger issues and their achievement, as envisaged by the senior hierarchy and a relatively slower bureaucratic approach at the middle hierarchical levels, relying on tradition. The knowledge and information disconnect between the officer and the other ranks is even worse and is not to be mistaken for poor officer-men relationship, which continues to be excellent. What is of concern is that despite matriculation being the minimum qualification, the standard of education in the country is so poor and acquiring the qualification so easy, that the level of awareness of most recruits continues to be of sixth standard or so. There is also a need to review the very structure of our armed forces to make these more attractive as a profession for the modern youth who are dissatisfied by the way we function, rather than the challenges we face. Thus, there is a need for a total review of our human resources development practices, from the manner in which we recruit, train and educate our soldiers and officers alike, to align these with modern military management techniques, for functioning in the information age. Similarly, the multiple capabilities required in soldiers to operate in the "Three Block" environment and peace projection operations envisaged in the paper, will require our soldiers to be much more than combatants, be global citizens, able to interact with civil society and bureaucracy in diverse countries and situations across the world.

Leadership capabilities for the future will have to include dynamic creativity to lead transformation, burying forever the debate of whether the armed forces require a leader or a manager, for modern militaries need kaleidoscopic, situation based traits in their leaders and/or managers. Ability to manage the political leadership and bureaucracy will also be one of the key capabilities needed in the military managers of tomorrow. The precedence debate has to be buried to grant equality of status based on functional requirements rather than orders drawn purely for ceremonial occasions but carried too far to govern decisions affecting development of in-service competencies in the long-term.

We also need to move from the sequential process of visualisation of concepts to experiment based actualisation of indigenous doctrines for war-fighting in the subcontinental environment. For operational concept development, experimental training as envisaged in the US Training and Doctrine (TRADOC) model, with battle labs testing concepts in live situations, needs to be implemented and the Army Training Command (ARTRAC) mandate modified, if need be. Concepts in training should also include cyclical readiness, through modular plug and play of units, thereby making available a slew of operational ready units while others carry out training. Exploiting the Internet as an open source training facility needs to be considered and can be adopted even with immediate effect, till other concepts fructify. All these facets of human resources development will enable us to operate effectively in a modern battlefield and peace-keeping environment in a globalised world.

Coalition Operations Capability

In a uni-multipolar world, coalition warfare will be the norm, rather than the exception, even in peace-keeping and stabilisation operations. This was demonstrated recently in Afghanistan, Iraq, and some time back, in Kosovo. The unipolar power, the United States, has been looking for militarily competent allies to assist its forces in underdeveloped states, such as Afghanistan and Iraq. Herein, its experience with its European allies in Kosovo had been poor and these forces were also unable to deploy in Afghanistan and were seen as militarily incompetent in Iraq.[12] Indian forces, with extensive operational experience, could well form the hub of such a coalition force with the United States, after political sensitivities have been ironed out. The recent operations launched by the Royal Bhutan Army to drive out ULFA insurgents from its territory comprise a significant example of successful conduct of coalition operations by a small yet motivated force. The bane of operating from a standard superiority-inferiority dyad needs to be avoided at all costs. The army must have the underlying capability to exploit political decisions arrived at for this purpose and should be able to support the same by immediate acceptance of these fleeting opportunities which will not only contribute to our military experience but also our national status.

Conclusion

India's goal is not to be a superpower, but a developed nation in all spheres by 2020. The Indian armed forces are on the threshold of ultimate transformation, a change which is not only technological but also organisational, doctrinal, and human resources based. With vision, strategy, organisation and processes in place, incremental improvements and evolutionary practices will have to be undertaken to fulfill national aspirations, by providing the nation a shield for unfettered growth. The armed forces have to think beyond the country's frontiers and look to our interests abroad. We have to think beyond the likely casualties abroad to what will be in the human interest, by creating alliances of networks with like-minded nations. While within our national frontiers, our efforts should aim at enhancing the effectiveness of the security forces, for which coordination and not competition with internal security agencies would be the order of the day. •

NOTES

1. Gautam Adhikari, "Unipolar No More," *The Times of India* (Lucknow), September 16, 2003, p. 10.
2. G.Parthasarthy, "Riding the Waves," *The Indian Express* (New Delhi), September 22, 2003, p. 6.
3. Manoj Joshi, *The Times of India* (Lucknow), November 15, 2003, p5.
4. Robert F. Hahn II and Bonnie Jezior, "Urban Warfare and the Urban War Fighter of 2025," *Parameters*, Summer 1999, p. 75.
5. Robert J. Bunker, "Non-State Threats and Future Wars," *Battlespace* (London:Frank Cass, 2003), pp. 97-98.
6. Interview by Mr. Jaswant Singh to *The Hindu*, November 29,1999. (Downloaded from Arms Control Today site.)
7. "The War on Terror." *Foreign Affairs* (New York), 2002. p. X.
8. "US Leaders Discuss Warfare Trends," *Defence News* Report, September 29, 2003. p.4.
9. Hahn II, n. 4.
10. Qiao Liang and Wang Xiangsui, *Unrestricted Warfare* (Beijing: PLA Literature and Arts Publishing House, February 1999). Downloaded from the Internet. Infowar.com. pp. 5-6.
11. Daniel Goure, "Battlefield Knowledge," *Defense News*, January 5, 2004, p.21.
12. *Defence News* Report, n.8.

VIEWS OF DISCUSSANT

Dr Brahma Chellaney

At first sight, a discussion on national aspirations and desired capabilities may seem like a distraction from the main theme of this seminar, but in reality it is essential for us to be clear on what India's national aspirations are and what they ought to be. Because it is very important to have the basics right and clear. We had four rich but varied presentations on this subject and each speaker had his own view on what India's aspirations ought to be. I think it is important to ask some questions. First, does India have a role in international affairs, commensurate with its size? After all, we are one-sixth of the human population. Do we have a say in international affairs, anywhere close to the size of this country, or do we have an important say, forget about the size? Are we an important player in international affairs? If we are not, why are we not? National aspirations are important, because ours is not a small country. This is an ancient, rich civilisation, with a unique history, a history that involves long periods of subjugation, of being repeatedly invaded by land and by sea, leading to exploitation of its people. And yet, I do not think we are clear even on the basics. On what our national aspirations ought to be. National aspirations are never static; they are evolving. They evolve with time, but a country, like a company, that doesn't have clear goals, would not go very far. National aspirations in my view are linked with four key elements. One, the strength of institutional processes of policy-making; two, a forward looking leadership; three, national ambition; and fourth, a sense of proportion in terms of priorities. If a country is too fixated on one issue or one threat or one neighbour, that can distort its own aspirations, its own strategy and its own outlook. I think that again the analogy with the corporate world is important. Reference was made to the aspirations of the people. I think that it is good to know what the people want, but in every democracy, aspirations are defined by the governing elites, and once defined, they become the aspirations of a whole society. But a society that doesn't have aspirations is not a good thing at all. Aspirations are linked with ambitions. It's like a game. My analogy is again with the corporate world. A corporate enterprise does well when it has clear goals and clear strategies. Its stock price will keep rising. Its productivity will rise. A nation state that doesn't have ambition, will certainly not have a clear set of aspirations.

So, I think that while we discuss capabilities, doctrines and other elements of the military structure, it is important to pay some attention to this. I am glad that we are spending some time on this important issue of what this country should aspire for, what it should seek to do. What role should it play in the larger world? I think that Brig Arun Sahgal pointed to the malaise within our system, and the malaise really is too much ad hocism. In fact, I was struck by his description of what passes as modernisation. He called it a product innovation or product improvement exercise, and that happens because we have not tried to define the fundamentals of our strategic environment. We have not tried to be clear about what constitutes our vital strategic interest and certainly we have not even tried to evolve a clear strategic vision. When you have these elements defined, then you know what kind of capabilities you should seek to pursue. But in the absence of a larger framework, you react to events, you react to moves by others and that, is something that we need to get out of, and have a longer-term perspective.

One of the speakers rightly spoke about development; in fact, Jasjit also began with poverty and growth, but a country that is wealthy but does not enjoy strategic autonomy – is that the path we want to follow or are we looking at an India that wants to be prosperous, wants to be secure and wants to maximise its decision- making autonomy? I think the key element is that while we need to grow rapidly in economic terms, in both technological terms and in our priorities, of late we seen to be getting it right, we need to be right. In that sense, economic modernisation is becoming the main focus of the government. We should not forget that economic modernisation has to be placed in a larger context. Our forces ought to have a technological edge to counter and defeat aggression of any kind. We often hear that despite the acknowledgement that a technological edge is necessary for our forces, our forces do not have that edge, even against immediate threats. The question is: who has failed, and what needs to be done to correct that situation? Or is this an alibi for lack of political will, because the two are linked: you can have any level of capability, but in the absence of the right leadership, of political will, that capability will lack credibility in the eyes of the enemy. So overall, it is not the issue of the level of defence spending; a higher defence spending does not mean a higher level of security. We all know that. We can keep sinking a lot of money into defence, but that may not buy us good defence, unless we get our act together, we have a clear set of priorities, a clear set of goals, To sum up, I think this is a country of very talented people. Fifty-seven years after Independence, however, I find that we are not clear on the essentials, the basics. It is not very clear even to those who seem to shape policy, what India's goals ought to be. I think it is important to debate, first, about what our vital strategic interests are. Have we defined our vital strategic interests clearly in any document? Two, we need to ask ourselves and debate this in a country of more than a billion people: what should be its aspirations? Aspirations in consonance with its heritage of a benign civilisation, that has been non-aggressive in nature, yet a civilisation that fell prey to foreign invasions. Therefore, it will be important for India to evolve a strategic vision that seeks to effectively defend peace. Unless India is able to defend peace, there is no way it can concentrate on economic modernisation, on social justice and on technological advancement. Thank you. •

INTERACTIVE SESSION

Lt Gen V.K. Nayyar

Right gentlemen, you have listened to a wide spectrum of aspirations, covering possibly all aspects of our national life. But I think if we keep our focus on restructuring of the army in 2020, you will find that all of them, in some manner or the other, have relevance. If there are any questions or any views on it, the house is open now.

Lt Gen K.K. Nanda

Mr. Chairman, there has been talk of poverty and there has been talk of lack of job opportunities, etc, but nobody has mentioned, surprisingly, anything about population control. If we do not control the population growth, we can develop economically, but will never have the means to catch up. So the focus must be on population control and the aim should be to attain zero per cent growth by 2020 or soon after. If that be so, quite a few things will fall into place automatically and you will have adequate amounts of money for your defence forces. In addition to that, I would like to make one more comment i.e. whatever our aspirations may be or whatever we may want to achieve, the mere fact that we are a soft state, will not let us proceed further. So our main aspiration should be to get out of the culture of being soft. From a soft-peddling nation, we must get onto a government which means business, has the grit to take hard decisions, and to pursue them. Thank you.

Brig P.K. Chakravorty

I would firstly, say, as Gen Nanda has correctly brought out, that I think all our problems can be solved by empowering our citizens. That empowerment comes through education. It is indeed surprising that where China today has a rate literacy of over 90 per cent, a country like Vietnam 95 per cent, all the ASEAN countries bordering around 97 per cent, we have a literacy rate of just over 60 per cent. Based on this, the next issue I come to is that you can get the best weapons but if the soldiers are not trained, and as the speakers brought out that the main stress in future will be on sensors and stand-off weapons, who would operate them? There are tremendous problems of technology embedded in this issue. The next point, which I think is extremely important, is that defence expenditure leads to spinoffs in other spheres. I do not think we should relate to the fact that we should only spend 2 per cent or 3 per cent of our GDP on defence. We have a very realistic threat. In 2020, we have to have dissuasive deterrence vis-à-vis China. If that be the case, whatever we need to meet the threat must be provided. Why are we today so focussed on this issue that we should only spend 3 per cent for the threat? Let us look at the USA: on each soldier, it spends $ 3,00,000 annually. Why are we so obsessed about this percentage issue when it comes to the army? There is no dearth of money for so many things, but when it comes to the security of the nation, as Prof Brahma Chellaney very correctly brought out, strategic vision can only come from an ambition – the ambition that we must prepare ourselves to cater for the Chinese threat. I would like to ask, why are we relating ourselves to such figures of 2 and 3 per cent? I do not think the people of India have laid down the figures. It is purely the governing elite who have come to this conclusion. Thank you.

Lt Gen S.K. Sharma

What matters is the people, whether they are in the government, in the public or in the armed forces. It is their development which is very vital, which should be done. Besides that, as Jasjit mentioned, the type of war we are expecting is an economic war, where proxy war is going to be the norm. So, you have to look at this aspect very carefully, as relations between people to people of India, Pakistan and China will become a very vital factor in future. Thank you.

Col (Dr) P.K. Vasudeva

There is a lack of accountability in the country, especially when we are talking about the armed forces. The MoD is not accountable for the large number of MiG crashes. The AJT has not been procured for the last so many years. We have no value for human life. Look at Israel. If one of its soldiers is targeted, Israel reacts immediately with punitive action.

Many people talk of human rights in Kashmir, in relation to the actions of the army. However, this is a state from where three lakh Kashmiri Pandits have been thrown out of their land, within their own country, no one talks of their rights. The National Human Rights Commission has instructed the armed forces to be exceedingly careful. If one person dies in custody or in operations, enquiries are held, people are taken to task, court-martialled and sent home. Why can't the politicians be accountable, why can't the bureaucrats be accountable for what they do? Why is the army held accountable even for their good deeds, which are called misdeeds?

Maj A.K. Punia

I would like to bring out one point regarding the man in uniform in 2020. Sir, by this, what I mean to say is that we may develop good relations or bad relations with the East or the West, or develop our technology in the fields of space and nuclear weaponry, but what about the selection of soldiers in 2020? We must see and study the changing psyche of our soldier, his expectations, his mental robustness, his home problems, and many linked issues. Let me tell you, sir, after all, it is the man behind the machine that counts, today, or in 2020, and beyond. The infantry will remain the queen of battle of 2020 and beyond. So we need to think in psychological terms and evolve a better selection procedure. The facilities for the army in 2020 need to be considered, so that the man behind the machine is mentally free, fit and full of knowledge, to use that machine of 2020, to protect India beyond 2020. I also want to bring out one more point: whatever is happening in India and in the army, I would like a proper psychological study to be carried out. Instead of ignoring incidents like that of a soldier running amuck, or a case of corruption, we have to go in for a psychological study. For example, in the Gulf War, the behaviour of the troops was studied, and remedial measures were taken by the US armed forces.

Brig Rajesh Singh

Sir, I wish to comment on the aspect of national aspirations as has been brought out, and to further reinforce it. Of the four countries in the world which have the necessary landmass and population, we are one of the four. So we have a legitimate right to be one of the four major powers of the world. Unlike China, which has been time and again articulating this view and imposing this particular aspect on the world community, we have not been doing it with particular conviction. Initially, Nehru had laid down this vision, but down the line, I think somewhere, it got lost. If we aspire to be one of the four major world powers, then obviously we have to have the capability of becoming one and then, automatically, you will find that things fall in line. For example, a glaring ambiguity I would like to point out is that we are the fourth largest country in the world, but we do not have a seat in the Security Council. On the other hand, China is a member of the Security Council. In the Fifties, China's military and economic capabilities were similar to those of India, so it is time for India to seek its place in the world order.

Lt Gen Vijay Oberoi

A number of speakers have brought out that the requirement for the future, for 2020, is that the army of the future will require a full spectrum capability so that it is capable of fighting in any type of war which may occur, from LICO to nuclear, and so on. How do we translate it into a force of 2020? Are we looking at the continuation of a manpower intensive army, which we have today, or are we looking at a technologically strong component in the army or all pervasive technology in the army? What type of downsizing or upsizing or rightsizing do we want? These are the questions to which we need answers. The second point is: are we looking for an incremental change or are we looking for something drastic in nature? These are the two questions which come to mind when we talk of capabilities, of what the army of 2020 should be.

Air Cmde Jasjit Singh

We have to, first of all, figure out that when we say the desired capabilities, are we mixing it with vision or a wish list? One has to be very careful in this, because even if you don't go in for a wish list, you go for whatever you think is pragmatic, the basis of the judgement itself has to be sufficiently rational, doable, as the Americans would say, feasible and relevant for 15-20 years from today. Anybody who looks at the question of capabilities, of 15-20 years ahead, including military capabilities, in a country that does not have the autonomy on military technology, even to a small extent, can see what problems we run into immediately. But if I may attempt an answer to you, sir, I think, this is at least my purpose in talking about military spending, not that merely military spending decides everything. It is one of the factors to make a judgement, to say what sort of resources will be available, because that will be a constraining factor. What sort of technology access will you have, given the fact that technology is not easily available? The old paradigm of your supplies coming from the former Soviet Union is no longer applicable. You may be very friendly with Russia, but the fact is and that is the point I was trying to tell Manoj earlier when he talked of 4 per cent, that for 30 years, we managed our defence in a reasonably successful way and had a certain set of capabilities post-Sixties, and there was no war, so whether the deterrence worked or didn't work was never proved. That was at an average of 3 per cent. The mere fact that the Soviet Union started to change under Gorbachev, affected the price structure which started to change; our costs of defence for the same capability must have now gone up at least 4 per cent, if not 6 per cent. You can keep complaining that the MiG-21 is not a good aeroplane. Its original cost was $ one million; its replacement cost for the lowest aircraft that we talked of is $ 23 million for a MiG-29. If you want to go West, which everybody wants, it is $ 65 million for the Mirage-2000. So, finally, somebody has to decide and that is the function of the leadership. This is the challenge you are faced with directly when you are dealing with the issue. That is the question Gen Oberoi has raised, and I think even if we do not manage to discuss it in this session or in today's seminar, this is the type of thinking that we should be doing. We may be right, we may be wrong. There may be no answer, we can palm off the blame to somebody else and say so and so is not accountable. Our accountability is to the men in uniform. Some of us have taken off the uniform, to be accountable to the nation, in terms of creating a capability within the resources available or then press for resources which are inescapable. What the trends indicate is that it is not going to be easy to get more resources financially. We are moving up on the technological side. So I think there is a balance that you have to choose, whichever capability you are looking at. It is too simplistic to say full spectrum capability, and that I think, in a way, was Gen Oberoi's second question. Many of us, I am sure Gen Oberoi himself in the past, and many others in the room, have battled with this idea: should the change be incremental or should it be drastic? Look at just one factor. I am of the belief, and I have argued that from 1987 onwards when Pakistan was not a nuclear weapon state: how do we fight and win against a country that has nuclear weapons? Can the old paradigm of 1971 be used? If you think it can be used, fine. You are the people dealing with it. I have reservations and, therefore, I have my questions to ask: what is the impact of this? Mere bravado, to say let us call

Pakistan's nuclear bluff is not enough, because, then, if I was to take the decision, would I risk New Delhi or Mumbai or any other city, just to call somebody's bluff? This is a game which can be horrendously destructive. It is not a question of simply saying that I can shoot down two aircraft and I will only lose this much. It is a different ball game all together. What has been impact of this so far? Seventeen years have gone by; have we thought of restructuring? Are we thinking of the overriding factors which are going to decide the nature of future war and capabilities? In my judgement, and I could be wrong, it is nuclear weapons. RMA is the solution, perhaps a part solution to this. Many other solutions exist. But what are the sort of capabilities we are thinking of to deal with what sort of war?

Brahma, I have slight differences with you. I do not think that we should rely only on the government elites to lay down the vision. I think it is also the responsibility and activity of the broad intelligentsia in and out of the government. There are a lot of people here who are in the government, in uniform, a lot who have served in the government and a lot who have not been in the government. The people in the streets do not make visions. I doubt if the political leaders and the governing elites have the time to make visions. It has to be done by people who have a part somewhere in the middle level, the media, the academia, the experts and that is where think-tanks become so crucial, because you are shaping and thinking the process. Of course, in an authoritarian state, it is much simpler. How did China get to that? When they decided on modernisation in 1980-82, a whole range of experts sat down and worked for two years to chart out a grand strategy for the next 20-30 years. Then they kept updating it. So their comprehensive national power is not something they just thought up the other day and came up with. It was part of a very substantive exercise; linked to that was recreation and regeneration of thinking, talking to hundreds of people on Sun Tzu and the *Art of War* and many other things. You do not see that here in this country, so we can blame the politicians, we can blame ourselves, we can blame the next generation too. But that is not enough, a broad-based strategic thinking process must start. I am so glad to be part of this exercise at the moment; this is what we are looking for. How do we build capabilities? It is going to take time and resources. And there are going to be conflicting demands from every quarter. It happens in a home, it happens in a family, it happens in a nation. How do you match the conflicting demands, that's the basic question. Thank you.

Dr Manoj Joshi

In continuation with this, if you look at 2020, I think all of us have a rough idea as to what kind of desired capabilities we need, such as space-borne sensors, long range precision strike platforms, and that kind of stuff. But I think if you work backwards from that you will realise that you simply cannot afford it because of the kind of manpower profile you have today or even the profile of individual Services today. For example, the air force. The other day, the air chief was speaking about a 60 squadron air force! I wondered who is going to authorise that. Earlier, the air force was based on the MiG-21 as the workhorse fighter. Jasjit has just given out the figure of how much it costs and, of course, the capabilities. Now if you are going to have much more capable aircraft replacing the MiG-21, you simply cannot have them in the same numbers. That is one thing. The second thing is, for example, if you look at the army, Gen Padmanabhan gave an interview two or three weeks ago on Operation Parakram, and he said that one of the problems was that holding formations could not do a cold start. Now the point is, if they cannot do a cold start, replace them. The army must, therefore, restructure. If the challenge of the future is that a formation must be able to do a cold start, then we must have that capability of doing a cold start, and frankly, I think, that is the way to go; the holding formation idea is way behind time. The way to look at it is a restructuring exercise. We know what the 2020 broad spectrum capabilities are. I certainly think that we ought to have a department of space and instead of going to the moon, they should be concentrating on enhancing military capabilities, which are pretty intense, because if you look at the kind of capabilities that are needed, a lot of joint effort is needed by all departments, including those which claim that they do not have any military role. If we work backwards, it is very clear that restructuring and drastic restructuring, is needed and that restructuring has to begin today, and for that, restructuring benchmarks have to be laid. Because, what Jasjit is saying, we already today have the GoM report; that is the first time in 55 years that politicians have actually sat down and conducted a certain exercise and that exercise has subsequently got Cabinet approval, meaning that it is government policy. Even if we can now set down benchmarks, in the coming years, the process of updating the GoM report and revising it, is something that ought to be undertaken and that should be the focus of our efforts. Thank you.

Brig Arun Sahgal

Sir, I disagree particularly on this issue of full spectrum capability. My view is that this issue of full spectrum capability has been the reason why our modernisation and our capability development have not been in consonance with our aims. Instead, what we should be looking at is the nature of the war, looking at the type of conflict and if we believe in our mind that it will be a J&K centric conflict, then for heaven's sake, let us get the core competence and the capability to take punitive actions against Pakistan in that area, and that should include effect-based operations; it should include long range activity; it should include air capability, it should include special forces. It should include the whole gamut of things. In the future, perhaps you cannot decide on going for a full-fledged war. It is going to be an incrementally increasing war. It will be a war in which you have to manage the ''escalation dynamics." If you have to manage the escalation dynamics of the war, you must ensure that you are always on the top of that escalation dynamics, that the control levers of the dynamics are with you. Therefore, I have recommended a strategy called "creeping escalation." What it essentially means is that if you have to take punitive action, there will be an action-reaction cycle, and the creeping escalation strategy is that the action-reaction cycle is always managed by you. I am not too sure whether the contours of our understanding of the capability we require are clearly understood. Today, everybody understands the names – the systems approach, the network centric warfare, and so on. What do they mean? Is it being implemented in our C^3I projects and the C^4I^2 projects? These are only names. There is nothing happening in terms of coordinated activity. For example, if an MI-17 acquires an all weather night sight, it picks up a large concentration of mechanised forces in an area, it has to pass the information all the way back to command headquarters, which filters down the channel from the air command down to the army channel. Where is the network centricity? We need capability that downloads information which is available. Just to give you an idea, the Blue Tracker Force, which the Americans used during the Iraq War, was not that successful. So it is not so simple. Even the Blue Tracker Force capability was only extended up to the brigade levels, they did not go beyond that. So when we are talking about our capabilities, my only submission is: look at operational conceptualisation or operationalisation of those capabilities. Let's not just talk about capabilities. And in terms of what you say about incremental or transformation, I personally feel we have done enough on incremental. If you get your ideas right in terms of our capability development model, and if you decide on core competence capability in a conflict spectrum, please go in for transformation, and the transformation also includes enhanced calibre improvement of officers and the troops. The Chinese model is based on this; China is not going in for full scale modernisation. The RMA concept is based on two concepts: one is a war against Taiwan; and the second is defeating American technological superiority. These are the two areas and they are working on them in an incremental fashion; the whole Chinese Army is not being modernised. They are nowhere near or close to modernisation. There is the School of People's War that continues to be dominant in the Chinese armed forces. Therefore, we have to be critical and focussed in planning our capability development.

Lt Gen K.S. Brar

Sir, when we talk of taking punitive action, are we prepared for nuclear retaliation from Pakistan? Are we prepared to absorb that first strike, regardless of the fact that in the second strike we are going to knock the hell out of them. But as Jasjit said, are we prepared to have Delhi and Bombay, etc attacked? You think the enemy will accept your punitive action and do nothing about it? I think we have to be little guarded when we talk of taking punitive action, knowing there is an irresponsible country as our neighbour and we may invite nuclear retaliation, because he would consider that you have crossed the threshold of his using the nuclear weapon. I think we have to build up our capabilities by all means. We must have our capabilities, as Gen Oberoi said, perhaps we must downsize our manpower and we must improve our technology and structure our armed forces in such a way that we deter our potential enemy from carrying out any adventurism against us. But I think we have to be very careful when we talk of taking punitive action and aggressive action against a nation, knowing that the nation is irresponsible and has a nuclear weapon. Thank you.

Brig Arun Sahgal

May I respond sir? There are two issues involved. Pakistan has very interestingly factored two issues in its nuclear doctrine thinking. One issue is cultivated and structural irrationality; it has produced that as a part and parcel of threshold determination tactics. It talks about structured irrationality in its nuclear thinking. It is talking of limited nuclear war in its strategic thinking. The point you are making is 100 per cent correct but we have done a number of scenario building exercises, whatever they are worth, and it is my personal perception, and it is a perception shared by a large number of people, at least those with whom we used to do the exercise, that the threshold issues are more overplayed than they are actually there physically. There is what we call cold rationality within the Pakistani strategic thinking, despite the fact that it might talk about irrationality.

Dr Brahma Chellaney

Sir, we can go back to Gen Oberoi's key question. The real issue is, how do we employ technology , doctrine and geography to our advantage? I think there is general agreement that we need to restructure our armed forces. It seems to mean that the vehicle of restructuring will be successful only after we restructure civil-military relations in this country. Keeping the military out of the policy-making loop has never been a good idea. Manoj referred to the GoM coming up with a report, approving it. The term of an entire government has ended without the recommendations actually being implemented. What happened to the much touted integration of the three Services with the Defence Ministry? Who is stopping this? And I think a country where the Services do not have a say in the affairs that affect the Services, will not be able to think long-term or carry out any kind of radical restructuring. The other thing that comes to my mind is that there is a very important deficiency in terms of our capabilities that we do not talk about, and we are very happy to go from one dependency to another dependency, as long as we are able to procure hardware. We do not ask ourselves, why does a country of a billion people, with 8 per cent plus annual growth rate, with fantastic industrial infrastructure, depend almost entirely on imports of high-tech military hardware? Why does this country not manufacture much of its hardware at home? What are the deficiencies that are to be overcome? Shouldn't there be a crash programme to reduce this dependency? For example, the way Israel in the last four-five years has emerged from nowhere, out of the sky literally, as a major supplier of military equipment to India; selling something like $ two billion worth of arms to India. This is a country whose population is only one-third the size of Delhi, and we are happy that now Israel is a major provider of arms. What's wrong with us? Why don't we make arms? When we talk long-term and when we talk of restructuring of the armed forces, of using technology to advantage, etc, how do we do all that unless we address this major drawback?

Col S.S. Rai

Sir, I want to make a point about the rate of absorption of technologies by the users. In the army, talk of C^3I and computers, etc had begun some 20 years ago.

As of now, the situation has not improved despite the introduction of a large amount of hardware. The computers are still being used for taking out reports and returns or making power point presentations. The strength of clerks has not gone down yet. In fact, you need not only clerks, you need computer operators along with them. So, the technologies that we are using today will form the basis of Army: 2020. Because this is the period it takes to absorb them. Perhaps due to the rise in the education level, this gap might reduce, but we have to factor this into our planning.

Brig Gurmeet Kanwal

Sir, to come back to the national aspirations, I think one of the major reasons for there being so much confusion and lack of clarity on the national aspiration front is that there never has been a debate on the subject. Nor is there a policy document, as is being amply brought out. Prime Minister Narasimha Rao had said in the Parliament over a decade ago that "lack of an official policy document does not mean the lack of policy." But we know what and where our policy is or has been so far. We all are aware of that. If one looks at the annual report of the Ministry of External Affairs (MEA) and the annual report of the MoD, put together side by side, sometimes, I wonder whether both these reports belong to the same country. There is so much difference in them. What I am suggesting is that there must be, possibly by legislation of the Parliament, a national security strategy and a national defence policy. My question to the panel is, how can this be brought about by the Services in general and by the strategic community in particular? Thank you.

Air Cmde Jasjit Singh

There are two problems here. One is you can have even a Parliament mandated national security strategy, but no willingness to implement it. I could give you dozens of examples where the law exists, but a Supreme Court ruling was required to make members of Parliament pay their electricity bills. I say it is wrong, but my saying so does not alter it at all. I think we also have to understand that in India it is not like, let's say the US, which does these things by law, so the president and the secretaries are obligated by law to put out an annual report. Even when we have to do this, one will not get very far on this because of the big question, and I know we faced that question five years ago when I was the convener of National Security Council (NSC) task force: why do we need an NSC? Can we identify the reasons why a Parliamentary democracy should not require an NSC? It has many other mechanisms, you can form many other ministerial groups, but why an NSC of this type? However, what was set up was not what we had recommended. It was totally different. What was, in fact, being criticised in the Parliament for the previous eight years was set up in 1990. So, this is part of the problem we are facing. An easy way to explain this would be that this is part of the developmental process. Development is not just a question of economic and the technological development, it is also the problem of our ability to govern ourselves in a variety of ways. Governance is complicated and, of course, in the process, there are other difficulties that keep coming up, whether it is corruption or anything else. This issue came up even at that time: is the problem institutional or cultural? Our conclusion at the task force was: both. And, therefore, what do we do about it? You can create an institution, you can mandate tomorrow that this or that should be done. I mentioned to you that the Finance Commission is a statutory body, but does the Finance Ministry listen to it? I am not talking about just defence planning, I am talking of actual allocation of resources, because politics comes in the way. Therefore, how do we, then, promote the strategic planning culture? At that time, the proposal, which is much easier to implement than setting up an NSC, was to create strategic planning divisions in at least six key ministries, including the MoD. I wouldn't say who all objected to that, but, of course, it was never set up. It has taken a long time and that is why I feel so happy that we have a think-tank, and we should use it in whatever way is possible, and not merely as a stick with which to keep on beating the past or the future, civil or military people. I think there are core issues to face. You and I were together at the IDSA; were we were able to draft out a national security strategy? You will find it is extremely difficult to do it. Then comes the question: will somebody listen to it and will somebody implement it? I think there are problems. We should move towards that in the future, but I would urge that there are so many more things that we have to achieve. The fundamental thing is better understanding of the issues, to find solutions for the future.

Lt Gen V.K. Nayyar

Right, gentlemen, after a very healthy discussion, I have only one thing to say. I think that after this discussion, two issues are very clear. The first one is that there is a definite need for restructuring. The second issue, which I think should be the focus of the fourth session is: which one of the core areas do we need to concentrate on, as far as technology is concerned? Taking into account the past experience, conventional amassing of troops and the threat of going to war is not going to fetch us any dividends. I wish everyone could read some of these papers, because there are some good thoughts in them. And I think one of the very interesting thoughts is, what will be the nature of escalation between us and Pakistan, how are we going to manage it, how is that window of opportunity going to be created and what sort of wherewithal will be required to make use of that opportunity? I think that is a start, but I am sure that in other areas, given the terrain configuration and the constraints, especially against China, what sort of scenario will build up? I am sure in the fourth session it will be deliberated upon.

I have only one thing to say as far as this business of how do we get the government to react is concerned. You will get the government reacting only to crises and nothing else, and to that extent, I think, you have to get a commitment or at least an assurance from the government on key issues, as to what their policies on these issues are. Otherwise, you will find, as everyone has, particularly Brahma has brought out, that you are totally out of the loop. I think it is only at critical timings, and I can give you a number of examples, that if you can foresee these critical timings and tell them in advance and ask for their views. Otherwise, it has always been a 'cold start', as far as we are concerned. I think, this is what the people in uniform will have to do and they have to themselves think ahead, visualise crisis situations and make the government commit themselves. Because, then you are going into a crisis by design, you are not going in by default. Thank you. •

Session III

Budgetary Aspects: Trends, Pragmatic Projections and Allocations and Revamping of Current Procurement and Other Procedures

Panel Chairman	:	Dr Mohan Guruswamy
Panel Discussant	:	Brig Gurmeet Kanwal (Retd)
Paper Presenters	:	Prof Badal Mukherji Col (Dr) P.K. Vasudeva (Retd)

PRELIMINARIES

Lt Gen Vijay Oberoi

Gentlemen, we will now start Session III. The subject of this session is "Budgetary Aspects: Trends, Pragmatic Projections and Allocations and Revamping of Current Procurement and other Procedures." I now request the chairman of the panel, Dr Mohan Guruswamy, the discussant, Brig Gurmeet Kanwal (Retd) and the two paper presenters, Col (Dr) P.K. Vasudeva(Retd) and Prof Badal Mukherji to please take their places on the dais. We had Dr Sanjaya Baru also on the panel, but he had to drop out at the last minute. So, we are going to have a little smaller panel, but I am sure they will make up by their expertise for the fewer numbers which they have on this panel. Over to the chairman, Dr Mohan Guruswamy.

Dr Mohan Guruswamy

Gen Sherman had said that war is hell; war is hell, but as many of you soldiers will testify, in peace getting the defence budget is hell, and what the generals, I suppose, in Army Headquarters and Air Headquarters do most of the time is fight for more appropriations. It's the same story the world over. I have been going through the literature on this and we have soldiers and generals fighting for more money, and politicians and bureaucrats saying you don't need so much money. Its the same old "guns and butter" discussion. We internalise this "guns and butter" argument. Actually, I think it is falacious logic, because it does not really apply. Governments waste enormous amounts of money, so if military expenditure is a waste, why not waste a little on the military also? Just to give you an idea, the total subsidy bill in India at this moment is over Rs 100,000 crore a year. The total wage bill of government employees of the Central and state governments is Rs 170,000 crore a year. That is not waste. So I don't see why military expenditure should be considered a waste. We keep advancing this "guns and butter" argument, because most of us have internalised this thing that war is bad, war is unthinkable. We don't like war and we have a tendency in this country to treat soldiers like Victorian children; they should be seen but not heard! Sometimes, with good reason, but you cannot ignore the realities either. The realty in India is that the total revenue collection of the Government of India is a little less than Rs 200,000 crore a year, the total budget is about Rs 400,000 crore a year, which means that the government each year borrows Rs 200,000 crore. The interest bill alone last year was Rs 120,000 crore. We are living like the old Maharajas, living it up after the sunset on borrowed money. Quite often, the appropriation on defence is stretched.

Today, I am happy to say that we have only two speakers. We have lots of room to manoeuvre and we have heavy armour on either side. Dr Badal Mukherji, director of the Delhi School of Economics to my left, Col Vasudeva, soldier scholar on my right, and they are going to have longer sessions, half an hour each, and then we will have a longer discussion. The Army Chief is also coming at 12.30 PM, so you know its time to be heard! We will start with Dr Mukherji.

THE THEORY AND PRACTICE OF DEFENCE BUDGETING

Prof Badal Mukherji

The Theory

I am very grateful to get this opportunity to meet, interact and share ideas with the top brass of the defence Services of this country, for this is something I rarely have the privilege to do. But, first of all, I must tell you that yesterday I came here straight from my class in the Delhi School of Economics, clad in a pair of trousers, a *kurta*, and slippers, and once inside the hall, I found that I was attracting a lot of attention for the wrong reasons. So, today (boots, trousers, tie and jacket), I hope, I get some attention for the right reasons.

But, let me remind you! Thomas Edison wrote, "All those years the scientists studied bats in dark rooms, they forgot that the bats were also examining them"!

However, I shall not start at the beginning of my paper because of something that Gen Oberoi said in his introductory remarks yesterday, which today makes me start with what my paper ends with. Gen Oberoi had said that there is need to think in terms of an "intellectual think-tank" such as the RAND Corporation in the USA. Gentlemen, if you are serious about it, then I shall request you to carefully examine the list of research papers and books that the RAND Corporation has financed. These include major contributions in probability theory, statistics, mathematics, linear and non-linear programming, and, as the heaviest user of mathematical programming, economics. The theory of linear programming was developed by George Dantzig, with the help of John von Neumann, to solve the assignment problem for the US Army. Indeed, the classic in the theory of infinite horizon efficient programmes of growth, by Dorfman, Samuelson and Solow , had nothing to do with defence research. It was funded by the RAND Corporation.

So, let me state the principle that the RAND Corporation has unflinchingly adhered to: knowledge is valuable for its own sake, and that the state has to support the search for knowledge, *irrespective of the proximate results*. This is the sole reason why the US is light years ahead of us in defence or any other research. They have invested very, very heavily in knowledge. I am not looking at any one of you in particular when I say, "Imagine that you are a dinosaur"; you have just woken up in this hall. You will see all the wrong things The lights, the seats, the power point, the sound system... You will not think of the knowledge industry that made all this possible. Which is why you are a museum piece and we are here in this conference!

Thus, the knowledge industry is at the heart of the modern defence systems and the state has to recognise and adjust to that fact. I remember a conversation I had with an erstwhile colleague and member of the Planning Commission, Babu Raj Krishna. He resigned after two years and I asked him, "Why?" I shall never forget his reply: "*Sarkar* is knowledge proof," he had said.

So, if you are thinking of the RAND Corporation, then you must have a research agenda that is comparable or better. You must be prepared to invest in knowledge, with no regard for the ultimate outcome, for only then will knowledge "pay".

Economists have always struggled trying to analyse defence expenditure. The security of a country is not a commodity; it is a service for sure, often the ultimate service, but it is difficult to imagine its being paid for individually, like one pays for the telephone service or the Internet. Security is enjoyed by the whole population and each one of us, in principle, enjoys the entire amount. In that sense, it is like the judiciary or clean air; one person's enjoyment cannot exclude someone else's. It is what we call a "public good", as opposed to a "private good", whose purchase provides the owner a legal right to use or consume it the way he or she pleases. Others can be excluded. Private goods can be priced, often using laws of demand and supply, but not public goods. One cannot assess the value of a public good by referring to how much people are willing to pay for it. A person buying a hundred rupee bus ticket to Agra is certainly not going to pay for the construction of the road from Delhi to Agra. However, the same person, paying a hundred rupees to go see the Taj might easily be willing to pay one thousand if his daughter was sick in Agra and the only transport available was an air-conditioned taxi.

This fundamental difference between 'public' and 'private' goods was first analysed by my teacher, Paul Samuelson, in two landmark papers in the 1950s.

But there are additional and subtler difficulties. First of all, pursuing the road example, the state can examine the cost of construction of the road length, make an assessment of the number of travellers and think of a 'reasonable' bus fare. But should that fare make the bus company a reasonable profit, who pays for the road? Observe that we are veering towards a user fee, a toll, that can be only enforced if the road has restricted access, limited entry, like the American turnpike. But what is the toll gate if it is not a means of exclusion? The turnpike is a private commodity, to those who are willing to pay for it.

Hence, comes the second problem. Defence expenditure cannot be evaluated like the toll road, because no citizen should be excluded. Nobody can be excluded. Everybody must be covered. Hence, the percentage of the government budget spent on defence must be determined by some other means!

But we are far from being out of the woods yet. In fact, we are getting in deeper. The noted jurist, Prof. Calabresi, of Yale University, U.S.A, was also a very senior consultant and adjudicator in automobile accident cases. In his famous book, *Tragic Choices*, he then commented on a life-time's work in a singular and striking bit of self-criticism, thus: "When you try to put an economic value to the damage done, say to a youngster, who is maimed for life in a car accident, you are trying to achieve the impossible." The arbiter, the judge, the society has to choose a number (so many rupees) but these are *tragic choices.*

I look upon the valuation of defence services in exactly the same light because Hanif died in Kargil without my knowledge, protecting me.

And, finally, even if a social contract is executed, taking all the national and international factors into account, churning out a NUMBER for the defence budget, a very serious logical problem still remains at the macro (national) level to which I now turn.

Why do we spend any money on defence at all? Why do we not spend nothing? The single, simple, compelling answer is that we have enemies who do. Let us analyse this answer, keeping in mind the fact that our "enemies" are likely to use exactly the same argument. I begin with a set of illustrative numbers. The story I am about to unfold is logically challenging.

Suppose there are two mutually antagonistic players (M and V) involved in a contest as follows. If they use strategies called (Friendly, Friendly) then they both earn (10, 10) – you can think of US$10 billion, if you want, for 10. If player M is Friendly and V is Hostile then the earnings are (0, 15). Likewise, if V is Friendly and M is Hostile. But if both are (Hostile, Hostile), neither has an advantage and both have spent large sums of money on "Hostility". They earn (.2, .2). What should they do?

The problem is best analysed with the following schematisation, now standard in Game Theory (Fig 1).

Fig 1

Player V

Player M

	F	H
F	10, 10	0, 15
H	15, 0	0.2, 0.2

Each player has two options (strategies): F and H. The bivariate matrix has two entries in each box (situation) indicating the payoffs to the two players in the situation concerned, the first entry being the pay-off to player M, the second that to player V.

Outcome (FF): Each has a very small defence budget, the money going to education (because I am writing this!). Social Welfare: 10 each.

Outcomes (F,H) or (H,F): Either case player playing F loses its sovereignty. It is taken over by the other country, gets zero, the rival is unequivocally better off.

Outcome (H,H): Both spend a lot of money on (nuclear?) deterrence, are back to where they would be if they were at (F,F) because nobody has any military advantage, and hence earn only (.2,.2).

Please note that (H,H) is the only logical outcome of this game. Whoever moves from (H,H) drops from (.2) to (0); and (F,F) is not an equilibrium outcome. Anyone who moves from F to H gains from 10 to 15. (H,H) is an example of a Nash equilibrium that John Nash identified and mathematically established in 1952, for which he got a Nobel Prize in 1997, and the particular game was due to Tucker in 1957 and is known as the Prisoner's Dilemma. The crunching point is that M and V have open to them an outcome better for both, which is (F,F) but by the inner logic of the problem must choose (H,H). The Nash equilibrium (H,H) is strictly worse for both the players than the social (international) optimum of (F,F)!. The beautiful mind of John Nash proved that a very ugly outcome is possible and destroyed Adam Smith's great theorem that individuals, chasing their own self-interest, would be guided by an invisible hand to a social optimum.

President Musharraf and Prime Minister Vajpayee might consider paying a little more attention to the power of logic than that of their respective dogmas.

But this is not the end of the problem. Economists worried if there is any way of getting out of this nasty outcome? Can these two idiots "learn", if they have to play this game many times? Let us examine this idea. Suppose they are told that they will have to play this 100 times. Can they look at the numbers and logically decide that they will move (F,F), say, 67 times? The answer, unfortunately is NO. Think of Round 100. There is no tomorrow, so they must move (H,H). But knowing this in the 99th round too, they must play (H,H), and so on. They will play (H,H) throughout!

The logical question then asked was, what if this is an infinitely repeated game? If M and V are told that they will confront each other forever? Notice that in the present context, a state must assume that it will last forever. I rest content,using a result proved by a student of mine, Prof. Dilip Abreu of Princeton University. If a Prisoners' Dilemma game is played an infinite number of times, then there is a "punishment strategy" that will sustain (F,F). I explain. In this situation, one player tells another, "I shall play F, as long as you do. But if after a few moves I find you deviated to H while I was in F so that I suffered, I shall immediately switch to H and stay there forever after." This threat sustains (F,F) forever. Why this obsession about (F,F)? Because it is socially optimal. Everybody is strictly better off than they are at (H,H). Why does the theorem work? Roughly because in infinite time the (discounted) cost of being selfish once (H,H) is greater than that of being cooperative (F,F).

Alas, neither M nor V bothered to ask John Nash.

I conclude with a telling quote from John Keegan, the greatest military historian of our time. In his BBC Reith Lectures of 1998 he writes, "Rational judgement underpins our attitudes to sickness and want. Man has equally rational reasons for mistrusting the power of reason to control human behaviour. While we recongnize that it is irrational to risk nuclear punishment in a world dominated by nuclear weapons, we recognise equally that we are a risk-taking species. In a sense we know ourselves too well to feel confident in the hope that man will behave any better in the future than he did in the past." There is something in us that makes a general war "some time, somewhere, inevitable." Keegan wrote this two and half years before September11!!

The Practice

So, let us take a defence budget as given. The percentage of Gross National Product

(GNP) spent has to be accepted as a politically given constraint that can only be relaxed under compelling verifiable circumstances. What percentage do we take?

I reproduce a table of defence expenditure in India from Air Cmde Jasjit Singh's "India's Defence Spending" (Institute for Defence Studies and Analyses (IDSA) 2000), acknowledging my regret that I did not have time to take written permis-

Table 1

India: Defence Expenditure Statistics

Year	Def Exp (bn. Rs.)	GDP Current Market Prices (bn. Rs.)	Population (mns)	Defence Forces' (1000s)	Central Govt. Exp (CGE)	DEI GDP (%)	DEI CGE (%)
1961-62	2.8954	171.77	455.0	490	14.765	1.69	19.61
1962-63	4.73,91	184.76	459.0	562	23.525	2.56	20.14
1963-64	8.1612	212.37	462.0	585	32.062	3.84	25.45
1964-65	8.0580	247.65	470.0	867	34.889	.25	23.10,
1965-66	8.8476	261.45	470.0	869	39.406	3.38	22.45
1966-67	9.0859	295.71	495.0	879	44.584	3.07	20.38
1967-68	9.6843	346.11	514.0	977	44.972	2.80	21.53
1968-69	10.3319	366.74	529.0	990	45.258	2.82	22.83
1969-70	11.0088	403.87	541.0	925	49.247	2.73	22.35
1970-71	11.9928	431.63	554.0	930	53.793	2.78	22.29
1971-72	15.2534	462.57	566.0	980	67.096	3.30	22.73
1972-73	16.5223	510.05	579.0	960	78.493	3.24	21.05
1973-74	16.8079	620.07	591.0	948	81.308	2.71	20.67
1974-75	21.1227	732.35	604.0	956	97.849	2.88	21.59
1975-76	24.7229	787.61	617.0	956	120.365	3.14	20.54
1976-77	25.6253	848.94	630.0	1,055	131.501	3.02	19.49
1977-78	26.3364	960.67	643.0	1,096	149.856	2.74	18.77
1978-79	28.6763	1,041.90	661.0	1,096	177.172	2.75	17.27
1979-80	33.5563	1:143.56	674.0	1,096	185.043	2.93	19.18
1980-81	38.6677	1,360.13	689.0	1,104	224.948	2.84	17.19
1981-82	46.5180	1,597.60	704.0	1,104	254.012	2.91	18.31
1982-83	54.0830	1,781.32	720.0	1,120	304.937	3.04	17.74
1983-84	63.0917	2,075.89	736.0	1,250	359.877	3.04	17.53
1984-85	66.6051	2,313.43	752.0	1,380	438.789	2.88	15.18
1985-86	79.8749	2,622.43	768.0	1,380	531.124	3.05	15M
1986-87	104.7746	2,929.49	784.0	1,380	640.231	3.58	16.37
1987-88	119.6749	3,332.01	800.0	1,380	703.046	3.59	17.02
1988-89	133.4102	3,957.82	812.0	1,360	814.023	3.37	16.39
1989-90	144.1617	4,568.21	825.0	1,260	950.494	3.17	15.17

1990-91	154.2648	5,355.34	843.0	1,200	1,040.729	2.88	14.70
1991-92	163.4704	6,167.99	858.0	1,200	1,127.307	2.65	14.50
1992-93	175,8179	7,059.18	877.0	1,150	1,259.269	2.49	13.96
1993-94	218.4473	8,769.52	892.0	1,150	1,457.880	2.49	14.98
1994-95	232.452	10,378.42	910.0	1,100	1,669.984.	2.24	13.92
1995-96	268:5629	12,179.63	934.2	1,100	1,852.328	2.21	14.50
1996-97	295.0508	14,098.49	950.6	1,145	2,112.596	2.09	13.97
1997-98	352.7799	15,635.52	973.9	1,145	2,320.680	2.26	15.20
1998-99	412:0000RE	17,668.14 E	981.0	1,100	2,819.120 RE	2.33	14.61
1999-00	456.940 BE	19,788.31 E	995.0	1,100	2,838.820 BE	2.31	116.10

Notes:

1 The revised GDP figures from 1993-94 to 1997-98 are in accordance with *The Economic Survey 1998-99*, Govt of India, 1999.

2. GDP for 1998-99 is estimated at 6 per cent annual real growth (CSO estimate, *The Economic Times*, July 1, 1999) and 7 per cent annual rate of inflation.

3. GDP for 1999-2000 is estimated at 7 per cent annual real growth (Planning Commission) and 5 per cent annual rate of inflation.

Sources: Defence Service Estimates, Govt. of India, for relevant years.
Economic Survey, Govt. of India, for relevant years.

sion from him. Since the sources cited are public documents, I feel that I shall be excused but if I publish this article, and then I shall surely take his approval.

I comment on the numbers, and on the problems of using them. Here is a list of the major problems that I face as an economist.

First, and foremost, how much of the expenses cited are due to contractual wages and salaries? Unlike the description of wages as "variable cost" in introductory economic theory, in all public sector appointments in our country, contractually settled wages and salaries are the fixed cost to which have to be added pensions and retirement benefits.

Incredibly valued friend and colleague Professor Suresh Tendulkar was a member of the last Pay Commission; his "note of dissent" is printed at the end of the report of the commission. He disapproved of the package being offered as it would be too high. But what was in fact given, was much more than what even the Central Government Employees' Union had asked for. The then PM, Mr. I. K. Gujral awarded a package far in excess, in the final meeting of the National Defence Council (NDC). That meeting will be celebrated by the fact that the then Finance Minister, Mr. Chidambaram did not attend it; he had to go to Chennai to meet the president of his party!

After the last Pay Commission awards, wages, salaries and pension benefits are bankrupting almost all state government budgets. A large standing army does just that to the defence budget; it chews up the defence department budget. Indeed, what varies enormously from year to year is capital expenditure. And

often they do not suffice. According to Air Marshal R. S. Bedi, (Retd) in the current financial year, the MoD will have an unspent sum of Rs.5,000 crore despite the $1.75 billion *Admiral Gorshkov* and $1.7 billion AJT purchases. (*Hindustan Times*, February, 19, 2004)

Air Marshal Bedi approves of the creation of a non-lapsable fund of Rs.25,000 crore for capital expenditure, as "this will free the defence procurement process from time constraints" but is that a good thing? Should we not rather have very severe time constraints on capital expenditures, alongside a serious audit of wages and salaries, and if a large percentage of Servicemen are sitting idle for a large percentage of their time of employment, then should we not work out a scheme of contract service with the state, keeping the option for recall in times of need?

Secondly, I worry about the coverage of the data. Thanks to the pressure of the Chinese, the Indo-Tibetan Border Police (ITBP) is a "police force" maintained by the Home Ministry. I am sure so is the Central Reserve Police Force (CRPF); I am not certain about the budgetary status of the Border Security Force (BSF), and the like. But, with the heightened threat of terrorism and suicide attacks, all the paramilitary forces are essentially defending the institutions of the country from invaders. Where are their costs being listed? Indeed, what is the extra cost being incurred by the police force to handle the threat of terrorist attacks, say, to the Parliament of the country?

The point I am trying to make is that the paramilitary forces are carrying out as much a task of defence of the country, in a terrorism infested world, as is the regular militia and the costing should reflect this, irrespective of what archaic government accounting practices reveal.

Thirdly, hardware. The land army, as well as the air force and navy, are locked into a specific set of suppliers for equipment and parts. The equipment is of various types and vintages, supplied by different agencies and some may have exceeded its life-time (MiG 21?). In each contract, the government is an "ignorant" principal facing a knowledgeable agent. How does the principal write the contract? There is no evidence in the literature that I have seen of the state being even remotely aware of this problem

Indeed, this has been a hectically researched area in the last decade or so; it is universally postulated that the principal offering the contract is the ignorant party, knows this, and hence, tries to write in clauses to safeguard against quality deterioration. This is the game of asymmetric information, for which Spence, Akerloff and Stiglitz got the Nobel Prize last year. How much of this holds true for *Admiral Gorshkov*? And who are the AJTs for? If they are meant to train pilots for the MiG 21s, then forget all caution. We have been had on a national scale.

To sum up, the defence budgets seem to be ad hoc. One needs first and foremost a clear perception of the needs of equipment. One needs to identify a set of alternative sources to buy from (if domestic production is either not possible or too expensive) – a package like this must balance the risk of being locked to one or a few sources, against the problem of having a heterogenous collection that makes the problem of spares and maintenance very complicated. Similarly, in terms of delivery lags, a heterogenous collection is better since the delay, if the equipment comes from a single source, might be unacceptably risky.

Thus, one has to solve a stochastic programming problem to find out the ideal basket in terms of variety and firepower. It is no accident that the theory of linear programming was worked out by Dantzig and Von Neumann to solve the US Defence Department's delivery problem during World War II. To this has to be supplemented by a manpower planning exercise that should try to work out the optimum mix of a standing army and reserves, of the standing army and paramilitary forces, and the regional distribution of each. This would also be in the nature of a programming problem. Unless these two exercises are worked out, no coherent and analytically justifiable defence budget can be constructed. •

BUDGETARY ASPECTS INCLUDING PAST TRENDS, FUTURE ALLOCATIONS AND PRAGMATIC PROJECTIONS TILL THE THIRTEENTH ARMY PLAN (2017-2020)

Col (Dr) P. K. Vasudeva (Retd)

Introduction

India is the only country in the world that has to protect its borders from high altitude areas in the north to the deep seas in the south, east and west. The Indian Army is the only army which has to carry out its operations in high altitudes, mountainous terrain, jungles, deserts as well as at sea. This means that Indian soldiers have to be expert in operating in all types of terrain, besides conducting anti-terrorist and counter-insurgency operations.

So far, there has not been any national defence and security policy formulated by the government. Even the Estimates Committee of the Parliament, in its 19th report on the MoD, regarding policy-making and system of higher direction, had deprecated the lack of strategic planning and thinking at the national level. The committee expressed deep concern at the absence of a national security doctrine, which would lead to strategic policy. It pointed out that directions and tasks must necessarily flow from a well-defined policy, or else the armed forces, guided by ad hocism, would flounder.

In view of the improvement of Indo-US military relations, the US government commissioned a study on "The Indian Strategic Thought" and entrusted it to the RAND Corporation, the prestigious American think-tank. George Tanham, after interviewing serving and retired senior and junior defence and civil officers, presented a thesis in a seminar held by the IDSA at Delhi in March 1994. Tanham came to the conclusion that India has no strategic tradition or culture. It is an inward looking country, and that tradition has been shaped by its geography, history, culture and civilisation. The Indian defence establishment does not look ahead and plan ahead. That country only reacts to threats as they arise, felt Tanham. It was brought out that the Chiefs of Staff and Services headquarters function outside the governmental set-up.

In 1990-91, the Committee of the Parliament and the MoD agreed to formulate a National Defence Policy. Unfortunately, that policy has still not been formulated, and no policy document is available so far. However, the Thirteenth Army Plan (2017-20) has given some useful inputs for the modernisation of the defence Services, with the allocation of an enhanced revolving fund.

Pursuant to the recommendations made by the GoM on Reforming the National Security System in February 2001, a separate, dedicated structure for defence procurement had been set up, known as the Procurement Board under the chairmanship of the secretary, MoD. It was expected to lead to better time cost management in the acquisition process, build up institutional memory, and help obtain better value for money. The new arrangement would ensure closer participation by the armed forces in the entire process of decision-making, leading to higher operational efficiency, better coordination and flow of information. That revised concept had been brought into effect for all activities, commencing financial year 2002-03. Its effectiveness is yet to be seen.

Streamlining Defence Planning

Taking the cue from recommendations made by the high-level GoM on reforming the national security system, the office of the Integrated Defence Staff (IDS) in the MoD was now busy improving the planning process.

The basic aim was to avoid the pitfalls ingrained in plans prepared in isolation by each of the three Services. On the 15-year Perspective Plan, the IDS had consolidated the inputs from the Services, keeping in view the GoM's recommendations of preparing a holistic and integrated defence perspective plan for 15 years. However, a plan of that time span would be speculative in nature, since it could not anticipate unforeseen developments that might necessitate massive re-prioritisation. A contemporary prototype would be that of the U.S. military and other armies of the developed countries.

The *leitmotif* of any budgeting process should be to plan and control expenditure; without any control being exercised, the entire process was undermined, making a mockery of the whole exercise. However, the Indian defence planning procedures continue to exist in an atmosphere of chaos, with the armed forces habitually submitting high projections of their requirements, yet huge sums of the funds earmarked for capital expenditure are left underutilised, and surrendered every year.

In 2001-02, more than Rs 7,700 crore was surrendered, while in 2000-01, the surrender was to the tune of almost Rs 9,000 crore. It should come as no surprise that the Standing Committee of Defence (2003), in a severe indictment of the entire process, declared the urgent need for reform, and recommended that the MoD formulate a long-term perspective plan – instead of the prevailing year-on-year basis system – so as to allow for the modernisation of the defence forces, and increased self-reliance. It also recommended that that long-term plan should indicate the funds requirement, so that a proper allocation of the scarce resources could be properly managed.

Currently, not only was the Tenth Defence Plan (2002-07) not finalised, but also, a rough indication of the financial commitment too was pending, despite the fact that the first two years of the plan are already over. The report blames the state of affairs on "slippage, slow progress of the work and non-finalisation of the deals and contractual commitments," though part of it is also due to the "Bofors Syndrome" and the more recent Tehelka expose, where fear of the stigma of corruption has paralysed the procurement process.

Seen in that light, the committee's recommendations of a multi-year Five-Year Defence Budgeting Plan deserves serious consideration, along with streamlining of the budgeting process. A look at some effective models existing in other countries would be of great help. Equally important was the case for an assured allocation of funds albeit after assessing the need for equipment requirement/upgradation, so as to ensure the full utilisation of the same.

Long-term defence planning for the procurement of arms and equipment is essential. Attempts at long-term planning have been handicapped due to the absence of adequate commitment of resources, even though it is common knowledge that projects of consequence, necessary to meet the undisputed needs of the armed forces, have very long gestation periods – the MBT, the LCA, Aircraft Carrier, AJT, and so on, are typical examples.

One is surprised at the manner in which the Five-Year Defence Plans have been, and continue to be, handled. There are cases on record when the Five-Year Defence Plan did not see the light of day during the Five-Year Plans. Such plans were as good as no plans.

As the Five-Year Defence Plans were not assured of any financial commitment, they were of no consequence. It is obvious that the deliberations of the Planning Commission, in relation to defence requirements, do not see the warranted considerations. Uncertainties of committed financial outlays are a mockery of planning and have been responsible for the ad hocism so evident in force planning and implementation.

Defence Budget

During the first 15 years of the Indian Independence, the country spent an average of 1.6 per cent of its GDP on defence. Parliamentary debates during that period suggested that our policy-makers deemed even that figure as too high, as it was felt that it was retarding socio-economic growth – a totally unwarranted posture, as global experience shows the reverse to be true. The 1962 Chinese invasion proved how wrong our policy was, as national honour had been compromised by not providing adequate resources in terms of budgetary support. National security policy-makers stood totally condemned and, unfortunately, so did the military leaders.

The Sino-Indian War of 1962 marked a watershed in relation to defence expenditure. As a result of that debacle, defence expenditure experienced a massive spurt, to register 3.8 per cent of the GDP.

The second time when the defence budget outlay was enhanced was after the Kargil operations in 1999. That shows that India was following a reactive rather than proactive policy, which was detrimental to national security. If further allocation in the defence budget is increased to 3 per cent of the GDP only after we fight another war, it would certainly be disastrous.

The details of Indian GDP growth and resource allocation of defence outlay are given in Table 1.

It is pertinent to note that progressively, the defence expenditure as a

Table 1

India's GDP Growth and Percentage of GDP Defence Expenditure

Year	GDP	Defence Expenditure (in crores)	DEI of GDP (%)	DEI of CGE (%)
1958-1959	3.49	0.275	2.3	23.50
1959-1960	3.50	0.283	2.2	21.75
1961-1962	5.37	0.289	1.6	19.61
1962-1963	5.17	0.473	2.5	2.14
1963-1964	3.50	0.816	3.8	25.45
1964-1965	2.40	0.805	2.2	23.10
1965-1966	2.78	0.884	3.3	22.45
1966-1967	3.28	0.908	3.7	20.38
1967-1968	2.80	0.968	2.8	21.53
1968-1969	2.91	1,033	2.8	22.83
1969-1970	2.53	1,100	2.7	22.35
1970-1971	2.48	1,199	2.7	22.29
1971-1972	2.56	1,525	3.3	22.73
1972-1973	2.53	1,652	3.2	21.05
1973-1974	2.52	1,680	2.7	20.67
1974-1975	2.78	2,112	2.8	21.59
1975-1976	3.86	2,472	3.1	20.54
1976-1977	3.91	2,562	3.2	19.49
1977-1978	3.73	2,633	2.7	18.77
1978-1979	3.69	2,867	2.7	17.27
1979-1980	3.86	3,355	2.9	19.18
1980-1981	6.10	3,866	2.8	17.19
1981-1982	6.15	4,651	2.9	18.31
1982-1983	6.20	5,408	3.4	17.74
1983-1984	6.10	6,309	3.4	17.53
1984-1985	6.13	6,660	2.8	15.18
1985-1986	6.11	7,987	3.5	15M
1986-1987	5.90	10,477	3.5	16.37
1987-1988	6.08	11,967	3.5	17.02
1988-1989	5.98	13,341	3.3	16.39
1989-1990	6.09	14,416	3.1	15.17
1990-1991	4.82	15,426	2.8	14.70
1991-1992	4.53	16,347	2.6	14.50
1992-1993	4.71	17,581	2.4	13.96
1993-1994	4.80	21,844	2.4	14.98
1994-1995	4.75	23,245	2.2	13.92
1995-1996	6.80	26,856	2.2	14.50

1996-1997	6.40	29,535	2.9	13.97
1997-1998	6.51	35,277	2.2	15.20
1998-1999	6.35	41,200	2.3	14.61
1999-2000	6.01	46,000	2.3	116.10
2000-2001	4.0	49,622	2.8	28.02
2001-2002	5.4	57,155	2.6	14.10
2002-2003	4.2	66,882	2.2	15.03
2003-2004	8.1 (e)	65,300	2.4	14.85
2004-2005	8.89 (e)	25,000*/66,000**	2.1	20.00

e- Expected, * - Non-lapsable, ** - Estimated

Sources: Economic Survey, Govt. of India, 2002-2003

proportion of CGE had been scaled down from around 29 per cent in 1955-59 to 14.13 per cent during 1995-96. It was only after the Kargil War that the defence expenditure was raised to 28.02 per cent, after losing more than 800 soldiers because of the lack of proper equipment, weapons and clothing.

No organisation, much less the armed forces, can function effectively and efficiently in the absence of well thought out long-term plans and strategies. Unfortunately, as things stand at the government level, we do not have an institutionalised structure which can evolve an integrated defence policy. That has not been possible because national security is erroneously deemed to be the preserve of the MoD. The Integrated Defence Planning and Staff, which has been created recently, is trying to do the job of strategic planning, but no results seem to have come forth.

Defence Budget 1998-99

After the Pokhran II nuclear explosion in May 1998, Prime Minister Atal Bihari Vajpayee had improved the national slogan of former Prime Minister Lal Bahadur Shastri, "*Jai Jawan, Jai Kissan*" to "*Jai Jawan, Jai Kissan and Jai Vigyan.*" But the increase of Rs 4,494 crore in the defence outlay, announced by Finance Minister Yashwant Sinha for 1998-99 marked a sharp decline in real terms. The "*Kissan*" and the "*Vigyan*" had been well looked after, but the "*Jawan*" seemed to have been neglected!

In the capital projects heads for the Bhabha Atomic Research Centre (BARC), the allocations had increased from Rs 58.20 crore in the 1998-99 revised estimates, to Rs 179.20 crore. BARC would cover the development of advanced plasma devices, and intense radiation source using these beams. A waste immobilisation plant was being set up at Trombay to process and solidify liquid wastes from the research reactors. Some undisclosed schemes were also to be pursued in the Ninth Plan programme.

The Department of Space also found some significant increase, which was likely to have a long-term impact on the country's future in mastering space. The plan capital outlay on the satellite system got an increase to an indicative Rs 60.49 crore. The plan outlay on space research got a whopping increase to Rs 325.39 crore. On the development side, the C-20 cryogenic stage development programme, for the future geo-synchronous launch vehicle (GSLV) got a more than

Table 2

Defence Expenditure Based on GDP Ratios of Various Countries

Country	GDP Ratio	Remarks
China	5.63%	Over Rs. 300 crore were spent on the maintenance and functioning of the MoD.
India	2.34%	
Israel	6.04%	
Pakistan	6.08%	
Thailand	6.00%	

double hike in allocation, but still a modest Rs 9 crore. There was an eight-fold increase for the second launch pad at Sriharikota, to Rs 83.25 crore, in order to cater for the requirement of the Polar satellite and GSLV. The G-Sat II & III satellites to be flown on GSLV development launches got a boost from Rs 1 crore to Rs 10 crore. And the second stage of the Indian remote sensing satellite programmes got an even greater boost of Rs 14 crore.

However, the Rs 45,694 crore defence outlay did not take into account even the prevailing inflation rate and the decline of the rupee against major international currencies or even the nominal increase in pay and allowances. It seemed that the defence forces were going to remain restricted to a slow march to the next millennium in modernisation. It might suffice to prevent slippage in modernisation and reequipment programmes, but would not contribute much to clearing the accumulated backlog on that front.

No major purchases were likely, going by the figures of capital outlay, which would be Rs 12,230 crore, an increase of Rs 2,043 crore over the revised estimate for 1998-99. The revenue expenditure being projected at Rs 33,464 crore, against the revised estimate of Rs 31,013 crore, an increase of Rs 2,451 crore. However, the modernisation programme could continue under the Indo-Russian deal, stretching up to 2010, largely under barter basis.

The budgetary statement on capital outlay pointed to an increase of Rs 500 crore for aircraft for the IAF, but that was not even sufficient for the payment of the SU-30 acquisition programme. There was no allocation for the long outstanding need of AJT for the training of air force pilots, who were to handle highly sophisticated aircraft, and to reduce accidents. An increase of Rs 17 crore for "heavy and medium vehicles" for the army suggested the finalising of the purchase of the Russian controversial T-90 S tanks. An increase of Rs 876 crore had been made for the army under the "other equipment" head. This might help the army for the purchase of 155 self-propelled guns, and night firing and detection devices for the infantry troops deployed along the borders, for ease of detection and destruction of infiltrators. The naval fleet would get Rs 2,431 crore in the capital outlay, an increase of Rs 171 crore from the previous year's provision of Rs 2,260 crore, which was not sufficient, as the navy was the most capital-intensive Service. The capital outlay for the ordinance factories had been drastically slashed from Rs 1,284 crore allocated the last year, to only Rs 892 crore, thereby meaning to encourage the private sector to participate in the manufacture of ordnance equipment and clothing.

According to a World Bank report, defence had claimed a higher share of spending in the developed and developing countries. Pakistan spent 6.8 per cent of the GDP on defence, China 5.63 per cent, Thailand 6 per cent, Israel 6.4 per cent and India merely 2.34 per cent GDP (Table 2). The World Bank appreciated the Indian defence outlay, hence, would be able to sanction more loans to India for the development projects.

That year's allocation of Rs 774 crore could be explained by large scale offloading of technology and products to the private sector. The outlay on defence research and development would work out to be Rs 2,780 crore, up by Rs 342 crore, which was only 6 per cent of the total outlay, when the Parliamentary Standing Committee had recommended that it be raised to 10 per cent. That needed serious consideration and revision as per the Parliament Standing Committee's recommendations.

Defence Budget 1999-2000: Inadequate for Modernisation of the Armed Forces

Referring to the Kargil issue, Gen V.P. Malik the then COAS said, "If we had satellite imagery and UAV surveillance platforms, despite human intelligence failure, we could have detected the Pakistan Army build-up and intrusion in those difficult terrain and climatic conditions much earlier." According to him, adequate night vision devices, laser-guided artillery, and weapon-locating radars could have reduced the total cost and duration of the war, as well as casualties. Gen Malik claimed that towards the end of the war, the IAF had safely and accurately used laser-guided weapons on Tiger Hill and a few other positions.

These views confirm that the deployment of a newly formed corps along the high altitude areas of Kargil during the winter months, like Siachen glacier, was unstrategic for three reasons. First, the landslides and the shifting of avalanches at Dras, the second coldest place in the world, next to Siberia, plummeting to minus 60 degree Celsius, would cause heavy casualties of deployed troops due to high altitude diseases like pulmonary odema and frostbites. Second, the aim of Pakistan, to tie down our forces and deplete our reserves, had been achieved. We played into the hands of the Pakistan grand strategy. Third, the expenditure on the maintenance of these troops was going to be around Rs 4 crore per month which could be saved by deploying high-tech equipment along the Kargil LoC for monitoring enemy movement and guns, as advocated by Dr. Kalam, as well as Gen Malik.

In order to cover up the immediate deficiencies in the arms, equipment and ammunition in the armed forces, the MoD had sought additional funds to meet defence hardware purchases planned for that year. That year the MoD had a Rs 46,000 crore budget, which experts feel was not sufficient to meet its weapons purchase plans. The government had contracted the construction of three warships to a Russian shipyard at a cost of Rs 2,500 crore and was negotiating the purchase of a couple of nuclear submarines worth Rs 15,000 crore. In addition, the MiG AJT planes and refurbishment of the *Admiral Gorshkov* aircraft carrier, which Russia had offered to gift to India, besides its upgradation, would cost another Rs 5,000 crore.

Of the total sanction in the 1999-2000 budget, barely Rs 15,000 crore was for defence hardware, with most of it already earmarked for ongoing purchases like that of the Sukhoi- 30 aircraft, for which a Rs 3,600 crore deal was concluded with Russia in 1996. The demand that year was for a lot more than Rs 15,000 crore, for if the nuclear submarine deal was clinched, it would mean Rs 2,000 crore spent on the advance alone.

The MoD had sought a 20 per cent hike in the budget allocation for the next fiscal year for replacement and management, and for fresh purchases of arms and ammunition following the Kargil conflict. That translated into an increase of around Rs 9,139 crore over that year's budget allocation of Rs 45,694 crore.

Arch-rivals India and Pakistan will spend around US$ 15 billion over the next ten years to maintain their arsenals. This is enough to feed and educate more than 37.5 million neglected children in South Asia, according to the Human Development in South Asia Report 1999. The Islamabad based Mahbubul Haq Human Development Centre had prepared that report. It says that India and Pakistan had increased defence outlays by 14 per cent and 8.5 per cent respectively after their tit-for-tat nuclear tests in 1998.

The Highest Outlay for Defence, 2000-01

In the steepest hike in defence allocation ever, Finance Minister Yashwant Sinha raised the allocation almost by Rs 13,000 crore to Rs 58,587 crore for the modernisation of the armed forces to meet the post-Kargil challenges. The defence budget for 2000-01 continued to be marginally below the prescriptive 3 per cent of the GDP, at about 2.8 per cent. For the last several years, the government had been spending 2.3 per cent of the GDP on defence, leading to the decline in real terms in defence expenditure.

A predictable steep rise in the pensions and payments towards war injury during the Kargil conflict, and a big increase in allocations for army "stores", made it necessary for the finance minister to increase allocation in the defence budget. The budget for 2000-01 saw the defence expenditure doubling from Rs 29,505 crore only five years earlier. The defence forces had been demanding such a hike keeping in view of the urgent need for state-of-art military hardware for the three Services and the electronic surveillance system. While in 1996-97, the budget allocation was Rs 29,505 crore, the subseqent years saw it increase to Rs 35,277 crore, Rs 41,200 crore, and Rs 45,694 crore in 1997-98, 1998-99, and 1999-2000, respectively.

According to the Kargil Review Committee headed by NSC Convener Mr. K. Subramanyam, a number of experts had suggested the need to enhance the defence outlay, as budgetary constraints had affected the process of modernisation and created a certain operational void. It said that among aspects of modernisation to which priority should be given was that of equipping the infantry with superior lightweight weapons, equipment, and clothing suited to the threats they face in the high altitudes. The defence needs further heightened after the Kargil conflict, which highlighted the gross inadequacies in the country's surveillance capability, particularly through satellite imagery. The committee recommended immediate acquisition of high altitude UAVs with night vision and thermal imaging capabilities. It also said that there was urgent need for communication interception equipment and satellite imagery capability of world standards.

The army, which suffered considerable losses during the May-July 1999 Kargil operations due to the paucity of advanced technology weapons, was allocated Rs 28,939.14 crore, more than Rs 5,000 crore over the previous year. The additional burden of deployment of troops in the high altitude Kargil sector would be met by Rs 1,800 crore allocation. The army would be able to acquire T-90 tanks, weapon locating radars, self-propelled guns and multi-barrel rocket launchers. It would also be acquiring UAVs and electronic warfare systems.

That year, a hefty allocation of Rs 11,012.20 crore over a budget estimate of Rs 7,893.28 crore for the previous year, for stores, suggested that a shortfall in ammunition reserves might be corrected that year. Capital allocations for the army also showed a big increase. For aircraft and aero-engines, the army had been allocated Rs 518 crore in that budget, while its budget for the previous year was Rs 189.86 crore. Similarly, heavy and medium vehicles to be purchased by the army had been allocated Rs 440.32 crore, which was roughly double the amount sanctioned to it in the last budget i.e Rs 281.72 crore. For other equipment, the army would get Rs 4,600 crore, while in the last budget it was Rs 2,763.91 crore.

Large allocations had also been made for air force stores. After the IAF lost two Mirages 2000 during the Kargil operations, and several MiG 21s to bird hits, the combat capability of the IAF had been severely affected. The IAF too was allocated an additional Rs 1,736.30 crore i.e. Rs 7,896.03 crore as compared to Rs 6,159.73 crore and a capital outlay of Rs 4,502 crore. The IAF has plans to acquire 60 AJT, Mirage 2000 fighters, midlife upgradation of some in its existing fleet of jets, and acquisition of other modern equipment.

A glaring lacuna in the budget was the low allocation to the Indian Navy, which was in a perilous state. Even if money had been sanctioned for the navy that year, the force would suffer a serious depletion of strength; from 134 ships , the number of ships in the navy would go down to 80 by 2007, because there had not been any perspective planning in the MoD. The money allocated for capital expenditure for the navy was disappointing. The Cinderella of the armed forces had been allocated Rs 1,610 crore for stores. Added to that, the capital allocation was about Rs 4,500 crore. That amounts to a little over Rs 6,000 crore. The 10th Finance Commission had recommended annual capital allocation alone of Rs 6,000 crore for the navy, considering the maritime threats to India's defence.

How the navy would fulfill its requirements was a big question mark. It hoped to go full steam ahead with new acquisitions like the *Admiral Gorshkov* aircraft carrier, the replacement of INS *Vikrant*, Tu-22 and Il-38 aircraft, the upgradation of Batch II of Project 15-A (Delhi class) and modernisation of the existing fleet and getting new electronic warfare equipment with that Rs 443.51 crore increase, apart from a Rs 682.50 crore increase in the capital outlay. It also needed nuclear submarines to counter the nuclear maritime threat from our adversaries.

The sharp increase in the defence outlay, to the extent of 28.2 per cent over the last year's budget estimates, had been widely commented upon both within and outside India. While criticism from abroad, especially from the USA and Pakistan, was understandable, the domestic criticism was a reflection of the failure of the government, the army and the intelligence agencies, particularly the MoD, in explaining the inescapability of that increase in expenditure.

Defence Budget Low Compared to GDP Ratio, 2001-02

The defence allocation in the union budget indicated that the government was satisfied with the security situation, and was happy with barely sustaining the post-Kargil modernisation of the armed forces. However, the modernisation still lagged far behind, because of bureaucratic hurdles and lack of integration and coordination between the armed forces and the MoD.

This budget was not actually a hike in allocation. It clearly reflected that a significant amount was unspent i.e. Rs 4,000 crore in the last fiscal year, because several defence contracts could not be clinched, which was quite alarming. Finance Minister Yashwant Sinha had made a nominal hike in the defence allocation by Rs 7,538.58 crore to Rs 62,000 crore for fiscal 2001-02. What was significant was that the revised estimates for 2000-01 turned out to be Rs 54,461.45 crore, marking an increase of a little over Rs 4,000 crore from the budget estimate of Rs 58,587 crore. Of that, Rs 4,000 crore or 75 per cent of the unspent amount was apportioned from the last year's outlay.

The overall increase of Rs 7,538.38 crore in the defence budget worked out to be 13.7 per cent as compared to the huge 28.2 per cent increase in the fiscal year 2000-01 due to the Kargil War. When adjusted against inflation, the increase worked out to only 8 per cent. That showed that the hike in the defence budget was marginalised, hovering at 2.6/2.7 per cent of the GDP, and represented a marginal increase of 0.02 per cent (repeat zero point zero two per cent) over the allocation in the previous fiscal.

Citing "drastic changes" in the international military situation, China announced plans to raise defence spending by 17.7 per cent that year, and to continue heavy construction spending to support economic growth. Chinese Finance Minister Xiang Huicheng said that a large share of the $ 17.07 billion military budget which the analysts felt represented only a portion of total defence spending, would go to higher salaries and improving weapons technology.

It is surprising that the defence experts, including the defence minister, have been time and again advocating for 3 per cent of the GDP for the defence budget, but it has remained around 2.5 per cent for the last two decades. The worst was that Rs 4,000 crore went unspent. That raises the need for a better defence management system in order to have better procedural arrangements for arms and equipment acquisitions.

The Indian Army, as usual, being the largest of the three Services, got the lion's share (56.28 per cent) of the defence budget with a 5.64 per cent hike from Rs 34,127.22 crore to Rs 35,895.96 crore. However, with the T-90 tank deal already clinched under controversies of its utility in Indian conditions, the army would not be able to purchase its long outstanding self-propelled gun, which was very much needed.

An analysis of Sinha's proposals reflected a greater focus on modernisation of the IAF and to some extent, of the army. The allocations for the navy would only maintain the status quo in terms of force levels. The defence outlay for the IAF had been hiked from Rs 11,300.92 crore in the current fiscal to Rs 15,172.72 crore, representing a 24.3 per cent jump. It meant that the purchase of the long outstanding AJT, mid-air refuellers, and air defence equipment might finally come through, especially with the frequent crashes, necessitating that the MiG 21 be phased out.

An indicator of the IAF's acquisition of the 66 AJTs was the steep raise (Rs 1,991.87 crore) in the capital outlay under the head "aircraft and aero-engines". The air force was negotiating purchases of AJTs with British Aerospace and of IL-78 M mid-air refuellers with Uzbekistan.

Defence Budget 2002-03

In view of the recommendations of the Standing Committee of Defence for the year 2003, India's defence spending in 2002-03 had been in synchronisation with the revised estimates approved by Parliament for the first time in recent years, signalling the fact that all equipment purchases planned for the defence forces had taken place. Actual expenditure on defence stood at Rs 66,125 crore, compared to the revised estimate of Rs 66,882 crore in 2002-03, according to government data compiled recently.

The original budget estimates were, however, significantly higher at Rs 76,611 crore. The figures include outlays on the capital and revenue accounts as well as pension payments. The capital expenditure on defence was projected at Rs 14,911 crore in the revised estimates, and actuals show these estimates as accurate. That was, however, nearly Rs 6,500 crore lower than the original budget estimate of Rs 21,410 crore.

The outlay on the revenue account was projected at Rs 41,088 crore in the revised estimates, as compared to the budget estimates of Rs 43,589 crore. The total non-plan expenditure on defence stood at Rs 56,000 crore in the revised estimates, as against the budget estimates of Rs 65,000 crore in 2002-03. The outgo on pensions was forecast at Rs 10,092 crore in the revised estimates, which was nearly Rs 600 crore, lower than the budget estimate.

The break-up showed that the allocations for the army, which also covered pay and allowances, were pruned to around Rs 29,619 crore in the revised estimates, compared to the budget estimate of Rs 30,690 crore. For the IAF, the outlay was revised downwards to Rs 7,419 crore as compared to the budget estimate of Rs 8,187 crore. Some marginal pruning was also done for the navy.

The army needed to purchase an additional 5,000 thermal imagers for the use of the RR – the specialised regiment for counter-insurgency operations in J&K. A light communication network was required for fast communications and quick action, which was the need of the hour for counter-insurgency operations.

Defence Budget 2003-04

For the last decade, the inadequacy/adequacy of the defence budget had been the subject of much debate and more controversies. The majority opinion had usually veered towards the need for a substantial hike in allocations, given the need to maintain a qualitative conventional weapon edge over our adversary, Pakistan, particularly after the formalisation of our nuclear capability so as to minimise the probability of a nuclear war, as threatened by Gen Pervez Musharraf from time to time.

In view of that, in India, due to political vacillation on key military hardware acquisition that weighed heavily on the armed forces, Finance Minister Jaswant Singh proposed a marginal increase in the defence budget. In his budget speech, Finance Minister Jaswant Singh said that shortage of funds would not be allowed to hit the modernisation of the armed forces. He also said the allocation could be raised if necessary for the purchase of armaments. While Singh might live up to his assurance, it was for the MoD to expedite the defence acquisition process by speeding up the decision-making process.

The defence budget for 2003-04 had not moved forward on account of the Rs 9,000 crore unutilised funds surrendered by the armed forces in the current fiscal. The proposed defence budget for the year 2003-04 was Rs 65,300 crore, Rs 300 crore more than the budget estimates of Rs 65,000 crore for 2001-02. Though a cap on the defence outlay would send positive signals to the international community, it would have a negative effect on the modernisation plans of the three Services.

The Services were supposed to return Rs 10,000 crore that fiscal. However, some last minute expenditure took up Rs 1,000 crore. The Rs 300 crore increase in the defence budget for 2003-04 was notional and did not cover military inflation of nearly 3-4 per cent more than the wholesale price index (WPI)-based inflation rate.

The budgetary proposals showed that the army got Rs 34,574.29 crore, as against Rs 34,509.32 crore for the last fiscal year. That translated into negligible increase in the outlay, even though the army needed at least a 15 per cent hike to maintain its existing equipment. The navy got Rs 11,744.68 crore, up from the last year's Rs 8,435.49 crore, signalling the much-needed modernisation of the naval fleet. The air force garnered more funds with Rs 15,410.45 crore, up from Rs

12,403.52 for the last year, indicating a decision on the AJT deal or that more Mirages could be on the cards.

The DRDO got a hike with Rs 3,647.6 crore, up from the last year's Rs 3,193.25 crore, and unlike in the past, was listed as a separate head in the budget.

The allocation for the year worked out to be nearly 2.4 per cent of the GDP, much lower than Pakistan's and China's defence spending at 4.6 per cent and 5.5 per cent respectively. India needed to spend at least 3 per cent of the GDP to keep its armed forces modernised and motivated against hostilities, especially counter-insurgency operations.

The record of the past two years did not provide sufficient confidence in our ability to spend the full budgeted amount. Actual expenditure for 2000-01 was Rs 49,622 crore (a whopping Rs 4,800 crore less than even the revised estimates) against the budgeted figures of Rs 58,587 crore, recording a spending level of 15 per cent less than the budgetary allocations. In the following year, 2001-02, we failed to spend Rs 5,323 crore, in spite of additional unforeseen expenditure on account of the poorly planned mobilisation of the troops. In that fiscal, as already stated, Rs 9,000 crore had been unspent and were included in the present budget proposals.

There was a need to induct a far more superior and substantial planning procedure within the procurement process. Instead of continuing the system of purchases dictated by short-term goals, there was an urgent need for a policy that would take into account the forces' needs in terms of medium and long-term objectives. It is in that context that a five years' perspective planning on the budgeting process becomes crucial instead of the prevailing year-on-year system, especially with regard to defence acquisitions. For example, the purchase of the AJT or *Admiral Gorshkov* aircraft carrier – involving future investments in related equipment, aircraft or a flotilla with the requisite fleet of defensive craft – cannot depend on an ad hoc budgeting system wherein a year of generous allocations is followed by a year of paucity.

It is high time that the prevailing system of arbitrariness is given a burial and a five years budgetary system is instituted. This would allow for effective planning and defence modernisation.

Non-Lapsable Defence Allocations: A Power to the Arsenal, 2004-05

In the defence budget (vote on account) for the year 2004-05, the government committed Rs. 25,000 crore for a non-lapsable defence modernisation fund, to cater to the procurement needs of the three armed forces. Paucity of funds would not come in the way of the defence establishments, modernisation and weapons acquisition plans. While hiking the country's defence outlay by Rs. 6,300 crore, the Vajpayee government had set up a non-lapsable fund. The move was expected to facilitate the purchase of Scorpene submarines and the Phalcon AWACS radar. Apart from the aircraft carrier *Admiral Gorshkov*, AJT Hawk 115Y, Embraer executive jets, thermal imagers and electronic warfare system had already been given the government's nod.

"The process of defence procurement often extends to over three years. Adequate and a committed availability of funds, over such a period, for defence modernisation and weapons systems acquisition need a satisfactory resolution. The fund would be made available to the MoD from the new financial year," Finance Minister, Jaswant Singh, said in his interim budget speech on February 4, 2004.

The move was to ensure that adequate funds were available to pay the installments for the purchase of the AJT for the IAF and the aircraft carrier *Admiral Gorshkov* for the navy. Both these deals were signed in the current fiscal, after years of delay. While the refurbished *Gorshkov*, along with its complement of two squadrons of MiG-29K fighter aircraft and Kamov helicopters, was likely to cost upwards of Rs. 7,200 crore, the 66 AJTs, to be purchased from British Aerospace, would come for about Rs. 8,000 crore.

The idea behind the fund was that it would not lapse annually but would be a permanent source that could be tapped by the MoD as and when the need arose. The MoD was often unable to utilise its entire allocation. It had to surrender substantial funds under the "Capital Expenditure" head. Concerned over the large amount of money allocated for the MoD going unspent every year, the government had finally agreed to establish a non-lapsable "defence modernisation fund" to enable the three wings of the armed forces to continue with their modernisation and upgradation drive without any hiccups.

The budgetary allocations for defence would be utilised through that fund, rather than surrendering crores of rupees unspent. Under the existing procedure, the Finance Ministry had not been able to accurately forecast expenditure or control the deficit accurately.

For instance, the last year's defence allocations were Rs. 65,300 crore, of which Rs. 500 crore had to be slashed in the revised estimates. That was more than 1 per cent of the total receipts for the year and around 4 per cent of the government's fiscal deficit. The other merit of the proposed fund was that it would result in the defence budget not increasing unduly. The allocation in the interim budget for 2004-05 was Rs. 66,000 crore, which was just Rs. 700 crore more than the last year's allocations.

Providing a large sum of Rs. 25,000 crore would have taken the defence budget to noticeable levels. At present, defence allocations were merely 2.1 per cent of the GDP. That was fully compatible with the nation's status as a peace loving, developing country, diverting more funds to agriculture, health, education, and so on.

India's neighbours, Pakistan and China, spend 4 and 6 per cent of their GDP respectively on defence. Adding Rs. 25,000 crore of the modernisation fund to the defence budget would have taken the defence allocations to almost 3.5 per cent of the GDP. It was not understood as to how the defence Services had been helped by that move. Firstly, the concept recognises that the system of annual budgetary allocations and mid-term review is not suitable for defence purchases. Modernisation of defence equipment is a long drawn out procedure. The requirements have to be quantified, circulated among possible vendors, the equipment has to be evaluated through comprehensive trials, and, finally, negotiations have to be conducted with the short-listed vendors, finalisation of suppliers, placing of orders, delivery of the equipment and payment to the supplier.

Under the best circumstances this can rarely be done during the budget period. Further delays occur because of the cautious attitudes of officials/decision-makers, following the various scams associated with defence purchases. The planned Defence Acquisition Council and the Defence Procurement Board are expected to help but only to a limited extent.

Secondly, developments in weapon technology have been rapid in the recent past. There is also greater appreciation among defence planners of the effect of technology on warfare. It is conceded that the side with the better equipment and the latest technology has better chances of winning a conflict rather than an army with older technology and devices.

Thirdly, India imports a large portion of its defence equipment. Defence deals involve large sums of money and it is natural to expect political pressures in these deals. The purchasers also have to assess whether the seller would maintain the supply of spares during the useful life of the equipment. All this further complicates the process of defence purchases and increases the time needed.

The demand for such a non-lapsable modernisation fund had been voiced for some time. It required the understanding of a former army major to give the idea concrete shape, and the problems of both the MoD and the Finance Ministry have been solved in one stroke.

Taking the cue from recommendations made by the high-level GoM on reforming the national security system, the office of the IDS in the MoD was required to improve the planning process.

In the past, growth of the Indian Army had been haphazard. As a reaction to contemporary crises, the declining budgetary support and archaic financial management procedures further aggravated the situation. Current financial allocations for defence are in the region of 2.1 per cent of the GDP. Most military organisations are sustained with a budget that varies between 3 and 4 per cent of the GDP. It had been analysed that a defence budget of over 4 per cent would have an adverse effect on the overall growth of the nation. On the other hand, sustained modernisation of the military was not possible with a defence budget of less than 3 per cent of the GDP.

The present non-lapsable fund of Rs 25,000 crore might still not be adequate as Rs. 7,000 crore have already been allocated for the purchase of the aircraft carrier *Gorshkov* from Russia and 66 AJTs for the IAF are yet to be procured. That would need another Rs. 2,000 crore. The requirement was for 15 years perspective planning and not ad hocism, as was the case projected in the budget.

Thirteenth Army Plan (2017-20)

The Thirteenth Army Plan (2017-20) is not a plan chalked out by the government. It is a plan given by the former COAS Gen S. Padmanabhan, during his tenure as army chief when the forces were mobilised on the borders for an offensive action against Pakistan. In his book, *Writing on the Wall: India Checkmates America 2017*, Gen S. Padmanabhan has given some utopian ideas which may not be palatable to most of the politicians as well as the defence personnel.

He has explained how Pakistan starts the war with India and in less than two days, its air force is nearly wiped out; its navy loses major ships with the ports of Karachi and Gwadar knocked out of action; the army succeeds in cutting Pakistan into two through Sind; and most of POK falls to India.

Alarmed, Pakistan's military ally, the US, fires seven Tomahawk cruise missiles from its carrier group, aimed at Hyderabad. These are intercepted and blunted by our National Missile Defence. We attack the US with powerful electromagnetic pulses (EMP) and computer viruses. Communications are completely snapped in Washington. In turn, the US attempts the same, but India is a step ahead.

The Writing on the Wall is about a 'rogue' state, a 'rogue' superpower, which would stop at nothing in the pursuit of her national interests. To India, that tendency of the US poses dangers to her hard-won Independence and her right to chart her own course to progress. The author believes that unless India acts now to deter the superpower from posing a threat to her national interests, it might not be possible for her to effectively resist the threat, when it matures – perhaps some time after 2008.

Apart from high agricultural output and major infrastructure projects like the National Highway Development Project and National Water Grid Project, India devotes large sums of money on the boosting of R&D generally and defence R&D specifically. A national missile shield is developed and the voids in both our order of battle and in terms of equipment are made up. As the book progresses, India achieves a higher degree of modernisation during the period 2003-17. By 2017, when India is forced to stand up to the US, she is almost evenly matched.

He further explains that the defence forces would get the highest priority for the allocation of funds for modernisation and also indigenisation. The latest weapons and equipment would be made available to the armed forces so that minimum casualties occur at the time of taking any offensive or defensive action. The non-lapsable funds, as have been created in the budget 2004-05, to the tune of more than Rs. 25,000 crore, would be available for the purchase of essential defence needs. That fund would not have to be surrendered being a non-lapsable fund, and it would be carried forward to the next year; and deficiency would be made up every year after the procurement of essential arms and equipment.

On the indigenisation front, the priority would be given to the domestic industries for the manufacture of weapons and equipment from within the country's resources. It has been established with the fast economic growth of the country that the country's firms and other enterprises are capable of manufacturing the most sophisticated weapons and defence equipment. Emphasis is on manufacturing 75 per cent of the defence needs from indigenous resources and only 25 per cent would be procured from foreign countries. However, it is yet to be seen if our industry will be able to meet the timely requirements of the defence forces and maintain the quality. So far, MiG-21 manufactured by Hindustan Aeronautics Limited (HAL) have proved to be defective and casualty ridden.

The process of procurement of arms and equipment in the MoD has already been streamlined. There will be no delay in the procurement of essential arms.

The process has already started and it will ensure that there will be no deficiency whatsoever in the defence forces. There will be no ad hocism and for any delay, the person concerned will be held accountable and taken to task.

Perspective planning for 15 years for the procurement of arms and ammunition would be carried out in advance and would be reviewed after every five years. That planning would be in line with other developed countries and it would be ensured that obsolete arms, ammunition and equipment are written off and the latest, modernised and sophisticated weapons are introduced into the Services from time to time.

Conclusion

Defence and development are complementary to each other. It would, thus, be in the fitness of the things to make some assertions about India 2020. In the next two decades, the border would be far better managed than at present. However, the boundary disputes are unlikely to get resolved. Peace and tranquillity is expected along the Sino-India border. China is expected to vigorously pursue its strategic game plan to keep India strictly confined to South Asia.

The economic reforms are in full flow; the Indian economy is expected to be the fourth largest in the world by 2020. By then, we would have also made our distinct mark in the field of frontier technologies – nuclear, space, missiles, information technology, latest weaponry, and so on. The sheer strength of India's numbers, their skills and expertise, their energy and enterprise would have propelled the country forward with adequate budgetary support.

Thus, notwithstanding the external and internal pressures, the year 2020 will see a far more confident India, an acknowledged nuclear power, and a permanent member of United Nations Security Council, deservingly having a greater say in the decision-making of world affairs.

If integrated finance in the MoD continues to be under the strict guidance and control of the Ministry of Finance, the defence projects (from the expenditure angle) will continue to malfunction on flimsy issues. The basic flaw in the system stems from the lack of accountability on the part of the Ministries of Defence and Finance. Consequently, the operational commander in the field becomes the scapegoat, who has to be content with the poor quality or deficiencies of spares, equipment and manpower. Someone has to take blame for such serious lapses, as also the large number of casualties during operations due to shortage of defence equipment and weapons.

In spite of good neighbourly relations and peace prevailing on the borders by 2020, India cannot lower its guard. It has to continuously keep its powder dry, including the nuclear deterrent, ready for the use as and when required. The budget allocation in the future years will have to be based on perspective 15 years planning, and the most efficient mode of procurement of arms and ammunitions has to be adopted.

As has been shown in the paper, most modern armies are sustained with a budget that varies between 3 to 6 per cent of the country's GDP. If India can allocate a defence budget to the tune of 3 per cent of the GDP, it will be able to meet requirements of both national development and military modernisation. Our capacity to spend enhanced allocations also needs to be upgraded by modernising our procurement procedures. •

REFERENCES

Ayesha Siddiqa-Agha, "Defence a Public Good? A Case Study of Pakistan's Military Expenditure, 1982-99," in P. R. Chari, Ayesha Siddiqa-Agha, *Defence Expenditure in South Asia, India and Pakistan*, RCCS Policy Studies 12 (Colombo: Regional Centre for Strategic Studies, 2000), p.23.

Economic Survey of India 2002-200.

George K. Tanham, *Indian Strategic Thought: An Interpretive Essay* (Santa Monica: RAND Corporation, 1993), p.28.

Jasjit Singh, "Trends in Defence Expenditure," in Jasjit Singh, ed., *Asian Strategic Review, 1988-99* (New Delhi: IDSA, 1999), p. 71.

Jaswant Singh, member of Parliament, *National Security: An Outline of Concerns* (New Delhi: Lancer Publications, 1996), p.58.

Mahbubul Haq Human Development in South Asia Report 1999.

O. P. Mehra, PVSM (Air Chief Marshal Retd.), "The Impact of Decreased Defence Spending on the Indian Armed Forces," *USI Journal*, January-March 1997, pp. 8 - 16.

Parveen Sawhney – Book Review – *Writing on the Wall: India Checkmates America 2017* by Gen (Retd.) S. Padmanabhan (New Delhi: Manas Publications, 2004).

Pervaiz Iqbal Cheema, "Defence Expenditure in Pakistan," in Pervaiz Iqbal Cheema and Jasjit Singh, *Defence Expenditure in South Asia*, RCCS Policy Studies 10 (Colombo: Regional Centre for Strategic Studies, 2000), p. 45.

Rahul Bedi, "India's Bizarre Arms Procurement Policy," *Economic and Political Weekly*, October 14, 2000, pp. 3716 - 3719.

Shalini Chawla, "Pakistan's Military Spending: Socio-Economic Dimensions," *Strategic Analysis*, Journal of Institute of Defence Studies and Analyses, Vol. XXV No. 5, August 2001, pp. 703-715.

Sidharth Mishra, *The Pioneer Sunday*.

V.K. Shrivastava, "Indian Army – 2020: A Vision Statement on Strategy and Capability," *Strategic Analysis*, Journal of Institute of Defence Studies and Analyses, Vol. XXV No. 6, September 2001, pp. 753- 763.

P.K. Vasudeva, "Defence Sans a Security Doctrine," *The Indian Express*, June 16, 1994 .

- "A Raw Deal For Defence Services," *The Indian Express*, March 25, 1994.
- "Join Army For What?," *The Tribune*, March 14, 1995.
- "More Teeth for Defence Services," *Sunday Observer*, February 6-12, 1994.
- "Non-Lapsable Defence Budget 2004-2005," *The Tribune*, March 6, 2004.

VIEWS OF DISCUSSANT

Brig Gurmeet Kanwal

Morning gentlemen. In the West, it is customary to begin with a joke ; in most of Asia, it is customary to begin with an apology! I will give you neither a joke, nor an apology, but I will give you the results of a survey which was carried out in Thailand. The question was very simple. Why do generals get up in the middle of the night? The survey revealed that 22 per cent get up to go to the toilet, 28 per cent get up for a glass of water, and 50 per cent get up to go home.

I am not going to really labour on the two presentations, both of which have been excellent. As far as Prof Badal Mukherji's presentation is concerned, the first part is the theoretical part, rather esoteric. You know, give a soldier a rifle, give him ammunition, give him food to eat, and he will fight. Teach him or try to teach him economics and there is a fair likelihood that he will run away from the battlefield, but with all the respect, sir, the second part was very interesting and some of the issues I will cover. I would like to begin my comments with a quote of Winston Churchill. I quote, "The armed forces are not like a limited liability company, to be reconstructed from time to time as the money fluctuates. They are not inanimate things, like a house to be pulled down or enlarged or structurally altered at the caprices of the tenant or owner. They are living things, if they are bullied, they sulk, if they are unhappy, they pine, if they are harried, they get feverish, if they are sufficiently disturbed, they will wither and dwindle and almost die, and when it comes to this last serious condition, it is only revived with lots of time and lots of money" (Churchill in the House of Commons 1923) unquote. I think Churchill's meaning is self-evident and I don't need to elaborate on what he said. Air Cmde Jasjit Singh has called the decade of the 1990s a decade of stagnation. Incidentally, most of the figures of the various budgets, which were used by the speakers today, come from an annual of the IDSA called the *Asian Strategic Review*, that has died unfortunately. IDSA is no longer publishing it. The first chapter in that used to be on the defence budget, not only of India but various Asian countries, comparisons, tabulations and a wealth of data was there, from year to year. I would like to recommend that CLAWS could perhaps do the same, at least for the army budget in the years to come, in the form of a monograph which can be brought out and updated regularly.

In this decade of stagnation of the 1990s, there was a massive decline of the defence expenditure, as a percentage of the GDP. From 3.17 per cent in 1989-90, it declined to 2.31 per cent in 1999-2000, just before the Kargil conflict. In this decade, every single finance minister, while presenting the budget, thumped the table in the Lok Sabha and said that the security of the nation will not be compromised and every single finance minister reduced the defence allocation in real terms i.e. "defence planning Indian style." There was a substantial decline in the current value of the rupee, due to inflation, in both rupees and more particularly in terms of US dollars. The inflation in terms of US dollars was almost 12 to 15 per cent, because that is how the rupee fell at that time. Dr Manmohan Singh as finance minister had carried out devaluation of the rupee in two steps within one month in early 1991. Naturally the Kargil conflict was waiting to happen. Pakistan sensed this degradation in India's conventional superiority and in India's planning for defence, and from that perhaps got the confidence that they would be able to carry into effect their intrusions into Kargil and achieve their tactical aims. The tactical aims were brilliant. It is at the strategic level that the intrusion faltered. During the Kargil conflict, the then COAS Gen V.P. Malik, made that famous statement on television for the entire nation to hear, "We will make do with what we have." This is what the Indian Army was reduced to in 1999 – we will make do with what we have! People from the Master General Ordnance (MGO) branch were flying to South Africa for 155 mm artillery shells while a war was on. Some of those decisions are now being questioned, by various committees, but that's okay, that happens in a democracy. There is this constant debate of defence versus development but I think there is historical evidence, empirical evidence, that shows us that to a certain extent, an increase in defence expenditure does lead to an increase in the economic strength of the country. To a certain extent, not beyond that, of course. There are several studies which have shown this empirically. So I think we should cut out the defence versus development argument and move on to defence and development as two sides of the same coin. The last point on the viewfoil is the gap between projection and allotment. I am sure you all are aware that each of the Services Headquarters makes a projection to the MoD every year. The MoD sometimes consults the Services Headquarters and reduces those projections, but mostly it doesn't, and the ministry then makes its own projections to the Finance Ministry, and what does the Finance Ministry do with them? In 1995-96, between the projections made by the defence Services and the allocations made by the MoD, the shortfall was almost 40 per cent – 40 per cent shortfall between projections made in 1995-96 and the allotment made in the defence budget! The next year it was 23.13 per cent from the Services allotment and 18 per cent or 19 per cent from the projections made by the MoD. These figures are from reports of the Standing Committees on Defence of various years. In 1997-98, the shortfall was 42 per cent from the projections made by the Services, and 27 per cent from the projections made by the MoD, and so on. What are the reasons? How is the Ministry of Finance legislating on behalf of the Services? How is MoD legislating on behalf of the Services? What special expertise does the MoD possess to decide willy nilly that the projections made by the Services are not going to be projected onwards to the Ministry of Finance? Why doesn't this exercise take place in consultation, as it happens in various other democracies? These are the issues to be pondered over. It is not only the MoD that is to be blame. What about the Services themselves? Do we have an institutionalised mechanism within the Services to decide our own priorities? We don't. Therefore, the MoD legislates on our behalf, because the three Services can't get their act together. Therefore, somebody has to sit down and act as a super commander in chief, a post that very unfortunately in this country has been enjoyed, and I make this statement very carefully, a post that very unfortunately has been enjoyed by the secretary of defence, a super commander in chief, who legislates on behalf of the Services. Why? Because the Services cannot get their act together. There is a Chiefs of Staff Committee(COSC), there is a chairman, COSC. It's a good club that meets every week, with all respect to everybody present here. I think some hard truths must be told. It took our COSC three years to approve a revised syllabus for the National Defence Academy. Can that committee ever agree on whether the *Gorshkov* is a priority or 40 additional Mirage 2000 or MiG-29s or SU-30s are a priority, or our 200 T-90s are a priority. Who is to legislate? Therefore, we must not blame only the MoD. The blame, gentlemen, rests mostly with us. There is now an IDS. There is a chairman of the IDS. The appointment is required to act as Chairman Integrated Staff Committee to Chairman COSC (CISC). The three Services are now making projections with Headquarters IDS, but there is no agreement in the meetings which are held. The IDS cannot make one single common projection to the MoD on behalf of the three Services, because we do not agree with each other. Part of the solution lies, I think, in the CDS, provided, he is given the authority. If he is not given the authority, we will be at square one. No progress.

Then there is the issue of management of the revenue budget: as you are well aware, more than two-thirds, almost three-fourths at least of the army's budget, is the revenue budget, and most of it is pay and allowance and other items, like rations and fuels, oils and lubricants, which cannot really be tinkered around it with. But who is managing it? The Services themselves? No. The MoD. There is a long standing demand of the Services that this revenue budget should be managed by the Services themselves. There are financial planning directorates within the Services, each one of them is quite capable of managing the budget. Of course, in the first few years there will be teething problems, but no, this has not been delegated to the Services. The GoM recommended integration of the MoD and the Services Headquarters. The Services Headquarters were attached offices to the MoD. Practically, they are still attached offices, no more.

There are continuing procedural delays for capital expenditure. There is a defence procurement board, but as one of the speakers mentioned, the Tehelka syndrome and the Bofors syndrome are still prevalent and no decisions are being made. All big ticket purchases have been postponed year after year. Then it is election time, in India it is always election time, "the great Indian tamasha," and then again, no decision can be made. Therefore, the Services need to get together and ensure that their voice is heard in the right quarters for early decision making; there should be a cut-off time for every decision. For the AJT, for the *Gorshkov*, for new aircraft, for tanks to come in, for modernisation of the infantry which is doing a grand job on the LOC and in dealing with low intensity conflict situations in Kashmir and in the Northeast and other places, but it does not happen. The Defence Modernisation Fund is a great idea. I will not say much on it as a lot of us have talked about the Defence Reserve Fund; it is the same. I won't say much on it because it has been just instituted. How it will play out remains to be seen. Will it be topped up every year? Will it be a part of the Consolidated Fund of India? Otherwise, it will lapse at the stroke of the midnight hour on March 31,2005. Rs 25,000 crore will lapse, regardless of all the lip-service that is paid, unless it is out of the Consolidated Fund of India.

Lastly, make or buy decisions – this again is something that is plaguing defence planning. Should we make a certain item of an equipment system or should we buy it? The DRDO always says that we will make it. They never say no. It is a great idea to go for self-reliance; of course, India must be self-reliant. Yesterday, Brahma Chellaney asked this question; why don't we manufacture our own defence equipment? We must do that, we have to invest in that and it takes a long gestation period to develop an AFV or an aircraft like the LCA, but at the same time, defence preparedness cannot be neglected. There must be a cut-off date, after which the Services must be allowed to import, and this is something that should be written into the system and only the Services can do it. The Services cannot be, must not be, allowed to be held hostage to various vested interests in the country. Prof Mukherji had mentioned paramilitary forces. Why are they not included in the defence expenditure? They have a specific duty to perform. The BSF, the CRPF have their roles of border guarding, anti-smuggling, anti-poaching, and so on, and as you would be aware, sir, when the army mobilises, some BSF battalions do come under command, but most of them pull back from the border. So, national security, yes, but not defence. I would like to make a distinction. After all, they are being used for policing, election duties and law and order such as at Godhra, Vadodra, and so on.

I think we are making a mistake by neglecting the aspirations of our men. There are just about 14 per cent of the men in peace stations who get married quarters for one year, and then it goes to the next one in the line. In any case, infantry battalions are not staying more than two years and 6 to10 months or so in a peace station. There are alarm bells ringing over there due to these hardships and if we do not pay heed, we are going to buy trouble for ourselves.

I would like to end with the great debate between qualitative upgradation and quantitative downsizing. I am sure that more than anybody else in this country, the army realises that 1.1 million is not an affordable strength, but there are the insurgencies to be fought, there are the LoC and Line of Actual Control (LAC)to be manned. So, if we want to upgrade our army qualitatively, the defence pie is going to remain what it is. Three per cent is a pipe dream today. Three per cent can only come about if there is another major upheaval. Otherwise, it is not going to happen. But even within the 3 per cent, qualitative upgradation and modernisation are not going to take place unless we downsize to some extent, so that some funds are available. I think in this seminar, the question that must come under serious debate is, which are the areas where we can downsize? How can we do it? Can we have a reserve where people can be mobilised quickly? Can we have a reserve located within the serving paramilitary forces, who revert to the army when the whistle is blown? We need to think very seriously of the issue of downsizing: 1.1 million in 2020 is not affordable, if we want to qualitatively upgrade the Indian Army. Thank you. •

INTERACTIVE SESSION

Dr Mohan Guruswamy

We have had two excellent presentations, and there is a lot we can discuss. Some of it must have been music to your ears. The need for bigger budgets, how armed forces have been ignored, all familiar tales. But the fact is that there is not enough money. You must learn to live with the system, which is very inefficient and just doesn't have enough money to allocate to its priorities. It also has very little time to decide its priorities. Can you imagine going into a room where the average minimum age of people is 75 and talking about a perspective plan of 30 years; they are just not interested. So, it adds to our problem, apart from their lack of knowledge. Once I ran into an old friend in North Block and asked him what was he doing. He said, look, I am the expenditure secretary. I said what do you do? He said I see that people don't spend money. That's what the expenditure secretary does!

I have gone through this process in the Finance Ministry. Around December, everybody wakes up and says the fiscal is looking bad, everything is looking bad, let's put a freeze on everything. So, you have financial advisers in other ministries. They are tied up with the Finance Ministry, so you call them up, and say, look, I want Rs 10,000 crore from you, or I want Rs15,000 crore from you. Chop, Chop. Which is how deparments, ministries lose their budgets. Naturally, everybody is geared to spending money between January and March and that's the time when you always get hacked, and the MoD also gets hacked like anybody else. It is not just you who surrenders money, the education department surrenders money, irrigation surrenders money, energy surrenders money, everybody surrenders money. The reality of life is that you know that the capital expenditure ratio of the Government of India is 11 per cent. It used to be 35 per cent in 1991 and it is 11 per cent now. It's going to get tighter and tighter. This is one reality you have to live with. Jasjit will tell you that when we bought the MiG 21 first, it cost Rs ten lakh a piece, the Sukhoi cost Rs150 crore each, and by 2020, an aircraft would cost about a Rs1,000 crore. You are going to be in a hell of a squeeze. Of course, we are an inward looking country. We don't have a strategic vision. That's because we have lots of problems inside. We have to look at our problems inwards, and that is bound to tell on our security planning.

Some of these points have been covered quite well. The DRDO was touched upon. I personally have very strong views on the DRDO. The DRDO has become a sacred cow for many reasons. Nobody questions what the DRDO does. A lot of money is ineffectively used. Programmes are delayed. The LCA is a bit of joke now; it has been going on and on forever. The missile programme. We have exaggerated notions about what our scientists are doing. The problem is we do not manage our resources effectively and nobody is responsible or answerable for non-performance.

As regards spending, I have noticed that there is a correlation between big ticket purchases and elections. Yesterday, the Cabinet met and cleared Rs 5,000 crore for long pending defence procurement. If you look at earlier big ticket items, these took place before the elections. The SU-30 purchase was decided on just before the 1996 elections. So, elections are good for defence procurement. It reminds me of what a Russian diplomat once told me. I asked, what do you think of this SU-30? He told me in Hindi (many Russian diplomats speak Hindi): "*Bahut achha aircraft hai Guruswamy Ji, magar wings jara heavy ho gaya hai.*" I said, what do you mean? He said, "*Woh teen government gaya hai isme.*" This is also a problem! This is something we have to live with. I am going to caution you about an excess of the RAND Corporation kind of thinking. I have studied under RAND Corporation trained people. Before that, I would like to say something about Prof Mukherji here. He went to the Massachusetts Institute of Technology (MIT) and I went to Harvard. My faculty advisor, said, "Look, whatever you do, do your courses here, do not go to MIT. At Harvard, we assume that if you are smart enough to get in here, you do not need much education. In MIT, they make sure that you learn something. They drill intelligence into your head. They make you work hard. Do not go there!" This advice I took very seriously, and didn't go there.

We have a serious problem here. We do not have a strategic vision. We do not have a notion of our place in the world. It's all true. But how does one bell the cat?

How does one get a room full of geriatrics interested in the future? A big problem. With that I throw the discussion open. Yes sir, Gen Vohra. I will come to the back rows after the chief arrives.

Lt Gen A.M. Vohra

A question was raised as to what should the armed forces be capable of and I suggest that we should have armed forces which have a deterrent capability and also possess the ability to carry out punitive raids, whenever needed. Now, to achieve this, one of the most important things is to get rid of our obsolescence, particularly in the way of tanks and aircraft. I am glad Gurmeet raised the point of indigenous production. In 1975, as the vice chief, I was connected with the qualitative requirement for the tank of the 1980s. It is still to come. Equally, there is a requirement for the introduction of new types of equipment, and certain steps have been taken to introduce radars, thermal devices and night vision devices of better quality. All that needs to be gone into in great detail. So that the armed forces that have to deter aggressors and carry out punitive strikes are well equipped. In this connection, the procurement board again is controlled by the defence secretary. Is it necessary to have everything centralised with the defence secretary? I believe that in Britain, the minister of state for defence deals with the procurement directly with the Services. I think this is something we ought to go into. In spite of the appointment of the procurement board, the process of procurement is very slow. Not only because of the Tehelka episode, because of many other ills that exist.

Lastly, I think, we give too much credit to Pakistan. What has Pakistan been able to achieve? It has been trying to get Kashmir for the last sixty years and got nothing. So let us not give too much credit to Pakistan. It is in a bad way and let us concentrate on equipping our armed forces properly. Thank you.

Dr Bharat Karnad

I have three comments. One is addressed to Dr Badal Mukherji's query about how the defence expenditure is spent. A perplexing issue which has bedevilled a lot of people. Now the Tenth Finance Commission actually did a report, the first by a civilian – and I was the one who did it. What was the theme we believe necessary for defence budgeting? This is what most advanced countries do, the need for mission role costing. If the three Services were to be budgeted on the basis of the missions and roles they perform, then you have a very clear idea of where the money goes. I did at times see this analysis in that so-called classified report. That's an awful thing, both good and bad reports get classified. So everybody is in the dark. Now, the thing about this report was that its recommendations were accepted in toto by the Tenth Finance Commission.

I will give you a rough idea of just how the defence budget breaks down over 40 years. Something like between 26 and 32 per cent annually goes to armour and mechanised forces, between 18-23 per cent is spent on the plain's infantry, between 11 and 14 per cent on mountain divisions. Compare the army break up with, say, air defence, including air defence missiles, which gets 6-7 per cent. The disparity is even greater when you get down to, say, sea denial with submarines, a meagre 2 per cent. Get down to sea control, because the navy likes visible large platforms, which goes up barely by 1 per cent. This is the kind of disparity I pointed out in the report. It was suggested to the government to promulgate changes in the budgeting system. Unless the Parliament knows where the money is spent and what is its outcome, it is difficult to bring in changes. Obviously, I can deduce from the reluctance of the Services and the government to change the system. The fact is there are vested interests. Now, I did not make that conclusion in my report. The obvious thing is, it has been ten years, since the recommendations of the Tenth Finance Commission, a constitutional body and the government has not thought it fit to implement the policy. Money management is really a very difficult road and there is no point in pointing fingers, as we readily do. This is a slightly longish answer to what should be done. This is how most advanced militaries and systems do it. Unfortunately, in our archaic system, there is no accountability. Therefore, if I may say so very bluntly, it is the prerogative of the Service chiefs to prioritise and this is the kind of power which others do not want to give up. Naturally, just because this falls into the same category as the CDS and everything else where the reforms haven't happened.

Secondly, Brig Kanwal talked about increased defence expenditure as having spillover benefits to the civilian economy and the national economy at large. The premise is that the bulk of the defence expenditure is going to be in-house, basically meaning within the economy. Now, the trouble with our acquisition system is precisely that it is all going to enrich the Soviet and Russian industry, the Israeli defence industry and every other industry you can think of. So we are subsidising the health of every other defence industry. As Prof Badal Mukherji would tell you, that is a wrong way of maximising any kind of benefit for yourself. Now we can again accuse the DRDO. Are the Services entirely not to blame, when they change General Staff Qualitative Requirements (GSQRs), whatever they have, at the drop of a hat? Are they willing to freeze the QRs somewhere down the line? Are they willing to say, well, whatever the technology trend, we will stop at that, purchase the first complement and let us have Mark II, Mark III and accept that. Someone mentioned that the AJT has taken forever. The AJT has taken forever because there was no interim aircraft after Marut, the HF-24. HAL pleaded with the air force and with the government to convince the air force that we should have an in-house follow-on to the HF-24, but the air force wanted foreign platforms. That is fine, all the Services want foreign platforms, preferably Western. So you have a real problem as to how you are going to gel your demands, your requirements, with your resources. It has been aptly said by Mohan Guruswamy and everybody else, there is only so much to go down. The question is not of the paucity of resources. The problem is wrong priorities, wrong requirements and, frankly, a wrong vision of what it is you are trying to accomplish with your armed forces, and the roles you have in mind. Thank you.

Lt Gen K. Balaram

Mr Chairman, firstly, I apologise to Gen Oberoi, because he is thinking in terms of 2020. I am sorry, I will be going back to 1985. And the point that I wish to make is as follows. Like everyone else, or every organisation, including a family, to answer the professor, our budget also consists of a capital budget and the revenue budget. You may say that how it is granted and how it is spent is questionable, as all three speakers mentioned. I will leave the capital budget alone and come to the revenue budget. Again, here, like some hints were thrown: are we making proper use of the money that is coming to us? In the revenue budget, basically the major portion is manpower costs, and in a manpower intensive environment these are quite considerable. Going back to 1985, that is the year I retired, I made a study at that point of time. The manpower costs then were 57 per cent; today, probably, they are much more and when I say manpower costs, it includes pensions. We may come to a stage when the pension budget is about equal to the pay budget. Why? Because of our benign army, in which, as some British general at one point of time has said, there is a system of outdoor relief. Talking of the Indian Army, perhaps we should keep that statement in mind. Every man who joins the army, retires on a pension. In most armies, very few are retained long enough to earn a pension. Are we doing the right thing? That was point one. The second is what I had studied at that time and had mentioned, was a minimal attempt to try and put this right. Till today, that paper has not seen the light of day. Now the conditions have changed, but the concept is perhaps still relevant and needs to be examined. When you are thinking of going forward, perhaps a smaller sized force with not too many or too much of commitment towards pensions is a thought that is worth considering.

The other point that didn't come out quite clearly was what was mentioned by the brigadier towards the end of his talk. We have to accept the concept of the territorial army (TA). I do not know whether I am making myself clear, when I say TA – it is a part time soldier, in the sense he does his training, keeps fit but is the sort of person to whom soldiering is not the primary means of livelihood. It is more of a hobby, like many of our students join the University Training Corps or NCC, and so on. Such units are kept in training or become embodied as regular units when required, and since they are in one locality, not spread all over India, they can be brought to strength pretty quickly. The pay liability occurs when they get embodied as a full unit. There are no pension liabilities. Many foreign forces, including in the Western countries, today use a similar concept. The TA comes from the British Army and the National Guards of the United States works on the same principle. That's what I wanted to say about manpower management in our army. Thank you.

Air Cmde Jasjit Singh

Thank you, Mohan. One basic thing we need to understand is, if you were to adopt any of the commercial principles of budgeting and the benefits that you get, defence is one thing where the inputs are clear, but the output is not clear. The output is a matter of judgement. This is sufficient. This will deter. This will not deter. Twenty nukes are enough; Bharat Karnad says 400 is the minimum. So it is matter of judgement, which is professionally exercised by the defence forces in India. How do we then look at this, because one can argue that we are in a situation when the defence forces themselves put in the demand and make the judgement. And then comes, as Mr Chairman said, not even the MoD, which at least has some involvement, but it is the Finance Ministry, which is a totally different set-up, which looks at it in a far more diffused way, simply as money. And the money saved is supposed to be great economy and better judgement. I think we need to look at this very carefully, and that is very essential. What criteria should we adopt for the judgement of the output? We are spending Rs 60,000-70,000 crore. What is it? Would there be an alternate judgement? So we simply add on to what we had in the past. And that in my judgement, is the problem, which we have followed for the last fifty years. An add on strategy. We have something and something new comes up, either in terms of technology and equipment or we need some more manpower, and we simply add on.

In terms of resources, I am glad and grateful that Gen Balaram mentioned this. If you want to look at the possibilities, this is roughly what we may get, the past can be an indication and the future is not going to be dramatically different. That is the point I was trying to argue yesterday. It is not a question of what I want or what I will argue for. I cannot see for 2020 an expenditure level of defence which is more than about 2.4 per cent of the GDP. The GDP is not growing at a great rate of 9 per cent, which the Planning Commission wants, but closer to a little less than 7 per cent. Whatever the figure is, or you take the percentage of the government expenditure, total or Central, there are ways of getting to a rough figure of what we are going to get between now and 2020. That's not going to be enough the way we are going, therefore, what is it that we need to do? What is it that we can do? If one looks at this funding problem, one can find all the faults with it and say where all it needs improvement for decision-making, that's one aspect of it. But let me just talk of one aspect, the expenditure on pensions, and I am not talking as a pensioner too. It used to be 2-3 per cent of the defence budget, and is now touching 16-19 per cent. We need to find a way of reverting it to something like 2-4 per cent of the defence budget, which, however, is not going to happen overnight, because you already have pensioners who are going to stay for a long time. But you could start a process. You could easily have at some point in the future, may be by 2020, something like 12-13 per cent of your defence budget available for modernisation, capital expenditure, high technology equipment, without touching the size of the manpower. Similarly, if you were to go back to the lower colour service, your manpower expenses could come down by as much as 20 per cent. I think this is where the future lies. The need is to look at the alternative choices and then the defence Services themselves can decide as to what they need or what they don't. As long as a solution is available, there will be a willingness to accept rather than to go on. This also needs a relook immediately and I was hoping that the Finance Commission would have done something to alter the budget structure. Bharat had access to a lot of documents, but even then, I am not too sure, we do not maintain our books that way. How much does an infantry division cost? Will we be better off with a mechanised division or we will be better off with an armoured division or what is the trade off between the cost and capability? That choice is not possible with today's budgeting, which is simply archaic. As early as the 1960s, the reforms committee had recommended a change, but we do not want to change. This is the issue of programme budgeting. What will it cost, at what period of time, because you remember, Mr Chairman, in the 1980s and even in the 1990s, 85 per cent of the budget was precommitted. At times, people say 90 per cent of the budget is precommitted. What do you do then? There is not much scope. My understanding of this modernisation fund is that it is not additional money. That it will be valid up to three years, that what you don't spend each year will be in the kitty the next year. But not in addition to the budget. But, in fact, at one level, it is a recipe for delaying decisions. Thank you.

Prof Badal Mukherji

Mr. Chairman, I will share with you a bit of personal experience. In 1973 or 1974, at ISRO, which was preparing to have the LANDSAT, scientists were pained because of the apathy of bureaucrats and politicians. So they asked me to do a paper. I said I am not a scientist, so you please explain to me the technicalities of the project.

Brig Kanwal, the response I got was esoteric. Fifteen years later, the Government of India is spending crores on programmes, along with the Americans. I had a very hard time trying to suggest that somehow we should be open to ideas. I am not trying to be esoteric, to waste your time. We must value the search. I was talking exactly about what you said, the user has to give the vector of commodity i.e. the variety of weapons and equipment and their desired priority. To me as an economist, that is the basic data. I cannot dictate that to the army, but if the user tells me about the requirements, priorities, resources and destinations, then I can work out the cheapest way to deliver the hardware needed for the country's defence. I am appalled to be told now that it is dictated by the MoD and not the Services, which is wrong. The user should tell us what is required and the ministry should accept it. Thank you.

Lt Gen Vijay Oberoi

Mr Chairman, I want to make two or three comments. The first is about downsizing. I sincerely believe, and always have, that there is a need to downsize, and we will be able to do it, but there is a problem. Suppose the army downsizes by a couple of divisions, the air force does so by a couple of squadrons and the navy does so by a couple of platforms, the danger is that the Finance Ministry will then say that now the armed forces do not need Rs 65,000 crore since they have downsized, so give them Rs 45,000 crore. So we are worse off that way, and that's a great danger. In fact, this was tried out by two army chiefs who volunteered to downsize by 50,000 troops, and a manpower cut was imposed. The units were crying for manpower. In every unit, there was a manpower shortage, when we needed the manpower, especially in J&K, and what happened thereafter. But the money saved did not come to us. It went to the Consolidated Fund of India. So why should the armed forces downsize, if these are the criteria?

My next comment is regarding prioritisation. We have been talking about it. A certain amount of modernisation is imperative for each of the Services. The prioritisation can only be done for the balance. Unfortunately, we do not have a system. The system which is required is that there must be a chunk allocated as the modernisation budget for all the three Services and then the prioritisation is left to the respective Service chief. Over and above, there should be a chunk which can be handled by the CDS or whichever agency, and this way we will probably be better off, because you cannot stop the modernisation of any force. Over a period of time, this has happened to us. I will give you a figure: when I was looking after the perspective planning in the early 1990s, the defence budget was around Rs 28,000-30,000 crore. The shortages in the modernisation budget amounted to Rs 30,000 crore. Firstly, there was a need to overcome the shortages, and then the modernisation undertaken. If you keep delaying the modernisation, the requirements will continue to grow, as well as their cost.

My third comment is regarding the indigenisation of defence equipment. It is not the Services which have always said that the defence equipment should always be made by the public sector. We have been asking that it should be privatised. In every country, the private sector participates in the manufacture of defence hardware but not in India. We want our own ordnance factories and the PSUs to do it. Unless we privatise, we cannot indigenise defence production. We will probably get our requirement earlier than we do now. An increased participation of the private sector in defence production will then help the domestic economy. I agree with Bharat Karnad that it does not help the domestic industry or economy at present. Hence, defence production needs to be decontrolled and decentralised.

A point regarding the Services. We always want the best. Whether it is a tank or a gun, we look around for the best weapon in the world and we want that. We need to be more pragmatic in our selection. We must analyse whether we need the best. Say, if we want 1,000 tanks and the budget allocation can only buy us 100 top of the line tanks because the money is not available, can we not accept slightly lower quality of tanks then? This way you will get what you want, at least nearly that much. Thank you.

Col (Dr) P.K. Vasudeva

Mr Chairman, I have got only one point to elaborate upon on indigenisation. The MoD, two years ago, had said that 70 per cent of defence equipment will be indigenised. Companies like Reliance, Kirloskar, and a couple of IT companies had then come forward. These were given a small range of defence equipment to produce. The private companies asked for a larger range of equipment, so that suitable infrastructure could be set up, which needed an investment of Rs 30,000-40,000 crore. The private sector will be able to help in manufacturing of the high end military hardware, when a wide range of defence equipment is decontrolled for production by the government. This was not agreed to. The result is that Indian companies are waiting in the wings. They want a bigger range of equipment for manufacturing, for which they are ready to invest. So, offload more defence hardware items for the private sector to manufacture, and they will do it. Sadly, it is not being done. The Indian companies are technologically competent to undertake this challenges. That is how a part of the defence budget can be ploughed back into the domestic economy. Thank you.

Lt Gen R.S. Shahrawat

Mr. Chairman, I am the director general of the ordnance services. There have been wonderful presentations by Col Vasudeva and Brig Gurmeet Kanwal. I have a few comments to make on both the presentations, particularly on what Col Vasudeva said, so that the junior officers who are sitting behind the aisle do not go with a wrong impression that has emerged from the presentations. The scene portrayed was somewhat dismal, and, I think that it needs to be dispelled.

First, a point was made that the equipment a soldier is using has generally let the army down. I do not agree with that. That may have been true in the 1960s or what happened in 1962. The equipment we had at that point of time perhaps was not suited for operations at that altitude. But today, I can very proudly say that the soldiers of the Indian Army are equipped with perhaps the best equipment available anywhere in the world. Siachen is the perhaps the finest example. Some of the other points which he brought out were about the defence procurement board and the revenue procurement board; these institutions came about as a result of the GoM recommendations, and these are very much in place and, yes, a beginning has been made. I believe that there are bound to be teething problems and, gradually, I think things are going to improve. We have a revenue procurement board in the MGO branch itself. The MGO himself chairs the procurement board. We have the representatives from the Defence and Finance Ministries, and, from user directorates. But there is no doubt that this process needs to pick up a greater momentum. I am very optimistic that things will not be as bad as they appear to be. Some of the points which Brig Kanwal brought out are very relevant, and they are definitely on the right track. Some of the issues which he referred to were particularly relevant to defence versus development. Yes, certainly that is not a very good argument. What is needed is defence and development, and I think that is very clearly visible today. If the defence industry progresses, there is bound to be a corresponding development, in both the private and public sectors.

We had the Defence Expo in Pragati Maidan recently. Earlier, we had a scant army-industry partnership. I have been seeing these Defence Expos over a period of time. Perhaps this was for the first time when such a close interface was witnessed.

As regards the gaps between projections and allocations, I couldn't agree with you more. Yes, we give out our projections to the ministry, and they are moderated there, many times without consultations. What happens at the Ministries of Defence and Finance has been very clearly brought out. That is one area that surely needs to be addressed, in case we have to modernise.

Management of the revenue budget was another point. I think we definitely need to have a greater say in this. Today, we are largely managing our revenue budget, but if we had a greater say and control over it, perhaps we would be able to utilise it more effectively and there would be absolutely no chance of any surrender of funds.

"Make or buy" again goes with defence and development. It is high time that we started making our own things. You have given examples of countries like Israel, a country as small as that, and look at the variety of defence equipment it is manufacturing. We have become the biggest buyers of its equipment. We have the knowhow, we have the technology and we have the resources. I think that is one area which we must target today. Certainly, there are delays in procedures, but overcoming these is easier said than done. It is a fact of life. For those who are operating these procedures have to be conscious of the environment that is obtaining today, Tehelka and Central Vigilance Commission (CVC) reports notwithstanding. Therefore , these delays are a part of the system and we have to accept them, but we are getting over these delays.

A point about the debate of quantitative versus the qualitative improvement. I tend to disagree slightly with the views. Look at the size of the country; everybody has been saying that if India has to become a global power, and our biggest competitor is China, then we have to have a big army. If we have to project ourselves and if we really want to guard our economic growth, we have to have defence forces which are absolutely competitive. Therefore, I do not look at the figure of 1.1 million as too huge. As a matter of fact, the size of our country can very well afford such defence forces. What is required is qualitative improvement; what needs to be addressed are aspects like obsolescence. As the head of the biggest logistic service, I think this is really an issue which concerns us. Because as we modernise, more and more equipment will come into this category. Today, the ordnance depots and establishments are bulging at the seams with obsolete equipment. We have to find ways and means to get rid of it. A very healthy trend has started about the growth and development of infrastructure. Let me tell the audience here that at one point of time, almost two-thirds of our ammunition was lying in the open. That is not going to be so 3-4 years down the line. We will have virtually no ammunition whatsoever lying in the open. It will be stocked under proper conventional accommodation. And as far as the accommodation for the men is concerned, it is very much on the anvil. I would like to correct the figures that were quoted by one of the speakers: it is not 14 per cent, it is going to be in the region of 33 per cent that our men will have married accommodation. We have a huge project, which is underway. Certainly, there is a lot of ground that needs to be covered, but things are surely not as dismal as somehow or the other they have been made to appear. Thank you.

Gen V.N. Sharma

Mr Chairman, I want to raise two points. One is about R&D and the other about manpower. I do not agree that the Services have a foreign platform syndrome. The Services want efficient equipment and in many cases, the R&D has not been able to produce it, the delays are too excessive, as has been brought out in the discussion. I can give hundreds of examples. The Arjun tank is one, the LCA is another. The Arjun tank is still not effective. The point at issue is that we spent a lot of money on it. Eventually, if you look at the cash outgo, it is cheaper to buy, let us say, the Soviet equipment than to buy the Indian equipment.

As regards the business of money and how it should be managed. We should have global markets at our disposal. If we get a good buy in India which is efficient, fine, buy it. But if we do not get a good buy and get a better buy outside, which is cheaper, I do not see any financial wizard telling us that is a wrong thing to do.

In the days when foreign exchange was scarce in our country, there was a problem, but today, that side of it is a little better than before, and I do not think that the Services can be accused of having a foreign syndrome. Let our private sector participate in the production of defence hardware, as suggested. But, certainly, we do not want a monopoly of the R&D, which exists at present.

There is a large amount of technology coming in from amongst our own people, within the Engineers, Ordnance, EME and the Services. The R&D refuses to accept this technology, because they want funds for getting it themselves. The technology is also available for the asking from institutions like IITs, and many of us have had that experience. But when these agencies ask for a trial, the R&D

refuses to accept them. There is a governmental or political syndrome of keeping certain things to themselves, like PSUs and R&D not opening up, because they have a large amount of money coming back, under the table, if you like. Since they are manpower intensive enterprises, politicians can oblige people from their constituencies. This is an important factor. The *Shaktiman* factory, for instance, is an example where engines of the vehicles were produced; it had ten workers where there were supposed to be two. Such over-staffing has made our PSUs economically unviable. So, we have to look at many other things, like the overall economic scenario, which will improve when the economy looks up.

I now come to manpower. We cannot say that the manpower of the military is large, especially the army, and the pension bill is large, so we must reduce the manpower. It is not going to work. This has been very rightly brought out. Our manpower is insufficient for our needs. We are amongst the few countries in the world having the smallest proportion of population in uniform. So, we cannot say that since we have the fourth largest army, please reduce. Look at the size of our borders, look at the enormity of our tasks. This is not the USA, where you have a coastal line so you do not have to guard borders, especially when you have politically quiet borders with Canada in the north, and the southern borders are managed by the police.

Unless our relations with our neighbours look up and the internal insurgency situation stabilises, we cannot afford to prune our manpower. A word about the question of whether a *jawan* should get a pension or not: this is a point which has been discussed again and again. Around 1965, the pension for a *jawan*, with his increased Service, was accepted against the grain of military thought. If a *jawan* is released early by reducing the colour Service, then he is without a job. He is an ex-Serviceman without a job in the village and these people have a tendency to join anti-social elements if they remain unemployed. So, it is better to retain a person longer in the Service so that he is not vulnerable to such temptation. Retiring a *jawan* at the young age of 25 is not a good idea either. Hence, the manpower should be managed centrally by the government. We alone will not be able to solve this problem.

Now what about central management of manpower? There was a time during the British Raj when the officers and men who left the Service were promptly absorbed in the government services. Today, that has stopped, because every Service wants to raise its own cadres. Why cannot the IAS and IPS for example, absorb some of our officer strength? They tend to get frustrated. Why? Because they do not go beyond the rank of major. There is no room for them. So why can't the IAS and IPS officers do five years in the army before joining their respective Services? If you do that, the number of officers will reduce straight away, and you will have people coming in and going out, like a short service commission. We are very keen on short service, because we want people to come in and go out. If you have a small cadre, the budget will be much less, the pensions will be much less.

We have been suggesting for the last 15-20 years that there should be the central management of armed forces cadres in all other services. But the bureaucracy turns it down, saying that there is an employment problem in the country. We have to employ a large number of people centrally and even if people retire after doing five years in service, at least they have employment for five years. So, we have to look into the aspect of manpower planning to sort some of these issues.

Brig Gurmeet Kanwal

I have a point regarding the modernisation and obsolescence. I would like to make a distinction between the replacement of obsolete equipment, which will be with a more modern equipment, like replacing the self-loading rifle (SLR) for the 5.56 mm INSAS (Indian Small Arms System) – this is not modernisation. We shouldn't confuse the two issues. Modernisation is a qualitative upgradation in the electronic warfare, surveillance and force multiplier equipment which we do not have. Things which make us a better army, which enable us to perform our operational tasks and roles more effectively. Therefore, just replacing obsolete equipment does not lead to modernisation. In fact, small ticket items should be part of the revenue budget.

As regards Gen Balaram's point about TA-isation, there was a committee headed by Shri K.P.Singh Deo. It made excellent recommendations for territorial forces for the army, the navy and air force. If those recommendations could be implemented, it would go a long way in reducing the manpower. Unfortunately , I do not think it will happen, because the committee made the mistake in the recommendations of saying that all government servants will first serve in the armed forces, in the territorial army. So there is no way that report is ever going to come out of the almirahs, where it is gathering dust!

Regarding downsizing, I think it is very clear that as long as the army is required to fight insurgency and militancy, which is a manpower intensive task, we cannot reduce the manpower, whether it is Rashtriya Rifles, Assam Rifles or additional infantry battalions, which are deployed in LICO. But, at the same time, I feel it should also be clear that we are not going to get a larger allocation in the defence budget. We do need to upgrade, qualitatively, the rest of the army as a conventional force, to meet the conventional threats. Unless we find ways and means of reducing the cost of the manpower, even if we cannot reduce the manpower,the objective will not be met.

Some years ago, when I was in the Military Operations Directorate, we used to work on an expenditure of Rs 100,000 per man per year, and when downsizing of 50.000 troops was ordered, it meant a saving of Rs 500 crore a year. This saving never came to the army's kitty, it just lapsed. But we must think of ways and means of reducing the cost of manpower. There are various ways, for example, sending a man after 6-7 years of colour Service to the BSF, CRPF, CISF, ITBP, where the retirement age is in the fifties, and, then having a lien on that man and getting him back when the chips are down. With a quick refresher course, he goes back to his unit. It can be done. This is just one measure; there are so many others which can be considered and adopted. Thank you.

Lt Gen V.K. Nayyar

I think during the discussion it was mentioned that we are an inward looking nation. From the discussion, I get an impression that we are making our army also inward looking. It is a case of serious wrong. I think this is not the forum for a discussion on budgeting and what type of army you want. That discussion should take place with the people who are decision-makers. We have had so many in-house discussions, but the people who need to take these decisions or need access to this knowledge are never available. Therefore, at the end of such a discussion, I feel very perturbed and I thought I would share my concern and anxiety with you. Thank you. •

Session IV

Force Restructuring and Doctrinal Challenges

Panel Chairman	:	Gen Shankar Roy Chowdhury, PVSM (Retd)
Panel Discussants	:	Cmde Ranjit B. Rai (Retd)
		Lt Gen G.K. Duggal, PVSM, AVSM, VrC (Retd)
Paper Presenters		Lt Gen V. K. Kapoor, PVSM (Retd)
		Lt Gen N.S. Narhari, PVSM (Retd)
		Dr Bharat Karnad

PRELIMINARIES

Lt Gen Vijay Oberoi

Gentlemen, we will now start Session IV, which is the last in the series of the sessions. The subject of the session is "Force Restructuring and Doctrinal Challenges". The chairman of the panel is Gen Shankar Roy Chowdhury (Retd) and the discussants are Lt Gen G.K. Duggal (Retd) and Cmde Ranjit Rai (Retd). The paper presenters are Lt Gen V.K. Kapoor (Retd), Dr Bharat Karnad and Lt Gen N.S. Narhari (Retd).

Gen Shankar Roy Chowdhury

Good afternoon gentlemen. We have an extremely distinguished panel here; really speaking, this is the apex of the discussions which you have been having so far. Before the paper presenters start presenting their papers, I will try to refocus ourselves on the subject of this session, and what we have discussed so far.

In the first session that we had, the general conclusions were that in 2020, China and Pakistan will remain our major adversaries. Major conventional wars are unlikely, but the threat of terrorism and low intensity conflicts will continue. Non-military issues like food security, energy security, environmental security and health security are going to dominate our concerns. So, in the context of what we have discussed and the background that has come out so far, we would like to know the future configuration of our army in 2020. By army, I mean the land component of the defence forces. What will it be like? Now, I invite Lt Gen V.K. Kapoor to present his paper.

ARMY 2020 – A PERSPECTIVE ON FORCE RESTRUCTURING AND DOCTRINAL CHALLENGES

Lt Gen V.K. Kapoor, PVSM (Retd)

India After The Cold War

The break up of the Soviet Union as a strategic entity did not provide the proverbial peace dividend to the subcontinent. The fundamental causes of conflicts in and around India did not change after the Cold War. On the other hand, new threat dimensions have emerged and these are yet to be fully analysed contextually. Moreover, with disputed land borders in the west with Pakistan and in the east with China, even the external military threats to India's territory cannot be seen as having receded despite the recent bonhomie. We will have to wait and watch the political developments.

The conduct of nuclear tests by India and Pakistan in May 1998 has added a new and important dimension to war planning on both sides, which needs to be factored into any study which attempts to understand future wars, doctrines and force structures.

The ongoing proxy war in J&K, advanced and encouraged by Pakistan since 1989, shows some signs of abating, with ameliorating utterances from Pakistan from time to time, based on international pressures. The Kargil misadventure followed by terrorist attacks on the Indian Parliament and J&K Assembly, among others, has hardened India's attitude, and India expects positive action by the Pakistan government in clamping down on all terrorist related organisations and activity before a meaningful dialogue is initiated. In the meanwhile, the growing strength and clout of militant organisations in Pakistan, encouraged and nurtured by the ISI, has been demonstrated by the recent attacks on President Musharraf. This, along with other factors, such as the growing sectarian violence between Sunnis and Shias, the high defence expenditure, and a poor economic status and growing poverty in Pakistan, together with the pressures from the US and the global community have forced Pakistan to review its internal and external policies. Strategically, the balance is tilting against Pakistan, steadily and inexorably. "As the Indian economy grows, as India strengthens her relationship with the West and Central Asian countries, as the long-term interests of India and US converge, as India's engagement with China gathers substance, Pakistan could find it tough to maintain its traditional position of hostility," states Tony Joseph in his essay in the *Business World.*

Such analysis on both sides has led to the successful SAARC discussions in

January 2004, which are now expected to pave the way for comprehensive discussions on all issues subsequently. Indo-Pak relations are heading towards a period of positive engagement. India has a vital stake in a stable and tranquil Pakistan, in order to have peaceful borders and reap the benefits of economic development.

As regards China, after more than four decades of strained relations, the recent breakthrough in India-China relations seems to be a result of a fundamental reappraisal of India by China, as apparent from the reports appearing in the Chinese newspapers. The report in the *People's Daily* of May, 21 2001, states, "Steadily warming Indo-US relations have resulted in widespread attention to the geopolitics of Asia. It is difficult to predict whether India will become a strategic ally of the US or China, but the sudden attractiveness of India will sooner or later, alter the regional balance of power between the countries."

In a paper presented at the Washington based Centre for Strategic and International Studies, visiting scholar Venu Rajamony says: "China's fear is that India might 'do a China on China'– that is to say, just as China and US put aside a history of hostility and ideological differences in the 70s to forge a tacit alliance against the Soviet Union, will India and the US, who have had a difficult and prickly relationship, find common ground by uniting against China?" Rajamony calls the India-China-US triangle a "soft balance of power system" in the making.

The CBMs with China started in 1993, when both countries signed the "Agreement on Maintenance of Peace and Tranquillity along the LAC in the India-China Border Areas." The two sides agreed to implement a number of CBMs to reduce the risk of actions through misperceptions. The above agreement was strengthened in concept and content by an additional agreement on December 29, 1996, during the visit of President Jiang Zemin to India. A number of additional CBMs were put into place consequent to the 1996 accord. However, what is of concern is China's incongruous and often confusing stand regarding the alignment of the LAC, and her unwillingness to define its alignment either on the ground or on maps. Till the boundary question is settled, misperceptions about each other's intentions are bound to occur from time to time. This fact, together with China's proclivity for military assistance to Pakistan in the nuclear and conventional fields, and Chinese patrolling and cattle grazing and at times provocative actions along the LAC makes India doubt China's peaceful intentions. Moreover, the 1962 conflict with China has left an impact on national psyche, which will take a long time to be erased and this needs to be understood when dealing with China.

It is expected that the visit of the Indian prime minister to China in 2003 and the subsequent meetings of the representatives of the two countries will help in establishing modalities for resolving the border dispute with China, which in the 21st century seems to be an anachronism

Future Threats and Challenges

In the future, there are three broad settings which need to be considered for force structuring and capability building. These are:

- Confront Pakistan and China and the emerging challenges.
- Confront emerging challenges only.
- Confront one adversary plus emerging challenges.

To get an idea of the military challenges that we are likely to face in the future, we need to examine these, away from the set scenario of Pakistan and China. Only then can the enormity of the challenge be visualised in real terms.

India's sphere of influence encompasses the region from the eastern sea board of Africa in the west to Malacca Strait in the east and includes Iran, the CARs and China. Hence, there is a variety of threats and challenges to national security, away from the set scenario of Pakistan and China, that needs to be factored in our planning process for the future. The challenges, which impact specifically upon the structure of the land component i.e. the army, are:

- Defence of our island territories separated by large distances from the mainland.
- Security of our off-shore and on-shore assets and resources rich area.
- Security of a large and unprotected coastline and the national assets and infrastructure along the coastline.
- Internal dissent and claims to autonomy and ethnic recognition by sub-national entities, who may be supported from outside.
- Demographic shifts in the South Asian region and other non-military threats which may impact upon the military.
- Inimical actions by powerful multinationals, which may affect own vital national interests and which may be supported by other states.
- The beliefs of a single, very powerful, state which views its security as more vital than that of the world.
- The proliferation of weapons of mass destruction and advanced delivery platforms such as missiles.
- Overspill of ethnic conflicts in the South Asian region into India.
- Global terrorism perpetrated by non-state actors, which may be aided or supported by other states.
- Military aid, in internal security, against:
  - Terrorist Activity
  - Narcotics
  - Antagonistic paramilitary groups
  - Large scale civil disobedience caused by a variety of reasons
  - Serious disturbances caused by ideological, ethnic and religious hatred, anarchy, food shortages and absence of governance.

The Impact of Economic Development

- Recent forecasts have placed India in the third or fourth position by 2020 along with the USA, China and Japan. The sudden attractiveness of India in the global economic sphere is evident. Recent forecasts by the Reserve Bank of India (2003-2004) have predicted a 7 per cent GDP growth rate with a continued upward bias.

- The logic of the Cold War that kept the US and India apart has withered away and the economic rise of India has given it a new eminence in the global market for power and influence, which is likely to facilitate settling of the border problems with both China and Pakistan.
- Such economic growth and a global/regional power status in the future necessitate autonomy in decision-making and safeguarding of sovereignty in a new global security environment whose contours are currently hazy and need to be analysed in greater detail, to ascertain their impact on our security.

Nature of Warfare in the Future, and the Basis of Force Structure

The basic nature of war never changes. For instance, we know that war is adversarial, dynamic, complex, uncertain and dangerous and it is rooted in individual and collective human behaviour. Hence, it needs to be studied to gain an insight into it and a clearer understanding. Even Clausewitz, Jomini, Mahan and Liddel Hart have all stated that the nature of war and strategy does not change i.e. the components and structure of the subject remain constant – only details change. Moreover, the nature of the subject does not permit precision and exactitude and, hence, we should be careful while predicting the future. The question that remains to be answered is: what is likely to change in the future, in our context?

The changes are likely to be in the detailed constitution of the war-waging apparatus and methodology. The changes, in our context, could be as follows:

- The method of preparing for, and conducting, war.
- The methodology of planning at higher levels.
- The war-fighting doctrine.
- The technology employed.
- Force structure and organisations.

What makes the future highly uncertain is that we cannot know precisely when, where, or for what ends war will be waged. This dilemma gets even more acute when and if the animosity against our traditional adversaries disappears. Thus, the issues related to doctrine, force structures and organisations have to be examined in relation to the role of the army in the total spectrum of war and viewed conceptually. The concepts should be broad and flexible enough to accommodate changes, as we move forward in time, depending upon the situation that may emerge.

Role of The Army

The role of the army is to preserve national interests, and safeguard the territorial integrity and unity of the country against any external or internal threat. In the future, the role may also include the preservation of sovereign rights, protection of innocents, preservation of environment and preservation of free trade.

Spectrum of War

The total spectrum of war includes the types of conflicts that the army is currently involved in and the ones it may be ordered to undertake in the future.

These include the following types of actions, both offensive and defensive (conventional and unconventional):

- Full scale conventional conflict.
- Limited and sectoral conflicts.
- Border skirmishes.

(Under the use of nuclear weapons)

- Defence of island territory and/or dislodging an adversary from our island territory
- Counter-insurgency (CI) and counter-proxy war operations.
- Global/regional terrorist actions including blackmail with WMD.
- Internal conflicts caused by internal dissent.
- Out-of-area contingency missions to assist friendly nations.
- Military reaction to an unforeseen contingency demanding a proactive (including preemptive) or reactive response, inside or outside the country.
- Other forms of warfare such as information war (including media war), psychological war, cyber and space wars
- UN peace-keeping operations.

Economic interdependence, international opinion and availability of nuclear weapons in the region may preclude full-scale conflicts (open wars) in the future. Hence, our responses to the future threats and challenges explained earlier, are likely to, broadly speaking, assume the forms of conflicts mentioned above.

The Changing Face of War: Land Warfare

While military development is a continuous evolutionary process, the modern era has witnessed three watersheds in which the change has been qualitative. The *first generation warfare* was reflected by the tactics of the era of the smooth bore muskets and the linear battle of lines and columns. The *second generation warfare* was a response to the rifled musket, breechloaders, barbed wire, and machine-gun and indirect fire. Tactics were based on fire and movement and they remained essentially linear. The *third generation warfare* was also a response to the increase in battlefield firepower. The Germans were, in World War I, aware that they could not compete in a contest of material because of their weaker industrial base; hence, they developed radically new tactics, which were based on manoeuvre rather than attrition.

The basic concepts of third generation tactics were in place by the end of 1918. The advent of the aircraft and tanks brought about a major shift at the operational level in World War II. This operation was named *blitzkrieg* by the Germans in which emphasis was placed on manoeuvre, speed and tempo to carry out wide outflanking movements, avoiding the enemy's defences to strike at his rear areas in order to cause his psychological collapse. The Germans exploited their tactical excellence to cause unprecedented defeats in the first two years of the war.

The Americans picked up from the Germans their ideas of "manoeuvre warfare," of simultaneous engagement of operational components of the enemy's defensive system, structured hierarchically along the entire depth of the opposing system, to cause *operational shock* and development of an operational momentum far exceeding the relative reaction capability of the opponent. The US Airland Battle concept developed along with principle of directing one's own main strike into the opponent's principal operational weakness. Military analysts in the USA are now deliberating and reflecting on a *fourth generation warfare* in which the target will be the whole of the enemy's society (ideology, culture, political, infrastructure and civil society). This generation of warfare, they say, will be characterised by dispersion, increased importance of actions by small groups of combatants, decreasing dependence of centralised logistics, high tempo of operations and more emphasis on manoeuvre. Masses of men or firepower may become a disadvantage, as they will be easy to target. Small, highly manoeuvrable, agile forces will tend to dominate. The aim would be to cause the enemy to collapse internally rather than physically destroying him. There will be little distinction between war and peace. It will be non-linear, possibly to the point of having no definable battlefields or fronts. Major military and civil facilities will become targets. Success will depend heavily on joint operations. If we combine these general characteristics with new technology, we see one possible outline of the new generation of warfare.

The Indian Army is organised, equipped and trained for second and third generation warfare. Our traditional methods favour deliberate set piece military operations against fixed defences, which are attrition oriented and tactically biased. The army excels in defensive operations and has considerable staying power and exceptional resilience. Over the past five decades or so, it has gathered exceptional experience in counter-insurgency operations. However, the higher leadership, by and large, remains mired in conservative attrition oriented methodologies. In the 21st century, the Indian Army, the Indian Navy and the IAF are still planning for conflicts essentially Service-wise, the way it was in the early years of World War II. We have not even started our journey for the type of integrated warfare contemplated in the future.

Army's Perspective on Air Power

Modern air power has certain characteristics that permit military power to be applied uniquely and in a different manner. The vital characteristics of air power are its reach, responsiveness, concentration and flexibility. Modern multi-role fighter aircraft can be configured to undertake any type of offensive role and deliver a wide variety of conventional or non-conventional munitions. Even transport aircraft and helicopters can be used to deliver weapons, in addition to their primary role of logistic support. The flexibility of air power is limited only by the imagination of the user. With the advent of precision guided munitions and target designation, modern technology has given air power the capability of destroying targets with a single digit circular error of probability (CEP) and with least amount of collateral damage. Given the wherewithal, these characteristics endow air power with the ability to psychologically imbalance an opponent and achieve strategic aims set by the national leadership with highly selective employment of land forces. Some areas to be accorded special focus as far as the army is concerned are:

- Airborne, heliborne, and air transported operations in the mountains (including high altitudes area).
- Intra and inter-theatre movement of troops and equipment.
- ISR operations of the battle space.
- Integrated theatre organisations for all operational commands.
- Integrated task force employment.
- Close support in CI and counter-terrorist operations and in conventional conflicts.
- Integration with special forces.

Approach to Force Structuring

From the brief examination in the foregoing paragraphs, we can draw an obvious conclusion, that in the next two decades, there are distinct possibilities of rapprochement in India's relationship with Pakistan and China, which would have a very significant impact on the Indian Army's organisation and force structure. In this new environment, away from the set scenario in which we have spent more than 50 years, we could downsize, restructure, and transform the army, based on new technologies and a new joint doctrine. This would have to be a holistic and joint effort of the three Services. However, should the expectations fail to materialise, then the approach to restructuring would have to differ. In the latter case, we would have to reengineer (reorganise, reorient and reequip) the existing force levels to acquire the additional operational capabilities desired. We could also be confronted with another scenario in which while Pakistan is marginalised, China continues to pose a military challenge. Such a setting would also require the adoption of the former methodology. Hence, the two basic methods identified, based on the emerging patterns of threat are:

- Downsizing (manpower) and transforming the army based on new technologies and new threats.

or

- Reengineering the existing force levels to acquire new capabilities.

Under these circumstances, and in view of our present operational culture, we should develop force structures that are capability based and not threat based and operationally integrate the three Services through reorganisation of our higher formations, and through joint training and joint procedures which will ensure coherence, synergy and success in war.

Capabilities Desired

Should the threat pattern demand the adoption of downsizing and transforming or reengineering of existing force levels, alternatives as stated above, then the force structure should be so designed that it is capable of operating across the spectrum of conflict. This would mandate the development of the following capabilities:

- Conventional force to fight limited wars.
- Rapid Deployment Force to deal with border skirmishes, and other types of

contingency missions.

- Amphibious task force (tri-Service) and special forces (trained for air-borne/air transported/heliborne role) for out-of-area missions and to cater for unforeseen contingency missions.
- Special forces, trained, equipped and organised for counter-terrorism (in all its manifestations including WMD).
- A substantial counter-insurgency force for fighting insurgencies, proxy wars and for internal employment.
- Strategic forces for deterrence. Land component to have multi-range missiles with nuclear warheads capable of a wide range of nuclear responses and options.
- Army Aviation and supporting arms to support the type of operations indicated above.
- Close integration of air power at strategic, operational and tactical levels.
- Be able to wage information wars (including media wars) and psychological wars.
- All capabilities to be integrated in the tri-Service context.

The second alternative, which relates to the existing set pattern of threat coupled with additional threats, requires a gradual transformation through reengineering (reorganisation with existing assets) to acquire the desired capabilities. This alternative will have to be assessed for its economic viability based on the availability/allocation of defence budget.

Power Projection

A regional/global economic status also bestows on India a responsibility of projecting military power to support her friends and allies and to safeguard her interests in the South Asian and in the IOR. This capability, which would essentially be integrated and tri-Service in nature, will have to be built into our future force structure. We would have to bear in mind that we have a strategic geography, which demands long-range power projection.

Technologies Desired

Effective employment of our forces on the battlefield will necessitate the use of some of the following technologies:

- Digital communication networks linking sensors, communication devices and weapons for real-time response.
- Ground and airborne surveillance with an array of manned and unmanned aircraft and UAVs sending data direct to the Integrated Command Headquarters with the intermediate units and formations receiving the data simultaneously.
- Situational awareness and identification friend or foe (IFF) for combat vehicles and tanks for receiving and transmitting important information and data and for IFF.

- Aircraft (fighters and bombers) fitted with compatible communication equipment and IFF, carrying precision-guided munitions.
- Digital imaging with GPS to allow commanders to draw up fresh battle plans with accurate and up-to-date information of enemy movements.
- Increased self-containment of logistics for combat elements
- Networked logistics with networked tracking system for functioning in a mobile and dynamic environment.
- Suitable transportation system (air and ground) for rapid movement of troops, equipment and logistics at strategic, operational and tactical levels.
- Accurate long-range firepower with a variety of munitions, including precision munitions.
- Lighter tanks with heavier firepower capable of strategic and operational mobility (between and within command theatres).
- Effective protection, firepower, and communications for the individual soldier.

Doctrinal Issues

Doctrine is a system of views adopted in given period on the aims and character of a possible war, on the preparation of a country and its armed forces for such a possibility as well as on the method of waging war should it break out. Changing circumstances (e.g. demography and technological changes) must be constantly evaluated because they can modify beliefs and necessitate changes to doctrine.

Considering the enlarged spectrum of war and the new dimensions of warfare, which are contextually relevant, some guiding principles or doctrinal precepts, which are central to our requirements, should be included in the joint doctrine so as to be prepared to win across the full range of military operations in any theatre of war or operations, in any contingency. Doctrinal precepts advocated for inclusion in the Joint Armed Forces Doctrine are:

- **Indian Way of Going to War**: There should be an Indian way of going to war. As citizens and soldiers of this great nation, we conduct military business in a peculiarly Indian way. This needs to be formalised. Currently there is no formal procedure followed. In fact, our political leadership, perhaps for political reasons, shies away from giving written directives to Service chiefs. On receipt of the political directive, the COSC convert abstract political aim(s) of war to achievable military aim(s) and objectives and if after analysis they come to the conclusion that the political aim set forth is not achievable, they must have the courage to say so. The nation must not go to war for an unachievable political aim. This process is called Regressive Planning because it moves from the highest strategic body to the lower echelons of command.
- **Operational Art as the War-Fighting Doctrine**:The essence of operational art is to convert the given political objective (strategic goals) into military objectives and to achieve these goals with least cost to own side
- **Effect Based Operation (EBO)**: Looks at our force structures from the

perspective of achieving the effects desired. At the strategic level, we may require to break enemy's will to fight or his cohesion, while at the operational level, we may wish to destroy the enemy's operational reserves. EBO requires superior military capabilities, to be built into the force structure, through the use of technology coupled with innovative operational art, to achieve these effects with the least cost to our side. Moreover in integrated operations, the most appropriate component(s) is used at each stage of the battle to ensure economy with least collateral damage.

- **Integrated Operations**: We should transcend from joint operations to integrated operations to unleash the full potential of combat power of joint operations. This demands integrated command structure at military strategic and operational levels in the context of the air-land battle.
- **Shared Fighting Culture**: Currently the planning for war is peculiar and exclusive to each Service. This must give way to joint training, joint planning and joint conduct of war. This will demand a culture change in the way we do things.
- **Address the Vulnerabilities and Weaknesses of the Opponent**: To avoid attritional warfare and to use the asymmetry of even a superior opponent to our advantage, we should concentrate on his vulnerabilities/weaknesses. To learn this art, we have to train ourselves through joint war-games in all possible scenarios.
- **Rapid Deployment and Environmental Mobility**: Future wars will demand such a capability to be used for proactive missions or as a reactive response. This capability will be required across the board at strategic, operational, and tactical levels.
- **Directive Style of Command**: For successful application of operational art, in future wars, the command style cannot be rigidly centralised as per our current practice. A more flexible style, which encourages risk taking and maximum initiative by subordinate commanders, will have to be adopted. This change of culture will also allow subordinates to conceptually grasp the higher commander's intention and the higher framework of war and facilitate the adoption of the manoeuvre approach to warfare in the Indian context, in all types of terrain.
- **Manoeuvre Approach:** There is an imperative need to evolve the manoeuvre approach as the key element underpinning our approach to war-fighting, in all types of terrain, including our mountainous regions. Our force development and organisations will have to cater for this offensive capability that in the future will involve close integration of air and ground troops.
- **Transformation Through Technology**: We should achieve faster transformation through use of new technologies and innovations coupled with operational art. This will not only change the methodology of war-fighting but confer distinct advantages which could be maximised through fusion of technology with training, organisational structure and force development.
- **Non-Linearity**: This calls for an attitudinal change in the military mindset

with regard to conventional/unconventional ground, air, sea and space operations. We should be able to translate our ideas of fighting the close, intermediate and deep battles in all five dimensions, including information war, in near simultaneity, and synchronise the destructive effects of battles on the ground, at sea, in the air, in space and in ether. This will require infusion of new technologies mentioned earlier.

- **Operational War-Gaming**: A tri-Service war-gaming centre should be established for strategic and operational level war-games to analyse issues such as emerging threats, new settings, new technologies, new concepts and war-fighting methodologies. Without such a facility, we will not be able to validate our concepts and doctrines. This is the most urgent requirement in our context.
- **Visionary Leadership**: Yet another requirement of the future is the need for enlightened leadership at military, strategic and operational levels with a large enough vision to fully comprehend the entire perspective of strategic and operational level of warfare without over-identification with tactical objectives. This mandates sound selection procedures and unbiased policies. The key attributes of operational and strategic level leaders are considered to be as under:
  - Professionally astute.
  - Vision.
  - Wisdom.
  - Contemplative/reflective approach.
  - Self-restraint/self-control.
  - Self-knowledge.
  - Ability to inspire/is a role model.
  - Sacrifice of personal interest.
  - Possesses all attributes of intelligence (IQ, emotional intelligence and spiritual intelligence).
- **Close Politico-Military Interaction**: Given the restrictive aspects of short duration wars, the nuclear backdrop and other factors, destruction of the adversary's strategic forces or capture of large tracts of territory will neither be possible nor desirable. War aims will have to be modulated, tempered and calibrated according to the environmental constraints. Therefore, translation of political aim(s) to achievable military objectives of war and skilful conduct of war will require a close politico-military interaction throughout.

Conclusion

Defence of a nation and its development are complementary. If we aspire to be a regional/global power, our military power must reflect that desire. In this context, the transformation of the army through technological improvements coupled with innovative operational art will give us a distinct advantage over a potential adversary, which is vital for preserving and furthering our national interests. •

DOCTRINAL CHANGES AND IMPERATIVES OF FORCE RESTRUCTURING

Lt Gen N.S. Narhari, PVSM (Retd)

Preamble

Maintenance of national interests is one of the main preoccupations of a nation. A nation's foreign policy and economic policy are closely intermingled with the dynamics of the geo-politics of the region and beyond. National security policy evolves out of these compulsions. The military strategy is the outcome of national security strategy and it should be realistic and achievable.

India's international land borders are around 15,000 km and it has a shoreline 7,500 km long. We have an Exclusive Economic Zone (EEZ), which is two and a half million sq. km and it is rich in natural resources. Peninsular India, and our island territories sit astride the East-West sea channels and are in a position to dominate the Malacca Strait, the main entry into the Indian Ocean. Two of our main adversaries are located on our International Boundary (IB) in the north, east and west. It is, therefore, incumbent on us to have both continental and oceanic (maritime) strategies. Both these strategies need now, and forever, the third dimensional force in modern warfare i.e air power. Unfortunately, these issues have been overlooked in the approach paper. I am sure it will be modified to suit our military strategy and land warfare studies.

Dynamics of Regional and Extra-Regional Situation till 2020

The Indian nation state shares the IB with Pakistan, China, Nepal, Bhutan, Myanmar and Bangladesh. Just across the narrow Palk Strait is Sri Lanka. Apart from Nepal and Bhutan, whose umbilical cord is in India, India has lukewarm to benign hostile relations with others. Only China is more than a match in national power and its strategic relations with Pakistan have for long been close, especially in supply and assistance in production of military hardware. Territorial disputes with China and Pakistan have resulted in four wars, besides a few minor conflicts. However, there appears to be change for better relations with both these countries. There may or may not be a final solution to the J&K issue by 2020, but border disputes with China are solvable if emotions take second place to realism. Both India and China do not have an open-shut case in this dispute. The Central government must be advised that the Indian armed forces have not got the potential military power to take on two fronts. While Indian strategic planners cannot rule out a Sino-Pak axis, they can plan a one front plus strategy or at the most a one and a half front strategy.

In the post-USSR era, the USA is continuously pushing its political, economic and military power, unilaterally and in a preemptive mode, eastwards towards Central Asia via Iraq, Iran and Pakistan. This is her strategy and it will continue to be so in the 2020 strategic scenario. In a US-Pak axis of this nature, India is unlikely to have the capacity or political will for preemptive strategy by 2020. Oil is a lodestone for the US' push towards Central Asia.

The EU less the UK, Russia and to an extent China, are indicating some resistance to these moves and the preemptive strategic doctrine. China, with its more monolithic political system and growing economic power and modernised (by 2020) armed forces will be a major factor to inhibit US moves closing up to the western flank of China. This could be one of the possible designs for the slowly emerging US-India strategic relationship. This, along with the longstanding Indo-Russian strategic relationship, could facilitate the equilibrium of Sino-Indian national power.

Strategy

China, India and Pakistan are nuclear weaponised countries, with nuclear weapon power asymmetry. The latter has not yet accepted the "no first use" doctrine because of lack of strategic depth and asymmetry in conventional military power, though the asymmetry is just marginal between India and Pakistan. India with the bigger territory, longer IB, and internal security problems does not enjoy adequate military superiority, international political support, as already discussed, or economic power for a preemptive strategy vis-à-vis Pakistan. Besides, it would provide Pakistan an early excuse to cross or threaten to cross the "nuclear threshold." So far as China is concerned, the balance of power is (deployable) in its favour vis-à-vis India and the terrain, which favours defence, precludes a preemptive/proactive strategy. India should adopt a "deterrent" offensive-defence strategy vis-à-vis Pakistan and a "dissuasive" strategy with a strong riposte capability vis-à-vis China. Either of these strategies would need preparation, readiness and will power, at the national and the armed forces level.

Changes in Doctrine at "Operational-Art" Level

Defence

Initial deployment for defence should cater for "damage control" in an NBC environment. We could plan on the adversary using a one kilo tonne (KT) theatre level weapon system. The existing ditch-cum-bund (DCB) system should be used as 'trigger', based on infantry companies and gaps being fought by mobile forces i.e. 'recce and support' units, equipped with battle field surveillance radars (BFSR) and ATGM, mounted on all-terrain vehicles and helicopters, backed by armoured squadrons/ regiments. The concept of DCB being "limit of penetration," as laid down in some commands in the Nineties, should be scrapped. As far as possible, the battle must be fought ahead of value objectives like Srinagar, Kargil, Jammu, Amritsar, Siliguri Corridor, Tawang, and so on.

Offensive Operations

The concept of concentrating counter-offensive forces close to the IB i.e. less than 50 km, should also be changed. Our road and rail communications, which have improved, must be further improved to cater for rapid concentration on the move from a dispersed mode. Manoeuvre, however, is a means to an end i.e. to give us the tactical superiority at the area of impact i.e. the adversary's strategic reserves/ value objective. Though the battle is not fought for territorial acquisition, unless we manoeuvre to threaten the value objective, the adversary's strategic reserves may not be exposed for battle. Unless that is done, at a time and place of our choosing, we cannot destroy his combat power. Positioning of our offensive forces in depth i.e. 150 to 200 km back, would give greater flexibility to choose areas of ingress and could put doubts in the minds of our adversary regarding the area of ingress.

Deception at theatre/operational art level should be deliberately planned. Positioning of our offensive corps in depth areas, ability for lateral movement and concentrating rapidly to the area of ingress, multiple bridgeheads, variable H hours and sophisticated active camouflage measures (both electronic and non-electronic) supplement deception plans. We have not put our minds in this direction after half-hearted attempts in the 1980s.

Till now there has been very little understanding of a "second no-mans land." Our adversary's combat potential is just adequate to have a 40 to 60 km belt of defensive system, wherein he has concentrated his defences and obstacle systems, beyond which is the second no-man's land. The concept of the so-called 'breakout' after the first obstacle system is breached was not even practised in World War II. Yet our armoured commanders think and practise in these terms. This is not viable and the potent armoured division could get stuck in fighting breakout and get attrited before the adversary's strategic reserves are brought into the battle. This is an adverse situation. Instead, armoured brigades available in the offensive corps and holding corps should be skilfully utilised till the second obstacle system is breached and the second no-man's land is reached. This will force the adversary's strategic reserve to be deployed earlier than own armoured division, which can then be manoeuvred into an advantageous position.

It is possible and viable to induct infantry and special forces at night, soon after the initial bridgehead is established so that they can position themselves 20 to 30 km beyond, or make a surprise raid on the depth obstacle system. They need not wait for bridge construction. There is an element of risk, but it can be minimised by the use of air power and SSMs.

Future Battlefield Milieu

The longer ranges of weapons and their operating destructive power, including non-conventional weapons, enforce greater dispersion. Better communication systems in the electro-magnetic spectrum, including the satellite based communication systems, now making their appearance with us should be the order of the day, along with BFSR, all linked by a C^4I^2 system, which will facilitate availability of time information/intelligence. Along with this, battlefield mobility should be increased to facilitate concentration of forces at the area of impact/ingress. This battlefield milieu will necessitate a change in the mindset of senior commanders. They must decentralise execution to company, unit and brigade commanders. Operational instructions rather than operation orders will be the order of the day. Senior commanders will have to rely on real-time information coming to them on the C^4I^2 System. There is a need, therefore, for greater stress on sub-unit /unit level and brigade level training. Higher formation exercises should conform to different forms of tactical exercises without troops, including computer aided war games.

Training

We have been paying lip-service to sub-unit level training and at best retaining 'cadre' type of training, despite the fact that from Leh to Lungleh, our army has fought 90 per cent of battles/conflicts, in both wars and CI situations at sub-unit and unit levels. If we have had success, then it is more due to the commitment and courage of our junior leaders than the systematic training organised at the unit level. I have had the fortunate experience to persuade and enforce sub-unit training in both peace and field areas. Sub-unit training hones the cutting edge of our army, builds better team work, creates a good base for the build up of junior leaders who should train their command in peace to lead them in conflict. Our field firing exercises and battle inoculations are a joke, despite the fact that the safety distances have been reduced, after the detailed 'live trial' by accepted by the MoD in 1986/87.

Our annual inspection system is outdated and our attitude towards it is merely 'spit and polish'. Even now, our erudite commands and staff, besides the unit, term it as "Admin Inspection." A look at the annual inspection format and the channel for these papers indicate that it is a General Staff (GS) matter. It is actually an operational efficiency audit. The IAF has had a centralised team to conduct these inspections since the late 1970s. The US Army has it too. This must be modified so that a systematic and objective methodology is arrived at assessing the operational efficiency of a unit and its battle worthiness.

Restructuring of Army

There is nothing fundamentally to be changed in the organisation of the army from the unit level. Some modifications would come based on the induction of BFSR, updating of electro-magnetic/satellite communications. However, the command system and staff procedures may have to be modified to suit C^4I^2.

It may not be cost effective to have a parallel force for CI operations and anti-terrorist operations. RR was created for this in the late 1980s. I believe there is some procedural problem in paramilitary forces working under RR formations. This should be solved at the Government of India level. The TA units raised initially as a second line of defence have not got the same statutory support as national guard units have in the US. TA battalions raised on regional basis and trained as army units can supplement forces for CI operations; they have been doing their bit now, including CI operations and disaster relief. Their mobilisation time should be refined and supported by an Act of Parliament.

Reappraisal of Logistics Units

This has been done earlier by Lt Gen Narasimhan's report. The requirement is of base workshop units, GS stock inventory, etc in view of the greater degree of indigenisation/privatisation, which will facilitate provision of spares, etc.

Our indigenisation plans are plagued by the intransigence of the DRDO, rigidity and lack of perception of the civil and military bureaucracy. If we do not indigenise, with progressive improvement of the product, India will always be dependent on foreign and politically controlled imports. The Arjun tank is a prime example of this. If we had accepted the MKI product in the mid-1990s, by now we would have had an ongoing production capability. Now we are dependent on import of T-90s, to upgraded T-72s till 2020 or more.

Every corps in the plains needs be rapidised, having one of the corps dedicated as reserve for mountain operations. All offensive corps should have a special operations brigade and one for Army HQ reserve for other tasks in holding role corps.

Employment of Air Power

Land power will be increasingly dependent on air power for all its traditional tasks. Where the two do not see eye to eye is in the employment of air power in counter-bombardment/achievement of air superiority role in a reactive strategic mode. More SSMs should be used for this role, thus, preserving flexible air power for the counter-offensive phase of the war.

Projection of own combat power in the region depends upon the maritime, merchant navy and air power.

Conclusion

Changes in the political and technological spheres in the next two decades will enforce changes in military strategy and doctrine, hence, equipment status too. We should, be mentally and attitudinally, ready for this. •

FIRMING UP THE CRITICAL CAPABILITY TRIAD: STRATEGIC MUSCLE, SUB-CONVENTIONAL PUNCH AND IT-ENABLED NETWORK-CENTRICITY AND ELECTRO-MAGNETIC WARFARE CLOUT

Dr Bharat Karnad

Emerging Challenges

Doctrine decides strategy which, in turn, dictates the shape and size of a force. But doctrine is premised on the perception of the emerging threats. For a country of India's potential superpower heft, the challenges to security have to be seen not only in terms of protecting territory but, more broadly, of their effect on the country's legitimate sphere of influence, international political leverage and bargaining power, and even self-respect. Since expansively is how all great powers and would-be great powers define their concepts of sovereignty and security, India is in danger because it is getting into a position to do just that.

On the cusp of becoming a great power, India is acquiring the expansive vision and the "critical mass", economically and technologically, but militarily the country is still confined in its thinking and, programmatically has yet to acquire the strategic thrust and momentum to enable it to wield distant influence and realise what it has sought for many decades now – a change in its rank order in the international system.

China and the United States, feeling threatened by the relative loss of power, will try and hinder India's rise.[1] After all, were it to acquire meaningful military capability with clout and reach to match its prospective economic muscle – a $27.8 trillion economy by 2050, the third largest in the world after China ($44.5 trillion) and the US ($35.2 trillion) according to a Goldman Sachs report[2] – India would gain international political leverage and influence mainly at the expense of these two countries.

Then there is Pakistan. It is in its interest, to the extent it possibly can, to retard India's advance, which it may continue to do either singly or jointly with its patrons, the US and China. This could take the form of material assistance of the kind Beijing provided to Pakistan's nuclear weapons programmes or diplomatic help that Washington has always offered Islamabad to protect it from the consequences of its own nuclear rogue state behaviour and even from American non-proliferation laws. More immediately though, the danger confronting India emanates from Pakistan's and China's aiding Indian insurgents in J&K and the Northeast respectively and encouraging the use of terrorism in order to keep the country unsettled.

With regular armies proving to be less than effective against guerrillas, as the historical record proves, the solution is to build up sizeable Special Operations Forces (SOF) capable of "fighting dirty"[3] to subdue assorted *jehadis* and "freedom-fighters" and, just as importantly, of expeditionary duty as an ideal quick reaction force. This last capability is what India will need to play a greater role in the extended IOR.[4] A beginning has been made in the last many years with an activist naval diplomacy – the spate of goodwill visits by Indian Navy ships, sailing of flotillas to the Gulf and as far east as Japan, annual naval meets of littoral navies, and joint exercises with them as also with the navies of Japan, South Korea and China. This role as the region's minder and *gendarme* has to be consolidated by a large and robust SOF.

In the event, the question – what kind of military capability India should have to fit its enhanced status and to deal with the emerging threats and challenges to its security – is easily answered. Given the fact that in the present day, large scale wars are frowned upon and redrawing the map, as Jaswant Singh warned when he was foreign minister, is infeasible, elaborate military wherewithal and the old fashioned ways of war-fighting with masses of armour and mechanised forces, mobile artillery and huge field armies active across a broad front, are becoming irrelevant. With the middle range in the conflict spectrum, thus, shrinking, the capability at the two ends – strategic and sub-conventional – will begin to matter more and more.

The two priorities are for India to acquire a safe, reliable, and size and quality-wise, consequential thermonuclear triad of intercontinental range missiles, strategic bombers and nuclear powered submarines firing nuclear-tipped missiles and SOF.[5] Substantial and comprehensive SOF to quell insurgencies, carry out expeditionary duties in the areas clearly within India's legitimate sphere of influence, and to deal with nuclear terrorism – the most lethal emerging threat– will have to be stressed. (The traditional conventional military instruments, namely, armoured and mechanised forces and heavy mobile artillery, *et al*, will have reduced salience but continue to be valued in the order-of-battle (orbat) but mainly as a conventional deterrent).

The third main priority is attaining an unassailable capability in electronic warfare and in IT-enabled network-centricity, which will decide the extent of the Indian military vulnerability to electronic preemption and bamboozlement in the future.

Nuclear Posture

The most prudent force structuring predicate is to plan for the worst possible contingency, which automatically guards against the less dire situations that might arise. The vast, versatile and launch-ready American thermonuclear arsenals, featuring strategic bombers, long range missiles, and nuclear powered submarines firing nuclear tipped missiles, and the IRBMs (intermediate-range ballistic missiles) in the Chinese Second Artillery Corps with standard warheads with yields of one megaton and 3.3 megaton, at once endow Washington and Beijing with escalation control and, therefore, decisive bargaining edge in any crisis, and render

India vulnerable to compulsion or coercion. Further, the incapacity of the present small yield 20 KT, short-legged Indian nuclear arsenal to reach target sets in CONUS (Continental US) and in the farthest reaches of Mainland China and to achieve high-destruction levels, will leave India open to serious arm twisting when it comes to Washington's and Beijing's pushing their agendas – non-proliferation, the violation of human rights,[6] Tibet, maritime power, or whatever.

The US is particularly dangerous because its incomparable thermonuclear, nuclear and conventional military capabilities are wedded to notions of absolute security and a strategy of preemption and preventive war articulated by President George W. Bush.[7] So far, nuclear preemption in the case of India is sought to be obtained by peaceful methods with the thinking of the Indian government and the armed forces on nuclear weapons and missile matters being sought to be influenced through various inducements (trade, high-technology transfer, etc.), strategic dialogue and with close engagement at the political and military-to-military levels.

Washington is confident it can cut deals, like the one cobbled together in 1998-2000 by the then Minister of External Affairs Jaswant Singh and President Bill Clinton's Deputy Secretary of State Strobe Talbott in their many rounds of talks, according to which Delhi agreed to not test and develop high yield thermonuclear weapons and intercontinental ballistic missiles threatening to the US or keep nuclear forces on launch-ready status. In exchange, the US promised technology transfers and cooperation. It is a deal the successor George W. Bush Administration has happily furthered by formalising the so-called "glide path" that is supposed to ease technology sale and transfer and collaborative projects in certain high-value sectors like civilian nuclear technology, space and missile defence.[8]

Prudent and legitimate Indian actions to firm up its nuclear deterrent have, thus, been forestalled very cheaply by Washington – by offering mere promises of cooperation in the area of critical military technologies. India, in effect, has sacrificed the immediate deterrence and political benefits from possessing a consequential thermonuclear arsenal in expectation of a commodity or good that realistically speaking may be realised, if at all, only in the very distant future.[9] But the problem for India is that there is no telling when the pursuit of the US' unbudging non-proliferation objective with such soft means will be replaced by coercive diplomacy and the use of hard economic and political-military measures.[10] And, realistically speaking, India will be in no position any time soon to militarily fight off the US, as Gen Padmanabhan has fantasised, except by having ready an intercontinental thermonuclear force with its implicit threat.

Two things have to be kept in mind. Senior US government officials, like Under-Secretary of State for Arms Control, John R. Bolton and Assistant Secretary of State for Non-Proliferation, John Wolff have consistently identified a nuclear weapon and missile armed India as a threat to the US. And, secondly, the US aggressive counter-proliferation policy can at any time lead to a strike by American precision conventional munitions vectored by satellite, aircraft and remotely piloted vehicles (RPVs)-based sensors against the extant limited Indian nuclear force deployed (?) in a disassembled form. Such a nuclear disarming strike can complicate an Indian riposte – will/can India go nuclear in retaliation with its residual supply of nuclear weapons (assuming any survive the preventive attack) to a conventional military strike, and if so, against what vital US targets? A dozen or so megapolis busting hydrogen bombs kept in launch-ready conditions will, however, always and invariably deter the US in any situation.[11] The less risk averse Chinese have to be deterred with a certain parity in numbers and weapons quality backed by a steely determination.[12]

Beijing too has begun to talk preemption. It is directed against Taiwan today,[13] but may be applied to India tomorrow, the latter's weaknesses permitting. Notwithstanding the upward trend of Sino-Indian relations, especially in the trade and economic sector, the PLA leadership has, for instance, unabashedly stated, "War is the continuation of politics, and more directly is the continuation of economics."[14] And, in a similar realist tone referred to the possibility of future conflicts on its periphery with India (and Russia, Vietnam and Japan).[15]

To compound India's strategic problems, these two great powers also perceive a limited nuclear armed Pakistan as an effective means of reining India in, keeping it tethered to the subcontinent. This explains their record of furtive nuclear aid and diplomatic assistance provided to Islamabad in all the years when its clandestine weaponisation programme was under development. Indeed, Gen Pervez Musharraf has conceded that the technical help available from, what he called, the "nuclear underground" consisting of European technology and component suppliers was chiefly responsible for Pakistan's securing uranium enrichment capability. He implied that insofar as the US and its West European allies – supposedly in the forefront of the international non-proliferation campaign – did nothing to stop the flow of technology to and from Pakistan, they were complicit in Pakistan's attaining nuclear weapons status, and party, in a sense, to its subsequent nuclear shenanigans. And that if Pakistan is to be held guilty on the proliferation count, then so should these other countries.[16] Indeed, investigations reveal that the nuclear black market in Europe had official sanction.[17]

Musharraf could, in fact, have gone further and acknowledged what is also equally widely known, namely, that China furnished his country with the original weapon design and the initial stock of enriched uranium and tritium required to make the bomb,[18] and that successive Administrations in Washington protected the Pakistani N-weapons programme from the US' own non-proliferation laws in the late 1970s onwards because it served the American interest.[19] It is a policy the US continues with by whitewashing Pakistan's role as a rogue state, transferring nuclear technologies and weapons designs in return variously for cash and missile technology to Libya, Iran and North Korea.[20]

The US and China will play the "Pakistan card" for strategic ends and readily take to nuclear coercion as long as India is saddled with a disaggregated and manifestly puny nuclear force that can do either of these countries little harm. The solution, as highest priority, is to secure at least a dozen armaments with the longest reach and the biggest clout, namely, megaton thermonuclear warheaded inter-continental ballastic missiles (ICBMs). Once these systems are in place, the balance of interests changes dramatically vis-à-vis the major nuclear states as China discovered when it secured missiles capable of reaching the US West Coast by 1967. Within a couple of years, a suddenly more respectful Washington had cemented a rapprochement with Beijing, President Richard Nixon had jettisoned the "Taiwan card" (the "Shanghai Declaration" reiterating the principle of "One China"), and once and for all, China freed itself from both American and Soviet nuclear pressures.[21] Indeed, it was the Chinese government's apparent readiness to go to war with the US over the "accidental" cruise missile strike on the Chinese Embassy at Belgrade in 2000 with the reminder by a PLA general that China would "destroy Los Angeles" that fetched Beijing the abject apology it had sought from the US government. Nuclear weapons have that kind of power in the hands of a state able to hold its nerve in a crisis.

Strategic independence (or "autonomy"), increased international political leverage and bargaining power, immunity from political-military pressure and from economic and technology sanctions, and a substantial role in shaping the world order are the primary reasons other than national security why India should have an all-azimuth thermonuclear deterrent. Because a small insignificant nuclear force, which has failed to even impress Pakistan, will beget only small returns as India's experience of forsaking rapid advance to acquire a whole range of proven, safe and reliable nuclear/thermonuclear weapons of different yield-to-weight ratios by an open-ended series of nuclear explosive tests and, hence, to genuine great power status in the wake of the 1998 test moratorium, has shown.

A mainly high yield thermonuclear force to be realised over 30 years featuring long range missiles with around 400 plus warheads/weapons (in the main, four ballistic nuclear powered submarine (SSBNs), 48 SLBMs, 25 ICBMs, 40 IRBMs, 20 Tu-22s both optimally sized and eminently affordable) will gain India entry into the nuclear second tier of states alongside of China and bring it, size-wise, within hailing distance of its Chinese counterpart with some 475 weapons/warheads. The achievement of "notional parity" will also serve as a warning to Beijing that India's accepting a differential in force strengths takes into account Chinese concerns about Russia. If, nevertheless, China decides for any reason to increase its weapons stockpile, India would do so too. [22]

Force Structuring Options and Nuclear Doctrines

There are two contrasting models – the American and the Soviet – of nuclear force structuring available. In the first flush of the Atomic Age, the US military endeavoured to reshape itself into a force uniquely capable of handling the revolutionary weapons in what was regarded as an entirely new kind of war in the offing. It was believed that nuclear weapons would play the part chemical explosives and munitions played in earlier conflicts. Between the Korea and Vietnam conflicts, the US Army, for instance, preparing to fight such wars, quickly alighted on three principles of warfare in a nuclearised "non-linear battlefield" akin to the fundamental notions of armoured warfare – "dispersion" (to avoid giving the enemy an attractive target to strike with tactical nuclear weapons), "flexibility" (as defined by "responsive" command and control) and "mobility" (construed as the ability to concentrate quickly to strike and then to disperse with equal alacrity).[23]

The US Army brass also agreed upon a "dual capable" force able to fight both conventional and tactical nuclear battles. Its principal fighting component was to be the battalion-sized "battle group" (thereby removing the regimental command echelon altogether) as the basic fighting unit configured around a tactical-use atomic weapon system – a battery of the 22 mile range, solid fuel, more rocket than the short range ballistic missile (SRBM) "Honest John." Organised according to a "pentomic" pattern, a division was formed with five battle groups, each of which comprised five companies, and each company was further divided into five platoons, and integral to the battle group as a whole was a battery of heavy mortars and a company providing signals, reconnaissance, maintenance, and medical support. Depending on whether the battle group was infantry, airborne or armoured, each had distinctive weapons platforms – tanks for the armoured battle group, helicopters for the airborne version, etc.

There was trouble though with operationalising the three principles of dispersion, flexibility and mobility. The airborne battle group, for example, was the only one to meet the mobility criterion but it could carry no conventional weapon larger than 105 mm calibre and, hence, lacked punch even for mopping up operations after "Honest John" had, as anticipated, blasted the way through the enemy's defences.[24] But the real problem in this scheme for war planning lay in the premise that nuclear weapons would be resorted to only when one's side started losing in the conventional military exchange.[25] The first use of nuclear weapons was, thus, implicit in the American military thinking. And dual capable meant that the force was forever strung out between the imperatives of going nuclear and the logic of persisting with conventional means in the hope that crossing the nuclear threshold is delayed if not altogether avoided. It tended towards deterring rather than fighting and for this and other reasons, the pentomic concept was discarded.[26] And the US Army ended up doing what its Soviet counterpart did, i.e. revert to a general purpose force with sea, land and air borne platforms and missiles able to mount tactical and strategic operations with nuclear weapons.

The Soviet model, which was copied by the Chinese, retained the basic conventional military fighting structure, equipped the various combat arms (motorised infantry, artillery, "frontal aviation" and air defence) within the Services (ground forces, air force and navy) with tactical/theatre-use nuclear weapons but also constituted a separate strategic fighting arm called the "strategic rocket forces" (the Second Artillery Corps in the case of the PLA) tasked with operating long range missiles with nuclear warheads "to carry out the main missions of war."[27] Nuclear weapons, while considered organic to the fighting forces, were nevertheless treated as defensive wherewithal and means of reacting and responding to the adversary's first use of nuclear weapons. Whereupon, the nuclear weapons possessed by all the Services and the combat arms within them were to be deployed so as "to enable the authorities to use these weapons simultaneously to inflict great losses on the aggressor's armed forces and to destroy his material and technical base for the conduct of the war and so disrupt his national and military administration." The Soviet strategy also conceived of situations in which nuclear weapons were employed "to destroy an opponent in any type of operation" other than "a war as a whole."[28]

The Soviet model minimised change for change sake and because of the continuity in the mode of operations, ensured better cohesion. It is the model the Indian Army has apparently adopted with the formation of the 333 Medium Regiment with the *Prithvi* SRBMs, the 444 Medium Regiment with the 700-900 km medium range ballistic missile *Agni-I* and the Medium Regiment with the 2,500 km range *Agni-II* IRBM. The difference is that the bulk of the nuclear weapons inventory consists of 20 KT weapons/warheads and what is envisaged by way of "strategic" weapons are 125-250 KT yield thermonuclear weapons. Once these latter hydrogen weapons are inducted it may be possible to make a distinction by assigning the lesser KT armament to tactical/theatre use.

As presently disposed, portions of the disassembled nuclear weapons are stored and under the control of different agencies – the nuclear cores or pits are with the BARC scientists, the warhead assembly with the DRDO engineers, and the missile and the launcher with the concerned Service. At a certain point in time during a crisis, the mated weapons will apparently pass into the hands of the Strategic Forces Command (SFC) acting under instructions of the prime minister and the NSC. (Once the CDS is installed, another decision and command echelon will, presumably, be inserted between the SFC and the NSC.) Difficulties will inevitably arise in actually employing these *Prithvi* and *Agni* regiments as part of the main force in operations. A flexible and responsive C^4I^2 system able to deal with the fluidity and vagaries of the nuclear battlefield, is one requirement. The more important thing is for the *Agni* and *Prithvi* units to continually exercise in the field with designated strike and defensive formations until the kinks in their interface are ironed out. In this context, the existing state of affairs involving nuclear weapon systems kept detached from the field formations, will become counter-productive. The troops and units as well as the C^4I^2 network have to become familiar with nuclear weaponry. It cannot be that the *Agni-III* regiment, say, is brought into the operational picture only when the unfolding situation in the war theatre or the strategic realm merits the firing of nuclear weapons as per the latest, updated Chiefs of Staff target list. This will, at a minimum, majorly increase the risks of unintended, inadvertent or accidental launch of missiles and the start of a nuclear exchange.

But the army may have a still more grievous problem on its hands. So far it has accepted, surprisingly without any qualms, what it has been told about the efficacy of the nuclear and thermonuclear warheads atop the *Agni-I*, *Agni-II* and, prospectively, the *Agni-III*, as well as these missile systems, or on the basis of computer simulated data. It has not been provided the opportunity to test these various systems physically and so satisfy itself. This was not the case with the *Prithvi* SRBM, which was put through some 19 field tests conducted by the army before it was inducted into its orbat. The army will have to likewise insist that the longer range versions of the *Agni* and their separate nuclear/thermonuclear warheads be physically tested and be required to perform as per their various design parameters to the satisfaction of the army rather than, as has been the case so far, of the scientists at BARC and the missile engineers in the Integrated Guided Missile Development Project alone. There is no other way of removing doubts about whether India, in fact, has a militarily usable fusion weapon considering that the lone thermonuclear test of 1998 was only partially successful.[29] It is precisely this hydrogen weapon the government hopes the military will, when the time comes, unquestioningly induct into their orbat.

As the senior armed Service, it is the responsibility of the Indian Army to convince the government about what is required by way of rigorous and extensive field tests before any weapon system is inducted into its orbat and why it cannot make an exception of a decisive armament like the thermonuclear bomb, which will only further damage its credibility. And that insofar as this will necessitate a resumption of physical explosive tests, that is what the government should in fact order but this time with the army/military in the testing and performance verification loop. If the army fails to carry the day on this issue, the lack of confidence and the uncertainty attending on the thermonuclear warheads/bombs will hobble the army as a strategic force.

A Nuclear Maginot Line?

That the Indian nuclear forces are being endowed with an overly defensive/reactive nature and that they are being reduced to a near tactical or theatre-level adjunct to a conventional military main force principally to deal with Pakistan, is an unfortunate development but evidenced by two facts. Firstly, the Indian nuclear armaments of the fission variety with miniscule yields in only tens of kilo tonnes and the extant delivery systems are all short to medium ranged missiles and aircraft – *Prithvi* SRBMs, Su-30 MKI and Mirage 2000. Further, the existing unready and disaggregated Indian nuclear deterrent may be adequate to deter a minor foe like Pakistan (which, conveniently for India, keeps its nuclear forces in a similarly unready state) but will be hugely insufficient to deal with the more potent threats like China and the US. Indeed, in case of a confrontation with say a Chinese force featuring the 1-3.3 megaton warheaded DF-21 mod 2 IRBMs or the versatile American thermonuclear arsenal, which will induct "fifth generation" fusion weapons in a few years, the existing Indian nuclear force make-up and its de-mated, de-alerted disposition is a recipe for self-deterrence.

And secondly, a string of self-contained nuclear fallout shelters are planned to be built along the border with Pakistan.[30] It suggests that what the Indian strategic planners have in mind is a nuclear Maginot Line. The Maginot Line, it may be recalled, was a heavily fortified line of mortar and stone defences with gun placements on its ramparts built by France on its eastern border in the inter-War years to blunt any German attack. The German Panzer Armies in World War II, however, made nonsense of it by simply outflanking it. The Indian Army too may be surprised in a future encounter by a daring adversary ordering its armoured and mechanised columns to rush past and around these static shelters full of troops seeking radiation protection under threat of imminent use of the enemy's nuclear weapons, occupy Indian territory, and even wrest the initiative of using nuclear weapons tactically or theatre-wise against Indian concentrations and rear area targets of opportunity to neutralise the possibility of a counter-attack or retaliatory strike.

The trouble is the Indian war planners do not think of nuclear weapons as war-fighting instruments. Time and again, senior military officers are heard to say what the former Army Chief Gen S. Padmanabhan recently said, albeit with a few flourishes of his own. "I do not see the (nuclear) weapon as a war-fighting one," he said. "It's like you make an expensive ornament for your wife. It may have taken years to make it, but she wears it once and keeps it in a vault. The Indian nuclear weapon is also to keep in a basement."[31]

Total wars between India and Pakistan have not been fought because of the close socio-political, religious and cultural linkages between them,[32] and nuclear war is for the same reasons unthinkable. There is, thus, a tendency in Indian military and civilian quarters to define the utility of nuclear weapons in any situation against any adversary in terms of the specific conditions and inhibitions operating with regard to Pakistan, which prevent the waging of wars of annihilation. This is a more serious liability than the nuclear bunkers strung out along the India-Pakistan border will prove to be in any nuclear war or near war or crisis. What use would these nuclear-proofed bunkers have against the threats posed by China or United States – the more probable scenarios in the future that may be actualised with ballistic and cruise missile strikes from the air and sea?[33]

Nuclear weapons are very like conventional military armaments in that the credibility of their use is only in terms of their utility in war. And this utilitarian quotient is high only when the forces are actually drilled in, and practise, nuclear war-fighting. Short of that, nuclear weapons *per se* may not deter a strong adversary and may, in fact, turn out to be mere "ornaments" that Gen Padmanabhan says they are. Barring such routinised drills and nuclear war-fighting practice by the field army, the resolve to use nuclear weapons will be doubted and the threat to activate nuclear weapons, even in a purely deterrent role, ring hollow. Ultimately a nuclear bomb "kept in the basement" will no more occasion dread than an entire formation of mothballed tanks.

As in the case of the conventional military, it is the operational readiness of a nuclear force constantly honed by war exercises that is critical to keeping a nuclear adversary honest. Gen Yuri Baluyevsky, first deputy chief of the Russian armed forces, for instance, justified the recent large scale nuclear war-games held in the country's six military districts, as necessary, he said, in order to "practis[e] strategic, including nuclear, deterrence" and to train for "preventing aggression and power pressure against Russia."[34] The Indian government and military likewise need desperately to see the nuclear weapon not merely as preventing "aggression" against sovereign territory but as shrugging off "power pressure" by the US and China or anybody else. This is the serious political value a country gets from owning a powerful nuclear arsenal of tested and reliable weapons – something India as yet cannot boast of.

All these aims will be realised only if India – and there is no way around it – obtains a fearsome nuclear orbat featuring a megaton thermonuclear-ICBM force and, on an accelerated schedule, an SSBN, the nuclear powered submarine capable of firing nuclear tipped ballistic and cruise missiles. And if it keeps the Indian forces in nuclear fighting trim, inducting at a minimum, for example, anti-contamination equipment and radiation resistant suits for troops for at least a three division equivalent of land forces. Presently, such equipment is available for about a brigade's worth of soldiers.

But to prove it's earnest, the Indian Army has to do more. Its operational nuclear war-fighting plans should aim to overwhelm the local nuclear adversary. Pakistan, in that sense, can be used for the purposes of "target practice." By itself it is not a serious threat to India and nuclear war-planning should not fixate on it. But intensive plans and preparations for nuclear war-fighting generally will signal to China and the US that India means business and is taking itself seriously as a nuclear military power and this will earn respect. Anything short of this will result in India's being continued to be bracketed with Pakistan in the nuclear sphere.

What should a credible nuclear war plan in the event look like? This writer has outlined an *ad interim* scheme until a consolidated peace with Pakistan is a reality to optimise the mobility and strike power of the Indian armoured and mechanised formations able to fight in a hatch-down mode. The scenario described as "Sialkot grab" envisions very rapid movements by armour to close with the enemy's defensive forces arrayed around cities like Sialkot, comprising the "strategic corridor" running south to north less than 30 miles from the border (which contains many of the most important of Pakistan's industrial and wealth-producing cities), which is arguably the centre of gravity of that state. Occupy critical parts of it and the Pakistani state falls apart.

Sticking close to the Pakistan Army, units will prevent Islamabad from doing what it says it will do – use tactical nuclear weapons in the first instance against ingressing Indian units on its own territory, because in that case these Pakistani Army units too will fall within its tactical nuclear fire zone and because it will end up targeting the Pakistani urban environs around which such Indian effort is concentrated. This may increase the pressures on Pakistan's National Command Authority to escalate by striking at Indian cities, according to the strategy Pakistan professes. But this decision will be an extremely difficult one to make because it would trigger a general nuclear war entailing the certain extinction of the Pakistani state. This is the exchange ratio the Pakistan Army will always be faced with.

The success in a nuclear confrontation lies precisely in confronting the adversary with impossibly difficult choices he cannot risk making. It is the only way to rein in GHQ, Rawalpindi's adventurousness and convince it that nuclear weapons have not made a whit of a difference to the natural and permanent military imbalance in the subcontinent unfavourable to Pakistan.[35] If such war plans are widely publicised and the appropriately equipped army formations are seen extensively to practise the execution of such operations, preferably with foreign, including Pakistani, military observers in attendance, it will have a salutary effect on Pakistan, of course, but also, as mentioned earlier on, China and the US as well. It will burnish India's reputation as a nuclear power that does not shy away from nuclear war-fighting. (This will require the Indian Army's hoary if impractical war plans of bisecting Pakistan on the Rahim Yar Khan axis in which lots of intellectual capital and material resources have been invested over the years, to be retired).

An India ready to fight a nuclear war if pushed, will add credibility to its inventory of high yield fusion (hydrogen) weapons equipping, say, the 666 Regiment hosting the thermonuclear-tipped *Agni-IV* ICBM, Tu-22 M3 strategic bomber fleet (to be acquired on lease) with air droppable H-bombs, and indigenously built and leased SSBNs. This force, moreover, will have to be deployed in the manner the great powers do, with a portion of it kept in launch-ready condition. Otherwise, however high value the force, it could be rendered inoperable by precision conventional munitions attacks on its constituent elements that the US is presently capable of launching and China will in a few years be able to do. In that case, it will be India that will face the dilemma of making the onerous decision of whether or not to cross the N-threshold in retaliation.

Special Operations Forces

At the other end of the conflict spectrum from the strategic arena where nuclear weapons are useable mainly as a strategic deterrent and as means of exerting political pressure are Low Intensity Warfare (LIW) and insurgency – the so-called "small wars" that Martin van Creveld says will increasingly encompass conflict within and between nations.[36] But nuclear weapons, far from making conventional military forces obsolete, in fact, require their build-up in more nuanced ways.

Gen Maxwell Taylor, for instance, was among the American military leaders in the 1950s who recognised that an intrepid enemy like the Soviet Union, would utilise the nuclear overhang as cover for prosecuting sub-conventional wars in the Third World to challenge the US by undermining friendly governments. The regular military opposed Taylor's emphasis insofar as it affected the growth and modernisation of the conventional military forces, but as John F. Kennedy's chairman, Joint Chiefs of Staff, he oversaw the accelerated expansion of the SOF.[37]

In the Vietnam War, even as the regular army floundered, battlefield successes were wracked up by SOF, like the Long Range Reconnaissance Patrols (LRRPs) who operating around the Ho Chi Minh Trail, disrupted supply lines and otherwise made life miserable for the North Vietnamese Army fighting in support of the Viet Cong in the south. That SOF continues to be strongly relevant in the US scheme of things for the new millennium is reflected in their deployment in Afghanistan to oust the Taliban regime and now to fight the Al Qaida terrorist organisation.

The Soviet military, from the time it was blooded in the revolutionary war, relied on *partizanskaia voina* (partisan warfare) described as "action behind the enemy lines by sympathetic irregular guerrilla forces"[38] to fight what the great Russian Gen Frunze, called "little wars" (*malaia voina*).[39] In Soviet military theory, the missions allotted to the partisan fighters, like harassing the enemy in the rear by interdicting his logistics system and communications channels, rendering "auxiliary" assistance to regular army units, gathering intellgence, and diverting hostile forces, read verily like those assigned to modern day SOF.[40]

During the Cold War, the Soviet Special Forces (*Spetznaz*) were geared to fill roles the regular military couldn't, and like their American counterparts in Vietnam, they had singular success in a losing cause in Afghanistan. But these forces are once again proving their mettle in Russia's counter-insurgency conflicts. In the First Chechen War, for instance, the Russian Army was mauled by the Chechen guerrillas, who inflicted casualties in the thousands with a whole division being virtually "wiped out." In the Second Chechen War, however, a brigade of the *Spetznaz* from Novosibirsk was sent in instead, and this time the Chechen freedom fighters were thoroughly beaten even as these Russian SOF suffered no more than two or three casualties during their entire deployment period.[41]

While bad governance compounded by divisive domestic politics has spawned numerous secessionist/separatist movements indulging in guerrilla warfare and terrorism in the country, the army is stuck with the responsibility of ending them. Terror has always been a traditional weapon of war except that now it is associated with "destructive warfare" attributable to *jehadis* and their ilk, as different from "progressive wars" boasting of certain norms and conventions that regular militaries supposedly wage.[42] The very different approaches to war-fighting in the two cases means that tasking the regular army for anti-guerrilla operations may be to incur the cost of considerable social collateral damage, as the Indian Army has recognised, in the physical sense of civilian casualties and destroyed homes and assets of the local people, "human rights violations" and, in the larger sense, of alienating the native populace, which fact is exploited by the insurgents to increase and strengthen their support base.

There is also the factor of external support. In Kashmir and in the northeastern states, the various insurgencies have been supported and sustained by Pakistan and China respectively with the result that India is politically distracted and the Indian Army tied down in sustained LIW and anti-guerrilla operations it is incapable of bringing to closure. Considering the huge returns on this low cost, low risk policy, neither Islamabad nor Beijing will be in a hurry to give it up, whatever undertakings their governments may give to New Delhi.[43]

Special forces capable of fighting the guerrilla on the latter's terms are, therefore, the only solution for a problem that is afflicting the nation as much as it is the Indian Army. The sub-conventional warfare ability of such forces to mount deep trans-border commando strikes (against terrorist training camps, supply depots, etc.) and generally to create mayhem in the enemy's rear areas, whether in a punitive retaliatory mode or as part of a larger policy strategically to discomfit an adjoining state offering support to Indian insurgents, will be critical in convincing the adversary to cease and desist. If a country faces no retribution, there is every incentive for it to continue supporting guerrillas and terrorist activity in India.[44]

The army has worsened the problem by showing no strategic sense in using such special forces it has – the five or six battalions of para-commando. Designated as Northern Army Reserve, the 9 Para and 10 Para, for example, are wasted in petty tactical strikes across the LoC. Moreover, despite every evidence to suggest that SOF are a far better bet to wipe out insurgencies, the Indian Army persists in its folly of using regular troops for this purpose and on insisting they fight according to some Marquess of Queensberry rules. Not only has it been determinedly against increasing the SOF strength, it does not even allow the RR units – manned by regular infantry troops who are processed through a short capsule of counter-insurgency training – deployed in the Srinagar Valley and elsewhere to grow beards and operate in mufti as irregulars. And it dissuades them from doing things like eliminating those identified as *jehadi* commanders in the field and their main supporters in the society. Indeed, RR commanding officers have been reprimanded for "fighting dirty" even if these tactics garnered success!![45] The negative attitude to any kind of SOF is apparently so great that a former army chief, whose antipathy is well known, reportedly turned down a proposal to configure the habitual "disciplinary cases," the misfits and the discards from the various regiments of the army into a crack irregular commando outfit. The army would rather that such people spend time in the Quarter Guard, in prison or continue disrupting normal unit cohesion than be gainfully employed in furthering the army's and the nation's objectives.[46]

But assuming that fatigue and shortage of resources will eventually persuade these groups of malcontents to make peace with the Indian state, as seems to be happening with the Naga secessionists, for example, sizeable SOF will still be required as the expeditionary arm in support of the more expansive role India is delineating for itself in the extended Indian Ocean region and Southern Asia. A far more significant role for a large-sized and multi-specialist SOF in the future will be to tackle the potentially horrific menace of nuclear terrorism.

A meaningful, multi-purpose SOF will have to have a comprehensive capability and be air and sea mobile. At the very least, a genuine expeditionary force would have to comprise two division equivalent forces, increasing over time to 5-6 division equivalent for distant deployment and built around a squadron of military air transport fleet and, perhaps, even a light 16,000 ton helicopter carrier. This is the irreducible minimum any credible SOF should have by way of retrieval, armed heliborne support and air and sea-lift capacities. And the SOF should be under command of a separate SFC at the Army Headquarters to control them and plan and direct them in the field, and to coordinate operations with the relevant theatre, corps and divisional commands as also with the SFC in-charge of the country's nuclear/thermonuclear weapons systems. If the Indian Army is not quick to seize the opportunity and reshape and enlarge its current para-commando units into a hefty and genuinely all-round SOF capability, other Services may fill the gap. After all, it was the IAF's lack of strategic vision and pusillanimity that allowed the Indian Navy to wrest the strategic bomber mission with the proposal to lease the Russian Tu-22M3 'Backfire'.[47]

The SOF in the advanced militaries are elaborate organisations divided between the sea, land and air components. Many of these then shear off into groups with specific regional and mission experience and, hence, operational specialisation – psychological operations, signals and electronic intelligence gathering, propaganda, sabotage, large scale demolitions, etc. For instance, the US Army's 5th Special Forces Group (Airborne), owing to its fluency in local languages and its familiarity with the native cultures, is usually called in when the operational area is in Asia.[48] This group was active during the time the Soviet occupation forces were in Afghanistan; more recently they ousted the Taliban regime from that country; and are now actively searching and destroying Al Qaeda cells within Afghanistan and in the NWFP and Baluchistan in Pakistan. Mission specialisation develops over time with sustained deployment of SOF units. Thus, the 157th Spetsnaz Brigade in Afghanistan had a special unit, *ohotniki karavana* (caravan hunters), to interdict *mujahideen* supply convoys and intercept and capture Westerners (mostly American covert operations agents, presumably) trying to sneak into Afghanistan.[49]

The Indian SOF are so far of a largely single mission character – para-commandos with high and low altitude parachuting competence, good survival skills once on the ground, and capable of sanitising and holding a designated area for short periods of time. The 1,000-odd strong Marine Commandos (Marcos) of the Indian Navy, created in the image of the US Navy's SEAL commandos, have proved their effectiveness in diverse milieus. Like in keeping the Wullar Lake in Kashmir free of both the *jehadis* and their handlers from across the LoC. But there is a void across the capabilities range, whether it be in mountain operations, specialist language skills, or the more demanding psyops, ELINT-SIGINT, propaganda, and so on. Units fluent in Pashtu, Balti, Tibetan and the Chinese languages will enable covert activities across the mountains in POK, NWFP, Baluchistan, in the Karakorams and Tibet, will have to be raised. And if operations are contemplated in Central Asia in cooperation with agencies of the CARs then knowledge of the Russian language is a minimum requirement.[50]

In this context, it would be prudent for the Indian Army to revive the Special Frontier Force (SFF), which was at the cutting edge of the clandestine war waged by the US Central Intelligence Agency and the Indian Intelligence Bureau involving Tibetan fighters against the Chinese Communist occupation forces in Tibet in the 1950s and 1960s.[51] With the passing from the scene of the current, the 14th Dalai Lama, there is every possibility of Tibetan nationalists taking to violence to regain independence for their homeland. It would be useful, at the very least, to have leverage in that situation of ensuring good Chinese behaviour in the Northeast by having a rebuilt SFF revolving around the night drop and other specialist capabilities and having a battalion of para-commando as the core of this composite SFF commando, as counter. And, in a more proactive mode, such SFF will be a powerful instrument for strategically unsettling the PLA on the Tibetan plateau.[52]

In the expeditionary role, other than the para-commandos, the army's 108 Brigade, which is part of the Andaman integrated command, should constitute the kernel of the country's amphibious capability. And it is this force that should be increased to division strength for rapid deployment anywhere in the Indian Ocean littoral to come in from the sea and firm up a lodgement on the littoral in strength. The aim of the country's SOF expeditionary capability would be to maintain law and order on the seas and in the proximal land areas, and to render help to friendly governments in the region facing threats from usurpers and the like.

It is the threat of nuclear terrorism, however, that needs to be urgently addressed by the Department of Atomic Energy (DAE) and the Indian military. The danger is from two sources. One is from the so-called "suitcase bombs," each weighing some 60 lb. Gen Alexander Lebed, secretary of the Russian State Security Council during a Washington visit in 1997 revealed that 132 of the 300 suitcase bombs in the Soviet arsenal were unaccounted for. It is also reported that the Chechen mafia have sold a number of these bombs to Osama bin Laden for $30 million in cash and two tons of Afghan heroin.[53] The other, still greater, danger comes from the most likely weapon in the hands of terrorists — radiological dispersion devices (RDDs). These last are packages of relatively easily available radioactive waste wrapped in conventional explosives, which, when detonated, spread lethal radioactivity. Both these threats may credibly emanate from Pakistan and other states in the region.[54]

In 1978, the US Department of Energy constituted the Nuclear Emergency Search Teams (NEST) of some 1,000 individuals trained in the main to detect, assess and disable nuclear bombs and RDDs. NEST stage out of the Nellis Air Force Base, Nevada, and in a contingency, assist the US SOF. Other US government agencies have similar outfits, for instance, the State Department has FEST (Foreign Emergency Search Team), the US Marines the CBIRT (Chemical, Biological Incident Response Team), and so on. The US DOE also has a Joint Technical Operations Team (JTOT) equipped with sophisticated instruments like the liquid abrasive cutter able to slice through any material without vibration and sparks and remotely operable at ranges of up to 1.2 km and portable hot spot mobile laboratories to analyse radiological samples to identify the kind of devices NEST may find.[55]

Russia has its secretive "Vympel" nuclear counter-terrorist commandos. American think-tanks, for instance, have conceived of situations in which NEST-SOF and the Russian Vympel join in "quick covert insertion to the sites (in Pakistan) to disable or even re-locate (Pakistani nuclear) weapons" and otherwise to "rescue the Pakistan arsenal of the need arises."[56] The Vympel organisation could, in fact, be the model for an Indian nuclear counter-terrorist commando outfit and its operating principles and tactics may be something this Indian outfit could, with appropriate changes, adopt.

War in the Electro-Magnetic Spectrum

Hardware is important but the software driving it is increasingly crucial. The so-called RMA, attributable to the micro-chip and semi-conductor, has been talked about for a decade and more. It is only with the application of these emergent technologies on the battlefield – in the First Gulf War, in Kosovo and the Balkans, in the Second Gulf War, and now in the successful hunt for Osama bin Laden – verily like finding a needle in a haystack – the IT generated advances have transformed war. It is now possible to engage in total war by simply jamming and spoofing radar and communications networks and otherwise causing so much disorientation as to make cohesive military action nearly impossible. Saddam Hussein's Iraqi Army was perhaps no great shakes as opposition but it is doubtful whether the Indian armed forces would have fared any better under the kind of electronic assault, followed by waves of air strikes succeeded by insertion of land forces, in effect, to conduct mopping up operations.

An overall architecture for network-centricity, what a former Chairman, Joint Chiefs of Staff, Admiral James Owen, called "a system of systems" which can bring intelligence data collected from innumerable platforms – satellites, RPVs and aircraft – high speed data processing, and the systems of vectoring appropriate weapon to stationary and mobile targets, is helping the US overwhelm its adversaries. In this field, the West European members of the NATO are thought of as lagging a generation behind their American counterparts. By this reckoning, the Indian military must be at least two generations behind the leading power. And because a clash of interests with the US may be on the cards, it is a gap the Indian defence forces cannot afford.

In this respect, instead of a single EW-network centric plan, each of the three Services is "doing its own thing." Without the electronic and IT interface and interoperability between their separate programmes optimised for different contingencies and situations, integrated military actions become difficult to launch and sustain. There is no reason why all the separate schemes cannot be brought under the COSC, pending the appointment of the CDS, the operating parameters defined holistically, taking into account the army's, navy's and air force's demands and requirements, and capital and effort mobilised to achieve a fairly effective system able to wage both offensive and defensive electronic warfare and to marshal all the resources available to fight wars of all kinds. India is regarded as an IT superpower and it will be central to the effort to involve the country's IT industry from planning stage onwards. This is very doable, considering the cutting edge work – algorithms, paradigms and solutions – our software engineers routinely produce to overcome very tricky and complex problems. Gen S. Padmanabhan's war-gaming scenario wherein Indian IT capabilities, logic bombs, computer viruses to disable sheltered American communications hubs, etc., are envisaged as defeating the US may not be as far-fetched as seems at first glance.[57] But this requires a strategic vision and the will and, of course, a genuinely combined effort by the three Services.

Making Hard Choices

If financial resources were not a constraint, the Indian government could have continued to fund and maintain the present army dominated by armour and mechanised forces as it has done since Independence. But the changing times and nature of war require a more discriminating approach. According to the blueprint advanced by the US Secretary of Defence Donald Rumsfeld, the US military of the future will be lighter-armed and more mobile and versatile, even as the American thermonuclear arsenal becomes more lethal and sophisticated. NATO has mooted a 21,000 strong Rapid Response Force as its cutting edge. Separately, Britain and France too are moving in the direction of configuring a force constituting small units trained variously to fight in distant jungles, urban locales, desert and mountains.[58] This London and Paris have decided to do after first safeguarding their top places in the rank order of countries by streamlining their respective modernised thermonuclear arsenals capable of delivering hundreds of megatonnage of destruction anywhere in the world.[59]

But there are roadblocks to realising a military that can pull its weight in 2020. The problem is not so much the paucity of financial resources as the correct use of the funds provided. If the Indian Army, in particular, means to retain the existing force structure of over 300 battalions divided between plains infantry and mountain warfare troops in the ratio 60:40 and armour and mechanised formations with well over 2,000 tanks along with a sizeable big callibre artillery, mobile and towed, in train and if, over and above this, the strategic thermonuclear arsenal and SOF are to be hugely augmented and a first-rate EW and network-centric system to be installed, then it becomes unaffordable. It has been persuasively argued by Col P.K. Vasudeva that even the regular military replacement and modernisation programmes on the anvil cannot be accommodated within the defence budget pegged at the 3 per cent of GDP level recommended by the 11th Finance Commission but that defence spending at the level of 4 per cent of GDP on national security would adversely affect the country's economic growth and is, therefore, inadvisable.[60]

It is for the army to make a correct appreciation of the kind of pressure situations it is most likely to face rather than stick with the idea of wars of yesteryears which will lead to wrong acquisition and force structuring decisions. It has to begin to associate its élan with the critical capability triad articulated here, and specifically with its strategic orientation and capability, with megaton thermonuclear weapons and *Agni* ICBMs and with the wherewithal to dominate the electromagnetic spectrum, instead of with tanks and field artillery. Wrong concepts of future wars and misplaced expenditure priorities may lead to the Indian Army doing a Pilsudski. Marshal Pilsudski, head of the Polish Army, distinguished himself by first sticking with the horse and then by leading a cavalry charge with drawn sabres against the Panzer tanks rushing towards Warsaw in 1939! •

Notes

1. Bharat Karnad, *Nuclear Weapons & Indian Security: The Realist Foundations of Strategy* (New Delhi: Macmillan India Ltd., 2002), pp.
2. Dominic Wilson and Roopa Purushothaman, "Dreaming with BRICs: The Path to 2050," *Global Economics Paper*, No. 99 (Goldman Sachs, New York), October 1, 2003.

3. Peter Harclerode, *Fighting Dirty: The Inside Story of Covert Operations From Ho Chi Minh to Osama bin Laden* (London: Cassell), 2001.
4. The writer has articulated an "Indian Monroe Doctrine" defining India's sphere of influence as encompassing the Indian Ocean and extending into Central Asia and Southeast Asia, east of the Malacca Strait. See Karnad, n.1, pp. 466-483. For an appreciation of India's more expansive foreign and military policy by an American security analyst, see Stephen Blank, "India's Grand Strategic Vision gets Grander" at http://www.atimes.com/atimes/South_Asia/EL25Df09.html
5. See Karnad, n. 1. For a concise treatment of the subject, see the author's, "To Pack a Good Wallop," *The Week*, Anniversary Special on India: Superpower 2020, December 28, 2003.
6. US President George W. Bush is expected to present an ambitious plan to promote democracy in the Middle East and South Asia. It would hold "Arab and South Asian governments" accountable for human rights violations. See "Bush to Unveil Greater Mideast, South Asia plans: Officials," Agencies, "World Focus", *The Statesman*, February 10, 2004.
7. This policy slant was reiterated by President George W. Bush in his most recent State of the Union address to the US Congress. America, he declared, "will never seek a permission slip to defend the security of our people." This quote and other parts of the presidential speech, reproduced in Elizabeth Bumiller and Richard W. Stevenson, "Bush Stresses Threat of Terror," *The New York Times, International Herald Tribune*, January 22, 2004.
8. Statement by President George W. Bush on "Next Steps in Strategic Partnership with India," issued on January 12, 2004, by the White House. http://www.whitehouse.gov/news/releases/2004/01/print/20040112-1.html
9. This is readily admitted by responsible US officials in private conversations.
10. Karnad, n.1, pp. 229-263, 545-557.
11. Ibid., pp. 549-556
12. Ibid., pp.540-548.
13. John Pomfret, "China General Warns Taiwan of Military Threat," *The Washington Post, The Asian Wall Street Journal*, December 4, 2004.
14. Lt Gen Li Jijun, "Notes on Military Theory and Military Strategy" in Michael Pillsbury (ed.), *Chinese Views of Future Warfare* (New Delhi: Lancer Publishers, 1998), Indian edition; (originally published by National Defense University, Washington, DC, 1997), p. 223.
15. Michael Pillsbury, "China's Strategic Outlook: A Case Study of Japan and India," paper presented at the 5th Asian Security Conference, New Delhi, January 27-29, 2003.
16. Statement by President Musharraf In *Pakistan TV News*, February 2, 2004. Regarding the "Father of the Pakistani Bomb" Dr Abdul Qadir Khan's confession that he had materially helped the nuclear weapons programmes of North Korea, Iran and Libya, see David Rohde and David E. Sanger, "Pakistani Admits Nuclear Transfers," *The New York Times, International Herald Tribune*, February 3, 2004.
17. Craig S. Smith, "Nuclear Black Market Had Roots in Europe," *The New York Times, International Herald Tribune*, February 20, 2004.
18. This is ancient knowledge. For more recent Press reports concerning China as the original proliferator emanating in the wake of Pakistan's now proven proliferation antics, see Joby Warrick & Peter Slevin, "Pak, Libya Nukes of Chinese Origin," *Los Angeles Times–Washington Post, The Indian Express*, February 16, 2004.

19. US Senator Larry Pressler discusses just why the US national interest in discomfiting the Soviet military occupation forces in Afghanistan led to the State Department turning a blind eye to Pakistan's acquisition of nuclear weapons. See his "The Restraint of Fury: US Non-Proliferation Policy and South Asia," in Bharat Karnad (ed.), *Future Imperilled: India's Security in the 1990s and Beyond* (New Delhi: Viking, 1994)
20. The US government has publicly accepted the Musharraf regime's explanation that the secret transfers of nuclear skills, technology, and hardware are attributable exclusively to Dr A.Q. Khan's greed and did not have the Pakistan Army's approval! Said the White House spokesman: "Pakistan was not involved in any kind of proliferation — I am talking about the government of Pakistan — and we value their assurances." See T.V. Parasuram, "US: We Value Pak Word on Proliferation," PTI, *The Asian Age*, February 5, 2004.
21. Moscow had contemplated a strike to take out China's nascent nuclear weapons industry in 1962 and even approached the US to join in this venture.
22. Karnad, n.1, pp. 612-645.
23. A.J. Bacevich, *The Pentomic Era: The US Army Between Korea and Vietnam* (Washington, DC: National Defense University Press, 1986), pp. 67-70, 105.
24. Ibid., pp.103-127.
25. Ibid., p.137.
26. Ibid., p.141.
27. Marshal V.D. Sokolovskii, *Soviet Military Strategy* (RAND Translation, Englewood Cliffs, NJ, Prentice-Hall Inc., 1963), p. 298.
28. Ibid., p.297.
29. For an in-depth analysis about why the 1998 tests were not all that they were cracked up to be and why the thermonuclear device was a dud, see Karnad, n.1, pp. 405-437.
30. Vishal Thapar, "N-Shelters on Border, LoC, in PMO,"*Hindustan Times*, February 10, 2004.
31. "Pak Nuclear Threat Worried Only me, says ex-Army Chief", *The Indian Express*, February 3, 2004
32. For an analysis of India-Pakistan Wars that suggests India cannot wage a war of annihilation against Pakistan but can only join Pakistan in fighting wars of manoeuvre because of the live and organic religious, social and cultural links which, in turn, translate into political inhibitions and limitations imposed on the military in the conduct of wars, see Karnad, n.1, pp. 561-562. This case was originally made by Bharat Karnad in "Key to Peace in South Asia: Fostering 'Social' Links Between the Armies of India and Pakistan," *The Round Table, The Commonwealth Journal of International Affairs*, April 1996, and in "Key to Confidence-Building in South Asia: Fostering Military-to-Military Links," *USI Journal*, April-June 1996.
33. The US as a threat is finally gaining adherents in the Indian military circles. See the future war scenario of India going up against the US in Gen S. Padmanabhan, *The Writing on the Wall: India Checkmates America 2017* (Delhi: Manas Publications, 2004)
34. Vladimir Radyuhin, "Russia Begins Large-Scale Nuclear War Games," *The Hindu*, February 11, 2004.
35. Karnad, n. 1, pp. 666-682.
36. Martin van Creveld, *On Future War* (London: Brassey's (UK), 1991).
37. Seymour J. Deitchman, *Limited War and American Defense Policy* (Cambridge, MA: Massachusetts Institute of Technology Press, 1964).

38. See the RAND study: Raymond L. Garthoff, *Soviet Military Doctrine* (Glencoe, IL: The Free Press, 1953), p. 442.
39. Ibid., p. 392.
40. Ibid., p. 393.
41. Comment by a Russian military attache.
42. The pros and cons about this typology of wars are discussed in John A. Lynn, *Battle: A History of Combat and Culture* (Boulder, CO and London: Westview Press, 2003), p. 327.
43. Thus, notwithstanding the apparent thaw in bilateral relations in the wake of the Vajpayee-Hu Jintao Accord and the ongoing efforts at resolving the border dispute, China continues to nurse the insurgency card to play against India. See Barry Hart, "Chinese Shadow Over Northeast!", *Sahara Times*, January 17, 2004. And Bhavatosh Singh, "ISI Ropes in Traders to Fund Militants," *The Statesman*, 31 July 2003.
44. This is the case the writer has made for over a decade now. For his more recent writings on the subject, see Bharat Karnad, "Obtaining Appropriate Military Capabilities, Post-Kargil: Special Operations Forces as the Cutting Edge," *Indian Defence Review*, October-December 1999 and *Nuclear Weapons & Indian Security*; pp. 405-512.
45. Several Rashtriya Rifles unit commanders who have been posted in Jammu & Kashmir; non-attributable personal communications.
46. A senior serving officer; unattributable comment.
47. Karnad, n.1, pp. 650-666.
48. Harclerode, n.3, p. 523.
49. Ibid., p. 558.
50. The government of Kazakhstan, for instance, has ordered an investigation of the active "nuclear black market" in that country. See "Kazakh Probe," AP, "World Focus", *The Statesman*, February 21, 2004.
51. Harclerode, n.3, pp. 332-393.
52. Interestingly, Humphrey Hawksley posits an Indian-aided Tibetan commando drop on Lhasa as the trigger for a future India-China nuclear war. See his *Dragonfire* (Basingstoke and Oxford: Macmillan, 2000).
53. See the *Jerusalem Report* story in http://www.jrep.com/Reporter/Article-46.html
54. See Bruce G. Blair, "What if the Terrorists go Nuclear?," Centre for Defence Information, last updated October 1, 2001, http://www.cdi.org/terrorism/nuclear,cfm
55. US Department of Energy, "Nuclear Incident Response," http://www.llnl.gov/nci/rdiv/nucinc.html
56. Blair, n.54.
57. Padmanabhan, n.33.
58. Judy Dempsey, "UK and France Join Forces on Combat Units," *Financial Times*, February 10, 2004.
59. Karnad, n.1. pp.524-526.
60. See P.K. Vasudeva, "More Money for Defence?," *The Tribune*, February 21, 2004.

VIEWS OF DISCUSSANTS

Cmde Ranjit B. Rai

The Indian Army is not dealing with the unknown. It is dealing with the weapons and equipment which are available today. The army bought the *Tanguska* before the Indian Navy bought the *Kashtan*. I did the commentary at your *Vijay Diwas* and I felt so proud of the army. I went around to meet *jawans* of the regiment of the Air Defence Artillery, whose knowledge was at par with any sailor of the technical branch of the navy. I was pleasantly surprised to see their technical efficiency. I know Indian troops can master any technology, but you have to have the tools. You gave them the *Tanguska*, a very difficult system. The Indian Navy took one year to commission the *Kashtan* in Russia. But the *jawans* did it here, in India. It means the technological aptitude of our *jawans* is good.

As I said, the army is not dealing with the "unknown." You can dabble with the latest technologies at Singapore, Indonesia and Malaysia. Army officers and men can and should interact with the foreign armies and jointly train themselves. Such interaction will give you the confidence and widen your horizons. Let me tell you that you are capable of learning the most complex technology or tactics through interaction and observation.

During such exposures, immense opportunities come your way. Last month in Singapore, I flew in a P–3C Orion for three hours and in a Euro Fighter for one and a half hours and got a chance to handle their controls. You should also avail such opportunities.

The Indian private sector is now taking defence production seriously. Larson & Toubro has made the control system for the *Brahmos* missile, and a Chennai based company is also closely associated with the development of its sub-systems. Similarly, Larson & Toubro has vastly improved upon the existing system of the *Pinaka* multi-barrel rocket launcher. Gen Kapoor has given you a full outline; I could not have done better. I would avoid nuclear issues, as I do not have first hand operational knowledge. Bharat said doctrine decides strategy. In a democracy, the army has to involve the political hierarchy, so please involve the leadership in this process. Gen Narhari mentioned about the relevance of holding and strike corps; this needs a closer look. Our attrition-oriented concept of warfare is outdated; aim for the enemy's centre of gravity instead. If, by 2010, the army does not evolve a fresh war-fighting philosophy, then, by 2020 it will be the same organisation, with some modern military hardware on its inventory. That's all.

Take into account the advantages of technology, firepower, communications, mobility, which will change the way we think, plan and operate.

No war can be fought without air superiority and that is why the Indian Navy pursued the case of acquiring the *Gorshkov* aircraft carrier. We may not understand the rationale behind it today, but, if there is a war, and the navy does not possess an aircraft carrier, no ship will be willing to engage the enemy. We all know the Indian Ocean is getting militarised, day by day; even a country like Singapore has four submarines, E2C Hawk Eye aircraft, F-16 fighters, and is toying with the idea of acquiring the Eurofighter.

Asymmetry is no disadvantage. 9/11 is ample proof, wherein a nation spending US $ 4,000 million over its defence was attacked by spending just US $ one million, and that war is still on. So, think of ways and means of turning asymmetry to your advantage. Special forces could be one, which will give us immense capability in terms of strategic clout and reach.

The modernisation and restructuring would need funds. The army is really very revenue intensive. Pay and pensions take most of the budget, so where is the money for capital expenditure? Meagre fund allocations of just 3 per cent of the GDP for the defence budget cannot support the kind of modernisation that we all have in mind. Perhaps, downsizing is the answer, as the revenue bill is only going to increase in the future, due to inflation.

Do not treat me only as a naval officer. I have worked with the army in Sri Lanka; I was DA in Singapore; I understand Siachen and other hot spots where the army is dealing with various conflict situations. Let me recommend that you must ask for a reduction from these deployments. Perhaps you are not aware of the size, capability and the wherewithal of the Central Police Organisations (CPO) and the Para-Military Forces (PMF). These are over 700,000 strong. They are getting Ml 17 helicopters, transport aircraft, speedboats and flat bottom ships. Some of them have their own para-commando battalions. They are not as naive as you think. Consider handing over homeland security and counter-insurgency tasks to the CPOs and PMF. The army must review its charter of duties, as it is over-committed. Most of the duties are not your tasks; reduce such involvement, so that you can concentrate on training, modernisation and integration.

I come back to the issue of exposure and interaction with foreign armies. We must forge defence cooperation and alliances, so that the officers and men get a chance to work, train and exercise with foreign armies. This will do a world of good to their confidence, thinking and vision. There are immense opportunities of learning for all of us through the inter-Services interaction at the level of officers and men. Most of us do not understand each other. Frequent visits and joint exercises would help.

As far as the modernisation is concerned, turn to the defence entrepreneurs, involve the private sector, have close interaction with the DRDO and the R&D facilities of the other two Services, to bring in synergy in your modernisation efforts. Do not change GSQRs frequently. Accept a developed equipment, its improved version will follow.

We all talk of power projection; it is fine – we must have such capability. But have we ever pondered over the issue of inter-Services command and control? There are many issues which need sorting out. In fact, we should have a system in place, wherein the inter-Services issues are not dealt with in an ad hoc manner, each and every time these crop up. The doctrinal aspect of this issue must be addressed with sincerity and settled once for all.

Clausewitz talks of the "fog of war." Today, I have tried to lift the "fog of technology" for you. These are known technologies, which the armies the world over are dealing with. Get your men to work in such an environment, so that their way of thinking and aptitude changes. The Duke of Wellington once said, "I have tried, all my life to learn and understand, what was there over the hill." Today, with the available technologies, you generals and your young officers can very well see what lies on the other side of the hill.

Technology absorption is another area you have to work upon; perhaps you find that the present educational standards of your men are not enough. Arrange for their additional education. I know it is a challenge to command educated and technically qualified troops but you have to meet this challenge in the future.

For 2020, you have to change the Indian Army. You have to rewrite that "war book;" politicians and bureaucrats will not ask you to change, because no one likes to lose power. Once you get your doctrinal bearings right, everything else will fall into place.

The greatest challenge for the army is ICK^2 (information based command and control). It is not the technology alone, but it also involves bringing in together the "community of communities" of all the three Services. This interaction will deconstruct old procedures and harness synergy and new opportunities. Homeland defence has wider implications. It is not confined to the deployment of troops alone. Approach the Home Ministry for better intelligence and redraw your tasks in internal security responsibility. Thank you, Mr Chairman, it was a total privilege for me to speak to this august gathering.

Lt Gen G.K. Duggal

Gentlemen, being the last speaker, I think one has both the advantage and the disadvantage. The disadvantage is that a lot of ground has been covered, many speakers have already spoken before me, and the advantage is that I can safely quote them. The three speakers have put across their points of view very effectively and convincingly and I will not go into commenting upon what they have said and what they have omitted. I would only speak on a couple of issues, which I consider important.

First, the mindset syndrome, which Shri Ranjit Gupta had mentioned in passing. I think it is human nature to resist change, to find it difficult to shed the beliefs and to shed the mindsets, which have been created over the years. The 1.5 million strong defence forces and our bureaucratic hierarchy are no exception. While working out and implementing RMA, I think it is food for thought that we need to bring in those elements, which will eventually usher in RMA.

Second, the pace of RMA. It is well known that to implement an RMA of the kind we are talking about will take many decades. The Americans started it in the early 1990s, and it is going to fructify by 2025. The Chinese commenced their programme way back in 1979, immediately after the Sino-Vietnam War and are likely to take time up to 2030. Therefore, what are we talking about? It has started just 6-7 years ago and where have we reached? I think, apart from some structural changes and a bit of modernisation in certain fields, our achievements have been none too impressive. For us to usher in RMA, the deadline should be 2040 and not 2020.

Third, our threat perceptions. I think we should not say what our target countries want us to say. We need to have our independent views. It was brought out by some speakers that by 2020, the USA will consider India as a potential threat. The Chinese perception will not be different either. I would recommend that we prepare ourselves to meet that particular threat. Such a situation may not arise by 2020 as envisaged, but by 2050, it could be a reality. So, while we talk about the time-frames, we need to evaluate threats pragmatically and work out our force restructuring, shape, size and own doctrine, in a meaningful manner.

By 2020, the world order would not change radically. China is going to be preeminent, the USA is going to be predominant and India will be working her way through to preeminence, in the shadow of such major players. We have to be prepared to deal with coercive diplomacy, and shall we say, gunboat diplomacy and blackmail. As far as our immediate neighbours are concerned, though our relations are improving, I do not foresee all our territorial disputes being resolved by 2020. During the interregnum, we should prepare ourselves for fighting short, swift and fast paced wars. Our strategic capabilities, commensurate to our capabilities, must be developed.

Fourth, which model should we follow? There is a tendency to follow the Western models, especially the American, which is not entirely compatible with our needs and environment. The USA does not have any live borders; they do not have any disputed territories. So, how can we transplant their model entirely? Yes, we can learn from their experience to create our own homegrown model for RMA, which can help us in restructuring and in dealing with future conflict requirements. In future, smaller forces, swifter forces with C^4I^2 capabilities and firepower will hold sway. So, in our restructuring exercise, we have to take into account the threats, the requirements, and the resources, and balance these accordingly. It will be a long-term perspective plan, to be implemented in stages, wherein some mid-course corrections will be applied from time to time. We should also take into account our advantages in certain areas of technology, which can give us a lead over others.

In stage 1, strengthen the C^4I^2 structures and exploit our advantages in IT. Improve capability in the field of mobility and restructure the special forces and field formations to enhance their performance in a short, swift and shallow depth war. All capabilities, which were recommended by our speakers, may not be achievable in the 2020 time-frame. We have to go in for a pragmatic prioritisation.

Gradually, we should delink from counter-insurgency and border management tasks. A doctrine dealing with counter- insurgency, border management, short wars, full-scale conflicts and conflicts in the nuclear backdrop will be voluminous. It cannot work.

Initiate steps for integration with the other Services. We cannot have complete integration in this time-frame. However, some steps could be taken to show our resolve for jointness. In order to fully realise reorganisation by 2020, structures and organisations must come into effect by 2010. By which time, equipping, modernising and technology introduction would have made inroads in our army and would continue till 2020. The assimilation of technology at doctrinal and formation levels will be an important aspect to this change. A meaningful downsizing by 2020 is neither realistic nor in sight. We should continue to work and improve our strategic capability against any blackmailing.

In stage II, which will go beyond 2020, and may reach up to 2040, our Services should achieve full integration. I think four decades are more than enough to forge all the three Services into one. Along with that, we would need to enhance our nuclear and space capabilities. Our strategic capabilities must be further enhanced and C^4I^2SR should be in position, both for conventional and nuclear forces. RMA planning for such a long period will have to be worked out, and the immediate, mid-term and long-term objectives will have to be identified and achieved. Thank you. •

INTERACTIVE SESSION

Maj Vivek Chaddha

Sir, at the end, one tends to get a feeling that defence is the responsibility of the army/armed forces. I think nobody does us a favour by giving us 3 per cent of the GDP. Spending on national security is as much the responsibility of the ruling elite, as of the armed forces. We should be very clear about it. We don't seem to be looking at the challenges of the future. Our thinking is focussed on Pakistan and China. India's economic progress by 2020 has been corroborated by many experts; the country is expected to be the fourth largest economy. If that be so, the military strength will flow from that, hence, we should be looking at the armed forces of 2050 and not only at the army of 2020. So our aim is just not adequate. We should look beyond.

India, should, therefore, mould its vision in the context of its future place in the world. Should it be neutral or should it be defensive or should it assert itself on the regional scene, if not the global one? This dilemma has been faced by all major powers in the past.

Irrespective of India's stance, the country will have adversaries in the neighbourhood and in the regions where its economic interests lie. With economic progress, our economic interests will also be growing far and beyond, especially to the Middle East and Central Asia. We will be bound to protect those interests.

Lt Col Vivek Bhatnagar

Sir, if we are looking at Army: 2020, then there is a requirement of changing our attitudes and mindsets. Our attitude is just not geared to accept such radical changes in the organisation, in the equipment and doctrines.

Brig Gurmeet Kanwal

Mr Chairman, given the theme of the seminar, I have a list of issues which I thought could have been included but perhaps for lack of time, they haven't been. Firstly, the strike corps and the holding corps: do these need to be restructured? Do we at all need three strike corps? The answer may be is yes, but it should have been battled out. Or do we need to give some divisions to the holding corps and convert them into the pivot corps and make these divisions self-contained for a limited offensive across the international border, under the nuclear umbrella?

Secondly, the firepower: we produced hundred guns per objective in Kargil and we could win that war. That was strategic vision on the part of some people and strategic risk taking on the part of other people. It is now amply proved that hundred guns per objective actually paved the way for victory. The infantry suffered less casualties because of that. We will be able to further minimise the casualties in the next war. Therefore, can we produce hundred guns per objective or per target in the plains? Do we have long ranges and the ability to concentrate that firepower? I think this has been completely glossed over, and should not have been.

Thirdly, the air assault. Bharat Karnad has adequately covered it. Sir, if you recollect, in Perspective Plan – 2000, the Indian Army was to have an air assault division but it didn't come about for various reasons. Is there an air assault requirement for 20-30 years hence? I definitely feel that there is a requirement for battalion sized air assault groups even now, and a brigade sized force later. Not only for contingency planning – we almost required one in Sierra Leone; mercifully things worked out – but definitely also for power projection. We will surely be in the power projection game in the next decade or so.

And lastly, cyber warfare units in the Indian Army. Do we want to take over our own cyber warfare related role or do we want to hand it over to some civilian scientists, and hope for the best? Thank you.

Lt Gen K. Balaram

Mr Chairman, I have only two points. This concerns what Mr Bharat Karnad said. I happened to have the opportunity of spending three days with the Pentomic Division in West Germany way back in 1956. I had gone there on an exercise, to try to understand what exactly they were doing. It was a colossal task and when I asked an American captain, of my rank, who was with me as liaison officer, about it, his answer was, "I know less about this than you do." That is point one. Mind you, the prevailing strategy at that time was not tactical use of nuclear weapons, it was the "trip wire strategy" – you cross the border, we will send off our ballistic missiles. That sort of idea prevailed at that time.

The second issue I would like to mention is that I think it was during the senior Bush's time, when the Berlin Wall came down. Tactical nuclear weapons were withdrawn from the American Army. I may be wrong, but I think it was around that time. Now, tactical nuclear weapons are no longer in vogue. The rest of it, as far as nuclear weapons are concerned, we are not discussing. We are not even in the know of these things, as far as I know. Perhaps the present day chief knows about this. I wonder if you would be permitted to play around with this, like a user trial of nuclear weapons. I do not think that it will be permitted. One advantage that we have for refining our nuclear weapons is that the USA has not ratified the CTBT. Therefore, it leaves the doors open for us to carry out more tests, if necessary. Thank you.

Lt Gen V.K. Nayyar

Mr Chairman, this session gives us a very good idea of what we really need to look at. Lt Gen V.K. Kapoor gave us a wide spectrum of things which we need to do, some immediately and some that can wait. Then Ranjit gave us a ground level view and, finally, Bharat provided us a view from space. The conflict spectrum which we need to look at is from strategic to low intensity. In this spectrum, one has to visualise about the vacant middle ground, how it will be played. Conflicts of the middle ground will draw on mobility, lethality and time for decision-making, in which the escalation factor will be predominant. To that extent, coupled with what Brig Gurmeet Kanwal said, we need to look at some of our large formations and what should be their size and shape for the task in the middle ground. This is what we need to look hard at. He also made a very valid point that the effort from the middle ground would come in, really speaking, wherever force projection is required. I am afraid that is one area where instead of being forward looking we have been backward looking. When I say backward looking, I mean that our air mobility and naval lift capability has gone down over a period of time. It is less today than what we possessed some fifty years ago. He also mentioned about the special forces. I have a different opinion. I want to make a distinction here. What do you want your special forces to do? One is force projection, trans-border operations... yes, for these we need the special forces of the type that was talked about. But when you are handling insurgencies and LICO within your country, I think the ethos changes. I say the ethos changes, because there is a problem. Unfortunately, everyone is spelling out the strategic vision, but no one is talking about the political vision, which has to go into resolving these problems. Unless that political vision is spelt out, laying down the politico-socio-economic vision for this country for various areas, you will find that we will be operating on an ad hoc basis, as we have been doing in the counter-insurgency environment. Even when such policy guidelines have not been given, I think that over a period of time our army has devised these for themselves. We need not deviate from them, but there are two basic requirements to be met. One is that you have to dominate the area and the population; for this, you have to understand the socio-political-economic background, and this cannot be done by inducting forces on a short-term basis. You are not conducting operations as the Americans are doing in Afghanistan. That is a foreign country, where they are not accountable for their actions, on a permanent basis, to their public. Therefore, this has to be done by the PMF or infantry or anyone else who stays in the area; though I am not in the favour of the infantry or the army getting involved. You have a basic template, wherein manning should be by the PMF, and the type of special forces operations which are to be undertaken are ones such as striking insurgents inside our territory or transborder pursuits. The magnitude of our problem is such that you can have two divisions of special forces. This is where both the wrong use and misuse of the special forces that we have had so far, has come into vogue. Thank you.

Brig B.K. Ponwar

Mr Chairman, this is regarding what has been said about power projection. Lt Gen V.K. Kapoor mentioned about strategic force projection. Just the other day, I had a battalion commander from Alaska, from the Striker Brigade, giving us a presentation on his Striker Brigade, as to where all in the world it can go. He mentioned that within 96 hours, this hi-tech mechanised force can be deployed anywhere on the globe, and the USA has about six such formations. These are the people who are coming to train with us. How far are we looking, as far as this strategic force projection is concerned in 2020? Gen Kapoor said that this force could get deployed into a friendly neighbourhood; but what will be its overreach? Which are the friendly nations we are looking at? Around the periphery of the Indian Ocean, in Africa, in the Middle East and in the CARs or are we also looking across the Atlantic Ocean? Thank you.

Lt Gen K.S. Brar

Mr Chairman, Lt Gen V.K. Kapoor gave us a very fine exposure as to what sort of force structures we would like to have in 2020. Just a word of caution; the first point by the speaker was that we should have conventional forces for a limited conflict. All I wish to say is that relationships can change, intentions can change and perceptions can change. In the Fifties, we had different relations and perceptions regarding the Chinese. In 1962, it was totally different. I would say that we must cater for the worst and we should build up our capability, whatever the budget permits. A mixture of technology and manpower is the answer. But let us not limit our thinking to only limited conflicts in 2020. We must be prepared for full scale conflicts, limited in duration perhaps, because there will be interventionist powers like the international community and the UN. There can be external pressures to halt the war or to reduce the time-frame of the war. But we should not have a mindset that the conflict will be limited. The danger is, if we tell the government or even project that our threat perception is going to be limited, they may not be very generous in providing us all the resources that we need. So let us not take it for granted that the conflicts will be limited. It could be limited in duration but it could be a full-fledged conflict, particularly in the context of China.

Gen Shankar Roy Chowdhury

I would like to make a comment, sir. I have read in the papers, as I am not privy now to what is going on, that the army has made a perspective plan, that is up to 2017, in which the army has apparently stated that they do not expect a conflict of the kind that you are talking about. I am just making a comment at this point.

Lt Col I.M. Singh

Sir, I would like to add to the discussion on special forces, and on specifically addressing Mr Karnad. I am looking at the general doctrine for emerging challenges in 2020. I would like to ask about these three divisions of special forces that you have mentioned. Taking off from what Gen Nayyar said, are we looking at these formations being employed across the borders or are these meant for internal security? Now, why I am asking this is to clarify whether we see the *jehadis* as special forces? In fact, why don't we see the *jehadis* as special forces? They are brilliant special forces. If this discussion was taking place in Islamabad and if they were discussing general doctrine for emerging challenges from or against India, they would have certainly taken into account the feasibility of employing *jehadis* in a future war against India, as such a force can be effectively employed in conventional, sub-conventional and non-conventional conflict scenarios. I am not too sure whether we look at special forces in the manner the Pakistanis look at the *jehadis*. Militarily that may be a great option, which a lot of people talk about in the army. Why don't we go across? But I do not know if the political leadership is there to support us in undertaking this sort of a thing. So, I would like you to elaborate on this, sir.

Col (Dr) P.K. Vasudeva

Almost all the speakers have said that insurgency, terrorism and low intensity conflicts will continue even beyond 2020. We have two types of ad hoc unified commands for coordinating the counter-insurgency operations. One, in J&K and the other in the Northeast. This aspect has been left out by all the speakers. I find the unified command concept, as established by the erstwhile Governor of Assam, Gen Sinha, working satisfactorily in the Northeast. Whereas, the unified command in J&K, where Gen Sinha is the governor presently, is functioning unsatisfactorily. It is very difficult to handle the PMF and the police, as both strive for one-upmanship. There should be a concept promulgated by law that these forces must come under the command of the army, which is deployed there, and the corps commander should be the boss of this unified command. Only then can the insurgency be controlled, otherwise the civilians and the security forces will continue to suffer casualties.

Gen Shankar Roy Chowdhury

Let me be very clear on this. This concept of unified command, as far as the PMF are concerned, is not acceptable to them. They do not accept coming under army command. I have had the same problem and we all have faced similar problems. In this peculiar Indian set-up, the only way you can integrate and control the PMF, the police and the CPOs is if you have a boss, like the chief minister of the concerned state, who heads the unified headquarters. It is a peculiar pattern which no other country has, except India.

The problem of Assam is different, as the chief minister did not want to be part of it. Mr Prafulla Mahanta did not want to go to his constituency, because he came to power on the promise that he would send the army back to the barracks. How could he be part of this unified command? These are the realities of the Indian situation, which the army, whether at the senior level or younger level, will have to understand.

Brig D.N. Verma

Sir, I cannot forget an article which I read in 1990 in the *Times*, wherein they said that the Indian Army is like an elephant. They move slowly, and when they come around, you come to know about them much earlier, and you can attack them from the rear, or from the sides. Only you should not confront them from the front.

There are certain grassroots problems we are suffering from, and if these are not removed, I am afraid what we are planning to achieve in 2020 will not be possible.

The place of pride which an Indian Army soldier had in 1950 and 1960, has deteriorated from 1970 onwards. Today, when I stand to observe a recruitment rally of the army and that of a paramilitary force, the material which is coming to get enrolled in the BSF, the civil police, the CRPF and the CISF is taller, steadier, more educated and hailing from a better background. What we are getting into our rank and file are weaker and shorter persons, hailing from a weaker background. This decay took place because we did not improve, while others, seeing us, improved and have gone ahead of us in certain areas like uniforms, training infrastructure and the amenities, which attract better manpower and instill more pride in them. First, we have to improve this. Why should an infantry man or for that matter a soldier of any arm or service not be physically fit, able to handle a variety of equipment? A police constable today can handle a vehicle, handle a weapon, use a radio set and he can read and write a little also. On the other hand, we have to have a separate MT Platoon, separate rifleman, separate radio operator; we do not have training facilities wherein a man can become a specialist at his job. As commandant of a regimental centre, I get letters from COs of para commando units for motivating recruits to volunteer for the parachute regiments. This is the state we have reached today that there are not enough volunteers for the parachute regiment, and they are looking to the infantry regimental centres to fill the rank and file of the parachute brigade.

Another point, which was put across by Gen Kapoor, and which has been oppressing the present environment of the army, is the load of the complete country on our shoulders. Whether it is an ecological task force, whether it is flood relief, whether it is relief to help somebody out, whether it is organising the Asiad, or organising and controlling any situation anywhere, for everything, the army goes in. The result is that today the soldier, except for the two months of annual leave, is running from pillar to post. He is not able to play games. He is not able to do the correct physical exercises. So much so, it is difficult to organise a range classification firing for him and then we expect him to shoot straight. These are the grassroots problems. If we do not eradicate them and bring back the army to a place of pride, I am afraid 2020, may see a rank and file which we may not be very proud of. We need to take stock of that. Thank you.

Gen Shankar Roy Chowdhury

I would like to make a few comments with the permission of the house. All the problems you mentioned in your second point are the fault of the army and the army alone. Why do you think an infantry soldier is happier to go to a field area? At a peace station, he is supposed to be in a place where he can be comfortable and gets some time to himself. But the routine in a peace station is over-busy, and it is the fault of the army set-up. Security duties, guard duties, organised sports, this that and the other, keep a soldier busy. As a matter of fact, it is the army which has to bring a different type of peace-time routine in the peace locations, so that when a soldier comes out of a field area, he gets a break, really gets a respite. Things are out of the hands of the army as far as married accommodation is concerned. Hopefully, that will come up in its own time. It is the routine, which is part of army culture, which needs a relook in order to give same respite to a *jawan*. This is my comment on what you said.

Lt Gen V.K. Kapoor

Sir, I have got just a few points. Regarding the "hundred guns" which Brig Gurmeet Kanwal mentioned, I think when we look to the future, we are looking for guns with greater lethality, precision and range. Therefore, we do not want a hundred guns. In fact, we want fewer guns to be able to do what a hundred guns can do today. The requirement of neutralising a target will continue, but in the future, this will be possible. With the type of ammunition that you are getting, and with the types of guns, it will be possible to achieve this with smaller numbers.

Secondly, the issue of cyber warfare, information wars, cyber wars and net wars, these are names which are interchangeable. That means net wars are to society what cyber wars are to the military. So when we say information war and cyber war, it is the same thing.

Next the issue of the police, CRPF, etc getting better manpower. It is a correct observation. I noticed it when I was a brigade commander in J&K. There was a very good friend there, the IG BSF, and I used to see that their manpower was much better. This is simply because these are highly corrupt forces, and people join them to make money. Believe me, I have interviewed them. They join to make money. Therefore, do not get frightened about it. In good battalions, this very manpower which you are getting, gets you the victory. So do not get too worried that the recruit is not tall enough or broad enough. Our soldiers are the most resilient soldiers in the world. There are no better soldiers. Your observation is right, but I do not think we should be worried, because in the units, the training and the upbringing they receive is very good, and I hope that continues.

Next, the issue of loading of the entire country's problem on your shoulders. When I joined the army in 1964, it was the same, except that what has happened now is this insurgency, and this seems to have increased year after year. So that is where we got over-burdened, but the army is the last pillar of the state and, to that extent, you have to bear this burden, whether you like it or not. I mean that's one way of putting it. The other is like it was mentioned... if the internal security problems are handled by the Home Ministry entirely, which may happen in due course. If we are able to prevail upon them, only then, I think, it can be taken off from our shoulders.

Regarding inclusion of strike corps, holding corps, or pivot corps in the discussion, gentlemen, if you look at the subject, it could have been tackled either at the conceptual level or at the tactical level, because of the time factor. Therefore, it was touched upon at the conceptual level. But I can assure you, if you have the time, I have the will, to tell you how restructuring of divisions and corps can be done. Thank you.

Dr Bharat Karnad

In answer to your question. As I said, the special forces are meant for internal use against the externally supported terrorism, and so on. I do not understand Gen Nayyar's apprehension. Either the threat is against the sovereignty of the state or it isn't. And it doesn't really matter whether he is a citizen or not. If the army is used, the collateral damage is so much larger. That's what we have learnt. That's the minimum lesson we ought to have learnt in the last fifty years. The collateral damage from alienated people is also large, when they are pitted against the regular army units. If you use special forces, which carry out very precision kind of operations and get the terrorists with relative ease and with less collateral damage, you get rid of the problem in that way. A special force can be used in counter insurgency, anti-guerilla operations and as an expeditionary force for distant use. One thing I did not mention – it is there in the paper, but I should mention it, in passing at least. In future, I think one of the major threats and dangers will be from nuclear terrorism, and for this we have to have nuclear specialist commandos. Again, that's the specialisation, I am talking about: the Russians have something called "*Vympel*" – some of you must have heard about it. It is a very specialised nuclear commando force equipped with Geiger counters and so on. They can do strikes, they can disarm nuclear and radiological dispersal devices. The Americans have something called NEST. These are virtually science commandos. They merge scientific talent, with commando skills, to be able to disarm nuclear weapons before they go off. You have to develop those kinds of capabilities. Something like the RDD is going to be a major threat, because it doesn't take much for an RDD to be activated, to create havoc in a city. That is the kind of damage it can do, given the ambient conditions, of course. I would suggest that we take up such specialisation very seriously.

There are specialised technologies being developed, at least in the advanced countries, for instance, high pressure liquid cutters, by which you can disarm nuclear weapons by cutting though the metal without disturbing the weapon's circuit. Then, there are mobile small hot labs – they can deduce from available data what the type of weapon, and its configuration, etc are. These are the types of capability we should think about in a realistic sense, or else we will be hostage to them. In fact, we may be outpaced by events or some crisis when we face it.

Gen Shankar Roy Chowdhury

Thank you, Dr Karnad. That brings us to the end of the session. As I had said earlier, this was the apex of all the discussions – what should the Indian Army: 2020 be like? It must be looked at as the land component of the integral Indian defence forces. We have to start thinking like that. The scenario that has come out so far in our discussions is that rivalry with China will persist, rivalry with Pakistan will persist. So, is there going to be any change in the geostrategic, geopolitical scenario? Can we do away with the DCBs along the borders with Pakistan, which consume upward of 70 per cent of our manpower? Can we do away with this by 2020? If that doesn't come through, then I do not think much of the manpower inten-

of the manpower intensiveness of our forces is going to change. If these things do not come through, can we prefer manoeuvre warfare over attrition warfare? Are you prepared for a scenario where, by 2020, the Pakistan problem is still unsolved? About China, I do not know how far we have gone. Are you prepared to dismantle the DCB and fall back, relying on manoeuvre warfare, with a string of your major cities – Jammu, Pathankot, Gurdaspur, Amritsar, Firozpur, Bikaner – all close to the border ahead of your deployment? Are you in a position to shed the attrition manpower? A lot depends upon how the geopolitical situation develops in 2020s. The majority of the speakers seem to say that it will not change much. If it changes, of course, it will be a different scenario. Even in the present scenario, are you prepared to hand over the LoC, assuming it persists 20 years hence? Are you prepared to hand over the LoC to the BSF and totally pull out of J&K. If the border problem with China is solved, are you prepared to hand over the entire Sino-Indian border to the ITBP and pull the army out? Otherwise, there is not going to be any change, so what do you do? Within the present structure of the army, which, as I see it, does not appear to be changing too much, what can we do? Firstly, I think we have to calculate our combat power or combat edge vis-à-vis Pakistan. What we are doing now is that we keep telling the government that our edge with Pakistan used to be 1.91 : 1 or 2 : 1 in 1971 and that is why we won. Now, it is only 1.1: 1, and, that is why we can't win. When you talk to the air force, they say no problem, we have 3: 1 superiority. The army says it is 1 : 1 superiority, the air force says it is 3 : 1, and the navy says it is 7 : 1. The combined combat power of the defence services, therefore, is how much? That is the point to make. Can we calculate the strength of our army on the basis of the combined combat power of all three Services? Are we prepared to accept that? That may mean right-sizing of the army. If this holding role of our formations does not go away vis-à-vis Pakistan, which is a major commitment of our army, are you prepared to have at least 50 per cent of manpower in the holding formations from the TA? Are you prepared to take that step? Yes, we will have holding formations, in every brigade we will have two battalions of TA and one regular battalion. I have tried it a couple of times. My army commanders were up in arms. So you have to take these decisions, otherwise the army will not change.

We must have nuclear capability, no doubt about it. I do not think Dr. Bharat Karnad has made his point very strongly, I do not know whether in the present day environment you can carry out megaton testing. Is there any possibility of doing it on the drawing board, by using computers? I do not know. But we do need a strong nuclear capability.

Internal security is our other bugbear. I was reading in a paper today that there are 17 lakh strong PMF and CPO forces, plus four lakh state police. Can you adopt a policy? One way to go about it is to pull the army out of internal security duties totally. Let CPOs and PMF handle these, but, I take the point Dr Bharat Karnad and other officers have made, which is to have very good special operation forces, which can support the blanket coverage by the PMF, which the army is doing now, and wherever required, insert your special operations forces to carry out specific tasks in support of the police/PMF. It may be one way to bring down your manpower.

We must work as integrated Services – the three chiefs have mentioned it yesterday, and I think this is coming out more and more clearly. Unfortunately, this comes out in the seminars. It must also come out on the ground. I think we really have to take these steps. The Defence Services Staff College teaches us enough integration, then what is the problem with the squadron leader of the air force being a Deputy Assistant Adjutant and Quarter Master General (DAA & QMG) of an infantry brigade? What is the problem with the lieutenant commander of the navy being a General Staff Officer-Grade 2 (GSO-2) of an infantry division? Unless we start off at that level, it will just never come about.

Finally, we must bear in mind that when the Americans went into Iraq, it took them seven-eight days of actual conventional war, but they have got bogged down in low intensity conflicts, suffering heavy casualties. With manpower intensive operations, they are appealing to all countries for troops. Low intensity conflict is manpower intensive. In our case, we are lucky that what we are suggesting is that the blanketing portion of the low intensity conflict operation be done by the PMF and the police and let us intervene only with the special forces. Similarly, look at Israel, they are fighting the *intifada*, they are again short of manpower. Manpower is important; the thing is how to do it cheaply and not at the cost of the defence budget. Therefore, what is the future structure of the infantry, the largest component of the Indian Army, and the land forces component of the integrated defence forces? Are you prepared to consider the infantry to be composed in various percentages of the TA, special forces and mechanised infantry? I mean, we must start thinking on these lines. Otherwise, nothing will change. We have to take a note of all these issues.

I would like to specially compliment Lt Gen Vijay Oberoi for this gathering we have had. This is the first occasion where I have seen the serving officers, particularly the younger generations and people like us, who have been in the Service earlier, come together on a formalised platform. This is an interchange and interaction which I think the army and the defence forces would do well to continue. Thank you very much. •

Concluding Session

Valedictory Address : Lt Gen J.J. Singh, PVSM, AVSM, VSM, ADC

Concluding Remarks : Lt Gen Vijay Oberoi, PVSM, AVSM, VSM (Retd)

VALEDICTORY ADDRESS

Lt Gen J. J. Singh, PVSM, AVSM, VSM, ADC
GOC-in-C Western Command

Esteemed former chief of army staff; Lt Gen Vijay Oberoi, Director CLAWS; panelists; distinguished guests; and the participants of this seminar.

I consider it a great privilege for me this afternoon, to be delivering the valedictory address on this maiden seminar of CLAWS and sharing some thoughts with you. I wish I had been present throughout the seminar and listened to the ideas and thoughts projected by all the eminent panelists and the discussions held during the interactive sessions. However, from what I have been briefed about and what I have heard during my brief sit-ins, including this concluding session, has indeed been thought-provoking and remarkable.

I always like to make this quote by Kautilya – I prefer to quote our own philosophers, thinkers and strategists. He says, "Societies that want to live in peace, should be always prepared for war." This is particularly relevant to the subject of this seminar, which has a very important bearing on our future operational capabilities and readiness to defend ourselves, as also, if need be, project our power across our shores.

Ladies and gentlemen, the subjects for this unique seminar of the CLAWS are not only of great relevance to the army, but to the entire nation. The armed forces have held a pivotal position amongst the various and varied instruments available to the nation, in practically all facets which impact on the security of the country. I have no doubt that this pivotal position will be retained, if not enhanced, by them in the coming years and decades.

Since Independence in 1947, the army has been engaged in active operations on a sustained basis, with only short periods of peace. These challenges have helped the army to earn a formidable reputation of a force that delivers, usually against heavy odds, with the exception of 1962. The professional capabilities of our officers and men are now recognised the world over. However, we cannot rest on our past laurels. The need is to look at, and be prepared for, the future, so that the army continues to have a high reputation in the future too. The topic of the seminar that has just concluded is, thus, of great importance. The army has to make the necessary changes in its structures and thinking, so that it is able to meet the challenges in the coming decades; with determination, advance planning and foresight. That is the *raison d'etre* of such deliberations.

The threats to our nation are both external and internal, and we have to focus on both.

Looking around us; our relations with China have improved in recent years. The Peace and Tranquillity Treaty has served to put the border dispute 'on hold', and both countries are now actively engaged in economic development. The momentum towards confidence building and improved relations is continuing. Talks between the two countries are in progress to arrive at a solution to the boundary problem.

As one speaker had highlighted, the need for controlled and continuous engagement with China is in our national interest. India's rapidly growing trade with China, worth over $ 7 billon today, is already impressive.

However, China is also continuing with its force modernisation and improvement of infrastructure in Tibet. To my mind, the best way to avoid a conflict is to be equally prepared and also that would contribute to strategic wisdom.

The current peace process with Pakistan, at both the Track-I and II levels, needs to be supported. There are obvious benefits of a rapprochement with an important neighbour like Pakistan. However, prudence demands that we continue to be careful and not let our guard down. We must, therefore, continue to plan and fight the proxy war and all its facets. The most important of all is infiltration. We have already taken many important steps in this direction, including a three-tiered counter-infiltration posture, a fence and deployment of surveillance equipment, besides the deployment of troops in depth, in a counter-insurgency role.

A nuclear stand-off now prevails in the subcontinent, as also in the larger region encompassing China. Irrespective of periodic Pakistani nuclear sabre-rattling, the fact remains that nuclear weapons are political and not military weapons. However, we have to ensure that nuclear deterrence remains in place. In addition, we should be prepared to fight through such areas where an NBC attack has been launched at a tactical level and in areas where it can happen, and not be caught unprepared when such a situation occurs. In this direction, certain steps have already been taken from the protective side, rather than the offensive side. I see no cause for undue concern on this account, as long as we continue with the endeavours in this direction.

The biggest danger today is that nuclear weapons or nuclear material that may well fall into the hands of non-state actors; this would be a major catastrophe. The recent revelation about the large-scale proliferation activities of both Pakistani individuals and institutions is a matter of grave concern for the entire global community. It cannot be overlooked.

On the conventional plane, while there is definitely space for conventional conflicts, there are likely to be more and more cases of increase in terrorism as an effective instrument of asymmetric war.

This is our biggest challenge today. While some countries have experienced it only recently, we have been living with, and fighting, terrorism and insurgencies for decades. We have had some successes in the past, but in every case, we have had to persevere over many years. This is likely to be the norm in the future too.

However, as has been brought out by some speakers, our capability for conducting conventional war in our environment should not be lost sight of.

As far as RMA is concerned, the rapid advancements in technology are changing the concept of warfare. In the information age, irrespective of whether it is nuclear, conventional or low intensity in nature, warfare will require highly complex planning and coordination, near real-time and total situational awareness, decision support systems and massive data-base and information-exchange capabilities, to tackle both friendly and enemy situations. We need to plan on creating appropriate structures for this.

India's military strategy needs to be effective across the entire spectrum of possible conflicts, from a high intensity conventional war under the backdrop of a nuclear threat to low intensity conflicts.

While the primary role of the army continues to be in the external arena, it cannot, for reasons well known, neglect major threats emanating internally. In any case, the trend today is that external and internal threats are now merging. This is likely to be accentuated in the coming years. Our army has been involved in countering terrorism, insurgency and militancy for years. My assessment is that the involvement of the army in tackling high-grade insurgencies, proxy wars, terrorism, and the like, is likely to continue.

Today, joint and combined operations are the norm. Information Warfare, including the creation of a favourable public opinion, is a necessary adjunct to the higher direction of war. Military planners will need to give considerable thought to the likelihood of terrorist threats also, while formulating plans for military operations. It is now difficult to divide operations into conventional and low intensity conflicts. The modern battlefield demands that wars and "Operations Other Than War" (OOTW) be fought in all six dimensions – space, cyber, air, land, sea and sub-surface.

Deterring war would continue to be the primary aim of the army. This is only possible if it maintains a potent force in being. Once deterrence fails to checkmate the adversary, then there should be no hesitation in selecting the military option. We need to build up our current missile capability substantially, so that the army is equipped with a full range of missiles, capable of reaching all possible targets. Credible conventional deterrence will continue to be important.

The structure of the army should be such that it is able to achieve the objectives the nation expects from it. The conventional capability of the army must be comprehensive against our likely adversaries. The army must also have the capability for punitive response to provocations short of war. The army needs to continue its support to the counter-insurgency strategy of the nation, without diluting its conventional capability. It must have adequate capability to fight high-grade insurgency in any part of India, as well as proxy wars of the type currently being waged by Pakistan in Jammu and Kashmir.

Some of the major points which have emerged from the deliberations of this seminar, which I wish to also highlight are:

- As our chief of army staff brought out yesterday, the focus in future conflicts would be on "joint operations." A number of speakers have also amplified on this particular aspect. Operations are unlikely to succeed unless they are planned and executed jointly. The need to bring about greater synergy of operations amongst the three Services through joint training and joint procedures has also been brought out.

- As highlighted by the chief of Naval Staff and other panelists too, it is imperative to modernise the man besides reshaping the organisation.
- Certain valuable ideas on force levels, restructuring and having a 'lean' army have been articulated by some speakers, which are being constantly examined and deliberated upon by the army.
- Increasing firepower and effective PGMs will help to achieve military objectives quickly and with minimum casualties. This had an impact on our war-fighting doctrine; a draft of which has been prepared as the COAS mentioned yesterday. The other day at the Mahajan Ranges, ladies and gentlemen, we had an assault by a combat team supported by the firepower of 17 batteries of guns. I am happy to say that the point was brought out by one of the speakers that we do not have to count the number of guns and, in fact, in Western Command, we have asked the artillery to put up a explanation of this concept of 'hundred guns'. It is not the physical number of guns, but the capability of bringing to bear that much of punishment on the target and, therefore, with precision ammunition or with less number of guns of heavier calibre, one can achieve the same effect. This is to understand the concept and not the nomenclature of 'hundred guns' *per se*. I must tell you when this firepower demonstration took place, it was a quantum jump from what we had in the last war. The kind of technology which has been fielded in the army in the last three-four years, including the force multipliers in terms of the UAVs, the satellites, the sensors, the surveillance radars and the night vision equipment, our night fighting capability has increased by night sights and an improved version of weapons and equipment. The T-90 tanks and the guns, all gave us the confidence that the enemy platoon locality was subjected to 170 tonnes of TNT, half an hour before it was attacked by the combat team. So, this is the kind of firepower which is available today and, therefore, it will result in a charge of our war-fighting doctrine.
- As brought out by some panelists, hi-tech and night-fighting capabilities will be the hallmark of any modern army. It is my firm conviction too. However, the air chief mentioned the aspect of budget constraints and cost of high-tech weapons and equipment has to be kept in mind.
- An eminent panelist rightly raised the question, do we have a role in this world, keeping in mind our size, location and resources? Do we have an ambition commensurate with our ancient civilisation and history, is an apt question too. We need to think about the need to develop the 'will for power', in addition to 'will for security.'
- I couldn't agree more with the speakers who have reiterated the importance

of the Indian Ocean, and Indian maritime role to safeguard our national interests, as also the concept of "homeland defence," which is engaging the advanced countries, which have no identifiable enemy along their borders.

- There is a need to substantially increase the army's special forces and evolve a doctrine for their employment, to achieve strategic objectives. Very few countries other than the US have the *savoir faire* or indepth knowledge of such employment of special forces.
- The success in future conflicts will be affected greatly by our ability to use IT in an optimum manner. The processing of the large amount of information, which would be available on the battlefield, requires the fielding of C^4I^2 systems. With the country's strength in the field of IT, this should not be a difficult task, provided we undertake it in a joint manner. I must mention here that we have made a lot of strides in training our commanders on computer simulated war-games. We have a centre for war games and that is training them and it is almost on par with the First World, as far as the techniques being used to train such commanders are concerned. And this may be brought further and taken down to the level of JCOs and NCOs in the future.
- Modernisation is a continuous process. Adequate funds need to be made available, and more importantly, we need to create an ability to vastly improve our methodologies for procurement. The recommendations made by some panelists regarding the increase of the defence budget to at least 3 per cent of the GDP has merit, and needs to be projected.
- Development of force structures that are capability-based and not threat-based is well understood.
- The need for projecting military power to support our friends and allies, and to safeguard our area of interest is another important recommendation. A country of our size and resources should have such a capability.
- In the doctrinal context, a number of issues which need to be followed up are "formalising an Indian way of tackling conflicts," "integrated operations," "directive style of command" and "a manoeuvre approach," "non-linearity," and "a proactive culture."
- Theatre-level deception is a force-multiplier, which needs to be dovetailed in all our plans.
- The Indian Army has been a major contributor to peace-keeping operations of the UN and has an excellent record. This trend is likely to continue and may well get enhanced in the coming years.

There is a symbiotic relationship between military security and economic development, and both must complement each other. Today, our economy is on the upswing, and the modernisation of the army has to keep pace. The recent decision to set up a non-lapsable fund will no doubt help, but we must also refine and modernise our procurement procedures. It would be in order to say that post-Kargil, modernisation and induction of various weapon systems, force multipliers and other hi-tech equipment has been significant.

Before I step down, let me say a few words about the CLAWS. The centre has been set up to encourage and initiate debate on national security and defence matters with special emphasis on the employment of land forces at the strategic and theatre levels encompassing the entire spectrum of conflict. It will also attempt to improve public awareness and understanding of "matters military." It is an independent and unencumbered "think- tank," which is being provided logistical support by the army. In due course, it will commence obtaining feed-back from the environment and offer frank and independent views related to issues of concern to the army. I would like to reiterate once again that the views expressed in this seminar and in the deliberations of CLAWS in the future are not the official views of the army or any other service or the Government of India.

This seminar was the first event organised by the centre. I would like to take this opportunity to thank Lt Gen Vijay Oberoi and his team for organising this event, on a subject which is of immense professional importance. I have no hesitation is saying that we are all richer by this experience. On behalf of the COAS of the Indian Army, I would like to convey the assurances that the army would continue to support such ventures in future too.

Thank you, ladies and gentlemen.

Jai Hind. •

CONCLUDING REMARKS

Lt Gen Vijay Oberoi, PVSM, AVSM, VSM (Retd)
Director, CLAWS

Ladies and gentlemen, I thank Lt Gen J.J. Singh, GOC-in-C, Western Command, for sparing the time to come and deliver the valedictory address, which needless to say was packed with a host of extremely important issues, in the brief time available. What the general has stated will hopefully be taken note of by all present and particularly the serving community. We do need to ensure that the army remains in a continuous modernisation mode and restructures itself where necessary, to face the challenges of the future.

I would also like to thank the participants of all the four sessions for their excellent presentations and the trouble they took to put all the papers together. I would also like to thank all the delegates and guests for their attendance and active participation in this seminar. The presence of GOC-in-C Army Training Command today is a matter of great honour for us.

In the final analysis, the success of this seminar can be directly attributed to the serving and retired officers of the three Services and our distinguished guests, who have taken time out to attend the seminar and have displayed great interest throughout the proceedings. I also thank the Army Headquarters, particularly the Director General of Military Training, Maj Gen H.S. Panag and the officers of the Military Training Directorate, who have interacted extremely closely with us to make this seminar a success. The same goes for Headquarters Delhi Area and the other formations which have spared their officers, lady officers and men, who have worked closely with us. Putting together, coordinating and tying up all the administrative details could only be achieved by the active support of these formations and their personnel. I must also not forget to thank my own staff, led by Col U. S. Rathore, who have done tremendous work towards the success of the seminar.

Ladies and gentlemen, this seminar is the first event of CLAWS. I have no doubt that there will be plenty more and the centre would continue to adopt a focussed approach to many security and defence issues of national and regional interests.

On this optimistic note, let me thank everyone once again for being with us for these two days and for their active participation in highly intellectual and cerebral discussions. Thank you very much. •